Annual Editions: Criminal Justice, 41/e

Joanne Naughton

http://create.mheducation.com

ISBN-10: 1259892697   ISBN-13: 9781259892691

Contents

Detailed Table of Contents

who died of abuse and neglect between 2009 and 2013 that were never brought into the state system at all. Social workers either dismissed reports of alleged maltreatment or never heard from concerned teachers, police, hospital workers or other mandated reporters at all.

More than 1,600 Women Murdered by Men in One Year, New Study Finds, *Violence Policy Center, 2015*
For homicides in which the victim to offender relationship could be identified, 94 percent of female victims nationwide were murdered by a male they knew. Of the victims who knew their offenders, 62 percent were wives, common-law wives, ex-wives, or girlfriends of the offenders. In 2013, firearms were the weapons most commonly used.

Human Sex Trafficking, Amanda Walker-Rodriguez and Rodney Hill, *FBI Law Enforcement Bulletin*, 2011
The United States not only faces an influx of international victims but also has its own homegrown problem of interstate sex trafficking of minors. Among the children and teens living on the streets in the United States, involvement in commercial sex activity is a problem of epidemic proportion.

He Was Abused by a Female Teacher, but He Was Treated Like the Perpetrator, Simone Sebastian, *The Washington Post,* 2015
Growing evidence shows that boys who are sexually preyed upon by older female authority figures suffer psychologically in much the same way that girls do when victimized by older men.

Male Victims of Campus Sexual Assault Speak Out, Emily Kassie, *Huffington Post*, 2015
Many men have difficulty with the language of sexual assault. There are words like "victim" and "survivor" that are hard for them to identity with because they find them antithetical to what it means to be a real man.

Unit 3: The Police

The Changing Environment for Policing, 1985-2008, David H. Bayley and Christine Nixon, *National Institute of Justice*, 2010
What are the differences in the environment for policing now compared with the 1985 to 1991 timeframe? Are the problems similar or different from one period to the other? Police today are considered to be performing well, but this assessment may be mistaken because the institutions that provide public safety are changing in profound ways that are not being recognized.

A Year of Reckoning: Police Fatally Shoot Nearly 1,000, Kimberly Kindy et al., *The Washington Post,* 2015
In a year-long study, *The Washington Post* found that the kind of incidents that have ignited protests in many US communities - most often, white police officers killing unarmed black men - represent less than 4 percent of fatal police shootings.

Police Chiefs, Looking to Diversity Forces, Face Structural Hurdles, Matt Apuzzo and Sarah Cohen, *The New York Times,* 2015
Though the history of discrimination and segregation looms large over American policing, many police chiefs are eager to hire minorities yet face structural hurdles that make it hard to diversity their departments. Those issues vary by state and city, making any single solution particularly elusive.

Training Officers to Shoot First, and He Will Answer Questions Later, Matt Apuzzo, *The New York Times*, 2015
When police officers shoot people under questionable circumstances, Dr. Lewinski is often there to defend their actions. He concludes the officer acted appropriately, even when shooting an unarmed person, shooting the person in the back, and when other testimony contradicts the officer's story.

Defining Moments for Police Chiefs, Chuck Wexler, *Police Executive Research Forum*, 2015
One central theme that grew out of the conference of police chiefs was the importance of developing a culture of policing that recognizes when officers should step in and when they should step back from encounters with the public.

The Supreme Court's Utah v. Strieff Decision and the Fourth Amendment, Joshua Waimberg, *Constitution Daily*, 2016
The Court held that evidence obtained from an unlawful police stop would not be excluded from court because the link between the stop and the discovery of the evidence was "attenuated" by the discovery of an outstanding warrant during the stop.

Excited Delirium and the Dual Response: Preventing In-Custody Deaths, Brian Roach, Kelsey Echols, and Aaron Burnett, *FBI Law Enforcement Bulletin*, 2014
Excited delirium syndrome (ExDS) is a serious medical condition that may lead to death if not recognized and treated. Typical ExDS subjects are males around the age of 30 and most have a history of psychostimulant use or mental illness. Law

enforcement or EMS personnel are often called to the scene because of public disturbances, agitation or bizarre behaviors and they should consider the possibility of ExDS when certain symptoms are present, and take the patient to the hospital.

Unit 4: The Judicial System

Unit 5: Juvenile Justice

came to light in 2007, Texas moved to reduce the number of incarcerated youth. During 2007 to 2012, the number of young people incarcerated dropped more than 60% and juvenile crime dropped more than 30%—evidence that safety was not compromised by changes in the law.

Juvenile Injustice: Truants Face Courts, Jailing without Legal Counsel to Aid Them, Susan Ferriss, *Center for Public Integrity*, 2014

Parents allege that children whose only infraction was struggling with a loathing for school were pulled into the criminal justice system, branded with permanent delinquency records and jailed with kids who had actually committed crimes. All of this happened without their kids having lawyers, and some dropped out rather than go back to school.

Level 14: How a Home for Troubled Children Came Undone and What It Means for California's Chance at Reform, Joaquin Sapien, *ProPublica*, 2015

The breakdown at FamiliesFirst, one of California's largest residential facilities for emotionally damaged kids, has helped spur California to rethink how it cares for its most troubled children, a question that for decades has confounded not just the state but the country.

Arrest of Tennessee Children Exposes Flawed Juvenile Justice, Sheila Burke, *The Associated Press*, 2016

A Tennessee police officer tried to prevent the arrests that would embroil his department in a national furor over policing in schools, but his colleagues and supervisors refused to change course. What followed was an unusually public examination of how police handle children suspected of wrongdoing.

Tribal Youth in the Juvenile Justice System, *U.S. Department of Justice, Office of Juvenile Justice and Delinquency Prevention*, 2016

Research has examined the juvenile justice system's disparate treatment of racial and ethnic minorities, including the disproportionate representation of American Indian and Alaska Native youth across the contact points in the system; as well as the lack of access to treatment, services, and other resources; and the risk factors that may increase their contact with the justice system.

Unit 6: Punishment and Corrections

The Archipelago of Pain, David Brooks, *The New York Times*, 2014

At the level of human experience, social pain is, if anything, more traumatic, more destabilizing, and inflicts crueler and longer-lasting effects than physical pain. What we're doing to prisoners in solitary confinement when we lock them away in social isolation for 23 hours a day, often for months, years, or decades at a time is arguably more inhumane than flogging them would be.

Meet the Ungers, Jason Fagone, *Huffington Post*, 2016

Several decades ago when they were young, 230 men and one woman were convicted of terrible crimes, but instead of spending their lives in prison, Merle Unger, one of the most notorious escape artists of our time, discovered an ingenious, legal, way to get them out. It was an unimagined second chance for them - and a nerve-wracking experiment for everyone else.

For Mentally Ill Inmates at Rikers Island, a Cycle of Jail and Hospitals, Michael Winerip and Michael Schwirtz, *The New York Times*, 2015

For years, Rikers has been filling with people who have complicated psychiatric problems that are little understood and do not get resolved elsewhere: the unwashed man passed out in a public stairwell; the 16-year-old runaway; the drug addict; the belligerent panhandler screaming in a full subway car.

States Struggle with What to Do with Sex Offenders after Prison, Monica Davey, *The New York Times*, 2015

Civil commitment for sex offenders gained support in the 1990s amid reports of heinous sex crimes by repeat offenders. Minnesota has the highest population of civilly committed offenders per capita - nearly all men - in the nation, and the lowest rate of release. And costs have soared to about $125,000 per resident per year, at least three times the cost of an ordinary prison inmate in Minnesota.

The Painful Price of Aging in Prison, Sari Horwitz, *The Washington Post*, 2015

Even as harsh sentences are reconsidered, the financial—and human—tolls mount.

Preface

In publishing *Annual Editions*, we recognize the enormous role played by the public press in providing current, first-rate information about a broad spectrum of Criminal Justice issues. Many of the articles in various magazines, newspapers, and journals are appropriate for students, researchers, and professionals seeking accurate, current material to help bridge the gap between principles and theories, and the real world. These articles, however, become more useful for study when those of lasting value are carefully collected, organized, indexed, and reproduced in a low-cost format, providing easy and permanent access when the material is needed. That is the role played by *Annual Editions*.

During the 1970s, Criminal Justice emerged as an appealing, vital, and unique academic discipline. It emphasizes the professional development of students who plan careers in the field, and attracts those who want to know more about a complex social problem and how the United States deals with it. Criminal Justice incorporates a vast range of knowledge from a number of different specialities, including law, history, and the behavioral and social sciences. Each specialty contributes to our fuller understanding of criminal behavior and of society's attitudes toward deviance.

In view of the fact that the Criminal Justice system is in a constant state of flux, and because the study of Criminal Justice covers such a broad spectrum, today's students must be aware of a variety of subjects and disciplines. Standard textbooks and traditional anthologies cannot keep pace with the changes as quickly as they occur. In fact, many such sources are already out of date the day they are published. *Annual Editions: Criminal Justice 41st Edition* strives to maintain currency in matters of concern by providing up-to-date information from the most recent literature in the Criminal Justice field.

This volume contains six units that treat Crime and Justice in America, Victimology, The Police, The Judicial System, Juvenile justice, and Punishment and Corrections. The articles in these units were selected because they are informative and provocative. The selections are timely and useful in their treatment of ethics, punishment, juveniles, courts, police, prosecutors, and other related topics.

Also incorporated are a number of features designed to be useful to students, researchers, and professionals in the Criminal Justice field. They include the *Table of Contents*, setting out the titles of the articles and the units in which they can be found and a list of relevant *Internet* sites. In addition, each unit is preceded by an overview that provides a background for informed reading of the articles, and each article is preceded by *Learning Outcomes*—a listing of goals for the reader to achieve after reading the article.

Finally, each article is followed by a section called *Critical Thinking*, containing questions designed to spur thoughtful consideration of the ideas raised in the article.

Joanne Naughton

Editor of This Volume

Joanne Naughton is a former member of the NYPD, where she encountered most aspects of police work as a police officer, detective, sergeant, and lieutenant. She is also a former staff attorney with The Legal Aid Society, where she represented indigent criminal defendants. In addition to her hands-on experience in criminal justice, she was an adjunct professor at John Jay College of Criminal Justice and has retired from Mercy College where she was an assistant professor. She received her BA and JD at Fordham University.

Academic Advisory Board Members

Members of the Academic Advisory Board are instrumental in the final selection of articles for each edition of *Annual Editions*. Their review of the articles for content, level, and appropriateness provides critical direction to the editors and staff. We think that you will find their careful consideration well reflected in this volume.

Harry N. Babb
Farmingdale State University of New York

Richard Baranzini
Liberty University

Joseph A. Bobak IV
Mount Aloysius College

Alton Braddock
University of Louisiana, Monroe

Frank Butler
La Salle University

James Byrne
University of Massachusetts, Lowell

Kelli Callahan
Park University

Terry Campbell
Kaplan University

Peter D. Chimbos
Brescia College at The University of Western Ontario

David Coffey
Thomas Nelson Community College

Bernard Cohen
Queens College

James Cunningham
State Fair Community College

Roger Cunningham
Eastern Illinois University

Michael T. Eskey
Park University

Bonnie Fisher
University of Cincinnati

David Forristal
Brown Mackie College

Paul Frankenhauser
Allied American University

Paul Fuller
Knoxville College

Peter Galante
Farmingdale State College

Alan Garcia
Bristol Community College

Arnett Gaston
University of Maryland

Barry Goodson
Columbia Southern University

Ken Haas
University of Delaware

Julia Hall
Drexel University

Bridget A. Hepner-Williamson
Sam Houston State University

Rick Herbert
South Plains College

Rosalee Hodges
Glendale Community College

Michael K. Hooper
Sonoma State University

Richard Hough
University of West Florida

Amanda Humphrey
Mount Mercy College

Larry Jablecki
Rice University

Gayle Jentz
North Hennepin Community College

Rachel Jung
Mesa Community College

Kim Kamins
Brown Mackie College

Scott Kelly
Penn State Altoona

William E. Kelly
Auburn University

Chandrika Kelso
National University

Steven Kempisty
Bryant & Stratton College

Lloyd Klein
St. Francis College/Hostos Community College

Kevin Kolbe
Solano Junior College

Jordan Land
Southwest Florida College

Michael A. Langer
Loyola University, Chicago

Barney Ledford
Mid-Michigan Community College

Matthew C. Leone
University of Nevada

Xiangdong Li
New York City College of Technology

Celia Lo
University of Alabama, Tuscaloosa

Jennelle London Joset
Sanford-Brown College

Mark Marsolais
Northern Kentucky University

Vertel Martin
Northampton Community College

Jon Maskaly
University of South Florida, Tampa

Suzanne Montiel
Nash Community College

Derek Mosley
Meridian Community College

James Murphy
College of Western Idaho

Bonnie O. Neher
Harrisburg Area Community College

Gary Neumeyer
Arizona Western College, Yuma

Michael Palmiotto
Wichita State University

Gary Prawel
Keuka College

Jeffrey Ian Ross
University of Baltimore

Michael P. Roy
Alpena Community College

Vincent M. Russo
Richard J. Daley College

Leslie Samuelson
University of Saskatchewan

Clifford L. Sanders Jr.
Clayton State University

Robin Sawyer
University of Maryland, College Park

Gary A. Sokolow
College of the Redwoods

Joseph A. Spadaro
Goodwin College

Darren Stocker
Cumberland County College

Michael Such
Hudson Valley Community College

Candace Tabenanika
Sam Houston State University

Amy Thistlethwaite
Northern Kentucky University

Al Trego
McCann School

Joseph L. Victor
Mercy College

Jason Weber
Rasmussen College, Bloomington

Lisa Grey Whitaker
Arizona State University

Larry Woods
Tennessee State University

Laura Woods Fidelie
Midwestern State University

Unit 1

UNIT

Prepared by: Joanne Naughton

Crime and Justice in America

The American justice system comprises three traditional components: police, courts, and corrections. In addition, special attention is also given to crime victims and juveniles. Crime continues to be a major problem in the United States. Court dockets are full, our prisons are overcrowded, probation, and parole caseloads are overwhelming, our police are being urged to do more, and the bulging prison population places a heavy strain on the economy of the country.

Clearly, crime is a complex problem that defies simple explanations or solutions. Although the more familiar crimes of murder, rape, assault, and drug law violations are still with us, international terrorism has become a pressing worry. The debate also continues over how to best handle juvenile offenders, sex offenders, and those who commit acts of domestic violence. The increasing prevalence of Internet crime also demands attention from the criminal justice system.

Article   Prepared by: Joanne Naughton

What Is the Sequence of Events in the Criminal Justice System?

Learning Outcomes

After reading this article, you will be able to:

- Name the agencies that make up the criminal justice system.
- State the various steps from the time someone is arrested for a crime.

The Private Sector Initiates the Response to Crime

This first response may come from individuals, families, neighborhood associations, business, industry, agriculture, educational institutions, the news media, or any other private service to the public.

It involves crime prevention as well as participation in the criminal justice process once a crime has been committed. Private crime prevention is more than providing private security or burglar alarms or participating in neighborhood watch. It also includes a commitment to stop criminal behavior by not engaging in it or condoning it when it is committed by others.

Citizens take part directly in the criminal justice process by reporting crime to the police, by being a reliable participant (for example, a witness or a juror) in a criminal proceeding and by accepting the disposition of the system as just or reasonable. As voters and taxpayers, citizens also participate in criminal justice through the policymaking process that affects how the criminal justice process operates, the resources available to it, and its goals and objectives. At every stage of the process from the original formulation of objectives to the decision about where to locate jails and prisons to the reintegration of inmates into society, the private sector has a role to play. Without such involvement, the criminal justice process cannot serve the citizens it is intended to protect.

The Response to Crime and Public Safety Involves Many Agencies and Services

Many of the services needed to prevent crime and make neighborhoods safe are supplied by noncriminal justice agencies, including agencies with primary concern for public health, education, welfare, public works, and housing. Individual citizens as well as public and private sector organizations have joined with criminal justice agencies to prevent crime and make neighborhoods safe.

Criminal Cases Are Brought by the Government Through the Criminal Justice System

We apprehend, try, and punish offenders by means of a loose confederation of agencies at all levels of government. Our American system of justice has evolved from the English common law into a complex series of procedures and decisions. Founded on the concept that crimes against an individual are crimes against the State, our justice system prosecutes individuals as though they victimized all of society. However, crime victims are involved throughout the process and many justice agencies have programs that focus on helping victims.

There is no single criminal justice system in this country. We have many similar systems that are individually unique. Criminal cases may be handled differently in different jurisdictions, but court decisions based on the due process guarantees of the U.S. Constitution require that specific steps be taken in the administration of criminal justice so that the individual will be protected from undue intervention from the State.

The description of the criminal and juvenile justice systems that follows portrays the most common sequence of events in response to serious criminal behavior.

Entry into the System

The justice system does not respond to most crime because so much crime is not discovered or reported to the police. Law enforcement agencies learn about crime from the reports of victims or other citizens, from discovery by a police officer in the field, from informants, or from investigative and intelligence work.

Once a law enforcement agency has established that a crime has been committed, a suspect must be identified and apprehended for the case to proceed through the system. Sometimes, a suspect is apprehended at the scene; however, identification of a suspect sometimes requires an extensive investigation. Often, no one is identified or apprehended. In some instances, a suspect is arrested and later the police determine that no crime was committed and the suspect is released.

Prosecution and Pretrial Services

After an arrest, law enforcement agencies present information about the case and about the accused to the prosecutor, who will decide if formal charges will be filed with the court. If no charges are filed, the accused must be released. The prosecutor can also drop charges after making efforts to prosecute (*nolle prosequi*).

A suspect charged with a crime must be taken before a judge or magistrate without unnecessary delay. At the initial appearance, the judge or magistrate informs the accused of the charges and decides whether there is probable cause to detain the accused person. If the offense is not very serious, the determination of guilt and assessment of a penalty may also occur at this stage.

Often, the defense counsel is also assigned at the initial appearance. All suspects prosecuted for serious crimes have a right to be represented by an attorney. If the court determines the suspect is indigent and cannot afford such representation, the court will assign counsel at the public's expense.

A pretrial-release decision may be made at the initial appearance, but may occur at other hearings or may be changed at another time during the process. Pretrial release and bail were traditionally intended to ensure appearance at trial. However, many jurisdictions permit pretrial detention of defendants accused of serious offenses and deemed to be dangerous to prevent them from committing crimes prior to trial.

The court often bases its pretrial decision on information about the defendant's drug use, as well as residence, employment, and family ties. The court may decide to release the accused on his/her own recognizance or into the custody of a third party after the posting of a financial bond or on the promise of satisfying certain conditions such as taking periodic drug tests to ensure drug abstinence.

In many jurisdictions, the initial appearance may be followed by a preliminary hearing. The main function of this hearing is to discover if there is probable cause to believe that the accused committed a known crime within the jurisdiction of the court. If the judge does not find probable cause, the case is dismissed; however, if the judge or magistrate finds probable cause for such a belief, or the accused waives his or her right to a preliminary hearing, the case may be bound over to a grand jury.

A grand jury hears evidence against the accused presented by the prosecutor and decides if there is sufficient evidence to cause the accused to be brought to trial. If the grand jury finds sufficient evidence, it submits to the court an indictment, a written statement of the essential facts of the offense charged against the accused.

Where the grand jury system is used, the grand jury may also investigate criminal activity generally and issue indictments called grand jury originals that initiate criminal cases. These investigations and indictments are often used in drug and conspiracy cases that involve complex organizations. After such an indictment, law enforcement tries to apprehend and arrest the suspects named in the indictment.

Misdemeanor cases and some felony cases proceed by the issuance of an information, a formal, written accusation submitted to the court by a prosecutor. In some jurisdictions, indictments may be required in felony cases. However, the accused may choose to waive a grand jury indictment and, instead, accept service of an information for the crime.

In some jurisdictions, defendants, often those without prior criminal records, may be eligible for diversion from prosecution subject to the completion of specific conditions such as drug treatment. Successful completion of the conditions may result in the dropping of charges or the expunging of the criminal record where the defendant is required to plead guilty prior to the diversion.

Adjudication

Once an indictment or information has been filed with the trial court, the accused is scheduled for arraignment. At the arraignment, the accused is informed of the charges, advised of the rights of criminal defendants, and asked to enter a plea to the charges. Sometimes, a plea of guilty is the result of negotiations between the prosecutor and the defendant.

If the accused pleads guilty or pleads *nolo contendere* (accepts penalty without admitting guilt), the judge may accept or reject the plea. If the plea is accepted, no trial is held and the offender is sentenced at this proceeding or at a later date. The plea may be rejected and proceed to trial if, for example, the judge believes that the accused may have been coerced.

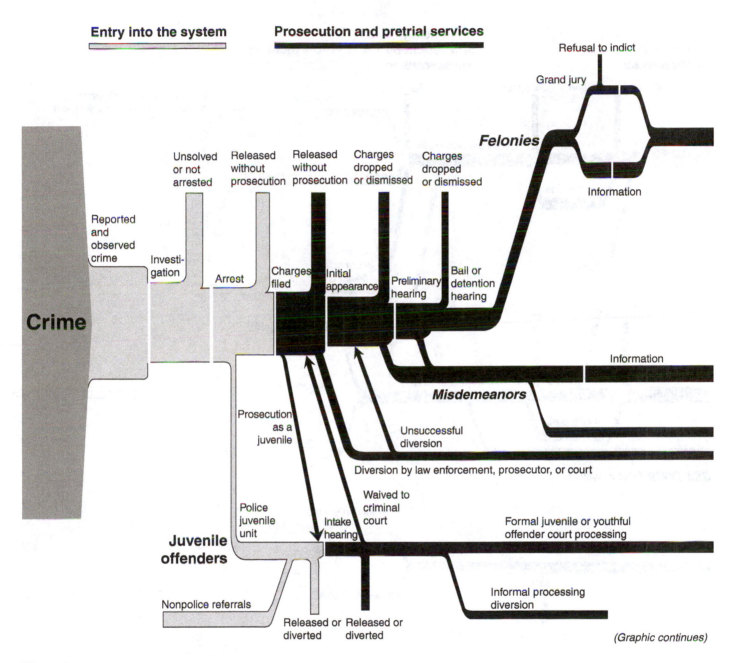

Figure 1

Note: This chart gives a simplified view of caseflow through the criminal justice system. Procedures vary among jurisdictions. The weights of the lines are not intended to show the actual size of caseloads.

If the accused pleads not guilty or not guilty by reason of insanity, a date is set for the trial. A person accused of a serious crime is guaranteed a trial by jury. However, the accused may ask for a bench trial where the judge, rather than a jury, serves as the finder of fact. In both instances the prosecution and defense present evidence by questioning witnesses while the judge decides on issues of law. The trial results in acquittal or conviction on the original charges or on lesser included offenses.

After the trial a defendant may request appellate review of the conviction or sentence. In some cases, appeals of convictions are a matter of right; all States with the death penalty provide for automatic appeal of cases involving a

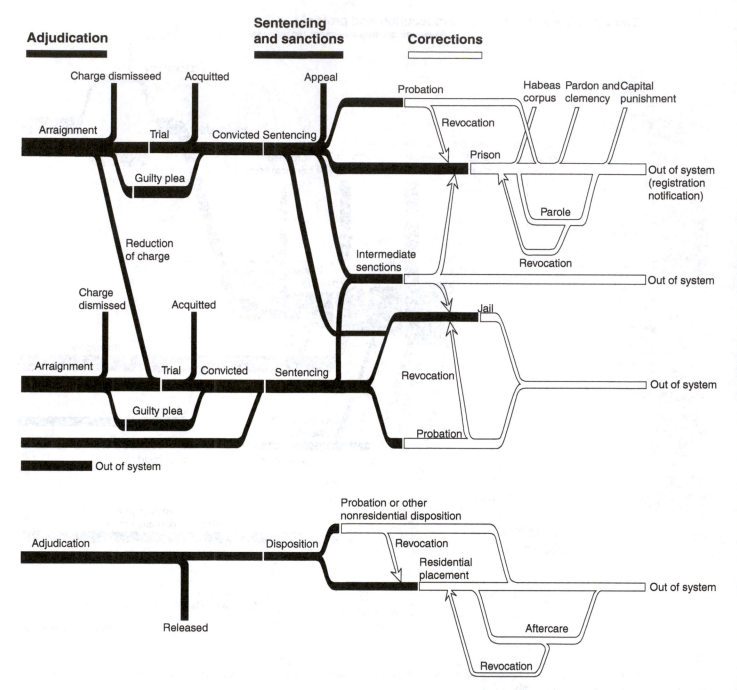

Figure 1 *(continued)*

Source: Adapted from *The challenge of crime in a free society*. President's Commission on Law Enforcement and Administration of Justice, 1967. This revision, a result of the Symposium on the 30th Anniversary of the President's Commission, was prepared by the Bureau of Justice Statistics in 1997.

death sentence. Appeals may be subject to the discretion of the appellate court and may be granted only on acceptance of a defendant's petition for a *writ of certiorari*. Prisoners may also appeal their sentences through civil rights petitions and *writs of habeas corpus* where they claim unlawful detention.

Discretion Is Exercised throughout the Criminal Justice System

Discretion is "an authority conferred by law to act in certain conditions or situations in accordance with an official's or an official agency's own considered judgment and conscience."[1] Discretion is exercised throughout the government. It is a part of decision making in all government systems from mental health to education, as well as criminal justice. The limits of discretion vary from jurisdiction to jurisdiction.

Concerning crime and justice, legislative bodies have recognized that they cannot anticipate the range of circumstances surrounding each crime, anticipate local mores, and enact laws that clearly encompass all conduct that is criminal and all that is not.[2]

Therefore, persons charged with the day-to-day response to crime are expected to exercise their own judgment within limits set by law. Basically, they must decide—

- whether to take action
- where the situation fits in the scheme of law, rules, and precedent
- which official response is appropriate.[3]

To ensure that discretion is exercised responsibly, government authority is often delegated to professionals. Professionalism requires a minimum level of training and orientation, which guide officials in making decisions. The professionalism of policing is due largely to the desire to ensure the proper exercise of police discretion.

The limits of discretion vary from State to State and locality to locality. For example, some State judges have wide discretion in the type of sentence they may impose. In recent years, other states have sought to limit the judge's discretion in sentencing by passing mandatory sentencing laws that require prison sentences for certain offenses.

Notes

1. Roscoe Pound, "Discretion, dispensation and mitigation: The problem of the individual special case," *New York University Law Review* (1960) 35:925, 926.
2. Wayne R. LaFave, *Arrest: The decision to take a suspect into custody* (Boston: Little, Brown & Co., 1964), pp. 63–184.
3. Memorandum of June 21, 1977, from Mark Moore to James Vorenberg, "Some abstract notes on the issue of discretion."

Bureau of Justice Statistics (www.ojp.usdoj.gov/bjs/). January 1998. NCJ 167894. To order: 1-800-732-3277.

Who Exercises Discretion?

These criminal justice officials . . .	must often decide whether or not or how to—
Police	Enforce specific laws
	Investigate specific crimes; Search people
Prosecutors	File charges or petitions for adjudication
	Seek indictments
	Drop cases
	Reduce charges
Judges or magistrates	Set bail or conditions for release
	Accept pleas
	Determine delinquency
	Dismiss charges
	Impose sentence
	Revoke probation
Correctional officials	Assign to type of correctional facility
	Award privileges
	Punish for disciplinary infractions
Paroling authorities	Determine date and conditions of parole
	Revoke parole

Sentencing and Sanctions

After a conviction, sentence is imposed. In most cases the judge decides on the sentence, but in some jurisdictions the sentence is decided by the jury, particularly for capital offenses.

In arriving at an appropriate sentence, a sentencing hearing may be held at which evidence of aggravating or mitigating circumstances is considered. In assessing the circumstances surrounding a convicted person's criminal behavior, courts often rely on presentence investigations by probation agencies or other designated authorities. Courts may also consider victim impact statements.

The sentencing choices that may be available to judges and juries include one or more of the following:

- the death penalty
- incarceration in a prison, jail, or other confinement facility
- probation—allowing the convicted person to remain at liberty but subject to certain conditions and restrictions such as drug testing or drug restrictions such as drug testing or drug treatment
- fines—primarily applied as penalties in minor offenses
- restitution—requiring the offender to pay compensation to the victim. In some jurisdictions, offenders may be sentenced to alternatives to incarceration that are considered more severe than straight probation but less severe than a prison term. Examples of such sanctions include boot camps, intense supervision often with drug treatment and testing, house arrest and electronic monitoring, denial of Federal benefits, and community service.

In many jurisdictions, the law mandates that persons convicted of certain types of offenses serve a prison term. Most jurisdictions permit the judge to set the sentence length within certain limits, but some have determinate sentencing laws that stipulate a specific sentence length that must be served and cannot be altered by a parole board.

Corrections

Offenders sentenced to incarceration usually serve time in a local jail or a State prison. Offenders sentenced to less than 1 year generally go to jail; those sentenced to more than 1 year go to prison. Persons admitted to the Federal system or a State prison system may be held in prison with varying levels of custody or in a community correctional facility.

A prisoner may become eligible for parole after serving a specific part of his or her sentence. Parole is the conditional release of a prisoner before the prisoner's full sentence has been served. The decision to grant parole is made by an authority such as a parole board, which has power to grant or revoke parole or to discharge a parolee altogether. The way parole decisions are made varies widely among jurisdictions.

Offenders may also be required to serve out their full sentences prior to release (expiration of term). Those sentenced under determinate sentencing laws can be released only after they have served their full sentence (mandatory release) less any "goodtime" received while in prison. Inmates get goodtime credits against their sentences automatically or by earning them through participation in programs.

If released by a parole board decision or by mandatory release, the releasee will be under the supervision of a parole officer in the community for the balance of his or her unexpired sentence. This supervision is governed by specific conditions of release, and the releasee may be returned to prison for violations of such conditions.

Recidivism

Once the suspects, defendants, or offenders are released from the jurisdiction of a criminal justice agency, they may be processed through the criminal justice system again for a new crime. Long term studies show that many suspects who are arrested have prior criminal histories and those with a greater number of prior arrests were more likely to be arrested again. As the courts take prior criminal history into account at sentencing, most prison inmates have a prior criminal history and many have been incarcerated before. Nationally, about half the inmates released from State prison will return to prison.

The Juvenile Justice System

Juvenile courts usually have jurisdiction over matters concerning children, including delinquency, neglect, and adoption. They also handle "status offenses" such as truancy and running away, which are not applicable to adults. State statutes define which persons are under the original jurisdiction of the juvenile court. The upper age of juvenile court jurisdiction in delinquency matters is 17 in most States.

The processing of juvenile offenders is not entirely dissimilar to adult criminal processing, but there are crucial differences. Many juveniles are referred to juvenile courts by law enforcement officers, but many others are referred by school officials, social services agencies, neighbors, and even parents, for behavior or conditions that are determined to require intervention by the formal system for social control.

At arrest, a decision is made either to send the matter further into the justice system or to divert the case out of the system, often to alternative programs. Examples of alternative programs include drug treatment, individual or group counseling, or referral to educational and recreational programs.

When juveniles are referred to the juvenile courts, the court's intake department or the prosecuting attorney determines whether sufficient grounds exist to warrant filing a petition that requests an adjudicatory hearing or a request to transfer jurisdiction to criminal court. At this point, many juveniles are released or diverted to alternative programs.

All States allow juveniles to be tried as adults in criminal court under certain circumstances. In many States, the legislature *statutorily excludes* certain (usually serious) offenses from the jurisdiction of the juvenile court regardless of the age of the accused. In some States and at the Federal level under certain circumstances, prosecutors have the *discretion* to either file criminal charges against juveniles directly in criminal courts or proceed through the juvenile justice process. The juvenile court's intake department or the prosecutor may petition the juvenile court to *waive* jurisdiction to criminal court. The juvenile court also may order *referral* to criminal court for trial as adults. In some jurisdictions, juveniles processed as adults may upon conviction be sentenced to either an adult or a juvenile facility.

In those cases where the juvenile court retains jurisdiction, the case may be handled formally by filing a delinquency petition or informally by diverting the juvenile to other agencies or programs in lieu of further court processing.

If a petition for an adjudicatory hearing is accepted, the juvenile may be brought before a court quite unlike the court with jurisdiction over adult offenders. Despite the considerable discretion associated with juvenile court proceedings, juveniles are afforded many of the due-process safeguards associated with adult criminal trials. Several States permit the use of juries in juvenile courts; however, in light of the U.S. Supreme Court holding that juries are not essential to juvenile hearings, most States do not make provisions for juries in juvenile courts.

In disposing of cases, juvenile courts usually have far more discretion than adult courts. In addition to such options as probation, commitment to a residential facility, restitution, or fines, State laws grant juvenile courts the power to order removal of children from their homes to foster homes or treatment facilities. Juvenile courts also may order participation in special programs aimed at shoplifting prevention, drug counseling, or driver education.

Once a juvenile is under juvenile court disposition, the court may retain jurisdiction until the juvenile legally becomes an adult (at age 21 in most States). In some jurisdictions, juvenile offenders may be classified as youthful offenders, which can lead to extended sentences.

Following release from an institution, juveniles are often ordered to a period of aftercare that is similar to parole supervision for adult offenders. Juvenile offenders who violate the conditions of aftercare may have their aftercare revoked, resulting in being recommitted to a facility. Juveniles who are classified as youthful offenders and violate the conditions of aftercare may be subject to adult sanctions.

The Governmental Response to Crime Is Founded in the Intergovernmental Structure of the United States

Under our form of government, each State and the Federal Government has its own criminal justice system. All systems must respect the rights of individuals set forth in court interpretation of the U.S. Constitution and defined in case law.

State constitutions and laws define the criminal justice system within each State and delegate the authority and responsibility for criminal justice to various jurisdictions, officials, and institutions. State laws also define criminal behavior and groups of children or acts under jurisdiction of the juvenile courts.

Municipalities and counties further define their criminal justice systems through local ordinances that proscribe the local agencies responsible for criminal justice processing that were not established by the State.

Congress has also established a criminal justice system at the Federal level to respond to Federal crimes such as bank robbery, kidnaping, and transporting stolen goods across State lines.

The Response to Crime Is Mainly a State and Local Function

Very few crimes are under exclusive Federal jurisdiction. The responsibility to respond to most crime rests with State and local governments. Police protection is primarily a function of cities and towns. Corrections is primarily a function of State governments. Most justice personnel are employed at the local level.

Critical Thinking

1. Explain discretion and how it is exercised in the criminal justice system.
2. What are the steps that follow once a suspect is arrested by police and charged with a crime?
3. How are young people who violate the law treated?

Create Central

www.mhhe.com/createcentral

Internet References

Bureau of Justice Statistics
   www.bjs.gov/content/justsys.cfm
The National Center for Victims of Crime
   www.victimsofcrime.org/help-for-crime-victims/get-help-bulletins-for-crime-victims/the-criminal-justice-system

U.S. Department of Justice, 1998.

Article   Prepared by: Joanne Naughton

Can a Jury Believe What It Sees?

Videotaped Confessions Can Be Misleading

JENNIFER L. MNOOKIN

Learning Outcomes

After reading this article, you will be able to:

- Discuss the advantages of videotaping confessions of criminal suspects.

- Explain what recent research shows about such recordings.

Los Angeles—Last week the FBI, the Drug Enforcement Administration and other federal law enforcement agencies instituted a policy of recording interrogations of criminal suspects held in custody. Only a minority of states and local governments have a similar requirement, but the new rule, which applies to nearly every federal interrogation, will most likely spur more jurisdictions to follow suit. It's not far-fetched to think that such recordings may soon become standard police practice nationwide.

Supporters of the practice present recordings as a solution for a host of problems, from police misconduct to false confessions. But while there are lots of good reasons to require them, they are hardly a panacea; in fact, the very same qualities that make them useful—their seeming vividness and objectivity—also risk making them misleading, and possibly even an inadvertent tool for injustice.

Support for electronic recording has been accelerating in recent years, and its backers now come from all sides of the criminal-justice process. Though some in law enforcement remain critical of the idea, firsthand experience with recording tends to turn law enforcers into supporters—it eliminates uncertainty about police conduct and lets investigators focus on the interrogation rather than taking detailed notes.

Likewise, criminal prosecutors find that when a defendant confesses or provides incriminating information, the video offers vivid and powerful evidence. At the same time, it aids defendants because the very presence of the camera is likely to reduce the use of coercive or unfair tactics in interrogation, and documents illegitimate behavior if and when it does occur. And a recording provides judges and juries with information about what took place in a more objective form.

Given this chorus of support, what's not to like?

The short answer is that, according to recent research, interrogation recording may in fact be too vivid and persuasive. Even seemingly neutral recordings still require interpretation. As advertisers and Hollywood directors know well, camera angles, close-ups, lenses, and dozens of other techniques shape our perception of what we see without our being aware of it.

In a series of experiments led by the psychologist G. Daniel Lassiter of Ohio University, mock juries were shown exactly the same interrogation, but some saw only the defendant, while others had a wider-angle view that included the interrogator. When the interrogator isn't shown on camera, jurors are significantly less likely to find an interrogation coercive, and more likely to believe in the truth and accuracy of the confession that they hear—even when the interrogator explicitly threatens the defendant.

Professor Lassiter and other psychologists have consistently shown this "camera perspective bias" across a substantial series of experiments, finding in one study that even professionals like judges and police interrogators are not immune.

Experiments like these feed a larger concern: whether the police, prosecutors, defense lawyers, judges, or jurors can actually tell the difference between true and false confessions, even with the more complete record of interactions that recorded interrogations provide.

We know that false confessions really do occur, even in very serious crimes, and probably more frequently than most people expect. But why? We know something about certain interrogation techniques, as well as defendant vulnerabilities like youth

Can a Jury Believe What It Sees? Videotaped Confessions Can Be Misleading by Jennifer L. Mnookin

19

or mental disability, that may create heightened risks for false confessions. But we don't yet know enough about the psychology of false confessions to be able to accurately "diagnose" the reliability of a given confession just by watching it.

The problem is that many of the red flags that frequently occur in false confessions—like unusually long interrogations, the inclusion of inaccurate details, or the police "feeding" some crime-related information to the suspect—can also occur in the confessions of the guilty. This means there's no surefire way to tell false confessions and true confessions apart by viewing a recording, except in extreme cases.

And yet by making confessions so vivid to juries, recording could paper over such complications, and sometimes even make the problem worse. The emotional impact of a suspect declaring his guilt out loud, on video, is powerful and hard to dislodge, even if the defense attorney points out reasons to doubt its accuracy.

This doesn't mean that mandating recording of interrogations is a bad idea. Routine recording will serve to make them fairer and less coercive—and this might well help reduce the number of false confessions.

But we need to recognize that by itself, video recording cannot stop all the problems with interrogations, prevent false confessions or guarantee that we will spot them when they do occur.

We are still a long way from fully understanding why the innocent confess during interrogations, and why we believe them when they do—regardless of what we see on camera.

Critical Thinking

1. What are some factors that may create heightened risks for false confessions?
2. Describe Lassiter's work regarding confessions.
3. How can false confessions be distinguished from valid ones?

Internet References

IZA
  ftp.iza.org
U.S. Department of Justice
  www.justice.gov

JENNIFER L. MNOOKIN is a professor of law at the University of California, Los Angeles.

Article Prepared by: Joanne Naughton

An Unbelievable Story of Rape

This story was co-published with The Marshall Project.

An 18-year-old said she was attacked at knifepoint. Then she said she made it up. That's where our story begins.

T. Christian Miller

Learning Outcomes

After reading this article, you will be able to:

- Understand that most victims of sexual attacks don't always behave as people would expect them to.

- Show why the police were wrong to rely on the minor discrepancies in Maria's statements when deciding she lied.

- Realize how it is possible for a crime victim to recant when faced with police who say she is lying.

March 12, 2009
Lynnwood, Washington

No one came to court with her that day, except her public defender.

She was 18 years old, charged with a gross misdemeanor, punishable by up to a year in jail.

Rarely do misdemeanors draw notice. Her case was one of 4,859 filed in 2008 in Lynnwood Municipal Court, a place where the judge says the goal is "to correct behavior—to make Lynnwood a better, safer, healthier place to live, work, shop and visit."

But her misdemeanor had made the news, and made her an object of curiosity or, worse, scorn. It had cost her the newfound independence she was savoring after a life in foster homes. It had cost her sense of worth. Each ring of the phone seemed to announce another friendship, lost. A friend from 10th grade called to ask: How could you lie about something like that? Marie—that's her middle name, Marie—didn't say anything. She just listened, then hung up. Even her foster parents now

doubted her. She doubted herself, wondering if there was something in her that needed to be fixed.

She had reported being raped in her apartment by a man who had bound and gagged her. Then, confronted by police with inconsistencies in her story, she had conceded it might have been a dream. Then she admitted making the story up. One TV newscast announced, "A Western Washington woman has confessed that she cried wolf when it came to her rape she reported earlier this week." She had been charged with filing a false report, which is why she was here today, to accept or turn down a plea deal.

Her lawyer was surprised she had been charged. Her story hadn't hurt anyone—no suspects arrested, or even questioned. His guess was, the police felt used. They don't appreciate having their time wasted.

The prosecution's offer was this: If she met certain conditions for the next year, the charge would be dropped. She would need to get mental health counseling for her lying. She would need to go on supervised probation. She would need to keep straight, breaking no more laws. And she would have to pay $500 to cover the court's costs.

Marie wanted this behind her.

She took the deal.

January 5, 2011
Golden, Colorado

A little after 1 p.m. on a wintry day in January 2011, Detective Stacy Galbraith approached a long, anonymous row of apartment buildings that spilled up a low hill in a Denver suburb. Snow covered the ground in patches. It was blustery, and biting cold. She was there to investigate a report of rape.

Galbraith spotted the victim standing in the thin sunlight outside her ground floor apartment. She was young, dressed in a brown, full-length coat. She clutched a bag of her belongings in one hand. She looked calm, unflustered. Galbraith introduced herself. Police technicians were swarming the apartment. Galbraith suggested that she and the victim escape the icy gusts in a nearby unmarked patrol car.

The woman told Galbraith she was 26 years old, an engineering student on winter break from a nearby college. She had been alone in her apartment the previous evening. After cooking green mung beans for dinner, she curled up in bed for a marathon of "Desperate Housewives" and "The Big Bang Theory" until drifting off. At around 8 a.m., she was jolted awake by a man who had jumped on her back, pinning her to the bed. He wore a black mask that seemed more like a scarf fastened tight around his face. He gripped a silver and black gun. "Don't scream. Don't call or I'll shoot you," he told her.

He moved deliberately. He tied her hands loosely behind her. From a large black bag, he took out thigh-high stockings, clear plastic high heels with pink ribbons, lubrication, a box of moist towelettes, and bottled water. Over the next four hours, he raped her repeatedly. He documented the assault with a digital camera and threatened to post the pictures online if she contacted the police. Afterward, he ordered her to brush her teeth and wash herself in the shower. By the time she exited the bathroom, he had gone. He had taken her sheets and bedding. She clearly remembered one physical detail about him: a dark mark on his left calf the size of an egg.

Galbraith listened to the woman with a sense of alarm. The attack was so heinous; the attacker so practiced. There was no time to waste. Sitting close to her in the front seat of the car, Galbraith carefully brushed the woman's face with long cotton swabs to collect any DNA traces that might remain. Then she drove her to St. Anthony North Hospital. The woman underwent a special forensic examination to collect more DNA evidence. Before she left with a nurse, the woman warned Galbraith, "I think he's done this before."

Galbraith returned to the crime scene. A half-dozen officers and technicians were now at work. They were knocking on neighbors' doors, snapping photographs in the apartment, digging through garbage bins, swabbing the walls, the windows, everywhere for DNA. In the snow, they found a trail of footprints leading to and from the back of the apartment through an empty field. They spraypainted the prints fluorescent orange to make them stand out, then took pictures. It was not much. But something. One officer suggested a bathroom break. "Just keep working!" Galbraith insisted.

As she headed home that night, Galbraith's mind raced. "Who is this guy?" she asked herself. "How am I going to find him?" Galbraith often volunteered to take rape cases. She was a wife, a mother. She was good at empathizing with the victims,

who were overwhelmingly women. Most had been assaulted by a boyfriend, an old flame, or someone they had met at a club. Those investigations often boiled down to an issue of consent. Had the woman said "yes"? They were tough for cops and prosecutors. Juries were hesitant to throw someone in prison when it was one person's word against another's. Rapes by strangers were uncommon—about 13 percent of cases. But there was still the issue of the woman's story. Was she telling the truth? Or fabricating a ruse to cover a sexual encounter gone wrong?

In that way, rape cases were unlike most other crimes. The credibility of the victim was often on trial as much as the guilt of the accused. And on the long, fraught trail between crime and conviction, the first triers of fact were the cops. An investigating officer had to figure out if the victim was telling the truth.

Galbraith had a simple rule: listen and verify. "A lot of times people say, 'Believe your victim, believe your victim,'" Galbraith said. "But I don't think that that's the right standpoint. I think it's listen to your victim. And then corroborate or refute based on how things go."

At home, her husband David had done the dishes and put the kids to bed. They sank down on separate couches in their living room. Galbraith recounted the day's events. The attacker had been cunning, attempting to erase any traces of DNA from the scene. Before he left, he showed the student how he broke in through a sliding glass door. He suggested she put a dowel into the bottom track to keep out future intruders. The victim had described him as a "gentleman," Galbraith said. "He's going to be hard to find," she thought.

David Galbraith was used to such bleak stories. They were both cops, after all. He worked in Westminster, some 15 miles to the northeast. Golden and Westminster were middle class bedroom towns wedged between Denver's downtown skyscrapers and the looming Rockies.

This time, though, there was something different. As David listened, he realized that the details of the case were unsettlingly familiar. He told his wife to call his department first thing in the morning.

"We have one just like that," he said.

Lynnwood, Washington

She does not know if she attended kindergarten.
She remembers being hungry and eating dog food.
She reports entering foster care at age 6 or 7.

The report on Marie's life—written by a mental health expert who interviewed her for five hours—is written with clinical detachment, describing her life before she entered foster care . . .

She met her biological father only once.

She reports not knowing much about her biological mother, who she said would often leave her in the care of boyfriends.
She was sexually and physically abused.

. . . and after, with:
adult caregivers and professionals coming in and then out of her life, some distressing or abusive experiences, and a general lack of permanency.

"I moved a lot when I was younger," Marie says in an interview. "I was in group homes, too. About two of those and probably 10 or 11 foster homes."

"I was on like seven different drugs. And Zoloft is an adult drug—I was on that at 8."

Marie has two brothers and a sister on her mother's side. Sometimes, she was placed in foster homes with her siblings. More often they were separated.

No one really explained why she was being moved, or what was going on. She was just moved.

After Marie became a teenager, her years of upheaval appeared at an end. Her foster family was going to adopt her. "I really loved the family and I made a lot of friends," Marie says.

The first day of the first year of high school fills many students with anxiety. Marie couldn't wait for it. She had gotten all the classes she wanted. She had a social circle.

She felt like she belonged.

But on the first day, a support counselor came to the school and told Marie the family had lost its foster care license. She couldn't live with them anymore. The counselor couldn't offer any more details.

"I pretty much just cried," Marie says. "I basically had 20 minutes to pack my stuff and go."

Until something more permanent could be found, Marie moved in with Shannon McQuery and her husband in Bellevue, a booming, high-tech suburb east of Seattle. Shannon, a real estate agent and longtime foster mom, had met Marie through meetings for kids with troubled pasts and had sensed a kindred spirit.

Shannon and Marie were both "kind of goofy," Shannon says. "We could laugh at each other and make fun. We were a lot alike." Despite all Marie had been through, "she wasn't bitter," Shannon says. She kept in touch with previous foster families. She could carry on a conversation with adults. She didn't have to be pushed out the door to school.

But no matter her affection for Marie, Shannon knew they couldn't keep her, because the foster child already in their home required so much care. "We were really sad that we weren't able to have her with us," Shannon says.

Marie left Shannon's home after a couple of weeks to move in with Peggy Cunningham, who worked as a children's advocate at a homeless shelter and lived in Lynnwood, a smaller suburb about 15 miles north of Seattle. She was Peggy's first foster child.

"I was preparing for a baby. I had a crib—and they gave me a 16-year-old," Peggy says, with a laugh. "And it was fine. I have a background in mental health and I've been working with kids for a really long time. And I think the agency just thought, 'She can handle it.' So."

At first, Marie didn't want to live with Peggy. Marie was used to being around other kids. Peggy didn't have any. Marie liked dogs. Peggy had two cats. "Our personalities didn't match at first either," Marie says. "It was hard to get along. For me it seems like people read me differently than I see myself."

Peggy, who had received a file two to three inches thick documenting Marie's history, was surprised at how well she was coping. Marie was into boys, drawing and music, be it rock, country, or Christian. "She was very bubbly and full of energy, but she also had her moments where she could be very intense," Peggy says. Like kids most everywhere, Marie wanted to fit in. She picked out a feminine white coat with a fur collar because she thought that's what girls were supposed to wear, but then kept the coat in the closet when she realized it wasn't.

Recognizing that Marie's high school wasn't a great fit—"pretty cliquey," Peggy says—Peggy found an alternative school that was. Marie settled in. She remained close with Shannon, who would joke that she and Peggy were raising Marie together—Shannon the fun one *(let's go boating)*, Peggy the disciplinarian *(be home by . . .)*.

Through friends, Marie met Jordan Schweitzer, a high school student working at a McDonald's. In time, they became boyfriend and girlfriend. "She was just a nice person to have around. She was always nice to talk to," Jordan says.

Marie figures her happiest years were when she was 16 and 17, and the happiest day may have been one she spent with her best friend, another high school student who was teaching Marie the fine points of camerawork.

"I would spend hours at the beach watching the sunset go down and that was one of my favorite things. There was a particular photo that I really liked that she took. We went to the ocean, it was like 7 o'clock at night, I don't know what we were thinking, I got in there and I jumped out and swung my hair back."

Instead of finishing high school, Marie went for her GED. She was 17, starting to stay out late, worrying Peggy, creating tension between the two. In the spring of 2008, Marie turned 18. She could have stayed with Peggy, provided she abided by certain rules. But Marie wanted to set out on her own.

Peggy, searching online, discovered a pilot program called Project Ladder. Launched the year before, the program was designed to help young adults who had grown up in foster care transition to living on their own. Case managers would show participants the dos and don'ts of shopping for groceries, handling a credit card, buying insurance. "The rules about life," Marie says. Best of all, Project Ladder provided subsidized housing, with each member getting a one-bedroom apartment.

"This was a godsend," Peggy says.

There were few slots, but Marie secured one. She was a little scared, but any trepidation was tempered by a sense of pride. She moved into the Alderbrooke Apartments, a woodsy complex that advertises proximity to a mall and views of the Cascades. She also landed her first job, offering food samples to customers at Costco. Six hours on her feet didn't bother her. She enjoyed chatting with people, free from pressure to sell.

So many kids, institutionalized, wound up on drugs or in jail. Marie had made it through.

"It was just nice to be on my own and not have all the rules that I had had being in foster care," Marie says. "It was just like, freedom.

"It was awesome."

January 6, 2011
Golden, Colorado

The morning after the rape in Golden, Galbraith hurried to work to follow up her husband's lead. At 9:07 a.m. she sent an email to the Westminster Police Department. The subject line was pleading: "Sex Aslt Similars?"

Westminster Detective Edna Hendershot had settled into her morning with her Starbucks usual: a Venti, upside-down, skinny caramel macchiato. She read the email and her mind shot back five months, to a crisp Tuesday in August 2010. She had responded to a report of a rape at a blue-collar apartment complex in the northwest corner of her city. A 59-year-old woman told her that she had been asleep in her home when a man jumped on her back. He wore a black mask. He tied her hands. He stole her pink Sony Cyber-shot camera and used it to take pictures of her. Afterward, he made her take a shower. He picked up a kitchen timer and set it to let her know when she could get out. "I guess you won't leave your windows open in the future," the man told the woman, who had recently been widowed.

There was more. Hendershot remembered that while investigating her case, an officer had alerted her to an incident in October 2009 in Aurora, a suburb on the other side of Denver. There, a 65-year-old woman told police that she had been raped in her apartment by a man with a black scarf wrapped around his face. He tied her hands with a ribbon. He took pictures and threatened to post them on the Internet. During the attack, he knocked a yellow teddy bear off a desk in her bedroom. "You should get help," the woman, a house mother at a local fraternity, told the man. "It's too late for that," he replied.

Cops can be protective about their cases, fearing that information could be leaked that would jeopardize their investigations. They often don't know about, or fail to use, an FBI database created years ago to help catch repeat offenders. Between 1/4 to 2/3 of rapists are serial attackers, studies show.

But Hendershot right away recognized the potential in collaborating and in using every tool possible. "Two heads, three heads, four heads, sometimes are better than one, right?" she said. So did Galbraith. Her department was small—a little more than 40 officers serving a town of about 20,000. It only made sense to join forces. "I have no qualms with asking for help," Galbraith said. "Let's do what we can do to catch him."

A week later, Galbraith, Hendershot and Aurora Detective Scott Burgess gathered around a conference table in the Westminster Police Department. They compared investigations. The descriptions of the attacker were similar. So, too, his methods. But there was a clincher: the woman in Galbraith's case had remained as focused as possible during her ordeal, memorizing details. She recalled the camera that the attacker had used to take photos. It was a pink Sony digital camera—a description that fit the model stolen from the apartment of the Westminster victim.

Galbraith and Hendershot hadn't known each other before the meeting. But the hunt for the rapist united them. As female cops, both women were members of a sorority within a fraternity. The average law enforcement agency in America is about 13 percent female. Police ranks remain overwhelmingly male, often hierarchical and militaristic. But both women had found a place for themselves. They had moved up in the ranks.

The two bonded naturally. Both were outgoing. They cracked fast jokes and smiled fast smiles. Galbraith was younger. She crackled energy. She would move "a hundred miles an hour in one direction," a colleague said. Hendershot was more experienced. She'd worked more than 100 rape cases in her career. Careful, diligent, exacting—she complemented Galbraith. "Sometimes going a hundred miles an hour, you miss some breadcrumbs," the same colleague noted.

Their initial attempts to identify the attacker faltered. Golden police obtained a surveillance tape showing the entrance to the apartment complex where Galbraith's victim had been attacked. A fellow detective sat through more than 12 hours of blurry footage. He laboriously counted 261 vehicles and people coming and going on the night of the incident. There was one possible lead. In the predawn hours, a white Mazda pickup truck appeared 10 times. Maybe it was the attacker waiting for the woman to fall asleep? But efforts to identify the vehicle's owner failed. The license plate was unreadable.

As the weeks passed, the dead ends continued. Hendershot turned to the database meant to capture serial rapists by linking cases in different jurisdictions. It turned up only bad leads. Frustration grew. "Someone else is going to get hurt," Galbraith worried to herself.

By late January, the detectives decided they needed to broaden their scope. Hendershot asked one of her department's crime analysts to scour nearby agencies for similar crimes. The analyst turned up an incident in Lakewood, another Denver suburb, that occurred about a month before the rape in Westminster. At the time, police had labeled the case a burglary. But in fresh light, it appeared very much like a failed rape attempt, committed by an attacker who closely resembled the description of the rapist. The analyst shot Hendershot a message, "You need to come to talk to me right now."

The report detailed how a 46-year-old artist had been accosted in her home by a man with a knife. He wore a black mask. He tried to bind her wrists. But when the man looked away, the woman jumped out of her bedroom window. She broke three ribs and punctured a lung in the 7-foot fall to the ground, but managed to escape.

Investigators at the scene uncovered a few, tenuous pieces of evidence. Thundershowers had soaked the area before the attack. Police found shoe prints in the soft, damp soil outside the woman's bedroom. On a window, they found honeycomb marks.

Honeycomb marks. Hendershot seized on them. Westminster crime scene investigators had discovered similar marks on the window of the victim's apartment. Hendershot asked for a comparison. The marks at the two crime scenes were the same. They also appeared similar to prints from a pair of Under Armour gloves that a Lakewood investigator, on a hunch, had discovered at a Dick's Sporting Goods.

Galbraith checked out the footprints left at the Lakewood scene. They matched the footprints in the snow outside her victim's apartment in Golden. She sent images of the shoe prints to crimeshoe.com, a website that promised to move an investigation "from an unidentified scene-of-crime shoeprint to detailed footwear information in one simple step." The site, now defunct, identified the prints as having been made by a pair of Adidas ZX 700 mesh shoes, available in stores after March 2005.

By the end of January 2011, the detectives had connected four rapes over a 15-month period across Denver's suburbs. The trail started in Aurora, east of Denver, on October 4, 2009, with the 65-year-old woman. It picked up nine months later and 22 miles to the west, when the rapist attacked the artist in Lakewood. A month after that the 59-year-old widow was raped in Westminster, some 10 miles to the north. And then, finally, in January 2011 came the attack on the 26-year-old in Golden, about 15 miles southwest of Westminster. If you drew a map, it was almost like the rapist was circling the compass points of Denver's suburbs.

Galbraith and Hendershot turned to DNA to identify the serial rapist. The detectives had thoroughly examined their crime scenes. Technicians had swabbed window panes, doorknobs, even toilet handles—anything that the attacker might have touched. But the man was familiar with the ways of law enforcement, perhaps even a cop. He knew to avoid leaving his DNA at the scene. He used wet wipes to clean up his ejaculate. He ordered the women to shower. He took their clothing and bedding with him when he left.

He had been punctilious. But not perfect. The attacker had left behind the tiniest traces of himself. The technicians recovered three samples of so-called touch DNA, as few as seven or eight cells of skin that can be analyzed with modern laboratory techniques.

One sample was collected from the kitchen timer in Westminster. A second came from the victim in Golden. And one came from the teddy bear in Aurora.

August 11, 2008
Lynnwood, Washington

A little before 9 on a Monday morning, two Lynnwood police detectives responded to a report of rape at the Alderbrooke Apartments. A couple of other officers were already there, protecting the crime scene. A K-9 officer was outside, his dog trying to pick up a scent.

The detectives, Sgt. Jeffrey Mason and Jerry Rittgarn, found the victim, Marie, on a couch, in a blanket, crying off and on. She was accompanied by her foster mother, Peggy Cunningham, and by Wayne Nash, her case manager with Project Ladder.

Marie, who had turned 18 three months before, told police she had been talking on the phone much of the night with her friend Jordan. After finally falling asleep, she was awakened by a man with a knife—and then tied up, blindfolded, gagged, and raped. The man wore a condom, she believed. As for what her attacker looked like, Marie could offer few details. White man, gray sweater. The attack seemed to last a long time, Marie told police, but she couldn't say for sure. It was all a blur.

Marie said that after the rapist left she had managed, with her feet, to retrieve some scissors from a cabinet's bottom drawer; she cut herself free, then tried calling Jordan. When Jordan didn't answer, Marie called her foster mother, then her upstairs neighbor, who came down to Marie's apartment and called 911.

Mason, then 39, had spent his years mostly in patrol and narcotics. His longest law-enforcement stint had been with a small police department in Oregon, where he served for almost nine years and received a medal of valor. He was hired by Lynnwood in 2003, and served on a narcotics task force. He was promoted to sergeant—and transferred to the Criminal Investigations Division—six weeks before the report of Marie's assault. He had previously worked only one or two rape cases. But this investigation was his to lead.

Rittgarn had been with the department for 11 years, the last four as a detective. He had previously worked as a technician in the aerospace industry. Before that, he had served in the Marine Corps, specializing in helicopter avionics.

The Lynnwood Police Department had 79 sworn officers, serving a city of about 34,000 people. In 2008, Marie's case was one of 10 rape reports the department fielded; with so few, the Criminal Investigations Division didn't have a separate sex crimes unit.

By the time Marie reported being assaulted, sex crime specialists had developed protocols that recognized the challenges and sensitivity of investigating rape cases. These guidelines, available to all police departments, detailed common missteps.

Investigators, one guide advised, should not assume that a true victim will be hysterical rather than calm; able to show clear signs of physical injury; and certain of every detail. Some victims confuse fine points or even recant. Nor should police get lost in stereotypes—believing, for example, that an adult victim will be more believable than an adolescent.

Police should not interrogate victims or threaten to use a polygraph device. Lie detector tests are especially unreliable with people who have been traumatized, and can destroy the victim's trust in law enforcement. Many states bar police from using them with rape victims.

Police, walking around Marie's apartment, discovered that the rear sliding glass door was unlocked and slightly ajar. It led to a back porch, with a wooden railing that was covered with dirt—except one part, about three feet wide, where it looked like maybe someone had brushed the surface while climbing over. On the bed officers found a shoestring—used, apparently, to bind Marie. On top of a computer monitor they found a second shoestring, tied to a pair of underwear, the apparent blindfold or gag. Both laces had come from Marie's black tennis shoes, in the living room. Next to the bed was a black-handled knife. Marie said the knife was hers—that it had come from the kitchen, and was what the rapist had used to threaten her. Police found Marie's purse on the bedroom floor, her wallet on the bed and her learner's permit, for some reason removed from her wallet, on a bedroom window sill.

Mason told Marie she needed to go to the hospital for a sexual assault examination. After Marie left, accompanied by her foster mom and case manager, the detectives helped process the scene. Looking for a condom or its wrapper, Rittgarn checked the bathroom, trash cans, and a nearby hillside, but came up empty. The dog, outside, had tracked to the south, toward an office building, but was unable to lead officers to anything that might identify the rapist.

At the hospital, medical staff collected more than a dozen swabs from Marie. Labs were taken for hepatitis, chlamydia, HIV. Marie received Zithromax and Suprax for possible exposure to sexually transmitted diseases, and an emergency contraceptive pill.

The medical report noted abrasions to Marie's wrists and to her vagina. The bruising on her right wrist measured 6.5 centimeters, or about 2.5 inches, the one on her left, 7 centimeters.

During the exam, the medical report said, Marie was "alert and oriented, and in no acute distress."

On the day she reported being raped, Marie phoned Shannon, her former foster mom, after getting back from the hospital. "She called and said, 'I've been raped,'" Shannon says. "There was just no emotion. It was like she was telling me that she'd made a sandwich." That Marie wasn't hysterical, or even upset, made Shannon wonder if Marie was telling the truth.

The next day, when Shannon saw Marie at her apartment, her doubts intensified. In the kitchen, when Shannon walked in, Marie didn't meet her gaze. "That seemed very strange," Shannon says. "We would always hug and she would look you right in the eye." In the bedroom, Marie seemed casual, with nothing to suggest that something horrible had happened there. Outside, Marie "was on the grass, rolling around and giggling and laughing," Shannon says. And when the two went to buy new bedding—Marie's old bedding having been taken as evidence—Marie became furious when she couldn't find the same set. "Why would you want to have the same sheets and bedspread to look at every day when you'd been raped on this bed set?" Shannon thought to herself.

Peggy, too, was mystified by Marie's demeanor. When Marie called her on that first day, before the police arrived, "she was crying and I could barely hear her," Peggy says. "Her voice was like this little tiny voice, and I couldn't really tell. It didn't sound real to me. . . . It sounded like a lot of drama, too, in some ways." At the time, Peggy had new foster children—two sisters, both teenagers. Not long before, Marie had accompanied Peggy and the sisters and Peggy's boyfriend on a picnic. To Peggy's mind, Marie had spent the afternoon trying to get attention—so much so that Peggy now wondered if this was more of the same, only more desperate.

After rushing to the apartment that morning, Peggy found Marie on the floor, crying. "But it was so strange because I sat down next to her, and she was telling me what happened, and I got this—I'm a big *Law & Order* fan, and I just got this really weird feeling," Peggy says. "It was like, I felt like she was telling me the script of a *Law & Order* story." Part of it was what Marie was saying. Why would a rapist use shoelaces to tie her up? And part of it was how Marie was saying it: "She seemed so detached and removed emotionally."

The two women who had helped raise Marie talked on the phone. Peggy told Shannon she had doubts. Shannon said she did, too. Neither had known Marie to be a liar—to exaggerate, sure, to want attention, sure—but now, both knew they weren't alone in wondering if Marie had made this up.

On August 12, the day after Marie reported being raped, Sgt. Mason's telephone rang. The caller "related that [Marie] had a past history of trying to get attention and the person was questioning whether the 'rape' had occurred," Mason later wrote.

Mason's report didn't identify the caller—but the caller was Peggy.

She called police to share her concerns. Mason then came to her home and interviewed her in person. When she told police of her skepticism, she asked to be treated anonymously. "I didn't want it to get back to Marie," Peggy says. "I was trying to be a good citizen, actually. You know? I didn't want them to waste their resources on something that might be, you know, this personal drama going on."

In addition, Mason had received a tip that Marie was unhappy with her apartment. Maybe, she was making up the rape to get moved to a new one.

On August 13, Marie met with Mason at the Lynnwood police station and turned in a written statement, describing what happened. The statement was only one page. But to Mason, there was one critical passage. Marie wrote that the attacker said she could untie herself once he was gone:

> *After he left I grabbed my phone (which was right next to my head) with my mouth and I tried to call Jordan back. He didn't answer so I called my foster mom. . . . She came right away. I got off the phone with her and tried to untie myself.*

This didn't square with what Marie had previously told Mason. Before, she told the detective she had tried calling Jordan after cutting the laces. In this written statement, she described calling him while still tied up.

Later that day, Mason talked to Rittgarn, his fellow detective, and said that—based on Marie's inconsistencies, and based on what he had learned from Peggy and Jordan—he now believed Marie had made up the story.

The fear of false rape accusations has a long history in the legal system. In the 1600s, England's chief justice, Matthew Hale, warned that rape "is an accusation easily to be made and hard to be proved, and harder to be defended by the party accused." Judges in the U.S. read the so-called Hale warning to juries until the 1980s. But most recent research suggests that false reporting is relatively rare. FBI figures show that police annually declare around 5 percent of rape cases unfounded, or baseless. Social scientists examining police records in detail and using methodologically rigorous standards cite similar, single-digit rates.

The next morning, Mason went to Jordan's home to interview him. Jordan told the detective that he and Marie had stopped dating a couple months back but remained good friends. He said nothing about doubting Marie's story, according to Mason's written summary. But he did say Marie had told him: When she tried calling him that morning, she had used her toes, because she was tied up.

Later that day—August 14, three days after Marie reported being raped—Mason called Marie, to ask if they could meet. He said he could come and pick her up, to take her to the police station.

"Am I in trouble?" Marie asked the detective.

February 9, 2011
Westminster, Colorado

On February 9, 2011, more than a dozen cops and agents from the FBI and the Colorado Bureau of Investigation gathered in a briefing room at the Westminster police station to discuss the state of the investigation.

The news was not great. After a five-week crush, there were few leads and no suspects. The analysis of the touch DNA produced mixed results. The samples narrowed the field of suspects to males belonging to the same paternal family line. But there was not enough genetic material to identify a single individual. Thus the results couldn't be entered into the FBI's nationwide DNA database to check for a match to a suspect.

Galbraith was hopeful. At least it was concrete now. The same person was at work. "It's huge," she said. "But not enough."

As the meeting drew to a close, a young crime analyst from the Lakewood police department stood up. She had conducted a search for any reports of suspicious vehicles or prowlers within a quarter mile of the Lakewood victim's home for the previous six months. She had turned up something. But she didn't know if it was important.

Three weeks before the attempted rape in Lakewood, a woman had called police late in the evening to report a suspicious pickup truck parked on the street with a man inside. Police checked it out, but the man was gone. The officer filed a brief report on the vehicle. What had attracted the analyst's attention was the location of the pickup. It was parked half a block from the Lakewood victim's house, by an empty field adjacent to her backyard.

The pickup was a 1993 white Mazda.

It was registered to a Lakewood man named Marc Patrick O'Leary.

The investigation instantly turned urgent. Could the detectives connect O'Leary's Mazda with the blurry image of the white Mazda in the surveillance footage from Golden? Aaron Hassell, the detective on the Lakewood case, raced back to his office. Lakewood patrol cars had cameras that automatically took pictures of every license plate they passed. The result was a searchable database of thousands of tag numbers indexed by time and location. Hassell typed in the license plate number from the Lakewood report: 935VHX. He got a hit. A Lakewood patrol car had snapped a picture of O'Leary standing by his white Mazda in the driveway of his house—only two hours after the August attack on the widow in Westminster.

Hassell transmitted the image to Galbraith. Carefully, she compared O'Leary's white Mazda to the surveillance tape. One freeze frame showed that her white Mazda had a broken passenger side mirror. So, too, did O'Leary's truck. Both vehicles had ball hitches on the back. Both had smudges on the back in the same place—perhaps a bumper sticker that had been torn off.

"That's our guy," Galbraith said.

Hendershot discovered the Lakewood patrol car had snapped its picture as O'Leary was headed to a nearby branch of the Colorado Department of Motor Vehicles. DMV records showed O'Leary sat for a driver's license mugshot about four hours after the Westminster attack. The photo showed a 6-foot-1 man with hazel eyes. He was 32 years old and 220 pounds. He wore a white T-shirt. The physical description closely matched the descriptions provided by the victims. And the Westminster widow had told Hendershot that her attacker wore a white T-shirt during her assault.

Hendershot did not want to be too hasty. "I'm encouraged, I'm excited," she said. But "I haven't made my decision yet, that yay, we've got the guy."

Over the next 24 hours, more than a dozen investigators threw their collective effort and experience into finding out everything possible about O'Leary. O'Leary had no criminal record. He was not a registered sex offender. He had served in the Army.

Galbraith and her husband David once again faced each other on the couches in their living room. They used laptops to search for any references to O'Leary, each using a different search engine. Before long, David stumbled onto something. O'Leary had purchased a pornography website in September 2008. They wondered whether it contained photos of his victims.

The investigators decided to try to get a sample of O'Leary's DNA. Though the degraded DNA lifted from the crime scenes could not definitively match O'Leary's DNA, it could show that a male from his family line had most likely committed the crime. If detectives could eliminate O'Leary's male relatives, they could place O'Leary at the scene of the crimes with a high degree of certainty. "We still have to make that definitive identification," Hendershot said.

On the morning of Friday, February 11, FBI agents were surveilling O'Leary's house. It was a small, single-story home with gray siding half a block from a gas station, an auto body shop and a carniceria in a beat-down neighborhood. A low chain-link fence surrounded it. Tall, winter-bare trees towered above the roof. Just after noon, the agents saw a woman and a man who looked like O'Leary leave. They tailed the pair to a nearby restaurant, and watched them eat. When they finished,

the agents raced in. They grabbed the drinking cups from the table. The rims would have traces of his DNA.

While the agents were following the man believed to be Marc O'Leary, another FBI agent knocked on the door of the home. He planned to install a surveillance camera nearby and wanted to make sure that nobody was around. Unexpectedly, a man came to the door. He looked like Marc O'Leary. Confused, the agent fell back on a practiced ruse. He told the man he was canvassing the neighborhood to warn of a burglar in the area. The man introduced himself. He was Marc O'Leary. His brother, Michael O'Leary, had just left to get lunch with his girlfriend. O'Leary thanked the officer for the information and closed the door.

Michael's appearance was confounding. The investigators hadn't known that Michael lived with his brother. Or that he looked so similar. They decided to run Michael O'Leary's DNA, collected from the restaurant glass, against the DNA found at the crime scenes. Analysts at the Colorado Bureau of Investigation got the samples. Usually, a DNA analysis took months. But in this case, they worked through the night. By 2 p.m. on Saturday, they had a result. The DNA from the cup matched the DNA collected from the victims. An O'Leary man was responsible. But which one?

Galbraith ruled out the brothers' father—he was too old and lived in a different state. But investigators could not yet rule out Michael as a suspect. It was possible that Michael had committed the rapes. Or even that Michael and Marc had worked together. They needed more information.

Galbraith hastily typed up a search warrant to enter the brothers' home. It was dark outside when she finished. She called the judge who was on duty for the weekend. He insisted on a fax. Galbraith rushed to a Safeway near her house to send the warrant. The judge signed it at 10 p.m. on Saturday.

She knew exactly what she was looking for. She trusted her victim's memory. The dark mark on his leg.

She emailed a crime analyst at another police department, "I so want to see this guy's leg! BAD."

August 14, 2008
Lynnwood, Washington

In Sgt. Mason's experience, when someone asked if they were in trouble, almost always, they were.

When Mason, accompanied by Detective Rittgarn, went to pick up Marie at about 3:30 p.m., they found her outside her apartment, sitting on the grass. The three went to the Lynnwood police station, where the detectives escorted Marie to a conference room.

From what Mason wrote up later, he wasted little time confronting Marie, telling her there were inconsistencies between her statements and accounts from other witnesses. Marie said she didn't know of any discrepancies. But she went through the story again—only this time, saying she believed the rape had happened instead of saying it for certain. Tearfully, she described her past—all the foster parents, being raped when she was 7, getting her own place and feeling alone. Rittgarn told Marie that her story and the evidence didn't match. He said he believed she had made the story up—a spur-of-the-moment thing, not something planned out. He asked if there was really a rapist running around the neighborhood that the police should be looking for. "No," Marie told him, her voice soft, her eyes down.

"Based on her answers and body language it was apparent that [Marie] was lying about the rape," Rittgarn later wrote.

Without reading Marie her rights—*you have the right to an attorney, you have the right to remain silent*—the detectives asked Marie to write out the true story, admitting she had lied, admitting, in effect, that she had committed a crime. She agreed, so they left her alone for a few minutes. On the form she filled in her name, address and Social Security number, and then she wrote, in part:

I was talking to Jordan on the phone that night about his day and just about anything. After I got off the phone with him, I started thinking about all things I was stressed out and I also was scared living on my own. When I went to sleep I dreamed that someone broke in and raped me.

When the detectives returned, they saw that Marie's new statement described the rape as a dream, not a lie.

Why didn't you write that you made the story up? Rittgarn asked.

Marie, crying, said she believed the rape really happened. She pounded the table and said she was "pretty positive."

Pretty positive or actually positive? Rittgarn asked.

Maybe the rape happened and I blacked it out, Marie said.

What do you think should happen to someone who would lie about something like this? Rittgarn asked Marie.

"I should get counseling," Marie said.

Mason returned to the evidence. He told Marie that her description of calling Jordan was different from what Jordan had reported.

Marie, her face in her hands, looked down. Then "her eyes darted back and forth as if she was thinking of a response."

The detectives doubled back to what she had said before—about being stressed, being lonely—and, eventually, Marie appeared to relax. She stopped crying. She even laughed a little. She apologized—and agreed to write another statement, leaving no doubt it was a lie.

I have had a lot of stressful things going on and I wanted to hang out with someone and no one was able to so I made up

this story and didn't expect it to go as far as it did. . . . I don't know why I couldn't have done something different. This was never meant to happen.

This statement appeared to satisfy the detectives. Rittgarn would later write, "Based on our interview with [Marie] and the inconsistencies found by Sgt. Mason in some of the statements we were confident that [Marie] was now telling us the truth that she had not been raped."

To Marie, it seemed the questioning had lasted for hours. She did what she always did when under stress. She flipped the switch, as she called it, suppressing all the feelings she didn't know what to do with. Before she confessed to making up the story, she couldn't look the two detectives, the two men, in the eye. Afterward, she could. Afterward, she smiled. She went into the bathroom and cleaned up. Flipping the switch was a relief—and it would let her leave.

The next day, Marie told Wayne Nash, her case manager at Project Ladder, that the police didn't believe her. Recognizing the jeopardy she was in, she said she wanted a lawyer.

The Project Ladder managers instead reached out to Sgt. Mason. He told them the evidence didn't support Marie's story, and that she had taken her story back.

But now, Marie wouldn't give. On August 18, one week after she reported being raped, she met with the two Project Ladder managers and insisted she had signed the recantation under duress. The three then went to the police station so Marie could recant her recantation—that is, tell detectives that she had been telling the truth the first time.

While the program managers waited outside, Marie met with Rittgarn and another officer.

Rittgarn asked Marie what was going on. Marie said she really had been raped—and began to cry, saying she was having visions of the man on top of her. She wanted to take a lie detector test. Rittgarn told Marie that if she took the test and failed, she would be booked into jail. What's more, he would recommend that Project Ladder pull her housing assistance.

Marie backed down. The police officers walked her downstairs, where the Project Ladder representatives asked if she had been raped. Marie said no.

After leaving the police station, Marie learned that she still wasn't through. There was something else she had to do. The Project Ladder managers told Marie that if she wanted to stay in the program—if she wanted to keep her subsidized apartment—she would have to confess to someone else.

Later that day a meeting was called at the housing complex, with all of Marie's peers gathered in a circle. Marie, as directed, told her fellow participants in Project Ladder that she had lied about being raped. They didn't need to worry, she told the group. There was no one out there who had hurt her and no one who might hurt them next.

If there was sympathy in the room, Marie sensed it from only one person, the young woman to her right. The rest was awkward, excruciating silence.

After the meeting, Marie started walking to a friend's place. On her way, she crossed a bridge. She considered jumping. "Probably the only time I just wanted to die in my life," she says. She called a friend and said, "Please come get me before I do something stupid." Afterward, Marie hurled her phone over the side.

Later that month, there was a final surprise. Marie got a letter, notifying her that she was wanted in court. She had been charged with false reporting, punishable by up to a year in jail. The criminal citation was signed by Sgt. Mason. Afterward, the paperwork went to a small law firm that Lynnwood had hired to prosecute misdemeanors.

For Mason, his decision to file the citation required no complicated calculus. He was certain Marie had lied. The police had spent a lot of resources chasing that lie. The law said her lie was a crime. Really, it was as simple as that.

There are no firm statistics on how often police arrest women for making false rape reports, nor on how often prosecutors take such cases to court. Nobody collects such data. But leading law enforcement organizations urge caution in filing such charges. The International Association of Chiefs of Police and the FBI stress the need for a thorough investigation before discounting a report of rape. Cops must work as hard to prove a falsehood as they do to prove a truth.

In practice, many police departments will pursue charges against women only in extreme circumstances—say, in a highly public case where a suspect's reputation has suffered, or where the police have expended considerable investigative resources. This reluctance stems from the belief that in rape cases, the biggest problem is not false reporting, but no reporting. Only about 1/5 to 1/3 of rapes get reported to police, national surveys show. One reason is that women fear police won't believe them.

Within days of reporting being raped, Marie had quit her job at Costco, unable to stand there, looking at people, lost in her head. Now, her losses mounted.

Project Ladder gave her a 9 p.m. curfew and doubled the number of times she had to meet with staff.

The media wrote about Marie being charged, without identifying her. (The Seattle Post-Intelligencer headline read, "Police: Lynnwood rape report was a hoax.") Marie's best friend from high school—the one who had taught her photography and had taken that picture of her emerging from the surf—created a webpage that called Marie a liar, with a photo from Marie's Myspace page, with police reports, with Marie's full name. Alerted to the site, Marie went into a frenzy, trashing her apartment.

Marie stopped going to church. "I was mad at God," she says. She lost interest in photography. She feared going outdoors.

"One night I did try to walk to the store by myself and felt like I hallucinated someone following me," she says. "It freaked me out. I didn't even get a half mile from my house. I ran home." At home she avoided the bedroom, choosing to sleep on the couch with the lights on.

"I went into this dark hole," she says.

Self-esteem gave way to self-loathing. She started smoking, drinking, gaining weight.

For Marie, this was a familiar drill, one she could trace to her years of being abused as a kid, and to her years in foster care, bouncing from home to home and school to school. Shut down. Hold it in. Act like nothing bad had happened, like nothing ever affected her. Because she craved normalcy, she would bury the hurt.

Neither Peggy nor Shannon abandoned her, but things weren't the same. Marie knew that both had doubted her story, even before the police had.

For Marie, Shannon's home had long provided an escape or respite. Marie and Shannon would walk in the woods, or take out the boat, then, at day's end, crash in Shannon's home. Now, fearful he could become the target of a wrongful accusation, Shannon's husband decided it would be best if Marie no longer spent the night. "When you become a foster parent, you're open to that," Shannon says.

It fell to Shannon to break the news. Delivering it crushed her. Receiving it crushed Marie.

In early October, less than two months after Marie was charged with false reporting, a 63-year-old woman reported being raped inside her condominium in Kirkland, east of Seattle. The stranger wore gloves. He held a knife. He tied the woman up—with her own shoelaces. He took pictures and threatened to post them on the Internet. For the last two or three months, the woman told police, she felt as if someone had been following her.

Shannon saw an account of the attack on the television news and was taken aback. Her father had been the chief of police in Kent, south of Seattle. She grew up with police, trusted police, knew how the police worked. She went to her computer, looked up the number, and called—immediately—to alert police in Kirkland to Marie's story, to advise them of all the parallels.

Shannon called Marie and suggested she also contact the Kirkland police. Marie never did.

"I was just too scared," Marie says. She'd gone through so much already. She couldn't bring herself to meet with the police again and say anything more. But she did go online and look up what happened to the woman in Kirkland. When she read the story, she cried.

A Kirkland detective eventually called Shannon back. Based on Shannon's tip, Kirkland investigators had reached out to their Lynnwood counterparts and had been told the Lynnwood victim was no victim, the story had been made up.

One of the detectives working the Kirkland case was Audra Weber. She remembers calling the Lynnwood detectives twice and being told they didn't believe Marie's account. "I just kind of trusted their judgment, in terms of it's their case, they know the details and I don't," Weber says. But she remembers being "kind of shocked" to learn that they had charged Marie. She let it go and hung up, thinking, "Okay, I hope that works out for you guys."

February 13, 2011
Lakewood, Colorado

At 8:15 a.m., Galbraith knocked on O'Leary's door.

"Police. Search warrant. Open the door," she shouted repeatedly. Seven cops stood behind her, pressed against the house, their guns drawn.

After a pause, O'Leary opened the door. He looked confused and shocked as he stepped out into the bright winter sun. Two dogs, a small pit bull and a Shar-Pei, tumbled out ahead of him. He wore a gray hoodie, baggy gray sweatpants and gray slip-on houseshoes. He was alone.

Galbraith pulled him to the side and patted him down. When she got to his legs, she raised his pant leg to look.

There it was, on O'Leary's left calf: a dark birthmark the size of a large chicken egg.

It was him. He was the rapist. Galbraith flashed a quick thumbs up.

As an FBI agent confronted him, O'Leary immediately invoked his right to an attorney. Galbraith had maneuvered herself to stand behind O'Leary. At 8:35 a.m., she handcuffed him. "You're under arrest for burglary and sexual assault which occurred in the City of Golden on January 5, 2011," she told him. O'Leary was put in a patrol car and transported to the Jefferson County Jail.

She was wearing new boots that day. Whenever she looked at them in the future, she would remember catching O'Leary. For Galbraith, it was important to be the one who made the arrest. "I wanted to see the look on his face, I guess," she said. "And for him to know that we figured you out."

The search of the home validated the detectives' investigation. Investigators found a pair of Adidas ZX 700 shoes in O'Leary's closet. The treads matched the footprints in the snow in Golden and outside the window in Lakewood. They discovered a pair of Under Armour gloves with a honeycomb pattern. In the bathroom was a black headwrap, tied to serve as a mask.

"He was military—so he was very organized," Galbraith said. "This was the cleanest house I've ever searched. It was so organized, we were like, 'Oh, thank God.'"

The victims' accounts were also borne out. Most had described a white man with green or hazel eyes, about 6-feet tall, weighing about 200 pounds. They talked about being tied up. They mentioned that he had stolen their underwear. In O'Leary's house, investigators turned up a black Ruger .380-caliber pistol, a pink Sony Cyber-shot camera and a large backpack, along with wet wipes and lubrication. Hidden inside a piece of stereo equipment in his closet, detectives found a collection of women's underwear, Trophies.

That night, Hendershot drove to break the news to her victim, the 59-year-old widow in Westminster. The woman had lost her husband to cancer the previous year. She had no family nearby. She was still emerging from the mental and physical suffering she endured during the attack. Hendershot met her at a Denny's restaurant. She found her in a back corner, eating dinner alone.

"I walked in, and she was super happy to see me, and I told her. I mean, I get shiver bumps thinking about it, just even now," Hendershot said. "I told her, I said, 'It's over. It's over. We have him.'"

By early March, a forensic computer specialist cracked into files that O'Leary had stored on his hard drive. He found a folder called "girls"—and pictures that O'Leary had taken of his victims in Golden and Westminster. Galbraith recognized them by sight.

But then Galbraith stumbled across an image of a woman she didn't recognize. It was a young woman—far younger than the Colorado victims, perhaps a teenager. The pictures showed her looking terrified, bound, and gagged on a bed. Galbraith felt sick. How would she identify her? How would she find justice for her?

After looking through the images, she found an answer. It was a picture of the woman's learner's permit, placed on her chest. It had her name. And it had her address.

Lynnwood, Washington.

August 11, 2008
Lynnwood, Washington

He arrived in the predawn hours, then waited outside her apartment, outside her bedroom, listening to her on the phone, waiting for her to fall asleep.

The night was dry, letting him settle in. The wall was thin, letting him hear her voice. A couple of times he left his position, for just a while, for fear of being spotted lingering.

He liked trees, for the cover they provided, and the Alderbrooke Apartments had plenty of them. Apartments didn't offer the privacy of a house, but still, there were advantages. All those windows, for one thing. And all those sliding glass doors—ridiculously easy to pick, when they weren't left unlocked, which so often they were.

She wasn't his type, not really. He'd realized that before while peeping into her bedroom. But he spent so much time hunting (that's what he called it, hunting), hundreds of hours, maybe even a thousand, that he conditioned himself to incorporate as many women as possible, young or old, into his fantasies.

That way his work wouldn't be wasted.

He had prowled before and broken into women's homes before, but following through was another matter. He had learned from past failures—one time, a guy walked in as he stood there, mask on, outside the bedroom door of the woman he planned to rape—so now, he did painstaking surveillance: peeking in windows, breaking in beforehand, gathering information. Years later, detectives would find notes on his cellphone from his surveillance of another target (his word) that detailed which room she was in and when, what lights were off or on, which windows and blinds were opened or closed, whether her boyfriend was there or gone. "BF in PJs, game over," he wrote in one night's entry.

He would rifle a target's personal documents. He would learn her date of birth and license plate number. He would watch her watching TV. And at the hunt's end, before he committed, he would take a final pass through the home, or what he called "precombat inspection," to make sure there weren't any weapons within the target's reach.

At a little before sunrise, he heard the phone conversation end. He waited a little longer, letting the silence stretch out, then climbed over the railing and slipped through the unlocked sliding glass door. For the next half hour or so, while she slept, he got ready while talking himself into following through.

He had first spotted her a couple of weeks before, through a window, while lurking outside her apartment. He had since broken into her place twice, both times through that same glass door.

He had a term for what he was about to do: "rape theater." Deviant fantasies had gripped him since he was a kid, way back to when he had seen Jabba the Hutt enslave and chain Princess Leia. *Where do you go when you're 5 and already thinking about handcuffs?* he would ask himself. He was only 8 the first time he broke into a home. It was such a rush. He had broken into more than a dozen homes since.

Now he was 30, an Army veteran—infantry, two tours in South Korea—who had enlisted in the Reserves, only he hadn't appeared for duty in months.

In the kitchen, he went to the knife block and removed a black-handled blade from the top row, far left.

In the living room, he removed the laces from her black tennis shoes and put the shoes back. One detective later wrote in a report, "The shoes were lying next to each other near the end of the couch and the bedroom door, on the soles as if placed there (not disturbed)."

He was just being neat and orderly, the way he was with everything.

He threaded one of the shoelaces through a pair of underwear.

Then he walked to the bedroom.

Around 7 a.m., he stood in her bedroom doorway, holding, at shoulder height, a knife in his left hand.

He watched as she awoke.

Turn away, he told Marie—and she did. Roll over onto your stomach, he told her. She did—and then he straddled her, putting the knife near her face.

Put your hands behind your back, he told her. She did. He bound her wrists and he covered her eyes. He stuffed cloth into her mouth to muffle any sound.

That was an interesting conversation you were having, he said, letting her know that he had been there, listening, waiting.

You should know better than to leave the door unlocked, he told her.

Roll back over, he told her—and she did, and then he raped her, and while he raped her he ran his gloved hands over her.

He put her learner's permit on her chest and took pictures of her.

When he was finished, he said that if she told the police, he would post the photos online so that her kids, when she had kids, could see them.

He took out the gag and removed the blindfold, telling her to avert her eyes and to keep her head in the pillow.

One of the last things he said was that he was sorry. He said he felt stupid, that it had looked better in his head.

He left the room, and walked to the front door, and he was gone.

Epilogue

O'Leary pleaded guilty to 28 counts of rape and associated felonies in Colorado. On December 9, 2011, almost a year after his arrest, O'Leary was sentenced to 327½ years in prison for the Colorado attacks—the maximum allowed by law. He is currently housed in the Sterling Correctional Facility in the barren, remote northeastern corner of Colorado. He will never be released.

In an interview with police after his conviction, O'Leary recounted his attacks in detail. He described the feeling after raping one elderly victim. "It was like I'd just eaten Thanksgiving dinner," he said.

He let spill some lessons for law enforcement. He boasted of the countermeasures he'd taken to avoid getting caught. He knew that the Army had a sample of his DNA. So he took steps to avoid leaving any traces of genetic material. He also realized police departments often did not communicate. So he deliberately committed each rape in a different jurisdiction.

The five other attacks—one in Washington, four in Colorado—all came after the attack on Marie.

"If Washington had just paid attention a little bit more, I probably would have been a person of interest earlier on," O'Leary said.

Working from Colorado, Galbraith not only linked O'Leary to the rape in Lynnwood, Washington, but to the rape in nearby Kirkland. She made the connection by working with a Washington state criminal analyst to search a database for unsolved cases similar to O'Leary's crimes. She then found the Kirkland victim's name on O'Leary's computer, attached to an encrypted file.

O'Leary pleaded guilty in both of the Washington cases. In June 2012, he was sentenced to 40 years for the rape in Kirkland and to 28½ years for the rape of Marie in Lynnwood.

After O'Leary was linked to Marie's rape, Lynnwood Police Chief Steven Jensen requested an outside review of how his department had handled the investigation. In a report not previously made public, Sgt. Gregg Rinta, a sex crimes supervisor with the Snohomish County Sheriff's Office, wrote that what happened was "nothing short of the victim being coerced into admitting that she lied about the rape."

That Marie recanted wasn't surprising, Rinta wrote, given the "bullying" and "hounding" she was subjected to. The detectives elevated "minor inconsistencies"—common among victims—into discrepancies, while ignoring strong evidence the crime had occurred. As for threatening jail and a possible withdrawal of housing assistance if Marie failed a polygraph: "These statements are coercive, cruel, and unbelievably unprofessional," Rinta wrote. "I can't imagine ANY justification for making these statements."

Jensen also ordered an internal review, which was similarly damning. Mason's judgment was unduly swayed by Peggy's phone call. The detectives' second interview with Marie was "designed to elicit a confession of false reporting." The false reporting charge arose from a "self-imposed rush."

Despite the reviews' tough language, no one in the Lynnwood Police Department was disciplined.

In a recent interview, Steve Rider, the current commander of Lynnwood's Criminal Investigations Division, called Marie's case a "major failing" that has left members of the department with a profound sense of regret: "Knowing that she went through that brutal attack—and then we told her she lied? That's awful. We all got into this job to help people, not to hurt them." Lynnwood Sgt. Rodney Cohnheim said of Marie, "She was victimized twice."

Sgt. Mason is now back in narcotics, in charge of a task force. Interviewed in the same room where he had confronted Marie seven years before, he said: "It wasn't her job to try to convince me. In hindsight, it was my job to get to the bottom of it—and I didn't."

Marie's case led to changes in practices and culture, Rider said. Detectives receive additional training about rape victims. Rape victims get immediate assistance from advocates at a local healthcare center. Investigators must have "definitive proof" of lying before doubting a rape report, and a charge of false reporting must now be reviewed with higher-ups. "We learned a great deal from this. And we don't want to see this happen to anybody ever again," Rider said.

Rittgarn, who left the Lynnwood Police Department before O'Leary's arrest, declined to be interviewed for this story. So did Zachor & Thomas, the law office that handled the prosecution of Marie on Lynnwood's behalf.

In 2008, Marie's case was one of four labeled unfounded by the Lynnwood police, according to statistics reported to the FBI. In the five years from 2008 to 2012, the department determined that 10 of 47 rapes reported to Lynnwood police were unfounded—21.3 percent. That's five times the national average of 4.3 percent for agencies covering similar-sized populations during that same period. Rider said his agency has become more cautious about labeling a case unfounded since Marie. "I would venture to say we investigate our cases a lot more vigorously than many departments do," he said. "Now, we're extra careful that we get the right closure on it."

Two and a half years after Marie was branded a liar, Lynnwood police found her, south of Seattle, and told her the news: Her rapist had been arrested in Colorado. They gave her an envelope with information on counseling for rape victims. They said her record would be expunged. And they handed her $500, a refund of her court costs. Marie broke down, experiencing, all at once, shock, relief and anger.

Afterward, Shannon took Marie for a walk in the woods, and told her, "I'm so sorry I doubted you." Marie forgave, immediately. Peggy, too, apologized. She now wishes she had never shared her doubts with police. "Because I feel that if I would have shut my mouth, they would have done their job," she says.

Marie sued the city and settled for $150,000. "A risk management decision was made," a lawyer for Lynnwood told The Herald in Everett, Washington.

Marie left the state, got a commercial driver's license and took a job as a long-haul trucker. She married, and in October she and her husband had their second child. She asked that her current location not be disclosed.

Before leaving Washington to restart her life, Marie made an appointment to visit the Lynnwood police station. She went to a conference room and waited. Rittgarn had already left the department, but Mason came in, looking "like a lost little puppy," Marie says. "He was rubbing his head and literally looked like he was ashamed about what they had done." He told Marie he was sorry—"deeply sorry," Marie says. To Marie, he seemed sincere.

Recently, Marie was asked if she had considered not reporting the rape.

"No," she said. She wanted to be honest. She wanted to remember everything she could. She wanted to help the police.

"So nobody else would get hurt," she said. "They'd be out there searching for this person who had done this to me."

Critical Thinking

1. Did Marie's age and background have an effect on whether she was believed?

2. How could Marie's case have been handled better by the police?

3. How did O'Leary's knowledge about police departments' communication practices help him avoid being caught?

Internet References

Coaches' Corner: The Story Behind "An Unbelievable Story of Rape"

http://www.poynter.org/2016/coaches-corner-the-story-behind-an-unbelievable-story-of-rape/390592/

People v. Gammage

http://law.justia.com/cases/california/supreme-court/4th/2/693.html

Pulitzer-Winning Reporting Highlights the Challenges of Reporting on Rape and How the Media Can Do Better

http://mediamatters.org/blog/2016/05/09/pulitzer-winning-reporting-highlights-challenges-reporting-rape-and-how-media-can-do-better/210312

Article Prepared by: Joanne Naughton

Criminals Should Get Same Leniency as Corporations, Judge Says

MATT APUZZO

Learning Outcomes

After reading this article, you will be able to:

- Describe how General Motors benefitted from a deferred-prosecution agreement with the Justice Department.

- Learn how America's prison population compares with that of China and Russia.

- Show how deferred-prosecution deals are attractive to companies that violate laws.

Washington—For years, when corporations paid big fines to escape prosecution for their misdeeds, critics fumed. Why, they asked, shouldn't big companies be treated like common criminals?

A federal judge turned that question on its head this week as he lamented being asked to approve yet another corporate settlement. Perhaps, he said, common criminals ought to be treated more like big companies.

Judge Emmet G. Sullivan, of the United States District Court for the District of Columbia, took aim at a favorite tool of the Obama administration for addressing corporate wrongdoing: a form of probation known as a deferred prosecution agreement. If companies behave for the length of the agreement, the matter is closed without any criminal record.

The judge said individual defendants should enjoy the same opportunities. While it is not uncommon for judges to criticize outcomes that they see as unjust, it is highly unusual for them to so explicitly advocate—and at such great length—a change in approach.

Judge Sullivan's 84-page opinion—in what could have been a short, straightforward decision—is the latest influential voice to join a growing chorus of both liberals and conservatives who see the American criminal justice system as fundamentally unfair.

The ruling comes amid a rapidly changing environment: The White House is approving clemency applications at historically high rates, support is coalescing on Capitol Hill to ease sentencing laws, and law enforcement leaders around the country have declared that too many Americans are in prison for too long. Though the federal prison population has declined for the first time in decades, America remains the world's largest jailer by far; its prison population nearly equals China's and Russia's combined.

Justice Department officials agree in principle with Judge Sullivan's critique and have encouraged Congress to ease tough sentencing laws that were passed at the height of the crack epidemic. Emily Pierce, a department spokeswoman, noted that under an initiative begun in 2013, prosecutors were already ordered to prioritize more serious crimes, while looking for alternatives to prison for low-level offenders. Fewer low-level criminals being charged means fewer people eligible for deferred prosecution. The department has also strongly supported drug courts, which essentially offer the same second chance that companies are given.

At the same time, the Justice Department recently promised to get tough on corporate executives after years of criticism in the aftermath of the financial crisis that bankers, in particular, escaped punishment because their companies agreed to pay big fines. It was that promise, followed days later by a deferred-prosecution agreement with General Motors (GM), that ignited Judge Sullivan's fury.

Judge Sullivan was appointed to the federal bench by President Bill Clinton. He previously served as a municipal judge and a local appellate judge in Washington, having been appointed by Presidents Ronald Reagan and George Bush.

He called GM's $900 million settlement "a shocking example of potentially culpable individuals not being criminally charged." GM admitted that it misled the public about auto defects, but neither the company nor its executives were prosecuted, "despite the fact that the reprehensible conduct of its employees resulted in the deaths of many people."

"The court is disappointed that deferred-prosecution agreements or other similar tools are not being used to provide the same opportunity to individual defendants to demonstrate their rehabilitation without triggering the devastating collateral consequences of a criminal conviction," Judge Sullivan wrote.

Justice Department figures show deferred-prosecution agreements are rare for both individuals and companies. But the number of cases against organizations and companies is so tiny—150 or so each year, compared with 160,000 or more individual prosecutions—that these deals occur at a much higher rate in corporate cases, which also tend to be higher profile.

Deferred-prosecution deals are attractive because they spare companies the consequence of criminal convictions, such as stock collapse and a loss of contracts. For people, the effects can be even more severe. The American Bar Association has identified tens of thousands of consequences of criminal conviction, which demonstrates how a single arrest can cost people their jobs and homes.

President Obama has indicated that he will make a criminal justice overhaul one of the most important issues of his remaining time in office. He became the first sitting president to visit a federal prison. On Thursday, he defended the Black Lives Matter movement, which has been criticized by police unions in particular as being antipolice. Mr. Obama plans to speak about changing the criminal justice system next week at the annual meeting of the International Association of Chiefs of Police in Chicago.

Much of the public debate has focused on reducing the prison population by cutting sentences for those serving long sentences for nonviolent crimes. Lost in the debate, Judge Sullivan said, has been the importance of keeping people out of jail in the first place. "This oversight is lamentable, to say the least!" he wrote.

He said criminal justice reform should offer people "the chance to demonstrate their true character and avoid the catastrophic consequences of felony convictions."

While Judge Sullivan cannot make policy from the bench, the opinion shows the momentum behind efforts to improve the system, said Norman L. Reimer, the executive director of the National Association of Criminal Defense Lawyers.

"It has finally seeped into the public consciousness that there is something wrong," he said. "All of a sudden, a nation wakes up and realizes we've created this unbelievable cadre of second-class citizens."

Critical Thinking

1. Is the American criminal justice system fundamentally unfair?

2. Why did Judge Sullivan say that perhaps common criminals ought to be treated like big companies?

3. Should corporate executives be treated the same as other criminals when they violate laws?

Internet References

ABA National Inventory of Collateral Consequences of Conviction
   http://www.abacollateralconsequences.org/map/

"Outside Box, Federal Judges Offer Addicts a Free Path"
   http://www.nytimes.com/2013/03/02/nyregion/us-judges-offer-addicts-a-way-to-avoid-prison.html?_r=0

Article   Prepared by: Joanne Naughton

We Have Lost the War on Drugs

The number of people who died of drug overdoses in 2014 is double those who died in 2000.

JEFF NESBIT

Learning Outcomes

After reading this article, you will be able to:

- State the findings of the CDC regarding drug overdoses.
- Show how the number of deaths has changed since 2000.
- Describe smoking addiction in an adolescent brain.

It's time, finally, to face the ugly truth. We've lost the war on drugs in America. We need a new playbook, now, before more lives are lost.

The Centers for Disease Control and Prevention (CDC) said last week that fatal drug overdoses in America were the highest in recorded history in 2014. The news is grim. But what the new CDC data say about certain aspects of American society more broadly right now is even scarier, to be honest.

CDC reported that fatal drug overdoses killed nearly 50,000 Americans in 2014, which is a new high. To put another way, more people died of drug overdoses than were killed in auto accidents last year.

More than half of the deaths involved either heroin or prescription narcotic painkillers like OxyContin. These two classes of drugs were responsible for more than 28,000 deaths in 2014, the CDC reported, or 61 percent of the fatal drug overdoses.

Despite an endless interdiction and criminal justice effort for seemingly forever, heroin and prescription painkillers are easy to find, easy to use, and relatively cheap to obtain on the street. No one in any demographic was immune. Men and women of every race and ethnic group, of all ages, were affected. If you want to get high, you're going to get high. The "war on drugs" isn't going to stop you.

But here's the truly scary part. That number—50,000 deaths from fatal drug overdoses—is double the number of Americans who died from drug overdoses in 2000.

Let that fact sink in for a moment.

After our government at the local, state, and federal level has declared that we would "win" the war on drugs on our streets—an effort that has cost taxpayers tens of billions of dollars, sent a significant proportion of young, black men to prison on drug convictions, and triggered violent police confrontations in known drug havens in urban areas—we have not only lost, we're getting overrun.

How in the world is it possible that the number of fatal drug overdoses in America has doubled in just 14 years? I mean, how is that really possible in the wealthiest country on Earth?

Here's how. We're playing a loser's game at every level with drug treatment and our societal response to what is happening inside people's brains when they enter the world of drug dependency. We're not recognizing just how victimized people are once they're on a path that, for 50,000 Americans annually leads to death from a fatal drug overdose.

These numbers won't get better–this killing won't stop–until we recognize the true nature of this tragedy. More police on the streets, in the air, on the waterways and in the train stations and airports won't reverse this trend. Putting even more, young, black men in prison on drug charges won't solve the equation. Only a deep, caring understanding of the true nature of drug addiction will set us free.

Once heroin "gets a hold of you," it never lets go, the son of a good friend of mine wrote in The Washington Post several years ago after he nearly died of a drug overdose. The only reason my friend's son survived is because his drug buddy—also high on heroin at the time—dialed 911 before he ran away, and paramedics arrived just in time minutes before his near-certain death from a heroin overdose.

My friend's son is incredibly lucky. Tens of thousands of Americans each year aren't.

Heroin takes all the pain away. And then it changes your brain. You don't worry about anything—whether you can pay the bills next month, whether you have the ability to raise a kid, whether your job might vanish next month—when you're on heroin. These types of drugs—heroin, and prescription narcotic painkillers—take hold of our brains and never truly let go.

This is the pain that we need to understand. This is what we must confront and deal with in society. An endless war on drugs will never deal with this. We can take away the cheap supplies of heroin, make it infinitely harder to obtain prescription painkillers, and people will still find a way to obtain something that "gets a hold" of your brain and never lets go.

There are many, varied examples of addiction across a broad swath of American society, addiction stories that all basically tell the same story—our brains are highly susceptible to things that take hold and don't let go.

For instance, while smoking rates are thankfully now the lowest in American history—about 17 percent of Americans still smoke—we finally understand nicotine is powerfully addictive and it takes considerable effort to quit smoking.

What's more, we now know that nearly 100 percent of smoking addiction occurs in an adolescent brain that's still being formed. Smoking "takes hold" of growing neurons and synapses in a teenaged brain and never lets go. Armed with that knowledge, families now understand what they're confronting with cigarettes and can help their kids.

This is the sort of knowledge we need to confront in what is clearly an epidemic with heroin and prescription painkillers. When the number of fatal drug overdoses is double the rate it was 14 years ago, despite a massive criminal and legal war on drugs, then something is terribly wrong.

To truly "win" this war, we need to focus on the victims, and give them what they need—which is compassion, understanding and knowledge about what it truly takes to break free of a narcotic that assumes control of our brain and never lets it go.

Critical Thinking

1. Why isn't the war on drugs working?
2. Would we be able to further reduce smoking by criminalizing tobacco use? Should we?
3. Would legalizing and regulating drugs for adults who want them be a more effective way to keep them away from young people?

Internet References

A Suburban Heroin Addict Describes His Brush with Death and His Hopes for a Better Life
https://www.washingtonpost.com/national/health-science/a-suburban-heroin-addict-describes-his-brush-with-death-and-his-hopes-for-a-better-life/2014/02/07/bd769b8e-8ea1-11e3-b46a-5a3d0d2130da_story.html

Centers for Disease Control and Prevention on Drug Overdoses
https://www.cdc.gov/drugoverdose/

JEFF NESBIT was the National Science Foundation's director of legislative and public affairs in the Bush and Obama administrations, former Vice President Dan Quayle's communications director, the FDA's public affairs chief, and a national journalist with Knight-Ridder and others. He's the executive director of Climate Nexus and the author of more than 24 books.

Article   Prepared by: Joanne Naughton

The Fine Print in Holder's New Forfeiture Policy Leaves Room for Continued Abuses

An exception for joint task forces allows evasion of state property protections.

Jacob Sullum

Learning Outcomes

After reading this article, you will be able to:

- Report how the Attorney General scaled back the Equitable Sharing Program.

- State whether drug cases qualify for the "public safety" exception.

- Explain what the author means by "A more serious problem" with the new policy.

Last week Attorney General Eric Holder scaled back the Equitable Sharing Program, which enables local law enforcement agencies to evade state limits on civil asset forfeiture. But he did not end that program, and the fine print in the new policy seems to leave a lot of leeway for continued abuses.

In the order describing the new policy, Holder says "federal adoption of property seized by state or local law enforcement under state law is prohibited, except for property that directly relates to public safety concerns, including firearms, ammunition, explosives, and property associated with child pornography." Although that exception sounds like it could be a pretty big loophole, the Justice Department seems to be construing it narrowly. A newly posted form says "Federal Adoptions of state or local seizures are limited to firearms, ammunitions, explosives, and child pornography instrumentalities." In other

words, drug cases do not qualify for the "public safety" exception, a point confirmed by a DOJ notice published on Friday.

A more serious problem with the new policy is that adoption, where a state or local agency seizes property and then asks the Justice Department to pursue forfeiture under federal law, is just one part of the Equitable Sharing Program. Holder's policy explicitly exempts "seizures by state and local authorities working together with federal authorities in a joint task force," "seizures by state and local authorities that are the result of joint federal-state investigations or that are coordinated with federal authorities as part of ongoing federal investigations," and "seizures pursuant to federal seizure warrants, obtained from federal courts to take custody of assets originally seized under state law."

Since there are hundreds of federally funded "multijurisdictional task forces" across the country, that first exception could prove to be very significant. Holder's order "does not prohibit the worst uses of the equitable sharing asset forfeiture program, particularly excepting seizures in which there is federal task force participation or direction," says Eapen Thampy, executive director of Americans for Forfeiture Reform. "As virtually every drug task force I know of has a federal liaison on call, this means business as usual by local law enforcement using civil asset forfeiture through the Equitable Sharing Program to enforce the Controlled Substances Act and other federal statutes. In other words, the exception swallows the rule."

On his *Washington Post* blog, my former *Reason* colleague Radley Balko highlights the same exception. "If it only applies to those investigations in which federal law enforcement personnel are actively involved," he says, "that's less troubling." Thampy is not sanguine on that point. "I do not read the Holder memo as requiring active participation," he says, "and if such a determination were to be made, it is hard to see the government defining 'active participation' narrowly." Thampy adds that "a substantial amount of equitable sharing is related to task force activity," since "most departments that receive a substantial amount of equitable sharing proceeds already do so through task force activity" that is overseen, assisted, or funded by the federal government.

The ban on forfeiture adoptions in drug cases nevertheless does some good. It puts an end to egregious abuses such as the slush fund created by police in Bal Harbour, Florida, with the proceeds of federally adopted forfeitures. *The Miami Herald* reported that the little town's cops raked in $19.3 million over three years, which they used for parties, trips, and fancy equipment such as "a 35-foot boat powered by three Mercury outboards" and "a mobile command truck equipped with satellite and flat-screen TVs."

The *Omaha World-Herald* reports that Douglas County, Nebraska, Sheriff Tim Dunning is fuming about the Justice Department's new forfeiture policy. "This benefits nobody but drug dealers," Dunning said. "Federal law is a tremendously bigger hammer. I don't see what hammer we are going to have over these people now." Dunning will sorely miss that hammer, because his state requires proof beyond a reasonable doubt to seize property allegedly linked to crime, while federal law requires only "a preponderance of the evidence"—i.e., any probability greater than 50 percent.

That low standard allowed Nebraska state troopers to take $124,700 in cash from a motorist named Emiliano Gonzolez in 2003. Gonzolez claimed the money was intended to buy a refrigerated produce truck, and there was no real evidence that he was involved in drug trafficking. In 2006 a federal appeals court nevertheless upheld the forfeiture, which would not have been possible under Nebraska law. The main impact of Holder's directive will be seen in cases like this one, where a single law enforcement agency seeks federal adoption because it makes highway robbery easier or more lucrative.

Addendum: In a statement posted on Friday, the Institute for Justice expresses a concern similar to Thampy's: "Today's announced policy would stop the process of adoption, where state and local officials use federal law to forfeit property without charging owners with a crime and then profit from those forfeitures, regardless of whether those forfeitures are permitted under state law. But the new policy leaves open a significant loophole, as state and local law enforcement can still partner with federal agents through joint task forces for forfeitures not permitted under state law, and state and local law enforcement can use such task forces to claim forfeiture proceeds they would not be entitled to under state law."

Addendum II: According to a 2012 report from the Government Accountability Office, "adoptions made up about 17 percent of all equitable sharing payments" in 2010, which suggests that Holder's new policy will affect less than one-fifth of cases in which state or local agencies profit from federal forfeitures. An estimate in the press release issued by the Justice Department on Friday suggests the share is even lower when measured by revenue. "Over the last six years," the DOJ says, "adoptions accounted for roughly three percent of the value of forfeitures in the Department of Justice Asset Forfeiture Program." By comparison, the DOJ's reports to Congress indicate that equitable sharing payments to state and local agencies accounted for about 22 percent of total deposits during those six years. That suggests adoptions, which the DOJ says represented about 3 percent of deposits, accounted for less than 14 percent of equitable sharing.

Note: An earlier calculation, based on data for fiscal year 2013, put the share at less than 10 percent. The six-year average is different because of variations in total federal forfeitures and the percentage going to the states.

Critical Thinking

1. How does the Attorney General's order allow abuses to continue?
2. What is Eapen Thampy's objection?
3. Why does Sheriff Tim Dunning object to the Justice Department's new forfeiture policy?

Internet References

Reason.com
http://reason.com/blog/2012/10/29/feds-investigate-asset-forfeiture-slush

The Washington Post
https://www.washingtonpost.com/news/the-watch/wp/2015/01/16/breaking-down-holders-move-to-limit-civil-asset-forfeiture-abuse/

US Department of Justice
http://www.justice.gov/afp/reports-congress

US Department of Justice
http://www.justice.gov/sites/default/files/opa/press-releases/attachments/2015/01/16/attorney_general_order_prohibiting_adoptions.pdf

US Department of Justice
http://www.justice.gov/sites/default/files/criminal-afmls/legacy/2015/01/16/request-for-adoption-form.pdf

Article

Prepared by: Joanne Naughton

FBI Admits Flaws in Hair Analysis over Decades

Spencer S. Hsu

Learning Outcomes

After reading this article, you will be able to:

- State which two organizations are assisting the government with the review of questioned forensic evidence.

- Describe the problem and show how the investigation came about.

- Discuss what Professor Garrett says about why the problem with faulty forensic evidence has gone on for so long.

The Justice Department and FBI have formally acknowledged that nearly every examiner in an elite FBI forensic unit gave flawed testimony in almost all trials in which they offered evidence against criminal defendants over more than a two-decade period before 2000.

Of 28 examiners with the FBI Laboratory's microscopic hair comparison unit, 26 overstated forensic matches in ways that favored prosecutors in more than 95 percent of the 268 trials reviewed so far, according to the National Association of Criminal Defense Lawyers (NACDL) and the Innocence Project, which are assisting the government with the country's largest post-conviction review of questioned forensic evidence.

The cases include those of 32 defendants sentenced to death. Of those, 14 have been executed or died in prison, the groups said under an agreement with the government to release results after the review of the first 200 convictions.

The FBI errors alone do not mean there was not other evidence of a convict's guilt. Defendants and federal and state prosecutors in 46 states and the District are being notified to determine whether there are grounds for appeals. Four defendants were previously exonerated.

The admissions mark a watershed in one of the country's largest forensic scandals, highlighting the failure of the nation's courts for decades to keep bogus scientific information from juries, legal analysts said. The question now, they said, is how state authorities and the courts will respond to findings that confirm long-suspected problems with subjective, pattern-based forensic techniques—like hair and bite-mark comparisons—that have contributed to wrongful convictions in more than one-quarter of 329 DNA-exoneration cases since 1989.

Flawed Forensic Hair Testimony from the FBI Lab

The FBI has identified for review roughly **2,500 cases** in which the FBI Lab reported a hair match.

- Reviews of **342 defendants' cases** have been completed. About 1,200 cases remain, including 700 in which police or prosecutors have not responded to requests for trial transcripts or other information.
- **268 trials** in which hair evidence was used against defendants.
- **268 trials** in which hair evidence was used against criminal defendants.
- FBI examiners gave flawed forensic testimony in **257 of those 268 trials,** or more than **95 percent.**
- **257 trials** with flawed forensic testimony.
- **32 death-penalty cases** with flawed forensic testimony.

NOTE: The FBI is completing reviews of about 900 lab reports.

Source: National Association of Criminal Defense Lawyers and Innocence Project analysis of FBI and Justice Department data as of March 2015, *The Washington Post*.

In a statement, the FBI and Justice Department vowed to continue to devote resources to address all cases and said they "are committed to ensuring that affected defendants are notified of past errors and that justice is done in every instance. The Department and the FBI are also committed to ensuring the accuracy of future hair analysis testimony, as well as the application of all disciplines of forensic science."

Peter Neufeld, co-founder of the Innocence Project, commended the FBI and department for the collaboration but said, "The FBI's three-decade use of microscopic hair analysis to incriminate defendants was a complete disaster."

"We need an exhaustive investigation that looks at how the FBI, state governments that relied on examiners trained by the FBI and the courts allowed this to happen and why it wasn't stopped much sooner," Neufeld said.

Norman L. Reimer, the NACDL's executive director, said, "Hopefully, this project establishes a precedent so that in future situations it will not take years to remediate the injustice."

While unnamed federal officials previously acknowledged widespread problems, the FBI until now has withheld comment because findings might not be representative.

Sen. Richard Blumenthal (D-Conn.), a former prosecutor, called on the FBI and Justice Department to notify defendants in all 2,500 targeted cases involving an FBI hair match about the problem even if their case has not been completed, and to redouble efforts in the three-year-old review to retrieve information on each case.

"These findings are appalling and chilling in their indictment of our criminal justice system, not only for potentially innocent defendants who have been wrongly imprisoned and even executed, but for prosecutors who have relied on fabricated and false evidence despite their intentions to faithfully enforce the law," Blumenthal said.

Senate Judiciary Committee Chairman Charles E. Grassley (R-Iowa) and the panel's ranking Democrat, Patrick J. Leahy (Vt.), urged the bureau to conduct "a root-cause analysis" to prevent future breakdowns.

"It is critical that the Bureau identify and address the systemic factors that allowed this far-reaching problem to occur and continue for more than a decade," the lawmakers wrote FBI Director James B. Comey on March 27, as findings were being finalized.

The FBI is waiting to complete all reviews to assess causes but has acknowledged that hair examiners until 2012 lacked written standards defining scientifically appropriate and erroneous ways to explain results in court. The bureau expects this year to complete similar standards for testimony and lab reports for 19 forensic disciplines.

Federal authorities launched the investigation in 2012 after *The Washington Post* reported that flawed forensic hair matches

might have led to the convictions of hundreds of potentially innocent people since at least the 1970s, typically for murder, rape and other violent crimes nationwide.

The review confirmed that FBI experts systematically testified to the near-certainty of "matches" of crime-scene hairs to defendants, backing their claims by citing incomplete or misleading statistics drawn from their case work.

In reality, there is no accepted research on how often hair from different people may appear the same. Since 2000, the lab has used visual hair comparison to rule out someone as a possible source of hair or in combination with more accurate DNA testing.

Warnings about the problem have been mounting. In 2002, the FBI reported that its own DNA testing found that examiners reported false hair matches more than 11 percent of the time. In the District, the only jurisdiction where defenders and prosecutors have re-investigated all FBI hair convictions, three of seven defendants whose trials included flawed FBI testimony have been exonerated through DNA testing since 2009, and courts have exonerated two more men. All five served 20 to 30 years in prison for rape or murder.

University of Virginia law professor Brandon L. Garrett said the results reveal a "mass disaster" inside the criminal justice system, one that it has been unable to self-correct because courts rely on outdated precedents admitting scientifically invalid testimony at trial and, under the legal doctrine of finality, make it difficult for convicts to challenge old evidence.

"The tools don't exist to handle systematic errors in our criminal justice system," Garrett said. "The FBI deserves every recognition for doing something really remarkable here. The problem is there may be few judges, prosecutors or defense lawyers who are able or willing to do anything about it."

Federal authorities are offering new DNA testing in cases with errors, if sought by a judge or prosecutor, and agreeing to drop procedural objections to appeals in federal cases.

However, biological evidence in the cases often is lost or unavailable. Among states, only California and Texas specifically allow appeals when experts recant or scientific advances undermine forensic evidence at trial.

Defense attorneys say scientifically invalid forensic testimony should be considered as violations of due process, as courts have held with false or misleading testimony.

The FBI searched more than 21,000 federal and state requests to its hair comparison unit from 1972 through 1999, identifying for review roughly 2,500 cases where examiners declared hair matches.

Reviews of 342 defendants' convictions were completed as of early March, the NACDL and Innocence Project reported. In addition to the 268 trials in which FBI hair evidence was used against defendants, the review found cases in which defendants pleaded guilty, FBI examiners did not testify, did not assert a match or gave exculpatory testimony.

When such cases are included, by the FBI's count examiners made statements exceeding the limits of science in about 90 percent of testimonies, including 34 death-penalty cases.

The findings likely scratch the surface. The FBI said as of mid-April that reviews of about 350 trial testimonies and 900 lab reports are nearly complete, with about 1,200 cases remaining.

The bureau said it is difficult to check cases before 1985, when files were computerized. It has been unable to review 700 cases because police or prosecutors did not respond to requests for information.

Also, the same FBI examiners whose work is under review taught 500 to 1,000 state and local crime lab analysts to testify in the same ways.

Texas, New York and North Carolina authorities are reviewing their hair examiner cases, with ad hoc efforts underway in about 15 other states.

Critical Thinking

1. Do you believe the "flawed testimony" given by FBI witnesses rises to the level of misconduct?

2. What does Peter Neufeld mean when he says "complete disaster" to describe the problem?

Internet References

The Washington Post
www.washingtonpost.com/

The Washington Post
www.washingtonpost.com/2

Urban Institute
www.urban.org

SPENCER S. HSU is an investigative reporter, two-time Pulitzer finalist and national Emmy award nominee.

Article

Prepared by: Joanne Naughton

Drug Offenders in American Prisons: The Critical Distinction between Stock and Flow

JONATHAN ROTHWELL

Learning Outcomes

After reading this article, you will be able to:

- Relate some of the problems of mass incarceration in the United States.
- Describe the criticisms of Alexander's claims.
- Show how Alexander's critics are mistaken.

There is now widespread, bipartisan agreement that mass incarceration is a huge problem in the United States. The rates and levels of imprisonment are destroying families and communities, and widening opportunity gaps—especially in terms of race.

But there is a growing dispute over how far imprisonment for drug offenses is to blame. Michelle Alexander, a legal scholar, published a powerful and influential critique of the U.S. criminal justice system in 2012, showing how the war on drugs has disproportionately and unfairly harmed African Americans.

Recent scholarship has challenged Alexander's claim. John Pfaff, a Fordham law professor and crime statistics expert, argues that Alexander exaggerates the importance of drug crimes. Pfaff points out that the proportion of state prisoners whose primary crime was a drug offense "rises sharply from 1980 to 1990, when it peaks at 22 percent. But that's only 22 percent: nearly four-fifths of all state prisoners in 1990 were not drug offenders." By 2010, the number had dropped to 17 percent. "Reducing the admissions of drug offenders will not meaningfully reduce prison populations," he concludes.

Other scholars, including Stephanos Bibas of the University of Pennsylvania, and some researchers at the Urban Institute, have made similar points in recent months: since only a minority of prisoners have been jailed for drug offenses, only modest gains against mass incarceration can be made here.

Stock versus Flow

There is no disputing that incarceration for property and violent crimes is of huge importance to America's prison population, but the standard analysis—including Alexander's critics—fails to distinguish between the stock and flow of drug crime-related incarceration. In fact, there are two ways of looking at the prison population as it relates to drug crimes:

1. How many *people* experience incarceration as a result of a drug-related crime over a certain time period?
2. What proportion of the prison population at a *particular moment in time* was imprisoned for a drug-related crime?

The answers will differ because the length of sentences varies by the kind of crime committed. As of 2009, the median incarceration time at state facilities for drug offenses was 14 months, exactly half the time for violent crimes. Those convicted of murder served terms of roughly 10 times greater length.

Drug Crimes Are the Main Driver of Imprisonment

The picture is clear: Drug crimes have been the predominant reason for new admissions into state and federal prisons in recent decades. In every year from 1993 to 2009, more people were admitted for drug crimes than violent crimes. In the 2000s, the flow of incarceration for drug crimes exceeded admissions for property crimes each year. Nearly 1/3 of total prison admissions over this period were for drug crimes:

State and federal prison admissions by offense type, 1993–2009

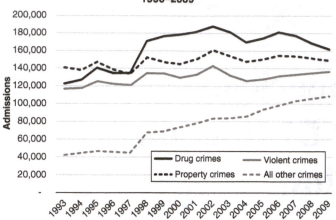

Note: Federal admissions data not included prior to 1998 because data were unavailable.
Source: Author analysis of various sources from the Bureau of Justice Statistics. 1993–2009 state admissions data from National Corrections Reporting Program and "National Corrections Reporting Program: Most serious offense of state prisoners, by offense, admission type, age, sex, race, and Hispanic origin"; 1998–2009 federal admissions data from Federal Criminal Case Processing Statistics.

Snapshot Pictures of Prison Populations Tell a Misleading Story

Violent crimes account for nearly half the prison population at any given time; and drug crimes only 1/5. But drug crimes account for more of the total number of admissions in recent years—almost 1/3 (31 percent), while violent crimes account for 1/4:

Prison by type of offense: Stock vs. flow

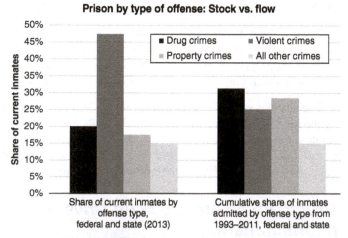

Note: Federal admissions data not included prior to 1998 in cumulative share. 2010 data omitted because not provided by sources. 16% of "all other crime" includes federal admissions for immigration offenses. Author analyzed various sources from the Bureau of Justice Statistics to make there calculations. Sources for current inmates share: "Prisoners in 2014" Tables 11 and 12 (state data is 2013, federal data is 2014). Sources for cumulative figure: 1993–2009 state admissions data from National Corrections Reporting Program and "National Corrections Reporting Program: Most serious offense of state prisoners, by offense, admission type, age, sex, race, and Hispanic origin", 2011 state admissions data from "Prisoners in 2012: Trends in Admissions and Releases, 1991–2012"; 1998–2011 federal admissions data from Federal Criminal Care Processing Statistics; total excluded unknown offense types.

Being Imprisoned and Being in Prison: The Wider Picture

So, as Michelle Alexander argued, drug prosecution is a big part of the mass incarceration story. To be clear, rolling back the war on drugs would not, as Pfaff and Urban Institute scholars maintain, totally solve the problem of mass incarceration, but it could help a great deal, by reducing exposure to prison. In other work, Pfaff provides grounds for believing that the aggressive behavior of local prosecutors in confronting all types of crime is an overlooked factor in the rise of mass incarceration.

More broadly, it is clear that the effect of the failed war on drugs has been devastating, especially for black Americans. As I've shown in a previous piece, blacks are three to four times more likely to be arrested for drug crimes, even though they are no more likely than whites to use or sell drugs. Worse still, blacks are roughly nine times more likely to be admitted into state prison for a drug offense.

During the period from 1993 to 2011, there were 3 million admissions into federal and state prisons for drug offenses. Over the same period, there were 30 million arrests for drug crimes, 24 million of which were for possession. Some of these were repeat offenders, of course. But these figures show how largely this problem looms over the lives of many Americans, and especially black Americans. A dangerous combination of approaches to policing, prosecution, sentencing, criminal justice, and incarceration is resulting in higher costs for taxpayers, less opportunity for affected individuals, and deep damage to hopes for racial equality.

Critical Thinking

1. Since blacks are three to four times more likely to be arrested for drug crimes, doesn't that prove they are more likely to use drugs than whites?

2. How does the author explain the difference between being imprisoned and being in prison?

Internet References

Bureau of Justice Statistics
http://www.bjs.gov/index.cfm?ty=pbdetail&iid=2056

Social Science Research Network
http://papers.ssrn.com/sol3/papers.cfm?abstract_id=2414596

The New Jim Crow
http://newjimcrow.com

Unit 2

UNIT

Prepared by: Joanne Naughton

Victimology

For many years, crime victims were not considered to be an important topic for criminological study. Now, however, criminologists consider that focusing on victims and victimization is essential to understanding the phenomenon of crime. The popularity of this area of study can be attributed to the early work of several criminologists such as Hans von Hentig and, later, Stephen Schafer, who examined victim-offender interactions and stressed reciprocal influences and role reversals.

Victimology focuses on the relationship of the victim to the criminal offender: whether they were strangers, mere acquaintances, friends, family members, or even intimates; and why a particular person or place was targeted.

The victim's role in the criminal justice process has received increasing attention from a growing number of criminologists in recent years, and as more criminologists focus their attention on the victim's role in the process, victimology will take on even greater importance.

Article   Prepared by: Joanne Naughton

How a $2 Roadside Drug Test Sends Innocent People to Jail

Widespread evidence shows that these tests routinely produce false positives. Why are police departments and prosecutors across the country still using them?

RYAN GABRIELSON AND TOPHER SANDERS

Learning Outcomes

After reading this article, you will be able to:

- Show that people often plead guilty to a crime even when they are innocent.

- Describe the effect a guilty plea to a drug law violation can have on a person's life even when the case is over.

- Explain the roles played by others, in addition to police, in drug arrest cases.

Amy Albritton can't remember if her boyfriend signaled when he changed lanes late that August afternoon in 2010. But suddenly the lights on the Houston Police patrol car were flashing behind them, and Anthony Wilson was navigating Albritton's white Chrysler Concorde to a stop in a strip-mall parking lot. It was an especially unwelcome hassle. Wilson was in Houston to see about an oil-rig job; Albritton, volunteering her car, had come along for what she imagined would be a vacation of sorts. She managed an apartment complex back in Monroe, Louisiana, and the younger of her two sons—Landon, 16, who had been disabled from birth by cerebral palsy—was with his father for the week. After five hours of driving through the monotony of flat woodland, the couple had checked into a motel, carted their luggage to the room and returned to the car, too hungry to rest but too drained to seek out anything more than fast food. Now two officers stepped out of their patrol car and approached.

Albritton, 43, had dressed up for the trip—black blouse, turquoise necklace, small silver hoop earrings glinting through her shoulder-length blond hair. Wilson, 28, was more casually dressed, in a white T-shirt and jeans, and wore a strained expression that worried Albritton. One officer asked him for his license and registration. Wilson said he didn't have a license. The car's registration showed that it belonged to Albritton.

The officer asked Wilson to step out of the car. Wilson complied. The officer leaned in over the driver's seat, looked around, then called to his partner; in the report Officer Duc Nguyen later filed, he wrote that he saw a needle in the car's ceiling lining. Albritton didn't know what he was talking about. Before she could protest, Officer David Helms had come around to her window and was asking for consent to search the car. If Albritton refused, Helms said, he would call for a drug-sniffing dog. Albritton agreed to the full search and waited nervously outside the car.

Helms spotted a white crumb on the floor. In the report, Nguyen wrote that the officers believed the crumb was crack cocaine. They handcuffed Wilson and Albritton and stood them in front of the patrol car, its lights still flashing. They were on display for rush-hour traffic, criminal suspects sweating through their clothes in the 93-degree heat.

As Nguyen and Helms continued the search, tensions grew. Albritton, shouting over the sound of traffic, tried to explain that they had the wrong idea—at least about her. She had been dating Wilson for only a month; she implored him to admit that if there were drugs, they were his alone. Wilson just shook his head, Albritton now recalls. Fear surging, she shouted that there weren't any drugs in her car even as she insisted that she didn't know that Wilson had brought drugs. The search turned up only one other item of interest—a box of BC Powder, an over-the-counter pain reliever. Albritton never saw the needle. The crumb from the floor was all that mattered now.

At the police academy four years earlier, Helms was taught that to make a drug arrest on the street, an officer needed to conduct an elementary chemical test, right then and there. It's what cops routinely do across the country every day while making thousands upon thousands of drug arrests. Helms popped the trunk of his patrol car, pulled out a small plastic pouch that contained a vial of pink liquid and returned to Albritton. He opened the lid on the vial and dropped a tiny piece of the crumb into the liquid. If the liquid remained pink, that would rule out the presence of cocaine. If it turned blue, then Albritton, as the owner of the car, could become a felony defendant.

Helms waved the vial in front of her face and said, "You're busted."

Albritton was booked into the Harris County jail at 3:37 a.m., nine hours after she was arrested. Wilson had been detained for driving without a license but would soon be released. Albritton was charged with felony drug possession and faced a much longer ordeal. Already, she was terrified as she thought about her family. Albritton was raised in a speck of a town called Marion at the northern edge of Louisiana. Her father still drove lumber trucks there; her mother had worked as a pharmacy technician until she died of colon cancer. Albritton was 15 then. She went through two unexpected pregnancies, the first at age 16, and two ill-fated marriages. But she had also pieced together a steady livelihood managing apartment complexes, and when her younger son was born disabled, she worked relentlessly to care for him. Now, their future was almost certainly shattered.

The officers allowed her to make a collect call on the coinless cellblock pay phone. She had a strained relationship with her father and with her son's father as well; instead she dialed Doug Franklin, an old friend who once dated her sister. No one answered. Near dawn the next morning, guards walked Albritton through a tunnel to the Harris County criminal-justice tower's basement, where they deposited her in a closet-size holding room with another woman, who told Albritton that she had murdered someone. Albritton prayed someone would explain what would happen next, tell her son she was alive and help her sort out the mess. She had barely slept and still hadn't eaten anything. She heard her name called and stepped forward to the reinforced window. A tall man with thinning hair and wire-rim glasses approached and introduced himself as Dan Richardson, her court-appointed defense attorney.

Richardson told Albritton that she was going to be charged with possession of a controlled substance, crack cocaine, at an arraignment that morning. Albritton recalls him explaining that this was a felony, and the maximum penalty was two years in state prison. She doesn't remember him asking her what actually happened, or if she believed she was innocent. Instead, she recalls, he said that the prosecutor had already offered a deal for much less than two years. If she pleaded guilty, she would receive a 45-day sentence in the county jail, and most likely serve only half that.

Albritton told Richardson that the police were mistaken; she was innocent. But Richardson, she says, was unswayed. The police had found crack in her car. The test proved it. She could spend a few weeks in jail or two years in prison. In despair, Albritton agreed to the deal.

Albritton was escorted to a dark wood-paneled courtroom. A guilty plea requires the defendant to make a series of statements that serve as a confession and to waive multiple constitutional rights. The judge, Vanessa Velasquez, walked her through the recitation, Albritton recalls, but never asked why she couldn't stop crying long enough to speak in sentences. She had managed to say the one word that mattered: "guilty."

Police officers arrest more than 1.2 million people a year in the United States on charges of illegal drug possession. Field tests like the one Officer Helms used in front of Amy Albritton help them move quickly from suspicion to conviction. But the kits—which cost about $2 each and have changed little since 1973—are far from reliable.

The field tests seem simple, but a lot can go wrong. Some tests, including the one the Houston police officers used to analyze the crumb on the floor of Albritton's car, use a single tube of a chemical called cobalt thiocyanate, which turns blue when it is exposed to cocaine. But cobalt thiocyanate also turns blue when it is exposed to more than 80 other compounds, including methadone, certain acne medications and several common household cleaners. Other tests use three tubes, which the officer can break in a specific order to rule out everything but the drug in question—but if the officer breaks the tubes in the wrong order, that, too, can invalidate the results. The environment can also present problems. Cold weather slows the color development; heat speeds it up, or sometimes prevents a color reaction from taking place at all. Poor lighting on the street—flashing police lights, sun glare, street lamps—often prevents officers from making the fine distinctions that could make the difference between an arrest and a release.

There are no established error rates for the field tests, in part because their accuracy varies so widely depending on who is using them and how. Data from the Florida Department of Law Enforcement lab system show that 21 percent of evidence that the police listed as methamphetamine after identifying it was not methamphetamine, and half of those false positives were not any kind of illegal drug at all. In one notable Florida episode, Hillsborough County sheriff's deputies produced 15 false positives for methamphetamine in the first seven months of 2014. When we examined the department's records, they showed that officers, faced with somewhat ambiguous directions on the pouches, had simply misunderstood which colors indicated a positive result.

No central agency regulates the manufacture or sale of the tests, and no comprehensive records are kept about their use. In the late 1960s, crime labs outfitted investigators with mobile chemistry sets, including small plastic test tubes and bottles of chemical reagents that reacted with certain drugs by changing colors, more or less on the same principle as a home pregnancy test. But the reagents contained strong acids that leaked and burned the investigators. In 1973, the same year that Richard Nixon formally established the Drug Enforcement Administration, declaring "an all-out global war on the drug menace," a pair of California inventors patented a "disposable comparison detector kit." It was far simpler, just a glass vial or vials inside a plastic pouch. Open the pouch, add the compound to be tested, seal the pouch, break open the vials and watch the colors change. The field tests, convenient and imbued with an aura of scientific infallibility, were ordered by police departments across the country. In a 1974 study, however, the National Bureau of Standards warned that the kits "should not be used as sole evidence for the identification of a narcotic or drug of abuse." Police officers were not chemists, and chemists themselves had long ago stopped relying on color tests, preferring more reliable mass spectrographs. By 1978, the Department of Justice had determined that field tests "should not be used for evidential purposes," and the field tests in use today remain inadmissible at trial in nearly every jurisdiction; instead, prosecutors must present a secondary lab test using more reliable methods.

But this has proved to be a meaningless prohibition. Most drug cases in the United States are decided well before they reach trial, by the far more informal process of plea bargaining. In 2011, RTI International, a nonprofit research group based in North Carolina, found that prosecutors in nine of 10 jurisdictions it surveyed nationwide accepted guilty pleas based solely on the results of field tests, and in our own reporting, we confirmed that prosecutors or judges accept plea deals on that same basis in Atlanta, Boston, Dallas, Jacksonville, Las Vegas, Los Angeles, Newark, Philadelphia, Phoenix, Salt Lake City, San Diego, Seattle, and Tampa.

This puts field tests at the center of any discussion about the justice of plea bargains in general. The federal government does not keep a comprehensive database of prosecutions in county and state criminal courts, but the National Archive of Criminal Justice Data at the University of Michigan maintains an extensive sampling of court records from the 40 largest jurisdictions. Based on this data, we found that more than 10 percent of all county and state felony convictions are for drug charges, and at least 90 percent of those convictions come by way of plea deals. In Tennessee, guilty pleas produce 94 percent of all convictions. In Kansas, they make up more than 97 percent. In Harris County, Texas, where the judiciary makes detailed criminal caseload information public, 99.5 percent of drug-possession

convictions are the result of a guilty plea. A majority of those are felony convictions, which restrict employment, housing and—in many states—the right to vote.

Demand for the field tests is strong enough to sustain the business of at least nine different companies that sell tests to identify cocaine, heroin, marijuana, methamphetamine, LSD, MDMA, and more than two dozen other drugs. The Justice Department issued guidelines in 2000 calling for test-kit packaging to carry warning labels, including "a statement that users of the kit should receive appropriate training in its use and should be taught that the reagents can give false-positive as well as false-negative results," but when we checked, three of the largest manufacturers—Lynn Peavey Company, the Safariland Group and Sirchie—had not printed such a warning on their tests. (Lynn Peavey Company did not respond to our request for comment. A spokesman for the Safariland Group said the company provides law-enforcement agencies with extensive training materials that are separate from the tests and their packaging. We asked John Roby, Sirchie's chief executive, about the missing warnings and requested an interview in May. He responded in writing a month later saying that the boxes carrying Sirchie's cocaine tests had been updated and now display a warning that reactions may occur with both "legal and illegal substances." After our inquiry, Sirchie added another warning to its packaging, listing at the bottom of its printed instructions: "ALL TEST RESULTS MUST BE CONFIRMED BY AN APPROVED ANALYTICAL LABORATORY!"

Even trained lab scientists struggle with confirmation bias—the tendency to take any new evidence as confirmation of expectations—and police officers can see the tests as affirming their decisions to stop and search a person. Labs rarely notify officers when a false positive is found, so they have little experience to prompt skepticism. As far as they know, the system works. By our estimate, though, every year at least 100,000 people nationwide plead guilty to drug-possession charges that rely on field-test results as evidence. At that volume, even the most modest of error rates could produce thousands of wrongful convictions.

After he arrested Amy Albritton, Officer Helms sent what remained of the crumb he found on the floor of her car to the Houston Police Department crime laboratory. He listed it as ".02 grms crack cocaine" and noted on the submission form that he was also sending a "syringe w/unknown substance .01 gr"—presumably, the needle Officer Nguyen reported pulling from the ceiling lining and that Albritton had not seen and still could not explain. (Helms's submission form, which was separate from the arrest report, said it came not from the ceiling but from the "suspect visor.") The last item Helms turned in was a ziploc bag of the "unknown wht powder" that had been removed from the BC Powder package.

"HOLD + ANALYZE FOR COURT," Helms wrote by hand. And then, with no court case pending, the evidence sat on hold, one of several thousand samples in the laboratory's backlog of untested pills, plants, powders and assorted crumbs and pebbles.

Albritton served 21 days of her 45-day sentence. When she was released, she took a taxi to the motel where she had planned to stay with Wilson, whom she never saw again after the arrest. (Helms and Nguyen would not comment for this article; Wilson did not respond to requests.) The manager had kept her clothes, so she took a room again and waited for her friend Doug Franklin to fly in from Louisiana. The plan was that he would lend her the money to get her impounded car and keep her company on the drive home. When they retrieved the car, it had been sitting in the summer heat for more than three weeks. Albritton was overwhelmed by the smell of rotting hamburgers.

When Albritton pleaded guilty, she asked Franklin to explain the situation to her bosses at the rental-property firm, but Franklin decided it was safer to say nothing. She was going to be fired in any case, he reasoned, and alerting an employer about the drug felony would only hurt her future prospects. Albritton had managed the Frances Place Apartments, a well-maintained brick complex, for two years, and a free apartment was part of her compensation. But as far as the company knew, Albritton had abandoned her job and her home. She was fired, and her furniture and other belongings were put out on the side of the road. "So I lost all that," she says.

Albritton's older son, Adam, then 24, had been living on his own for years and learned of his mother's arrest only after she had begun her sentence. While Albritton was incarcerated, her younger son, Landon, remained with his father, who had threatened in the past to seek custody but never followed through. Albritton's father, Tommy Franklin (no relation to Doug), was openly skeptical about her claim of innocence. "If the law said you had crack, you had crack," she recalls him telling her.

Albritton gave up trying to convince people otherwise. She focused instead on Landon. Using a wheelchair, he needed regular sessions of physical and occupational therapy, and Albritton's career managing the rental complex had been an ideal fit, providing a free home that kept her close to her son while she was at work, and allowing her the flexibility to ferry him to his appointments. But now, because of her new felony criminal record, which showed up immediately in background checks, she couldn't even land an interview at another apartment complex. With a felony conviction, she couldn't be approved as a renter either. Doug Franklin allowed Albritton and Landon to move in with him temporarily, and Albritton took a minimum-wage job at a convenience store.

Through all of this, the crumb of evidence remained in storage in the Houston crime lab. It was a closed case, and the

prosecutor, as was standard practice, had filed a motion to destroy the evidence. Only some final paperwork—a request from the lab and a judge's signature—was needed. But this was an extremely low priority in a complex bureaucracy.

By 2010, the lab had been discredited by a decade of botched science and scandal. Thousands of untested rape kits were shelved from unsolved assaults. Errors in fingerprint matches were discovered in more than 200 cases. The lab had lost key blood samples; employees had tampered with or falsified other evidence. And it was continuing to struggle with a significant backlog of drug-test evidence—one that stemmed from what amounted to an epic experiment in field testing.

When Hurricane Katrina struck the Gulf Coast in August 2005, more than 250,000 mostly black refugees streamed into Houston, and local authorities openly anticipated a crime surge in which the refugees were portrayed as would-be perpetrators. Charles McClelland, who retired in February as Houston's police chief and was then an assistant chief, says the department decided that pursuing drug-possession charges would also help suppress the number of predicted robberies and burglaries. "Anecdotally, it makes sense: Where does a person who has a substance-abuse problem get the money to buy drugs?" McClelland argues. "One could easily make the connection that they're committing crimes." The city distributed thousands more of the color field tests than usual to patrol officers, and drug evidence swamped the controlled-substances section of the lab. Even as the Katrina refugees gradually left Houston, the emphasis on low-level drug enforcement remained. By 2007, annual submissions to the lab had climbed to 22,000, even as budget cuts had reduced the staff, leaving the scientists with far more samples than they could competently analyze.

In 1972, the Department of Justice published a training guide for forensic chemists in the nation's crime labs, emphasizing that they were "the last line of defense against a false accusation," but 40 years later, that line had largely vanished. A federal survey in 2013 found that about 62 percent of crime labs do not test drug evidence when the defendant pleads guilty. But the Houston crime lab, for all its problems, would not be among them.

James Miller, the lab's controlled-substances manager, had long practiced a kind of evidentiary triage. Evidence tied to pending drug manufacturing, sale or possession cases—50 a year on average—would receive immediate attention, because only laboratory analysis would be admissible in court. But evidence from cases in which the defendants pleaded guilty before going to trial—the overwhelming majority of the remaining thousands of submitted drugs samples—would also be tested. The city had no legal requirement to confirm that the substances were the illegal drugs the police claimed they were. But in Miller's lab, everything would be checked, even if it took years. "All along, we've said we're about the science," he says—not securing convictions. So the evidence sat, waiting.

The forensic scientists in Miller's lab keep untested samples in Manila envelopes locked in cabinets below their work benches. Some sat there for as long as four years, lab records show. Albritton's evidence stayed locked up for six months. On February 23, 2011—five months after Albritton completed her sentence and returned home as a felon—one of Houston's forensic scientists, Ahtavea Barker, pulled the envelope up to her bench. It contained the crumb, the powder and the still-unexplained syringe. First, she weighed everything. The syringe had too little residue on it even to test. It was just a syringe. The remainder of the "white chunk substance" that Officer Helms had tested positive with his field kit as crack cocaine totaled 0.0134 grams, Barker wrote on the examination sheet, about the same as a tiny pinch of salt.

Barker turned to gas chromatography–mass spectrometry analysis, the gold standard in chemical identification, to figure out what was in Albritton's car that evening. She began with the powder. First, the gas chromatograph vaporized a speck of the powder inside a tube. Then, the gas was heated, causing its core chemical compounds to separate. When the individual compounds reached the end of the tube, the mass spectrometer blasted them with electrons, causing them to fragment. The resulting display, called a fragmentation pattern, is essentially a chemical fingerprint. The powder was a combination of aspirin and caffeine—the ingredients in BC Powder, the over-the-counter painkiller, as Albritton had insisted.

Then, Barker ran the same tests on the supposed crack cocaine. The crumb's fragmentation pattern did not match that of cocaine, or any other compound in the lab's extensive database. It was not a drug. It did not contain anything mixed with drugs. It was a crumb—food debris, perhaps. Barker wrote "N.A.M." on the spectrum printout, "no acceptable match," and then added another set of letters: "N.C.S." No controlled substance identified. Albritton was innocent.

Inger Chandler oversees the small conviction-integrity unit of the Harris County district attorney's office, where she has been a prosecutor for 12 years. Conviction-integrity units are a fairly new concept in law enforcement: prosecutors reexamine convictions in light of new evidence, often in the form of previously unavailable DNA tests. Conviction-integrity units originally focused on murder and rape cases, but they also increasingly investigate drug convictions.

In early 2014, Chandler took a call while sitting at her desk, encircled by stacks of case files and pictures of her toddler twins. Eric Dexheimer, a reporter at The Austin American-Statesman, told her he had noticed a series of unusual exonerations coming out of the Texas Court of Criminal Appeals. He'd tracked 21 drug convictions across Texas that had been reversed

because labs had found that the drugs in question weren't really drugs. The laboratory results came after defendants had already pleaded guilty. Did Harris County have any other bad drug convictions beyond what the courts had overturned? Chandler didn't know, but she said she would try to find out.

Chandler called Miller, the controlled-substances manager at the lab, and asked him if there was something wrong with any of their drug convictions. Miller was not surprised to hear from Chandler. He explained that the lab had indeed found problems with their drug convictions; when his forensic scientists found discrepancies in the evidence—officially labeled "variants"—they sent the details by email to the district attorney's office, and they had been doing so for years. Chandler hadn't known any of this. She found the email inbox for lab notices, and it did indeed contain hundreds of messages that were sent from the lab. One after another, the lab notices said, "No Controlled Substance." In cases involving drug possession, that meant the defendants were not guilty. (Drug manufacturing and selling charges can hold even if the underlying substance is not illegal.)

It was unclear if anyone had ever followed up on the notices. When Chandler entered several of the court case numbers into the district attorney's records-search system, however, she found that a majority of the convictions remained in place. She started a list. Over the course of the following year, she found that the district attorney's office had failed to correct 416 "variants" between January 2004 and June 2015, all of them in cases that ended in guilty pleas. Some variants were legally ambiguous—the field test was positive, but for the wrong drug; the drug weights were incorrect; or there was too little of the evidence to analyze—but in 251 cases, the results were simple: "No Controlled Substance."

Under the 1963 Supreme Court opinion in Brady v. Maryland, prosecutors must provide defendants with exculpatory evidence, even after a conviction. Chandler could have met that mandate simply by alerting the convicting court and the defense attorneys to the lab reports—"Every other Brady situation, as long as I give notice, I'm done," she says—but in these cases, Chandler says, she knew very few of the wrongful drug convictions would be reversed if she let the system handle each of them individually. The exoneration effort needed to be centralized, so that someone would become responsible for finding the defendants themselves. Chandler took the list to Devon Anderson, Harris County's district attorney.

Anderson, a former district-court judge, had been the top prosecutor for only seven months. Her husband, Mike Anderson, who took office as district attorney in January 2013, died of cancer eight months into his term, and Gov. Rick Perry appointed her to replace him. Now, as Chandler described the problem, Anderson felt sickened. The litany of wrongful convictions was not just enormous—it was still growing. Her office, she says, was to blame for "a breakdown at every point in the system." She hired a former prosecutor to research the cases and find the defendants. "It may sound corny, but it's true: Our duty under Texas law is to seek justice," she says. "A lot of people think it's convictions, but it's justice."

In April 2014, The American-Statesman published Dexheimer's story, which focused on 21 wrongful drug convictions across Texas caused by lab delays. But prosecutors in Harris County were still uncovering the scale of their own problem.

Based in part on the information gathered by Marie Munier, the former prosecutor Anderson hired to examine the drug convictions, we determined that 301 of the 416 variants began as arrests by the Houston Police Department, with the rest coming from surrounding municipalities, and that 212 of those 301 arrests were based on evidence that lab analysis determined was not a controlled substance, or N.C.S.

In our own examination of those 212 cases—thousands of pages of arrest reports, court filings and laboratory-testing records, along with interviews of prosecutors, police executives, officers, defense attorneys and innocent defendants who pleaded guilty—we saw a clear story about both who is being arrested and what is happening to them. The racial disparity is stark. Blacks made up 59 percent of those wrongfully convicted in a city where they are 24 percent of the population, reflecting a similar racial disparity in drug enforcement nationally. Patrol units, not trained narcotics detectives, appeared to be the most prolific field-test users.

The kits, or the officers interpreting them, got it wrong most often when dealing with small amounts of suspected drugs. Sixty-three percent of the N.C.S. cases involved less than a gram of evidence. The smallest possession cases are the ones in which a field test can be of greatest consequence; if officers find larger quantities of white powder in dozens of baggies or packaged in bricks, they have sufficient probable cause to make an arrest regardless of what a color test shows. (Though in those cases, too, they are generally required to test the drugs.) It's widely assumed in legal circles that these wrongfully convicted people are in fact drug users who intended to possess drugs. Barry Scheck, a founder of the Innocence Project, a nonprofit group that seeks to overturn wrongful convictions, says some who work toward exoneration have complained to him that those exonerated of drug charges often are just accidentally not guilty, and shouldn't be added to the National Registry of Exonerations. The assumption is not entirely without basis—162 of the 212 N.C.S. defendants had criminal histories involving illegal drugs. However, 50 had no criminal history involving drugs at all.

All of the 212 N.C.S. defendants struck plea bargains, and nearly all of them, 93 percent, received a jail or prison sentence. Defendants with no previous convictions have a legal right in Texas to probation on drug-possession charges, even if they're convicted at trial. But remarkably, 78 percent of defendants entitled to probation agreed to deals that included incarceration. Perhaps most striking: A majority of those defendants, 58 percent, pleaded guilty at the first opportunity, during their arraignment; the median time between arrest and plea was four days. In contrast, the median for defendants in which the field test indicated the wrong drug or that the weight was inaccurate—that is, the defendants who actually did possess drugs—was 22 days. Not only do the innocent tend to plead guilty in these cases, but they often do so more quickly.

On July 29, 2014, Munier sent a letter to Amy Albritton. It was a form letter, one of hundreds Munier was sending to exonerated defendants, opening with the salutation "Dear Sir or Madam," but the contents were highly personal. It stated that the Harris County district attorney's office had learned that the drug evidence in Albritton's case was not a controlled substance: "Accordingly, you were prosecuted for a criminal drug offense and convicted in error." Munier mailed the letter to the address on Albritton's driver's license, but Albritton did not receive it. She had long since moved on.

She had struggled to rebuild her life as a felon. The hours at the convenience store were erratic, so she started waiting tables and tending bar as she tried to find work in property management again. In 2013, she heard about a small set of rentals in Baton Rouge that needed someone to run them day to day. The pay was low compared with what she had made at Frances Place, and there was no free apartment. But the owner agreed to interview Albritton, even with her drug felony, and quickly hired her. She had almost nothing to pack besides her clothes and Landon's before relocating to the state capital. The reason this property owner was willing to hire a drug felon became apparent soon enough. The apartments were in disrepair, with broken heaters and plumbing, and the owner forced his property manager to deal with angry tenants. She had gone to work for a slumlord.

Albritton quit and took a bartending position at the restaurant attached to a Holiday Inn near Louisiana State University. Tips included, she was earning about $15,000 a year, but she liked her coworkers and impressed her bosses. One of them tried to promote her to shift supervisor, Albritton recalls, but the promotion was denied when a criminal-background check by the hotel chain's corporate office flagged the Houston conviction. She could pour drinks and do nothing more. She remembers how desperate she had been to leave her jail cell, naïvely believing that the punishment for pleading guilty would end with her sentence. "No," she says. "You're not ever free and clear of it. It follows you everywhere you go."

In the two years, since the efforts to overturn wrongful convictions began at the Harris County district attorney's office, Inger Chandler and her colleagues at the integrity unit have struck 119 N.C.S. convictions from the record. At least 172 remain. They haven't been able to locate all of the wrongly convicted, at times even after hiring private investigators, and some defendants they have reached have declined to interact with the courts, even to clear their record. Last year, as we examined records in Harris County, we came upon Albritton's file and decided to search for her ourselves to find out what had happened to one representative figure out of hundreds. Her case fit the larger pattern of convictions for no controlled substance: It moved rapidly, with Albritton pleading guilty within 48 hours of her arrest, and it involved an exceedingly small amount of supposed drugs. We searched for Albritton in public databases, finding likely relatives but no phone numbers or a current address. We called her sister, who said that Albritton was in Baton Rouge and provided a cellphone number. It was disconnected. But knowing where Albritton lived now, we found a Facebook profile she had been updating regularly with details of her life, including her work. Interestingly, we also found that Albritton had pleaded guilty to a 2008 misdemeanor, a D.U.I. conviction in Louisiana, despite breathalyzer results showing her blood-alcohol level at 0.0. When we asked her about this, she said that she had caused a collision by pulling onto the wrong side of a two-lane highway, and because she was guilty of that, she did not protest the other charges; she's still unable to explain why she confessed to a crime there was no evidence she committed.

In August, we called and left a brief message for Albritton at the Sporting News Grill. She returned the call a couple of hours later, her voice small, wondering what this was about. When we described the details from the lab report and the letter from the district attorney that she never received, Albritton gasped. She didn't make a sound for several seconds before shouting into the phone: "I knew it! I told them!"

If Albritton's case is one of hundreds in Houston, there is every reason to suspect that it is just one among thousands of wrongful drug convictions that were based on field tests across the United States. The Harris County district attorney's office is responsible for half of all exonerations by conviction-integrity units nationwide in the past three years—not because law enforcement is different there but because the Houston lab committed to testing evidence after defendants had already pleaded guilty, a position that is increasingly unpopular in forensic science.

Crime labs have been moving away from drug cases to focus on DNA and evidence from violent crimes. In some instances, the shift has been extreme. The Las Vegas Metropolitan Police Department's forensic laboratory analyzes the evidence in, on average, just 73 drug cases a year, internal records show. Nearly all of its 8,000 annual possession arrests rest exclusively on field-test results.

The United States Department of Justice was once among the leading voices of caution regarding field tests, and encouraged all drug evidence go to lab chemists. But in 2008, the Justice Department funded a program developed by the National Forensic Science Technology Center, a nonprofit that provides crime-lab training, to reduce drug-evidence backlogs. Titled Field Investigation Drug Officer, the program consisted of a series of seminars that taught local police officers how to administer color field tests on a large scale. In its curriculum, the technology center states that field tests help authorities by "removing the need for extensive laboratory analysis," because "the field test may factor into obtaining an immediate plea agreement." The Justice Department declined repeated interview requests.

Field tests provide quick answers. But if those answers and confessions cannot be trusted, Charles McClelland, the former Houston police chief, says, officers should not be using them. During an interview in March, McClelland said that if he had known of the false positives Houston's officers were generating, he would have ordered a halt to all field testing departmentwide. Police officers are not chemists, McClelland said. "Officers shouldn't collect and test their own evidence, period. I don't care whether that's cocaine, blood, hair."

Judges, too, have the power, and a responsibility, some argue, to slow down the gears of the system. Patricia Lykos, the Harris County district attorney from 2009 to 2013, says that when she served as a criminal-court judge in the 1980s and 1990s, she would ask the defendants questions about their lives and the crimes they were accused of committing. If she wasn't satisfied that the defendant was guilty of the charge, Lykos says, she wouldn't accept the plea. At times the situation is even easier to decipher, says David LaBahn, president of the Association of Prosecuting Attorneys. The defendant can be heard arguing his or her innocence to the appointed attorney. In such drug-possession cases, when the prosecutor doesn't have a lab report, "if I'm that judicial officer, this case is continued"—adjourned—"until everybody can do their job," LaBahn says.

But that means the defendant, depending on his or her custody status, could go back to jail until the case proceeds, presenting a significant dilemma. Last year, Devon Anderson, the current Harris County district attorney, prohibited plea deals in drug-possession cases before the lab has issued a report. The labs issue reports in about two weeks, but defendants typically wait three weeks before they can see a judge—enough time to lose a job, lose an apartment, lose everything. And yet since Anderson implemented the rule, case dismissals have soared 31 percent, primarily because the lab has proved defendants not guilty.

People plead guilty when they're innocent because they see no alternative. People who have just been arrested usually don't know their options, or even that they have an option. "There's a fail-safe in there, and it's called the defense lawyer," says Rick Werstein, the attorney now representing Albritton as she seeks to finalize her exoneration. Defense lawyers can demand a lab analysis, and they exist to help defendants navigate the consequences of the jail time while they wait, even as they explain the even higher costs of a felony conviction. They are fully authorized to pursue alternative deals.

In fact, Richardson, Albritton's original court-appointed lawyer, says the prosecutor offered her a deferred adjudication, in which she may have been able to wait for the results of a lab test outside the walls of a jail cell. Richardson, who first said he had no memory of their conversations, says he told her about the offer but she refused it. Albritton says she has never heard of anything called deferred adjudication. Neither could explain what actually happened. Perhaps they simply accepted that the field test, with its promise of scientific inevitability, would eventually convict her. "The entire country works on these field-test kits, right?" Richardson asks.

In the past three years, people arrested based on false-positive field tests have filed civil lawsuits in Sullivan County, Tennessee; Lehigh County, Pennsylvania; Atlanta, Georgia; and San Diego, California. Three of the four cases also named the manufacturers Safariland Group or Sirchie as defendants. Three of the cases have already been settled. In one of them, the Sullivan County case, Safariland secured a gag order on the plaintiff, explicitly to prevent media coverage, before entering settlement negotiations. The plaintiffs in each of the suits were people who were arrested, refused to plead guilty and were detained for a month or longer. So far, we have been unable find anyone who pleaded guilty based on field-test results and later filed suit, though Werstein said he and Albritton are considering their additional legal options.

The Texas Criminal Court of Appeals overturned Albritton's conviction in late June, but before her record can be cleared, that reversal must be finalized by the trial court in Houston. Felony records are digitally disseminated far and wide, and can haunt the wrongly convicted for years after they are exonerated. Until the court makes its final move, Amy Albritton—for the purposes of employment, for the purposes of housing, for the purposes of her own peace of mind—remains a felon, one among unknown tens of thousands of Americans whose lives have been torn apart by a very flawed test.

Correction: July 17, 2016

An article on July 10 about roadside drug tests described incorrectly one aspect of the procedure involving a closed drug-possession case. As was standard practice, the prosecutor—not the Houston Police Department—filed a motion to destroy the evidence.

Correction: August 7, 2016

An article on July 10 about roadside drug tests erroneously included an analysis of cocaine field-test results used by the Las Vegas Metropolitan Police Department. The sampling did not represent a broad submission of results to the department's lab—it was an isolated group of field-test failures including officer mistakes and false positives—and the data should not have been used to calculate an error rate. The article also misstated the average number of drug cases analyzed by the police department. It was an average of 1,757 cases per year, not 73. And the article overstated the role field tests play in Las Vegas's possession arrests. According to the Las Vegas Metropolitan Police Department, forms of evidence other than field tests can lead to drug-possession arrests. They are not based exclusively on field-test results.

Critical Thinking

1. Do you believe Albritton was treated fairly?
2. Is our desire to curb drug use worth the harm done to people who are arrested for drug crimes? Even when they are guilty?
3. Who else besides the police share blame for what happened to Albritton?

Internet References

Austin American Statesman
http://www.mystatesman.com/news/news/state-regional/lab-delays-create-texas-unknown-exonerees/nfdTW/

Common Sense for Drug Policy
http://www.drugwarfacts.org/cms/Crime#sthash.5hU4P4f0.edjvqnXz.dpbs

National Archive of Criminal Justice Data
http://www.icpsr.umich.edu/icpsrweb/NACJD/studies/2038?q=state+court+processing+&amp%3Barchive=NACJD

RYAN GABRIELSON AND TOPHER SANDERS are staff reporters at ProPublica.

Article   Prepared by: Joanne Naughton

Out of the Shadows

The untold stories of 110 child abuse and neglect fatalities, and one state's failure to learn from tragedy.

JENIFER MCKIM

Learning Outcomes

After reading this article, you will be able to:

- Discuss the importance of CORI.
- Describe the two-tier system.
- Show how children can be missed completely by the system.

Christopher Berry's troubles started long before he killed his infant son in 2013. After surviving a suicide bombing and returning from Afghanistan with posttraumatic stress in 2011, Berry racked up arrests for allegedly shoving his teenage girlfriend, deliberately running over pigeons, and stealing from his employer.

Yet, when state social workers got a report that the Lowell couple was neglecting month-old William James Berry in the spring of 2013, records show they assigned the family to the "lower risk" category of state protection for children they believe are not in immediate danger. These families are targeted for increased social services rather than a full abuse investigation.

A month later, Christopher Berry lost his temper over the baby's crying, shaking him for 30 seconds until his body went limp.

"I was holding him, and I was like, 'Oh, my God, oh my God, what did I just do?'" Berry told police in a recorded confession.

William is one of at least 110 children 17 and younger whose deaths were linked to abuse and neglect between 2009 and 2013 in Massachusetts, a third of whom had at some point been under the watch of the state Department of Children and Families (DCF). Many others were likely known to the state but never subject to DCF supervision. The rest died without ever having a chance at state protection.

Records obtained by the New England Center for Investigative Reporting (NECIR) show that the vast majority of the dead were under the age of three, beaten, drowned, smothered or otherwise abused or neglected by caretakers. And their numbers have steadily increased, records show, from 14 reported abuse and neglect deaths in 2009 to 38 in 2013—and state officials say numbers will likely remain elevated when the 2014 death toll is made public.

Most of these children's stories have gone untold, either because their plight wasn't known to the state until they died, or because the state's missteps and failures to protect dozens of them was long concealed by confidentiality laws and secrecy. An examination of these sad cases shows that mistakes occur at all levels of the child welfare process—from at-risk youths the system failed to catch, to infants with open social services cases who fell through the cracks, to babies like William who were funneled into a program meant for lower risk youths that couldn't save them.

DCF already has faced harsh criticism for failing to protect children under its watch, including Jeremiah Oliver, the Fitchburg toddler who disappeared and was later found dead by a highway in 2014 and 7-year-old Jack Loiselle of Hardwick who fell into a coma in July after his father allegedly starved and beat him. Just September 18, DCF faced more criticism with the revelation that Baby Doe, the child found dead in a garbage bag on Deer Island this summer, was Bella Bond, a 2-year-old who had twice been under supervision of state social workers. Earlier this month, Gov. Charlie Baker held a press conference to say that DCF "has many systemic problems and we are going to fix them . . . No one is standing here and saying everything is fine."

But many child specialists worry the state swings from one tragedy to the next without learning from past mistakes or implementing lasting reform. The state's own child fatality data is faulty, review teams set up to analyze fatalities don't often meet, and DCF social workers say they often are kept from learning anything about what went wrong when a child dies, the Center's review found.

"It's a very dysfunctional system. Not only is DCF failing, but the other eye of the state, the child fatality review teams, are largely nonfunctional," said Dr. Robert Sege, vice president at the Boston-based nonprofit Health Resources in Action who sits on a county-level review team in Suffolk County that has not met for over a year. "How do you make improvements if you don't open your eyes and look at what is going on?"

The New England Center and the Boston Globe obtained information about child abuse and neglect deaths caused by parents and caretakers through a public records request that took seven months to complete and cost nearly $4,500 to obtain. Center staff also spent months reviewing court and police records, interviewing families and child experts for this story, and found that:

- Thirty-eight children who died between 2009 and 2013 had received services from state social workers, and 26 of those were under state supervision at the time of their deaths. Other deceased children undoubtedly had contact with DCF, either to receive voluntary services or because their family was the subject of a complaint that social workers dismissed. But DCF declined to release information about complaints that had been rejected.

- A six-year-old DCF intake system for maltreatment complaints—opposed by the union that represents social workers—divides children into high-risk and lower risk categories, with less risky cases assigned to workers with less required training. Between 2009 and 2013, 10 children on the lower risk track died, including 7 in 2013, records show, raising questions about whether the system has enough safeguards to protect children.

- The DCF screening system does not require social workers to do criminal background checks of a child's caretakers when analyzing neglect and abuse complaints—an oversight that some child advocates say leaves a huge gap in assessing risk.

- The state keeps shoddy data on child deaths and its child fatality review system is crippled by lack of funds and resources. The New England Center found 10 children who were not included in state data even though their deaths were ruled to be homicide and, in most cases, parents or other caretakers were implicated.

Not Learning from Mistakes

Commissioner Linda Spears, named to run DCF in January, would not discuss individual cases that predated her tenure, but said that, much as a hospital emergency room has to determine the patients in most urgent need, DCF has to better identify and protect the most vulnerable children.

DCF faces a daunting task: responding to more than 92,000 child abuse complaints last year alone and figuring out which situations are so dire that children need to be removed from home, even though that could mean sending to foster homes that have their own problems. Last year, social workers substantiated 62,452 maltreatment complaints, a 34 percent increase over 2013, records show.

What needs refinement, Spears said, is "how do we make decisions based on risk factors that we know in the case ... I'm taking a very broad systemic view."

In contrast to the headlines about Oliver and Loiselle, most abuse and neglect victims die with little public notice. That includes Dejalyse Alcantara of Boston, who was put under state watch at birth in 2011 because of her mother's drug abuse. She died six months later in an overheated car, her mother asleep or unconscious in the front seat. Two-year-old Yarelis Rosario-Pereyra of Boston died allegedly of abuse and neglect in 2013 even though social workers had confirmed that she suffered bouts of maltreatment throughout her life. No one yet has been charged in her case.

Peter MacKinnon, DCF chapter president of the SEIU union local 509, said social workers are devastated when a child dies on their watch, but seldom learn from their managers about what went wrong or how they could improve their work.

"If you are truly looking to get a sense from DCF about what you did well, what you might have missed, you need to see what that analysis is," he said. "If you don't know what you are doing, how can you fix it? It goes into this black hole."

Child fatalities—from natural and abuse-related causes—are supposed to be reviewed by a panel of experts, but that system has ground to a halt. The state review team, chaired by the Office of the Chief Medical Examiner, has filed only four reports since its launch 15 years ago, even though state law requires it to file findings and recommendations annually.

State officials say the review teams lack funding to do their work, but regular appeals for more money from the state Office of the Child Advocate have gone nowhere.

Informed of 10 homicide cases of children not included in the 2009–2013 data, DCF officials acknowledged that they sometimes miss maltreatment deaths entirely—because they don't always hear about them. In some cases, they said, medical examiners did not always alert DCF when a child's death was linked to abuse and neglect as required by law. As a result, the agency has undercounted child abuse deaths and may be leaving abusive parents with other children.

Spears called the increase in child maltreatment deaths "tragic but not surprising," blaming the jump on affects of the state's opioid crisis as well as an increase in reporting of infants who die suddenly due to unsafe sleep practices, like sleeping with an adult, which state officials consider a form of neglect.

Sixteen child deaths in 2013 were sleep-related, state records show, five of those had histories of maltreatment.

And Spears said she expects 2014 death levels, not yet finalized, to remain elevated. "I don't think anything in the caseload and the community would give me any indication that the number will go down," she said.

Social Worker's Dilemma: Is A Case Lower or Higher Risk?

William James Berry's shaking death, some say, points to weaknesses in a system launched in 2009 to help social workers separate cases where children are in imminent danger from those where the family simply needs help.

The policy, part of a national movement, was quickly embraced in Massachusetts: in 2013, 38 percent of child abuse reports were assigned to the lower risk group, DCF records show.

The higher-risk cases, including allegations of sexual or serious physical abuse or neglect, are referred to social workers whose "primary purpose" is to investigate and "determine the safety of the reported child," state documents show. Social workers are supposed to "engage and support families" when the child is in the lower-risk group.

The state social worker's union opposed the state's two-tier system from the onset, MacKinnon said, because of concerns that families considered lower-risk may get short shrift. The social workers who do the full child abuse investigations are provided more training on how to interview children and ferret out signs of child abuse, he said, leaving people with less specialized training to handle lower-risk cases.

Currently, caseworkers who handle lower-risk cases are less likely to interview the child away from parents—often a key to getting at the truth, explained Taunton DCF social worker Laurie Cyphers. They are less capable, she said, of pushing parents to cooperate if they refuse state help. She worries that social workers with less experience and less training won't be able to accurately assess safety risks.

"They don't have the training and they don't have the experience to fall back on," said Cyphers, a 14-year DCF veteran who mainly oversees lower-risk cases.

There is no national data tracking deaths of children who had been placed on the lower risk track. But there have been enough incidents, here and elsewhere, to lead some child welfare advocates to question the idea of a two-tier system. In Minnesota, for example, the murder of a 4-year-old boy who had been placed on the lower-risk track prompted statewide scrutiny and recommendations to narrow, and perhaps do away with, the program.

In Massachusetts, 3-year-old Alyvia Navarro was put on the less severe track months before the autistic preschooler drowned in a pond behind a Wareham trailer home in a death DCF ascribed to neglect, state records show. There's also 10-year-old Isaiah Buckner from Athol who died from abuse and neglect-related injuries in July 2013, according to DCF, a case that remains unsolved. At least four other children on the lower-risk track died of what DCF determined are neglect-related unsafe sleep issues, records show.

Sharon Crawford, Buckner's maternal grandmother, said she was not aware that her daughter was being visited by social workers, much less in what is considered a lower-risk track. She said the state should have taken special care since her grandson was deaf and legally blind. She's angry that social workers never reached out to her, since she was very involved in Isaiah's life.

"Something is not right here," said Crawford, 53, who lives in Whitinsville. "Why would he be (placed on the lower-risk track) if he couldn't hear and couldn't talk?"

Before taking charge of DCF, Spears last year oversaw a critical report on the agency by the Child Welfare League of America. The report found that DCF's budget cuts, lack of staff support and growing caseloads compromise the effectiveness of the two-tier system. The report also said DCF needs to put a higher priority on a "child's right to basic safety."

Now, Spears says the two-tier program needs to be tightened up. She noted that, when the system works properly, children can be shifted to the higher risk group as social workers learn more about the families.

"We may walk in and find that something else is going on, at which point the case can then go back over to the investigation response track," said Spears. "The paths are not so distinct."

A new DCF review on Loiselle, the Hardwick boy now in a coma, showed that social workers had dismissed multiple allegations of abuse and neglect as far back as 2008. But when they finally opened a case on the boy in February 2015 in response to two new complaints, the social workers placed him in the lower-risk category, records show.

Elizabeth Bartholet, a Harvard law professor and national critic of the two-track program, said the Hardwick report "screams out" that social workers involved with the family were more concerned with keeping the family together than ensuring the boy's safety.

Especially for children in the lower risk category, Bartholet said, "Best interest of the child is clearly not the standard."

Missing Cues: No Criminal Background Check

William Berry's case, which did not get the same kind of public scrutiny as Loiselle's, also raises questions about how closely social workers studied the baby's home life before concluding he was at low risk of harm.

When a maltreatment call comes in, individual caseworkers must decide which track to place a family on based largely on agency files and phone conversations, according to DCF documents. They can also request a criminal background check—a "Criminal Offense Record Information" or CORI—though it's not required.

DCF won't say whether staffers checked Christopher Berry's CORI when they received a neglect complaint in 2013. If they did, the record would have shown Berry was facing a series of pending criminal cases, including an allegation that he repeatedly shoved Tabatha Cupan, his 18-year-old girlfriend who was pregnant with William, during a dispute in their Lowell apartment.

Mary McGeown, president of the Boston-based Massachusetts Society for the Prevention of Cruelty to Children, said simply knowing that Berry was a veteran should have prompted a closer look at the family, because so many people return home suffering from mental issues, leading to increases in domestic and child abuse.

In the end, DCF assigned the family to the lower risk group a month before Berry killed his son, state records show.

Boston pediatrician and child abuse expert Eli Newberger said he was "appalled" to learn that social workers are not required to request a person's criminal history as part of a screening—saying that the state is ignoring key evidence that puts a child at risk.

Commissioner Spears said that DCF hasn't traditionally believed every neglect case requires that level of scrutiny, but agrees that the agency needs to re-examine the role CORI checks play in evaluating abuse and neglect complaints.

"We need to look at when CORI should be done and we should make those things routine," Spears said.

Of course, even a full-scale investigation by DCF is no guarantee children will be safe. Dejalyse Alcantara, for instance, died in March 2012 even though she had been under state supervision since birth because of her mother's substance abuse, DCF documents show.

D.J. Alcantara of Boston, Dejalyse's father, had separated from the girl's mother before the child's birth to deal with his own drug problems. But now he can't stop thinking of what he could have done to save his baby, who died of heat exposure in the back seat of a car while her mother was seemingly passed out in front. He said he told Boston police a month before Dejalyse's death about his concerns about his daughter's safety, because of the mother's drug use. But the police report shows the concern was not relayed to DCF.

Marivette Morales, the mother, declined requests to comment for this story. But Alcantara wonders how social workers could have failed to see that his daughter was in danger. He said the baby didn't even have a crib and slept on the couch for months.

Some argue that, until DCF makes a clear commitment to put child safety above all else, including keeping families together, child deaths like Dejalyse's will continue to be a troubling problem.

"Strengthening families and keeping children safe are both vital, but child safety must always take precedence," said Gail Garinger, former head of the state Office of the Child Advocate. "In some cases it may not be possible for vulnerable infants, especially those born prematurely or with drugs in their systems, to be safely maintained in their homes."

Children the System Completely Missed

Perhaps as troubling as children who die under the watch of social workers tasked to protect them are the stories of the children who died of abuse and neglect between 2009 and 2013 that were never brought into the state system at all—there were 72 of them.

Social workers either dismissed reports of alleged maltreatment or never heard from concerned teachers, police, hospital workers or other mandated reporters at all, records and interviews show.

Some cases reviewed by NECIR include clear signs that the state missed opportunities to save them. For example, state officials knew that Alexis Medina Sr. had repeatedly assaulted his baby daughter—he served 18 months behind bars for that crime. But, released on probation, he suffocated his three-month-old son from a new relationship in 2013. State officials at the time said Medina's case had been closed and social workers were not aware he was again living with children.

It's also unclear how many times social workers dismissed abuse and neglect claims about children who later died of abuse and neglect. The state, citing legal issues, refused to provide this information for the children who died between 2009 and 2013. NECIR is appealing this decision to the Secretary of State. But it's likely that many had been known to state agencies: A 2013 state report, for example, found that in 65 percent of all child maltreatment deaths between 2001 and 2010, families were known to DCF.

For Laura Cyphers, the Taunton social worker who handles low-risk cases, each new tragedy is a painful reminder of problems that front line workers know only too well. She wishes the agency would be more transparent and introspective, but, in her experience, that has not been the case.

When a child dies, she says, coworkers are interrogated by higher ups about what happened, but never see a final report or learn about findings—unless it involves losing their jobs.

"They go in saying, 'I did nothing wrong,' and they come out devastated," she said. "If we can learn from something, it is important."

Critical Thinking

1. Why does the author say DCF is not learning from their mistakes?

2. Why did the social workers' union oppose the state's two-tier system from the start?

3. Why aren't child fatalities being reviewed by a panel of experts, as required by law?

Internet References

Information Denied, Children Endangered
   http://eye.necir.org/2015/09/19/information-denied/

Unexplained Infant Deaths to be Reported to State Social Workers
   http://eye.necir.org/2014/11/30/sids-report/

JENIFER MCKIM is a senior investigative reporter at the New England Center for Investigative Reporting—an independent, nonprofit investigative reporting newsroom that holds the powerful accountable and trains a new generation of reporters.

Article   Prepared by: Joanne Naughton

More than 1,600 Women Murdered by Men in One Year, New Study Finds

Learning Outcomes

After reading this article, you will be able to:

- State which states have the highest rate of women murdered by men in 2013.
- Relate what was the most common weapon used.

Study Ranks the States on the Rate of Women Murdered by Men in Advance of Domestic Violence Awareness Month in October

Washington, DC—More than 1,600 women were murdered by men in 2013 and the most common weapon used was a gun, according to the new Violence Policy Center (VPC) study *When Men Murder Women: An Analysis of 2013 Homicide Data*.

This annual VPC report is being released in advance of Domestic Violence Awareness Month in October. This year's study applies to 2013, the most recent year for which data is available.

The study also ranks the states on the rate of women murdered by men. In 2013, South Carolina had the highest rate, followed by Alaska, New Mexico, Louisiana, and Nevada. (A list of the 10 states with the highest rates of women murdered by men follows below.)

The study covers homicides involving one female murder victim and one male offender, and uses data from the Federal Bureau of Investigation's Supplementary Homicide Report.

Nationwide, 1,615 females were murdered by males in single victim/single offender incidents in 2013, at a rate of 1.09 per 100,000. The study found that nationwide, 94 percent of women killed by men were murdered by someone they knew.

Of the victims who knew their offenders, 62 percent were wives or other intimate acquaintances of their killers.

The study also found that black women are disproportionately impacted by fatal domestic violence. In 2013, black females were murdered by men at a rate of 2.36 per 100,000, two and a half times higher than the rate of 0.95 per 100,000 for white women murdered by men.

Nationwide in 2013, out of the 1,615 female homicide victims, 1,086 were white, 453 were black, 36 were Asian or Pacific Islander, 21 were American Indian or Alaskan Native, and in 19 cases, the race of the victim was not identified.

"Women are dying every day as a result of domestic violence, and our state and federal laws are insufficient in the face of this crisis," states VPC Legislative Director Kristen Rand. "State and federal policymakers should take immediate action to help protect women from abusers and prevent future tragedies. This should include ensuring that men with a history of domestic abuse do not have access to guns."

"When men murder women, the most common weapon used is a gun," says Julia Wyman, executive director of States United to Prevent Gun Violence. "Closing gaps in state and federal gun laws will save women's lives."

The Violence Policy Center has published *When Men Murder Women* annually for 18 years. During that period, nationwide the rate of women murdered by men in single victim/single offender incidents has dropped 31 percent—from 1.57 per 100,000 in 1996 to 1.09 per 100,000 in 2013.

Below is the complete list of the 10 states with the highest rate of females murdered by males in single victim/single offender incidents in 2013:

For each of the top 10 states, the study offers a detailed summary including the number of victims by age group and race; the most common weapons used; the victim to offender relationships; and the circumstances of the homicides.

For homicides in which the victim to offender relationship could be identified, 94 percent of female victims nationwide

Ranking	State	Number of Female Homicide Victims	Homicide Rate per 100,000 Females
1	South Carolina	57	2.32
2	Alaska	8	2.29
3	New Mexico	21	2.00
4	Louisiana	47	1.99
5	Nevada	27	1.95
6 (tie)	Tennessee	55	1.65
6 (tie)	Oklahoma	32	1.65
8	Vemont	5	1.58
9	Maine	10	1.47
10	Michigan	73	1.45

were murdered by a male they knew. Of the victims who knew their offenders, 62 percent were wives, common-law wives, ex-wives, or girlfriends of the offenders.

Firearms—especially handguns—were the weapons most commonly used by males to murder females in 2013. Nationwide, for homicides in which the weapon used could be identified, 53 percent of female victims were shot and killed with a gun. Of the homicides committed with guns, 69 percent were killed with handguns.

The overwhelming majority of these homicides were *not* related to any other felony crime, such as rape or robbery. Nationwide, for homicides in which the circumstances could be identified, 85 percent of the homicides were not related to the commission of another felony. Most often, females were killed by males in the course of an argument between the victim and the offender.

The study calculates the rate of women murdered by men by dividing the total number of females murdered by males in single victim/single offender incidents by the total female population and multiplying the result by 100,000. This is the standard and accepted method of comparing fatal levels of gun violence.

The study urges state legislators to adopt laws that enhance enforcement of federal legislation and ensure that guns are surrendered by or removed from the presence of abusers. In addition, the study urges the U.S. Congress to adopt stronger legislation to protect victims of domestic violence, such as: the "Protecting Domestic Violence and Stalking Victims Act of 2015" introduced by Sen. Amy Klobuchar (D-MN); the "Lori Jackson Domestic Violence Survivor Protection Act" introduced by Sen. Richard Blumenthal (D-CT); and, the "Zero Tolerance for Domestic Abusers Act" introduced by Reps. Debbie Dingell (D-MI) and Robert Dold (R-IL).

To view the full report, please visit http://www.vpc.org/studies/wmmw2015.pdf.

Critical Thinking

1. Where the relationship could be identified, were the men who killed women likely to be loved ones?
2. Is Julia Wyman's conclusion about gun laws accurate?
3. Do you agree with Kristen Rand's statement?

Internet References

30 Shocking Domestic Violence Statistics
http://www.huffingtonpost.com/2014/10/23/domestic-violence-statistics_n_5959776.html

National Coalition against Domestic Violence
http://ncadv.org/learn-more/statistics

When Men Murder Women
http://www.vpc.org/studies/wmmw2015.pdf

The Violence Policy Center (VPC) is a national educational organization working to stop gun death and injury. Follow the VPC on Twitter, Facebook, and YouTube.

States United to Prevent Gun Violence (www.CeasefireUSA.org) is a national nonprofit organization working to support state-based gun violence prevention groups and help build new state-led organizations. States United believes that all Americans deserve to live in a country free from the fear, threat, and devastation caused by gun violence.

Article Prepared by: Joanne Naughton

Human Sex Trafficking

AMANDA WALKER-RODRIGUEZ AND RODNEY HILL

Learning Outcomes

After reading this article, you will be able to:

- Outline the scope of human sex trafficking.

- Describe how victims are recruited into the business of human sex trafficking.

H uman sex trafficking is the most common form of modern-day slavery. Estimates place the number of its domestic and international victims in the millions, mostly females and children enslaved in the commercial sex industry for little or no money.[1] The terms *human trafficking* and *sex slavery* usually conjure up images of young girls beaten and abused in faraway places, like Eastern Europe, Asia, or Africa. Actually, human sex trafficking and sex slavery happen locally in cities and towns, both large and small, throughout the United States, right in citizens' backyards.

Appreciating the magnitude of the problem requires first understanding what the issue is and what it is not. Additionally, people must be able to identify the victim in common trafficking situations.

Human Sex Trafficking

Many people probably remember popular movies and television shows depicting pimps as dressing flashy and driving large fancy cars. More important, the women—adults—consensually and voluntarily engaged in the business of prostitution without complaint. This characterization is extremely inaccurate, nothing more than fiction. In reality, the pimp *traffics* young women (and sometimes men) completely against their will by force or threat of force; this is human sex trafficking.

The Scope

Not only is human sex trafficking slavery but it is big business. It is the fastest-growing business of organized crime and the third-largest criminal enterprise in the world.[2] The majority of sex trafficking is international, with victims taken from such places as South and Southeast Asia, the former Soviet Union, Central and South America, and other less developed areas and moved to more developed ones, including Asia, the Middle East, Western Europe, and North America.[3]

Unfortunately, however, sex trafficking also occurs domestically.[4] The United States not only faces an influx of international victims but also has its own homegrown problem of interstate sex trafficking of minors.[5]

The United States not only faces an influx of international victims but also has its own homegrown problem of interstate sex trafficking of minors.

Although comprehensive research to document the number of children engaged in prostitution in the United States is lacking, an estimated 293,000 American youths currently are at risk of becoming victims of commercial sexual exploitation.[6] The majority of these victims are runaway or thrown-away youths who live on the streets and become victims of prostitution.[7] These children generally come from homes where they have been abused or from families who have abandoned them. Often, they become involved in prostitution to support themselves financially or to get the things they feel they need or want (like drugs).

Other young people are recruited into prostitution through forced abduction, pressure from parents, or through deceptive agreements between parents and traffickers. Once these children become involved in prostitution, they often are forced to travel far from their homes and, as a result, are isolated from their friends and family. Few children in this situation can develop new relationships with peers or adults other than the person victimizing them. The lifestyle of such youths revolves around violence, forced drug use, and constant threats.[8]

Among children and teens living on the streets in the United States, involvement in commercial sex activity is a problem of epidemic proportion. Many girls living on the street engage in formal prostitution, and some become entangled in nationwide organized crime networks where they are trafficked nationally. Criminal networks transport these children around the United States by a variety of means—cars, buses, vans, trucks, or planes—and often provide them counterfeit identification to use in the event of arrest. The average age at which girls first become victims of prostitution is 12 to 14. It is not only the girls on the streets who are affected; boys and transgender youth enter into prostitution between the ages of 11 and 13 on average.[9]

The Operation

Today, the business of human sex trafficking is much more organized and violent. These women and young girls are sold to traffickers, locked up in rooms or brothels for weeks or months, drugged, terrorized, and raped repeatedly.[10] These continual abuses make it easier for the traffickers to control their victims. The captives are so afraid and intimidated that they rarely speak out against their traffickers, even when faced with an opportunity to escape.

Today, the business of human sex trafficking is much more organized and violent.

Generally, the traffickers are very organized. Many have a hierarchy system similar to that of other criminal organizations. Traffickers who have more than one victim often have a "bottom," who sits atop the hierarchy of prostitutes. The bottom, a victim herself, has been with the trafficker the longest and has earned his trust. Bottoms collect the money from the other girls, discipline them, seduce unwitting youths into trafficking, and handle the day-to-day business for the trafficker. Traffickers represent every social, ethnic, and racial group. Various organizational types exist in trafficking. Some perpetrators are involved with local street and motorcycle gangs, others are members of larger nationwide gangs and criminal organizations, and some have no affiliation with any one group or organization. Traffickers are not only men—women run many established rings.

Traffickers represent every social, ethnic, and racial group.

Traffickers use force, drugs, emotional tactics, and financial methods to control their victims. They have an especially easy time establishing a strong bond with young girls. These perpetrators may promise marriage and a lifestyle the youths often did not have in their previous familial relationships. They claim they "love" and "need" the victim and that any sex acts are for their future together. In cases where the children have few or no positive male role models in their lives, the traffickers take advantage of this fact and, in many cases, demand that the victims refer to them as "daddy," making it tougher for the youths to break the hold the perpetrator has on them.

Sometimes, the traffickers use violence, such as gang rape and other forms of abuse, to force the youths to work for them and remain under their control. One victim, a runaway from Baltimore County, Maryland, was gang raped by a group of men associated with the trafficker, who subsequently staged a "rescue." He then demanded that she repay him by working for him as one of his prostitutes. In many cases, however, the victims simply are beaten until they submit to the trafficker's demands.

In some situations, the youths have become addicted to drugs. The traffickers simply can use their ability to supply them with drugs as a means of control.

Traffickers often take their victims' identity forms, including birth certificates, passports, and drivers' licenses. In these cases, even if youths do leave they would have no ability to support themselves and often will return to the trafficker.

These abusive methods of control impact the victims both physically and mentally. Similar to cases involving Stockholm Syndrome, these victims, who have been abused over an extended period of time, begin to feel an attachment to the perpetrator.[11] This paradoxical psychological phenomenon makes it difficult for law enforcement to breach the bond of control, albeit abusive, the trafficker holds over the victim.

National Problem with Local Ties
The Federal Level

In 2000, Congress passed the Trafficking Victims Protection Act (TVPA), which created the first comprehensive federal law to address trafficking, with a significant focus on the international dimension of the problem. The law provides a three-pronged approach: *prevention* through public awareness programs overseas and a State Department-led monitoring and sanctions program; *protection* through a new T Visa and services for foreign national victims; and *prosecution* through new federal crimes and severe penalties.[12]

As a result of the passing of the TVPA, the Office to Monitor and Combat Trafficking in Persons was established in October 2001. This enabling legislation led to the creation of a bureau within the State Department to specifically address human trafficking and exploitation on all levels and to take legal action against perpetrators.[13] Additionally, this act was designed to enforce all laws within the 13th Amendment to the U.S. Constitution that apply.[14]

U.S. Immigration and Customs Enforcement (ICE) is one of the lead federal agencies charged with enforcing the TVPA. Human trafficking represents significant risks to homeland security. Would-be terrorists and criminals often can access the same routes and use the same methods as human traffickers. ICE's Human Smuggling and Trafficking Unit works to identify criminals and organizations involved in these illicit activities.

The FBI also enforces the TVPA. In June 2003, the FBI, in conjunction with the Department of Justice Child Exploitation and Obscenity Section and the National Center for Missing and Exploited Children, launched the Innocence Lost National Initiative. The agencies' combined efforts address the growing problem of domestic sex trafficking of children in the United States. To date, these groups have worked successfully to rescue nearly 900 children. Investigations successfully have led to the conviction of more than 500 pimps, madams, and their associates who exploit children through prostitution. These convictions have resulted in lengthy sentences, including multiple 25-year-to-life sentences and the seizure of real property, vehicles, and monetary assets.[15]

Both ICE and the FBI, along with other local, state, and federal law enforcement agencies and national victim-based advocacy groups in joint task forces, have combined resources and expertise on the issue. Today, the FBI participates in approximately 30 law enforcement task forces and about 42 Bureau of Justice Assistance (BJA)-sponsored task forces around the nation.[16]

In July 2004, the Human Smuggling Trafficking Center (HSTC) was created. The HSTC serves as a fusion center for information on human smuggling and trafficking, bringing together analysts, officers, and investigators from such agencies as the CIA, FBI, ICE, Department of State, and Department of Homeland Security.

The Local Level

With DOJ funding assistance, many jurisdictions have created human trafficking task forces to combat the problem. BJA's 42 such task forces can be demonstrated by several examples.[17]

- In 2004, the FBI's Washington field office and the D.C. Metropolitan Police Department joined with a variety of nongovernment organizations and service providers to combat the growing problem of human trafficking within Washington, D.C.
- In January 2005, the Massachusetts Human Trafficking Task Force was formed, with the Boston Police Department serving as the lead law enforcement entity. It uses a two-pronged approach, addressing investigations focusing on international victims and

those focusing on the commercial sexual exploitation of children.

- The New Jersey Human Trafficking Task Force attacks the problem by training law enforcement in the methods of identifying victims and signs of trafficking, coordinating statewide efforts in the identification and provision of services to victims of human trafficking, and increasing the successful interdiction and prosecution of trafficking of human persons.
- Since 2006, the Louisiana Human Trafficking Task Force, which has law enforcement, training, and victim services components, has focused its law enforcement and victim rescue efforts on the Interstate 10 corridor from the Texas border on the west to the Mississippi border on the east. This corridor, the basic northern border of the hurricane-ravaged areas of Louisiana, long has served as a major avenue of illegal immigration efforts. The I-10 corridor also is the main avenue for individuals participating in human trafficking to supply the labor needs in the hurricane-damaged areas of the state.
- In 2007, the Maryland Human Trafficking Task Force was formed. It aims to create a heightened law enforcement and victim service presence in the community. Its law enforcement efforts include establishing roving operations to identify victims and traffickers, deputizing local law enforcement to assist in federal human trafficking investigations, and providing training for law enforcement officers.

Anytown, USA

In December 2008, Corey Davis, the ringleader of a sex-trafficking ring that spanned at least three states, was sentenced in federal court in Bridgeport, Connecticut, on federal civil rights charges for organizing and leading the sex-trafficking operation that exploited as many as 20 females, including minors. Davis received a sentence of 293 months in prison followed by a lifetime term of supervised release. He pleaded guilty to multiple sex-trafficking charges, including recruiting a girl under the age of 18 to engage in prostitution. Davis admitted that he recruited a minor to engage in prostitution; that he was the organizer of a sex-trafficking venture; and that he used force, fraud, and coercion to compel the victim to commit commercial sex acts from which he obtained the proceeds.

According to the indictment, Davis lured victims to his operation with promises of modeling contracts and a glamorous lifestyle. He then forced them into a grueling schedule of dancing and performing at strip clubs in Connecticut, New York, and New Jersey. When the clubs closed, Davis forced the victims to walk the streets until 4 or 5 A.M. propositioning customers.

The indictment also alleged that he beat many of the victims to force them to work for him and that he also used physical abuse as punishment for disobeying the stringent rules he imposed to isolate and control them.[18]

As this and other examples show, human trafficking cases happen all over the United States. A few instances would represent just the "tip of the iceberg" in a growing criminal enterprise. Local and state criminal justice officials must understand that these cases are not isolated incidents that occur infrequently. They must remain alert for signs of trafficking in their jurisdictions and aggressively follow through on the smallest clue. Numerous websites openly (though they try to mask their actions) advertise for prostitution. Many of these sites involve young girls victimized by sex trafficking. Many of the pictures are altered to give the impression of older girls engaged in this activity freely and voluntarily. However, as prosecutors, the authors both have encountered numerous cases of suspected human trafficking involving underage girls.

> **Local and state criminal justice officials must understand that these cases are not isolated incidents that occur infrequently.**

The article "The Girls Next Door" describes a conventional midcentury home in Plainfield, New Jersey, that sat in a nice middle-class neighborhood. Unbeknownst to the neighbors, the house was part of a network of stash houses in the New York area where underage girls and young women from dozens of countries were trafficked and held captive. Acting on a tip, police raided the house in February 2002, expecting to find an underground brothel. Instead, they found four girls between the ages of 14 and 17, all Mexican nationals without documentation.

However, they were not prostitutes; they were sex slaves. These girls did not work for profit or a paycheck. They were captives to the traffickers and keepers who controlled their every move. The police found a squalid, land-based equivalent of a 19th-century slave ship. They encountered rancid, doorless bathrooms; bare, putrid mattresses; and a stash of penicillin, "morning after" pills, and an antiulcer medication that can induce abortion. The girls were pale, exhausted, and malnourished.[19]

Human sex trafficking warning signs include, among other indicators, streetwalkers and strip clubs. However, a jurisdiction's lack of streetwalkers or strip clubs does not mean that it is immune to the problem of trafficking. Because human trafficking involves big money, if money can be made, sex slaves can be sold. Sex trafficking can happen anywhere, however unlikely a place. Investigators should be attuned to reading the signs of trafficking and looking closely for them.

Investigation of Human Sex Trafficking

ICE aggressively targets the global criminal infrastructure, including the people, money, and materials that support human trafficking networks. The agency strives to prevent human trafficking in the United States by prosecuting the traffickers and rescuing and protecting the victims. However, most human trafficking cases start at the local level.

Strategies

Local and state law enforcement officers may unknowingly encounter sex trafficking when they deal with homeless and runaway juveniles; criminal gang activity; crimes involving immigrant children who have no guardians; domestic violence calls; and investigations at truck stops, motels, massage parlors, spas, and strip clubs. To this end, the authors offer various suggestions and indicators to help patrol officers identify victims of sex trafficking, as well as tips for detectives who investigate these crimes.

Patrol Officers

- Document suspicious calls and complaints on a police information report, even if the details seem trivial.
- Be aware of trafficking when responding to certain call types, such as reports of foot traffic in and out of a house. Consider situations that seem similar to drug complaints.
- Look closely at calls for assaults, domestic situations, verbal disputes, or thefts. These could involve a trafficking victim being abused and disciplined by a trafficker, a customer having a dispute with a victim, or a client who had money taken during a sex act.
- Locations, such as truck stops, strip clubs, massage parlors, and cheap motels, are havens for prostitutes forced into sex trafficking. Many massage parlors and strip clubs that engage in sex trafficking will have cramped living quarters where the victims are forced to stay.
- When encountering prostitutes and other victims of trafficking, do not display judgment or talk down to them. Understand the violent nature in how they are forced into trafficking, which explains their lack of cooperation. Speak with them in a location completely safe and away from other people, including potential victims.
- Check for identification. Traffickers take the victims' identification and, in cases of foreign nationals, their travel information. The lack of either item should raise concern.

Detectives/Investigators

- Monitor websites that advertise for dating and hooking up. Most vice units are familiar with the common sites used by sex traffickers as a means of advertisement.
- Conduct surveillance at motels, truck stops, strip clubs, and massage parlors. Look to see if the girls arrive alone or with someone else. Girls being transported to these locations should raise concerns of trafficking.
- Upon an arrest, check cell phone records, motel receipts, computer printouts of advertisements, and tollbooth receipts. Look for phone calls from the jailed prostitute to the pimp. Check surveillance cameras at motels and toll facilities as evidence to indicate the trafficking of the victim.
- Obtain written statements from the customers; get them to work for you.
- Seek assistance from nongovernmental organizations involved in fighting sex trafficking. Many of these entities have workers who will interview these victims on behalf of the police.
- After executing a search warrant, photograph everything. Remember that in court, a picture may be worth a thousand words: nothing else can more effectively describe a cramped living quarter a victim is forced to reside in.
- Look for advertisements in local newspapers, specifically the sports sections, that advertise massage parlors. These businesses should be checked out to ensure they are legitimate and not fronts for trafficking.
- Contact your local U.S. Attorney's Office, FBI field office, or ICE for assistance. Explore what federal resources exist to help address this problem.

Other Considerations

Patrol officers and investigators can look for many other human trafficking indicators as well.[20] These certainly warrant closer attention.

General Indicators

- People who live on or near work premises
- Individuals with restricted or controlled communication and transportation
- Persons frequently moved by traffickers
- A living space with a large number of occupants
- People lacking private space, personal possessions, or financial records
- Someone with limited knowledge about how to get around in a community

Physical Indicators

- Injuries from beatings or weapons
- Signs of torture (e.g., cigarette burns)
- Brands or scarring, indicating ownership
- Signs of malnourishment

Financial/Legal Indicators

- Someone else has possession of an individual's legal/travel documents
- Existing debt issues
- One attorney claiming to represent multiple illegal aliens detained at different locations
- Third party who insists on interpreting. Did the victim sign a contract?

Brothel Indicators

- Large amounts of cash and condoms
- Customer logbook or receipt book ("trick book")
- Sparse rooms
- Men come and go frequently

Conclusion

This form of cruel modern-day slavery occurs more often than many people might think. And, it is not just an international or a national problem—it also is a local one. It is big business, and it involves a lot of perpetrators and victims.

Agencies at all levels must remain alert to this issue and address it vigilantly. Even local officers must understand the problem and know how to recognize it in their jurisdictions. Coordinated and aggressive efforts from all law enforcement organizations can put an end to these perpetrators' operations and free the victims.

Notes

1. www.routledgesociology.com/books/Human-Sex-Trafficking-isbn9780415576789 (accessed July 19, 2010).
2. www.unodc.org/unodc/en/human-trafficking/what-is-human-trafficking.html (accessed July 19, 2010).
3. www.justice.gov/criminal/ceos/trafficking.html (accessed July 19, 2010).
4. Ibid.
5. www.justice.gov/criminal/ceos/prostitution.html (accessed July 19, 2010).
6. Richard J. Estes and Neil Alan Weiner, *Commercial Sexual Exploitation of Children in the U.S., Canada, and Mexico* (University of Pennsylvania, Executive Summary, 2001).

7. Ibid.

8. http://fpc.state.gov/documents/organization/9107.pdf (accessed July 19, 2010).

9. Estes and Weiner.

10. www.womenshealth.gov/violence/types/human-trafficking.cfm (accessed July 19, 2010).

11. For additional information, see Nathalie De Fabrique, Stephen J. Romano, Gregory M. Vecchi, and Vincent B. Van Hasselt, "Understanding Stockholm Syndrome," *FBI Law Enforcement Bulletin,* July 2007, 10–15.

12. Trafficking Victims Protection Act, Pub. L. No. 106–386 (2000), codified at 22 U.S.C. § 7101, et seq.

13. Ibid.

14. U.S. CONST. amend. XIII, § 1: "Neither slavery nor involuntary servitude, except as a punishment for crime whereof the party shall have been duly convicted, shall exist within the United States, or any place subject to their jurisdiction."

15. U.S. Department of Justice, "U.S. Army Soldier Sentenced to Over 17 Years in Prison for Operating a Brothel from Millersville Apartment and to Drug Trafficking," www.justice.gov/usao/md/Public-Affairs/press_releases/press10a.htm (accessed September 30, 2010).

16. www.fbi.gov/hq/cid/civilrights/trafficking_initiatives.htm (accessed September 30, 2010).

17. www.ojp.usdoj.gov/BJA/grant/42HTTF.pdf (accessed September 30, 2010).

18. http://actioncenter.polarisproject.org/the-frontlines/recent-federal-cases/435-leader-of-expansive-multi-state-sex-trafficking-ring-sentenced (accessed July 19, 2010).

19. www.nytimes.com/2004/01/25/magazine/25SEXTRAFFIC.html (accessed July 19, 2010).

20. http://httf.wordpress.com/indicators/ (accessed July 19, 2010).

Critical Thinking

1. Do you believe prostitutes are victims of human sex traffickers?

2. How can sex traffickers compel anyone to become a sex worker against his or her will?

3. What laws have been enacted to deal with sex trafficking?

Create Central

www.mhhe.com/createcentral

Internet References

Polaris Project
www.polarisproject.org/human-trafficking/sex-trafficking-in-the-us
Science Daily
www.sciencedaily.com/releases/2013/09/130925132333.htm

From *FBI Law Enforcement Bulletin* by Amanda Walker-Rodriguez and Rodney Hill, March 2011. Published by Federal Bureau of Investigation. www.fbi.gov.

Article   Prepared by: Joanne Naughton

He Was Abused by a Female Teacher, but He Was Treated Like the Perpetrator

SIMONE SEBASTIAN

Learning Outcomes

After reading this article, you will be able to:

- Consider the effects on young men of sexual abuse by older female authority figures.

- Show what usually happens when such cases get to court.

- Discuss the research regarding male suffering as a result of sexual abuse.

Cameron Clarkson was a 16-year-old football player when he suddenly landed in the middle of a sex crime investigation at his St. Paul, Minn., high school. Lawyers grilled him on the details of his sexual history. School officials, in a statement to the press, cited him for not invoking the school's sexual harassment policy and said he "bragged to fellow students about what had happened." His car was vandalized with red-dyed tampons and smeared with peanut butter, to which he is fatally allergic, by an unknown assailant. The shape of a penis was burned into his front lawn with bleach.

"People kept reminding me that I ruined that poor girl's life," Clarkson says.

The "poor girl" was a teacher at his school. Gail Gagne, a 25-year-old basketball and lacrosse coach, was a full-time substitute teacher at Cretin-Derham Hall High School and a couple of months away from becoming a regular physical education instructor. One day, she offered to give Clarkson a ride home after he left the school gym, leading to what he describes as the first of a series of sexual encounters between them in 2008—in Gagne's car, in their homes, in hotels. He says their relationship ended two months later; another student told school officials about it the next spring.

Gagne was fired and charged with two felony counts of criminal sexual conduct with a student. But in the investigations that followed, Clarkson was treated more like the perpetrator than the victim. Gagne, meanwhile, faced an easier path in some ways. She denied any sexual contact with Clarkson but entered an Alford plea, in which a defendant does not admit guilt but recognizes that prosecutors have enough evidence to convict her. The deal reduced her charges to a fifth-degree gross misdemeanor with a one-year sentence, which was suspended—a far lighter punishment than the possible four-year prison sentence for the felony charges she faced. (Gagne's lawyer still says there was no sexual contact.)

For male victims of sexual abuse, this is how it goes. Growing evidence shows that boys who are sexually preyed upon by older female authority figures suffer psychologically in much the same way that girls do when victimized by older men. But in schools, courts and law offices, male victims are treated openly with a double standard, according to interviews with a dozen experts in law, psychology and social work. Some say boys should get the same protective care that girls do; other people who work with these cases argue that male teens are driven by raging hormones and are only too happy to explore their new sexuality with older women. But all of the experts agree that the discrepancy in the treatment of victims of nonviolent sexual abuse by their high school teachers is real. And it shows: Male victims typically receive lower awards in civil cases, the experts say, and female perpetrators get lighter sentences.

There is a clear hierarchy in courtrooms, lawyers say. Cases involving a male teacher and a female student result in the most severe punishments and the highest damages. Los Angeles-based lawyer David Ring, whose firm Taylor & Ring represents plaintiffs in sexual abuse suits, has worked on hundreds of teacher–student cases and says it's not unusual for those against male teachers to end with judgments of more than $1 million. In one example, a jury awarded $5.6 million to a high school girl in a sexual abuse case involving her 40-year-old teacher. The teacher was convicted of a felony, sentenced to a year in jail and ordered to pay 40 percent of the civil damages to the student, who was 14 at the time of the encounters. (Chino Valley High School was ordered to pay the other 60 percent.)

But jurors and prosecutors don't have nearly the same outrage for abusive female teachers, Ring says: " 'So what? Good for him.' That's how society looks at it." Male students, in his experience, rarely collect damages of more than $200,000. In November, Clarkson settled his case against Cretin-Durham Hall High School for $75,000. The case against Gagne settled for just $1.

Clarkson's attorney, Sarah Odegaard, says her team made a strategic choice: They stood to win a larger award from the school, so they agreed to a token gesture from Gagne in lieu of a trial in which she would have denied the sexual relationship. In cases like this—with "an attractive, young female" defendant—jury bias doesn't work in favor of the victim, Odegaard says. "It's not a bias we want to acknowledge, but we have to," she says. "There have been some successes involving female teachers and coaches, but more often, you see lower verdicts."

Exact comparisons between cases are difficult to make; every case is unique. Sentences and monetary damages are shaped by the number and type of sexual encounters, the age of the victim relative to the state's age of consent, and—rightly or wrongly—the level of suffering the victim displayed during the investigation, among other factors. But while there's no data tracking the nationwide disparity in how male and female sexual abuse victims are treated (one possible reason: male abusers tend to be significantly older than their female victims, which leads to larger penalties, according to several lawyers who work on these cases), everybody seems to agree that the disparity exists.

The problem, rather, is that not everyone sees a problem with it. "I think they *should* be treated different," says Minneapolis-based defense lawyer Joe Friedberg. "Every high school boy had some kind of fantasy about some female teacher. I walk away from these cases and say, 'That would have been my finest hour.' I don't know that I see the damage to the victim in those cases."

Many more studies track female victims than male ones, but the research matches experts' anecdotal observations about the severity of male suffering. In a 2004 study, researchers in Australia reviewed the psychiatric histories of more than 1,600 people who had been sexually abused as children. They found that both male and female victims had higher rates of psychiatric treatment for personality, anxiety and other disorders compared with the general population. Nearly one in four male victims had received treatment, compared with 10 percent of female victims.

In another 2004 study, researcher Myriam Denov, then at the University of Ottawa, conducted in-depth interviews with 14 victims of sexual abuse by females. Both male and female victims reported experiencing damaging long-term effects, including depression, substance abuse, self-injury, dysfunctional relationships with women and even suicide attempts.

"I'm sick of life and how I'm lying / I'm sick of this earth and what I'm trying to do," a 16-year-old boy wrote in a seemingly suicidal poem to Denise Keesee, then a 32-year-old teacher at Sherwood High School in Oregon with whom he had sex, according to news reports. Last April, a judge sentenced Keesee to just one month in jail for sexual abuse of the student. Her lawyer declined to comment.

Girls are four times more likely to be victims of sexual abuse than boys, according to the National Center for Victims of Crime. That imbalance has meant that sexual assault policies are not applied to the 1 in 20 abused boys with the same urgency they are applied to female victims. "You are laughed at and not believed," says Denov, the researcher who conducted the 2004 study.

The victims are disbelieved precisely because they are so rare, and the failure to be heard adds another layer of trauma. "Because of our views of mothering and nurturing," Denov adds, people wonder: "'How is it possible that a woman can commit a sexual offense?' People can't get their head around what that means."

Evidence of arousal is often used against boys, too. Clarkson says, "I was asked [by lawyers] how something that ended in me ejaculating could possibly be abuse," he recalls.

That's a common mistake, says psychiatrist Brian Jacks. Even if a boy cooperates in the sexual encounter—and brags about it to friends—that doesn't mean the experience won't have long-term, negative effects. "They are swaggering around at this point," Jacks says. "You don't realize the consequences until later in life. You realize that you were taken advantage of. . . . I promise you, it's going to mess up your life."

Clarkson said the psychological effects of his relationship with Gagne caught up with him soon after it ended. He started skipping school, spending the day sitting in his bedroom in the dark. He lost interest in the activities most important to him and gave up on his dream of playing football in college. In his first year of college at Howard University, he smoked marijuana heavily, drank copiously and struggled to engage in social activities. Psychiatrist Raymond Patterson diagnosed Clarkson with depression, saying it was "directly related to the sexual abuse he suffered," according to court documents.

"There are people who believe that I cannot possibly be a victim of abuse because of my appearance," says Clarkson. Gagne's lawyer struggled with exactly this point during an interview. "He looks like he is 35. And Gail looks 20," he says.

Clarkson believes that race compounded the discrimination against him. He is black; Gagne is white. Society views black men as sexual predators rather than as victims, he wrote in a summary of his experience. "I was referred to as simply a physical body, with no regard for the development of my mind or soul."

Critical Thinking

1. Why do you think Cameron Clarkson wasn't treated the way a victim of sexual abuse is usually treated?

2. Do you agree with attorney Joe Friedberg's statement about every high school boy?

3. What are some of the reasons male victims are often disbelieved?

Internet References

Administration for Children & Families
Child Abuse & Neglect | Children's Bureau | Administration for Children and Families

Sage Publications
http://jiv.sagepub.com/content/19/10/1137.short

The National Center for Victims of Crime
http://www.victimsofcrime.org/media/reporting-on-child-sexual-abuse/child-sexual-abuse-statistics

SIMONE SEBASTIAN works for *The Washington Post* as deputy editor for PostEverything and is an assistant editor of *Outlook*.

Article   Prepared by: Joanne Naughton

Male Victims of Campus Sexual Assault Speak Out

EMILY KASSIE

Learning Outcomes

After reading this article, you will be able to:

- Relate how likely it is that rape victims will attempt suicide.
- Report what studies show about victims of sexual violence.

Note: The following story contains descriptions of sexual assault that some readers might find upsetting.

It was Andrew's sixth night of freshman year at Brown University when he was assaulted by a male student in his dorm bathroom. When Andrew brought on-campus charges, his assailant was expelled.

Unlike myriad students who report mishandled cases in the burgeoning national campaign against sexual assault, Andrew initially believed his case was handled appropriately.

But after *The Huffington Post* discovered Andrew's assailant had previously been found responsible for assaulting two other students and had not been expelled, Andrew was devastated.

Andrew has decided to share his story in hopes that victims of assault—and specifically male victims—be taken more seriously.

"It's time to include male survivors' voices," he said. "We are up against a system that's not designed to help us."

In the early hours of Sept. 5, 2011, Andrew, who asked that his last name be withheld, was up late excitedly chatting with his hallmates in Keeney Quad, one of two main freshman housing units. Jumping from room to room, Andrew admired the varied displays his classmates had on their walls. In his room, Andrew had put up Art Deco travel posters and a screen print of neighborhoods in his hometown of Washington, D.C.

Around 5 A.M., his classmates returned to their rooms while Andrew headed to the communal bathrooms to brush his teeth. Halfway down the hall, a male student he didn't recognize passed him. Not thinking much of it, Andrew entered the bathroom and began to wash his hands.

A knock on the door surprised him. The bathroom required a dorm key, so anyone who lived in the building should have been able to get inside. Andrew opened the door. It was the same student he had seen in the hall.

Andrew went back to the sink, and the student approached him. "You're hot," Andrew remembers him saying. The student propositioned him but Andrew politely declined.

"Nobody has to know," the student said.

He came up behind Andrew, grabbed his crotch and moved him into the bathroom stall. Frozen, Andrew protested but did not fight back, scared of what would happen if he did.

For 15 minutes the stranger assaulted him.

Andrew has a hard time articulating what he felt during the assault. All he remembers is being unable to speak or act. "I just remember focusing on the stall door, knowing that he was between me and my escape."

When the assault was over, the assailant "just left." Andrew remembers resting his head against the bathroom stall and listening to the buzz of the fluorescent lights as he tried to reconcile what had just happened to him.

"I didn't even know his name," Andrew said. "I didn't know who he was. Nobody saw anything."

Andrew later found out the assailant's name through a mutual friend. During the hearing process he also learned that his assailant was a sophomore who had been visiting a residential adviser in the dorm earlier that night.

The day after the assault, Andrew told his friends what happened, but joked that it was a "5 A.M. hookup in the bathroom." It was easier to deal with the shame if he felt control over the situation. At 8 P.M. Andrew and his classmates were required to attend a mandatory orientation meeting entitled "Understanding Sexual Assault."

Andrew remembers feeling isolated in the auditorium populated by his peers. "It was a sad twist of irony," he said.

At first, Andrew berated himself, wondering if he could have done more to stop it. But after a couple months he started feeling like himself again, excelling in his introductory course on Urban Studies and joining groups like the Queer Alliance, the Brown University Chorus and a coed literary fraternity.

Things took a turn in the spring when Andrew was cast in a campus production of "Don Pasquale" and attended rehearsals nightly on the north side of campus, where his assailant lived—and seeing him "almost every single time" he was there.

On the morning of Feb. 29, 2012, he had a panic attack. "I got in the shower and suddenly started shaking and could only see in front of me and probably couldn't have told you where or who I was."

Andrew started meeting regularly with a counselor, but initially chose not to share the assailant's name, as he was not ready to pursue a campus hearing. But in May, after a couple months of counseling, he decided to file a formal complaint with the university. The hearing was held the following November.

Andrew's assailant participated via phone as, unbeknownst to Andrew, he was on suspension for two other cases of sexual assault.

The two other victims, Brenton (who would only give his first name), and another student who requested to remain anonymous, said they filed a joint complaint in December 2011. They had hearings for their cases in March 2012; the university found the assailant responsible for sexual misconduct in both cases and suspended him until the following December.

"I was happy that he got suspended, but I didn't think it was enough. I knew there were even more people he had gotten to," Brenton said.

After Andrew's hearing in November, the university found the assailant responsible for a third case of sexual misconduct and expelled him. The assailant appealed all three sanctions and was rejected. He declined to comment for this article.

The timeline of all three assaults was as follows:

After this story was published, a fourth student came forward and told *HuffPost* that the same perpetrator had harassed him, stalked him and threatened his life after a sexual encounter. According to documents obtained by *HuffPost,* the encounter occurred in September 2011, and the harassment resulted in a university no-contact order between the two students. This means the university was aware of the perpetrator's history of harassment during the first two sexual misconduct hearings and still only imposed a one-semester suspension on the perpetrator.

Brown has recently been in the news for accusations of mishandled cases of sexual assault, notably that of Lena Sclove, which prompted a federal Title IX investigation.

In Sclove's case, the accused student was found responsible for two counts of sexual misconduct and suspended for two semesters. Similarly, the student who assaulted Brenton and the anonymous victim was merely suspended for just over one semester.

Brown's failure to impose a sufficient sanction was unsurprising to Andrew but upsetting nonetheless. "I wish they had taken it seriously the first one or two times," he said. "The process weighed on me from April to November. … I could've had days of my sophomore year that I didn't have to drag myself out of bed every morning. … To know that [the hearing process] could have been prevented if they had expelled him the first time is incredibly upsetting. My sophomore year could have been totally different."

Brown's president, Christina Paxson, recently sent a letter to the Brown community outlining revisions to Brown's sexual assault policy, including that a student given a sanction that includes separation from the university would be immediately removed from campus residences (though not necessarily barred from campus). The letter also included clearer guidelines on how the university determines a sanction, but it didn't determine specific sanctions for violations of sexual misconduct, leaving Andrew's concern unaddressed.

In a statement emailed to *The Huffington Post,* Brown University said it could not comment on the individual cases.

"The circumstances of each case are taken into account by the conduct board and adjudicated under our current sanctioning guidelines, which are reviewed regularly," the statement said. "We believe our process is the right one for our University and we remain committed to doing all we can to keep our community safe and to being a leader in establishing best practices."

For all the focus on campus sexual assault in recent years, male victims have been frequently absent from the news coverage, except for the most tragic cases, like that of Trey Malone, an Amherst College student who committed suicide after his assault.

One study shows rape victims are 13 times more likely than non-crime victims to have attempted suicide. Jennifer Marsh, vice president of victims services at Rape, Abuse & Incest National Network, the largest anti-sexual-assault organization in the nation, said both men and women who survive sexual assault face similar psychological effects—but there are some differences. "Male survivors who are suicidal tend to use more lethal means," Marsh said.

Studies show that one in five women has been the victim of attempted or completed rape in her lifetime, and that approximately 50 percent of transgender people experience sexual violence at some point in their lifetimes. But statistics vary on the incidence of sexual assault against men. According to a study by the Centers for Disease Control and Prevention, of 5,000 college students at over 130 colleges, one in 25 men answered "yes" to the question "In your lifetime have you been forced to submit to sexual intercourse against your will?" Other organizations, such as 1in6, an advocacy group for male survivors, put the estimate much higher, at one in six males before the age of 18.

Steve LaPore, founder and director of 1in6, believes male sexual assaults are underreported because the issue is still taboo. While women have "really moved the ball forward," resulting in a heightened awareness about sexual assault against women and children, it's an awareness that doesn't include men as victims, he said.

"Culturally we still don't want to see men as vulnerable or hurt," LaPore explained. "We tell little boys and men to pull themselves up by their bootstraps." Because of the stigma, he said, there are fewer resources available for male victims.

LaPore was not surprised by the fact that Andrew's assailant initially received a lighter punishment. "In many cases we find that it's more difficult for men to be believed, or to take their case seriously," he said. "I think we've done a pretty good job of seeing men's roles as bystanders and preventers, but we don't recognize men who are survivors of sexual assault and abuse."

Clayton Bullock, psychiatrist and co-author of *Male Victims of Sexual Assault: Phenomenology, Psychology, Physiology,* found that male victims are also less likely to come forward or be taken seriously because of their physiological response to assault.

"It is possible for men to get aroused and ejaculate when being assaulted," Bullock said. "What's particularly bewildering for the males is that if they ejaculated or were aroused during the assault, it adds a layer of shame or confusion in their culpability of their own victimization."

Men also have difficulty with the language of sexual assault, according to Jim Hopper, instructor of psychology at Harvard Medical School and a founding board member of 1in6.

"There are words like 'victim' and 'survivor' that are hard to identify with, especially for men," Hopper said. "For many men, they don't want to be a 'victim' because it's antithetical to what it means to be a real man."

A friend of Malone's at Amherst, who identified himself as Eric for this article, said he was raped by his freshman-year roommate. After feeling dissatisfied with the school's handling of his case, Eric attempted suicide by overdosing on Benadryl, but it didn't work.

"I remember waking up to [my roommate] kissing the back of my neck, and I feel his erect dick behind me," Eric recalled.

"I turn around and am like, 'What are you doing?' And he says, 'What are you doing in my room?' And I said, 'No, dude, you're in my bed.'"

Eric feels he was targeted because of his sexuality. "I was very open about being gay, so I think that's a big part of it; he assaulted me because he knew I was gay," Eric said. "After that I felt like I couldn't be as out as I was. He thought that was an invitation."

Andrew, who identifies as queer, believes it's more difficult for people to talk about queer victims of assault. "They don't want to think that queer people exist to begin with, so the idea that sexual assault happens in those communities is something people don't want to talk about," he said. "There are some people who also believe [sexual assault] is punishment or retribution for being queer."

The 2010 National Intimate Partner and Sexual Violence Survey from the Centers for Disease Control and Prevention found about 40 percent of gay men, 47 percent of bisexual men and 21 percent of heterosexual men in the U.S. "have experienced sexual violence other than rape at some point in their lives."

Bullock says gay men are often targets of sexual assault because of gay-bashing, or because of conflicted feelings about the assailant's own attraction to other men in which they are "exorcising their internalized homophobia."

And since the LGBTQ community is often perceived as promiscuous, it can be difficult for victims to come forward.

"The sentiment I hear the most and feel the most is that because we're being open about our sexuality, when someone assaults us it's not an assault," Eric said. "Like, 'Oh you were kind of asking for it,' or 'Are you surprised you got assaulted?'"

Eric struggled at Amherst in the immediate aftermath of his assault, eventually dropping out when the administration allowed his assailant to remain on campus. After leaving college, he joined the military and became an engineer. He's feeling optimistic about what's next, but he still feels the impact of what happened to him.

"You know 'Carry That Weight'?" he asked, referring to Columbia University student Emma Sulkowicz's campaign to raise awareness of college sexual assault by carrying a mattress around campus until her rapist is expelled. "How I imagine carrying my weight is physical weight. I actually gained a lot of weight, and part of that was intentional. It's comforting for me being heavier and less looked at as a sex object. In my life I want to be smart, I want to finish college, I want to be good at my job. But I don't want to be attractive."

According to Marsh, Eric's sentiment is typical of both male and female victims.

"The idea that they don't want any type of attention, or anything remotely resembling sexual advances," Marsh said. "I think there's a fear that this could happen again. And if they make themselves so unappealing, they won't get hurt the way they've been hurt before."

Like many other victims, Eric doesn't think the punishment for sexual assault at colleges is sufficient.

"If we treated rape the way we treated plagiarism on college campuses, there would be minimal rape," Eric insisted. "They expel people all the time for plagiarism."

However, punishment for rape is just one part of the solution. LaPore, founder of 1in6, believes resources need to be more easily accessible for men, including the way clinics and programs are named and advertised. "If we could become willing to be inclusive, we would see more men willing to come forward and say we would like some help," he said.

Michael Rose, who was in the same coed fraternity as Andrew at Brown, believes the role of bystanders is also integral. "Making sure every space is a safe space" is important, he said. "If more people can be trained as bystanders, and feel comfortable intervening. That's huge."

Rose was surprised when Andrew told him about the assault. Despite Rose's involvement in Brown's Sexual Assault Peer Education program, Andrew was the first male survivor he had met.

"We were just together in the lounge and we had been talking about consensual sex and life on campus, and he mentioned to me he'd been assaulted his first semester," Rose said. "I was shocked at first. You never want it to happen, but especially not to someone you know."

Rose was one of the first people Andrew told about his assault. He told his parents about it the following summer and came out as a survivor to his friends on Facebook during his junior year, when he participated in an online campaign for sexual assault survivors called Project Unbreakable.

He also participated in "Carry That Weight" in solidarity with Sulkowicz's campaign by carrying a stall door, since his assault occurred in a bathroom.

Both experiences helped Andrew in his healing process. Upon sharing his story, he received encouragement from his friends and family. "My parents were pretty supportive," he said. "They reiterated the points that I was still valuable and it had no impact on how they thought of me."

Andrew is now a senior at Brown. He's finishing his concentration in Urban Studies, writing a thesis on suburban poverty and completing an applied music program. A sign on his dorm door reads, "Hi! Come talk to me about sexual assault, consent, relationships or really anything."

Walking along the campus green, Andrew seems energized. He talks about the campus buildings and how they provide a great microcosm for exploring urban planning. Specifically, he likes to think about transportation and how it connects people.

As Andrew passes the auditorium where he had his freshman orientation on sexual assault, he says he wants to continue advocating for sexual assault victims. He believes telling his story could make a difference, especially for men. "There are a lot of male survivors who haven't found someone they can relate to," he said. "I want to break the silence, and I want other men to know that they're not alone."

This article has been updated with new information regarding an incident in 2011 involving a fourth student who had made a complaint to the university about the same perpetrator. The complaint resulted in the university issuing a no-contact order between the two students. Brown declined to comment on the incident.

Critical Thinking

1. Why do you think schools like Brown don't simply expel students who have harmed other students?

2. Does it surprise you to read about male victims of sexual violence on college campuses?

3. Do you think it would be better to report all these incidents directly to the police?

Internet References

LA Times

http://www.latimes.com/local/lanow/la-me-ln-california-teacher-sex-students-20150122-story.html

NJ.com

http://www.nj.com/news/index.ssf/2013/04/a_look_at_teacher-student_sex.html#incart_m-rpt-1

S.E.S.A.M.E.

http://www.sesamenet.org/survivors/male-survivors/12-survivors/male-survivors/1-male-victims

TDCAA

http://www.tdcaa.com/node/1277

Unit 3

UNIT

Prepared by: Joanne Naughton

The Police

Police officers are the guardians of our rights under the Constitution and the law, and as such they have an awesome task which, in turn, requires furnishing police with immense powers. They are asked to maintain order, prevent crime, protect citizens, arrest wrongdoers, aid the sick, control juveniles, control traffic, and provide emergency services on a moment's notice. Sometimes in the service of these duties, police officers may sustain injuries or lose their lives.

In recent years, the job of the police officer has become even more complex and dangerous. Illegal drug use and trafficking are still major problems; racial tensions are explosive; and terrorism is now an alarming reality. As our population grows more numerous and diverse, the role of the police in America becomes ever more challenging, requiring skills that can only be obtained by greater training and professionalism. It is also vital that the public be aware of how their various police departments are carrying out their duties, providing citizen oversight.

Article   Prepared by: Joanne Naughton

The Changing Environment for Policing, 1985–2008

DAVID H. BAYLEY AND CHRISTINE NIXON

Learning Outcomes

After reading this article, you will be able to:

- State the differences between the policing environments in 1985 and 2008.

- Relate some of the challenges facing police executives today.

- Show how the growth of private security affects policing.

Introduction

In 1967, the President's Commission on Law Enforcement and the Administration of Justice published *The Challenge of Crime in a Free Society*. This publication is generally regarded as inaugurating the scientific study of the police in America in particular but also in other countries. Almost 20 years later, the John F. Kennedy School of Government, Harvard University, convened an Executive Session on the police (1985–1991) to examine the state of policing and to make recommendations for its improvement. Its approximately 30 participants were police executives and academic experts. Now, 20 years further on, the Kennedy School has again organized an Executive Session. Its purpose, like the first, is to combine professional with scholarly appraisals of the police and their contribution to public safety.

So the question naturally arises, what are the differences in the environment for policing between these two time periods? Are the problems as well as the institution of the police similar or different from one period to the next? Our thesis is that policing in the mid-1980s was perceived to be in crisis and there was a strong sense that fundamental changes were needed in the way it was delivered. In contrast, police are considered to be performing well 20 years later by both practitioners and outside observers. Crime has been falling for almost 18 years and any new challenges, including terrorism, appear to be manageable without the invention of new strategies for the delivery of police services. Past experience contains the lessons needed for the future. In our view, this assessment may be mistaken, not because existing policies are defective in controlling crime but because the institutions that provide public safety are changing in profound ways that are not being recognized.

The Policing Environment in 1985

Policing in the United States was under siege in the 1980s for two reasons: (1) crime had been rising from the early 1960s, and (2) research had shown that the traditional strategies of the police were ineffective at coping with it. In 1960, the serious crime rate was 1,887 per 100,000 people. In 1985 it was 5,224, almost a threefold increase. This trend peaked in 1990 at 5,803. Violent crime (i.e., murder, rape, robbery and aggravated assault) rose from 161 per 100,000 people in 1960 to 558 in 1985, on the way to quadrupling by 1991 (Maguire and Pastore, 2007). Crime was, understandably, a big issue, feeding what could properly be called a moral panic.

Prompted by the President's Commission on Law Enforcement and the Administration of Justice in 1967, researchers in universities and private think-tanks began to study the effectiveness of standard police strategies. In the ensuing two decades, studies were published showing that crime rates were not affected by:

- Hiring more police (Loftin and McDowell, 1982; Krahn and Kennedy, 1985; Koenig, 1991; Laurie, 1970; Gurr, 1979; Emsley, 1983; Silberman, 1978; Reiner, 1985; Lane, 1980).

- Random motorized patrolling (Kelling et al., 1974; Kelling, 1985; Morris and Heal, 1981).

- Foot patrols (Police Foundation, 1981).
- Rapid response to calls for service (Tien, Simon and Larson, 1978; Bieck and Kessler, 1977; Spelman and Brown, 1981).
- Routine criminal investigation (Laurie, 1970; Burrows, 1986; Greenwood, Petersilia and Chaiken, 1977; Eck, 1982; Royal Commission on Criminal Procedure, 1981).

These conclusions, despite challenges to some of them on methodological grounds, were considered authoritative. They were so well accepted, in fact, that Bayley could say in 1994 that "one of the best kept secrets of modern life" was that the police do not prevent crime. "Experts know it, the police know it, and the public does not know it" (Bayley, 1994:3).

No wonder, then, that the first Executive Session concluded that fundamental changes were needed in police strategies. The Session took the lead in developing and legitimating a new model for the delivery of police services—community policing. The key recommendation was that police needed to be reconnected to the public in order both to enhance their crime-control effectiveness and to increase public respect. The strategy for doing this was community policing, including problem-oriented policing (Trojanowicz and Bucqueroux, 1990; Goldstein, 1990). Of the 17 studies published by the first Executive Session as *Perspectives on Policing,* eight featured "community" or "community policing" in the title, and several others discussed the importance of community. George Kelling and Mark Moore, members of the session, argued that the evolution of American policing could be described as movement from a politicized system to professionalism, then to constitutionalism, and ultimately to community policing (Kelling and Moore, 1988).

The first Executive Session also encouraged a new management style for policing, namely, one based on the analysis of crime and disorder problems and the evaluation of remediation programs. This process of description and analysis was to be carried out jointly by police and outside experts, such as academic scholars and management consultants.

The Policing Environment in 2008

When the second Executive Session met in January 2008, crime in the United States had declined dramatically since 1990. The serious crime rate (Part I crimes) had fallen to 3,808 per 100,000 people by 2006, a decline of 34 percent (Maguire and Pastore, 2007).[1] Even though the violent crime rate was still three times higher in 2006 than in 1960 (474 versus 161 per 100,000 people), it had declined by 37.5 percent since its peak in 1991, a huge change for the better. The police, in particular, feel that the decline vindicates their crime-control efforts, notably the strategy attributed to Bill Bratton of New York City, of the strict enforcement of laws against disorder and the management technique known as *zero tolerance,* managed through COMPSTAT (Bratton and Knobler, 1998; Eck and Maguire, 2000).

The decline has been so dramatic that it offset the continued questioning by analysts of the importance of police action in controlling crime (Eck and Maguire, 2000). Furthermore, there are now positive findings about the efficacy of certain police strategies. The most authoritative summary of this research comes from a panel of the National Research Council (Skogan and Frydl, 2004).

Reviewing all research conducted since the President's Commission (1967) and available in English, the panel reaffirmed the findings of the 1970s and 1980s that the standard practices of policing—employing more sworn officers, random motorized patrolling, rapid response and criminal investigation—failed to reduce crime when applied generally throughout a jurisdiction. It should be noted that most of the research on these topics, except for analysis of the effect of the number of police employees on crime, dated from the earlier period. At the same time, the panel found that police could reduce crime when they focused operations on particular problems or places and when they supplemented law enforcement with other regulatory and abatement activities.

The strongest evidence for effectiveness was some form of problem solving, especially when focused on "hot spots," that is, locations accounting for a high volume of repeat calls for police service. Nonenforcement options included changing the physical design of buildings and public spaces, enforcing fire and safety codes, providing social services to dysfunctional families, reducing truancy and providing after-school programs for latch-key children.

By 2008, police executives could feel much happier about their efforts to control crime than they had 20 years before. Scholars, too, agreed that strategies used since the 1980s were efficacious, by and large.

This is not to say that police leaders currently feel that they can rest on their laurels nor that the environment for policing is entirely benign. Police executives understand that they are confronting several challenges, some new and some old:

- **Declining budgets and the rising cost of sworn police officers.** The cost of policing has quadrupled between 1985 and 2005, according to the Bureau of Justice Statistics (Gascón and Foglesong, 2009). The causes are rising labor costs for both sworn officers and civilian personnel, increased demand for police services and the growing complexity of police work. As a result, police budgets are increasingly at risk, with some cities reducing the number of police officers per capita.

- **Terrorism.** The primary impact of the Sept. 11 terrorist attack on state and local policing in the United States has been to improve their capacity for risk assessment of local vulnerabilities and first-responding in the event of terrorist incidents (Bayley and Weisburd, 2009). Although threat assessment and first-responding are understood to be core responsibilities of local police, their role with respect to counterterrorism intelligence gathering and analysis is more problematic. At the moment, most intelligence about terrorism comes from federal sources. Some observers take the view that local law enforcement, especially in the United States with its radically decentralized police system, does not have the personnel or skills to collect operational intelligence in a cost-effective way. Others argue, however, that local general-duties police who work among the population are essential for detecting precursor terrorist activities and building cooperative relations with the communities in which terrorists live (Bayley and Weisburd, 2009). Many police executives are critical of the federal government, therefore, for downgrading its law enforcement attention from nonterrorist crime and for reducing its support for local community-responsive and crime-prevention activities.

- **New immigrants, both legal and illegal.** Until recently, most American police departments took the view that enforcing immigration was a federal rather than a local responsibility. They took this view, in part, because they wanted illegal immigrants to feel free to approach police when they were victims of crime, particularly when they were exploited by employers. Police executives felt that even people who were in the country illegally deserved protection under the law. Recently, however, driven by growing anti-illegal immigration feelings in their jurisdictions, some police departments have begun to enforce immigration regulations. As anticipated, this has alienated these communities at the very moment when the importance of connecting with immigrants—legal as well as illegal—has become imperative as a response to terrorism. Not only may foreign terrorists take cover in immigrant communities but these communities, especially if they are disadvantaged and marginalized, may produce their own home-grown perpetrators. Great Britain and France have both experienced this phenomenon. Thus, the threat of terrorism raises difficult questions about the scope, intensity and methods of law enforcement in immigrant communities.

- **Racial discrimination.** Charges of unequal treatment on the basis of race have been a continual problem for police since the rise of civil rights consciousness in the 1960s. Concerns raised about the substantial amount of discretion possessed by frontline police was one of the first issues taken up by police researchers more than 40 years ago. Various aspects of policing have been implicated—arrests, use of force, shootings, street stops, search and seizure, offense charging and equality of coverage (Fridell et al., 2001; Skolnick and Fyfe, 1993; Walker, 2003). Not only is racial discrimination an enduring issue for police executives to manage but its potential for destroying the reputation of police agencies and the careers of officers is hard to exaggerate. It is the allegation that every police chief dreads.

- **Intensified accountability.** Oversight of police performance, with regard to effectiveness in controlling both crime and personal behavior, has grown steadily in the past few years. The monitoring of institutional performance has been part of a governmentwide movement to specify measurable performance indicators. External oversight of individual behavior has involved complaints commissions, citizen review panels and ombudsmen. Many would argue that the quality of policing with respect to crime control and personal behavior has improved over the last half of the 20th century as a result of these developments. The public, however, seems more skeptical, especially with respect to the behavior of individual officers. At least that would be a fair reading of the fact that in the United States as well as other English-speaking countries, the demand for greater oversight of police behavior continues to grow, fed by the media's insatiable appetite for stories about police misdeeds.

There are two aspects to what is being asked for: (1) holding the police to account for performing the services for which they were created—crime prevention and criminal investigation and (2) disciplining officers who behave improperly in the course of their duties. Today, more than 100 of America's largest cities have some sort of civilian oversight of police behavior compared with only a handful in the early 1990s (Walker, 2003). Independent civilian review of complaints against the police has been established in the last three decades in Great Britain, New Zealand, Australia and Canada. But this is only the most visible tip of a larger iceberg. Oversight has also intensified in the form of tighter financial auditing, performance indicators mandated by governmental and quasi-governmental bodies, enactment of more stringent legal standards and federal consent decrees. This is in addition to what seems to police to be an unappeasable media appetite for revelations about police, and even ex-police, misbehavior.

- **Police unions.** While acknowledging the reasons that led to the growth of police unions, police executives complain about its impact on management. In particular, they criticize the reflexive defense of work rules that inhibit strategic innovation and organizational change, the elaborate procedures required to discipline poorly performing officers, and the inculcation of an occupational culture preoccupied with tangible rewards.

Although all of these current challenges certainly complicate their work, police executives do not view them as a crisis for policing as was the case in the mid-1980s. These challenges are complex and difficult but manageable within the competence of experienced executives. With the arguable exception of terrorism, they do not require a shift in the strategies of policing.

Embedded in this sense of achievement among police professionals is frustration with the gap between objective measures of public safety and public perceptions. Although crime may have declined, the public's fear has not. Police commonly attribute this discrepancy to the exaggeration of crime by the media and the failure to give credit where credit is due.

The Looming Watershed

We believe that policing may be approaching, if not well into, a period of change that will significantly affect what police do and how they do it. It may be as significant as the period after 1829 when Sir Robert Peel created the London Metropolitan Police. The choice of 1829 as the reference point is not rhetorical. This year marked the beginning of the gradual monopolization of the police function by government. Starting in 1829, governments in Anglo-Saxon countries, much earlier in Europe, assumed responsibility for policing—for hiring, paying, training and supervising. What is happening now is the reverse of that: nation-states are losing their monopoly on policing.

The pressures eroding the monopoly of governments within national boundaries to create and manage policing come from three directions:

- The internationalization of policing.
- The devolution of policing to communities.
- The growth of private policing.

In short, policing is being pushed up, down and sideways from its traditional mooring in government.

The Internationalization of Policing

Policing has shifted away from national governments because of the development of a genuinely international police capacity and increased international collaboration in law enforcement. The United Nations now has more than 11,000 police recruited from about 118 countries and deployed in 13 missions. The United States currently contributes 268 police to UNPOL (formerly CIVPOL). Although UNPOL's primary mission is "to build institutional police capacity in post-conflict environments" (Kroeker, 2007), its officers have been armed in Kosovo, Timor-Leste and Haiti and enforce laws alongside the local police. It is worth mentioning that this is part of a broader development of international institutions of justice, including the development of a portable international criminal code, courts and tribunals authorized to try individuals, and prisons for persons both convicted and under trial.

The United States now collaborates widely with law enforcement agencies abroad. As of February 2010, the FBI has offices in 70 cities overseas and the DEA has offices in almost 90 (see FBI and DEA home pages). The United States trains more than 10,000 police a year at its four International Law Enforcement Training Academies (located in Budapest, Bangkok, Gaborone and San Salvador) and brings many more trainees to the United States. The United States also participates in a host of international task forces and ad hoc law enforcement operations that focus on drugs, terrorism, trafficking in people and, more recently, cyber-crime, including pornography. The United States has also encouraged—some would say "pressured"—countries to bring their laws into conformity with American practice, for example, with respect to wiretapping, the use of informants, asset forfeiture, and the Racketeer Influenced and Corrupt Organizations Act (Nadelman, 1997; Snow, 1997). American influence, direct and indirect, has been so powerful that Chris Stone says there has been an "Americanization of global law enforcement" (Stone, 2003). The United States, furthermore, has begun to create a reserve force of police and other criminal justice experts that can be deployed at short notice to countries emerging from conflict.

If policing is a fundamental attribute of government, along with external defense, then the world has begun to create a world government of sorts. Although seeds of this movement preceded the first Executive Session, a major impetus was the fall of the Berlin Wall in 1989 and the subsequent implosion of the Soviet Union (Bayley, 2006).

The Devolution of Policing to Communities

The attitude of police generally in the Western world, but especially in its English-speaking democracies, toward collaborating with members of the public who act voluntarily to improve public security has undergone a major change since the 1980s. No longer viewed as nuisances or dangerous vigilantes, these people are now seen as "co-producers" of public safety. This transformation of view is attributable in large part to the acceptance of community policing, which the first Executive Session was instrumental in promoting. Police in democratic countries now actively encourage citizen participation by sharing information, training volunteers, consulting the public about priorities, mobilizing collaborative crime-prevention programs, enlisting the public as informants in problem solving, and soliciting help from city planners, architects and the designers of products to minimize criminal opportunities. Neighborhood Watch is probably the best known police-citizen partnership. Others include Business Improvement Districts, mobile CB-radio patrols, and private-sector programs for providing equipment and professional skills to police departments.

It has become axiomatic in policing that the public should be encouraged to take responsibility for enhancing public safety. As police themselves now recognize, they cannot do the job alone. Public participation is seen by police and academics alike as a critical contributor to police effectiveness and thus to public safety.

The Growth of Private Policing

Policing is being pushed sideways by the growth in the private security industry. Estimates of its strength are not exact because "private security" covers a wide range of activities—e.g., guarding, transporting valuables, investigating, installing protective technology and responding to alarms—and is supplied by companies commercially to others as well as by businesses to themselves. The U.S. Department of Labor estimated that there were slightly more than 1 million private security guards in 2005 (U.S. Bureau of Labor Statistics, 2005). That would be 49 percent more than the number of full-time sworn police officers in the same year (673,146). A report issued by the International Association of Chiefs of Police (IACP) and the Community Oriented Police Services (COPS) Office estimated, however, that in 2004, the number was about 2 million (IACP, 2005). If that were true, there would be almost three times as many private security personnel as full-time police officers. The discrepancy between figures of the Department of Labor and those of IACP-COPS may have arisen because the larger estimate includes in-house security provided by private organizations, whereas the Department of Labor figures only include the personnel of companies providing security services commercially. The larger figure is the one most often cited in commentaries on private policing (Cunningham and Taylor, 1985; Singer, 2003).

The growth of private security appears to be a phenomenon of the last quarter of the 20th century (Nalla and Newman, 1991). It was first documented in *The Hallcrest Report: Private Security and Police in America* (Cunningham and Taylor, 1985), which estimated the number at 1.5 million. This was more than twice the number of public police at that time. Although the use of private security was certainly visible to police officials in the 1980s, the number of *commercial* private security personnel has grown by as much as two-thirds. Their

number rose sharply immediately after the Sept. 11 attack, fell in 2003 (although not to pre-Sept. 11 levels) and has continued to increase (U.S. Bureau of Labor Statistics, 2007). It is reasonable to assume that the number of *in-house* private security personnel has also increased, though perhaps not as much.

Worldwide, there are now more private police than government-run police: 348 versus 318 per 100,000, according to a survey by Jan Van Dijk (2008). The highest rates are in the United States, Canada and central Europe. Britain and Australia also have slightly more private security personnel than public police (Australian Bureau of Statistics, 2006; European Union, 2004). In the European Union, only Britain and Ireland have more private than public police (European Union, 2004). Statistics are not available for Latin America, Africa, and South and Southeast Asia, but private security is certainly very visible there.

The point to underscore is that worldwide, and dramatically in the United States, there has been a steady growth in the number of private "police." If visible guardians are a deterrent to crime, as the routine-activities theory of crime asserts and as police themselves strongly believe, then one reason for the decline in crime in the United States since the early 1990s might be the growth in private security. As far as we are aware, analyses of the crime drop in the United States have not tested for this possibility.

The effect of these three changes in the environment for policing is to diversify the providers of public safety. Governments, especially country-based governments, no longer direct or provide public safety exclusively. The domestic security function has spread to new levels of government but, more important, to nonstate actors, volunteers and commercial providers. The police role is now shared. This is not simply saying that there are now both public and private police. Public and private policing have blended and are often hard to distinguish. Governments hire private police to supplement their own police; private entrepreneurs hire public police. We are in an era of what Les Johnston refers to as hybrid policing (Johnston, 1992).

Until now, assessments of the police have focused on two questions: How can they be made more effective, and how can the behavior of individual officers be improved? Now, we suggest, a third question has arisen: Who is responsible for policing?

Changes within Public Policing

Not only are changes occurring in the environment that may affect the structure of policing but police themselves are in the process of changing the way they work. The factors driving this are (1) the threat of terrorism, (2) intelligence-led policing and (3) DNA analysis. Each of these developments transfers initiative in directing operations to specialists who collect and analyze information and away from both general-duties police and the public. Ironically, these changes could undo the signature contribution of the 1980s—community policing.

The Threat of Terrorism

Although many anti-terrorism experts understand the importance of working with communities, especially immigrant ones, counterterrorism centralizes decision making, shifting it upward in police organizations and making it less transparent. In the aftermath of Sept. 11, a new emphasis has been placed on the development of covert intelligence gathering, penetration and disruption. In the United States, the development of covert counterterrorism capacity has been unequally distributed, being more pronounced in larger police forces. Where it occurs, important questions arise about legal accountability as well as operational payoff. These issues are familiar to police, having arisen before in efforts to control illegal narcotics and organized crime.

Intelligence-Led Policing

Intelligence-led policing[2] utilizes crime mapping, data mining and the widespread use of closed-circuit television monitoring, which all rely on analysis based on information collected from impersonal sources. It thereby empowers senior commanders to develop their own agendas for law enforcement rather than consulting with affected communities.

DNA Analysis

DNA analysis allows crimes to be solved without witnesses or confessions. Research in the 1970s showed that the identification of suspects by victims and witnesses was essential to the solving of most crimes (Greenwood, Petersilia and Chaiken, 1977). Detectives, contrary to their fictional portrayals, work from the identification of suspects by the public back to the collection of evidence to prove guilt. DNA changes that, emphasizing forensic evidence over human testimony, promising a technological solution to criminal identification.

The effect of these developments—the threat of terrorism, intelligence-led policing and DNA analysis—impels the police to rely more on their own intellectual and physical resources and on centralized decision making for agendas and strategies. It lessens the importance of consulting with and mobilizing the disaggregate resources of communities. It also favors enforcement as the tool of choice over preventive strategies of regulation and abatement. These changes in orientation may be necessary and may raise police effectiveness, but they also represent a return to the sort of insular professionalism that characterized policing before the 1980s.

The Challenges of Change

The changes described both inside and outside the established police structures and functions create issues that will have to be confronted. With the expansion of private policing, public safety may become more inequitably distributed on the basis of economic class. The affluent sectors of society, especially its commercial interests, may be more protected, and the poor sectors less protected (Bayley and Shearing, 2001). This trend could be exacerbated if the tax-paying public at the same time withdraws its support from the public police in favor of private security. There are indications that this has already occurred in public education, where people with the means to pay for private schools are increasingly reluctant to support public education. If this should occur in policing, a dualistic system could evolve—responsive private policing for the affluent, and increasingly underfunded public policing for the poor (Bayley and Shearing, 2001). The political consequences of this could be calamitous.

Furthermore, who is to hold private policing to legal and moral account? Public police in the United States and other democracies have been made accountable in many ways. Public police executives themselves often argue that they are too accountable, meaning they are scrutinized too closely, too mechanically and at a substantial cost in reporting. Private policing, however, is imperfectly regulated and it is unclear whether existing law provides sufficient leverage (Joh, 2004; Prenzler and Sarre, 2006).

So, an ironic question arises: Is there a continuing role for government in ensuring an equitable and lawful distribution of security at the very time that government is losing its monopoly control? Should it accomplish by regulation what it no longer can by ownership? If so, how should this be done? In particular, what agency of government would be responsible for it?

The internationalization of policing also raises issues of control and legitimacy. Simply put, whose interests will be served by policing under international auspices? Will it be collective interests articulated by constituent states and powerful organized interests, or by the needs of disaggregate populations represented through participative institutions? Democratic nation-states emphasize the needs of individuals in directing police. It is not at all clear that international institutions will do the same, although they have taken impressive steps on paper to articulate comprehensive standards of police conduct (U.N. High Commissioner for Human Rights, 1996).

Finally, we submit that policing may be facing a clash of cultures as the public increasingly demands participation in the direction and operation of policing while at the same time police agencies become more self-directing and self-sufficient in their use of intelligence resources. This issue is not new. It is the same issue that policing faced in the 1980s and that was tackled in the first Executive Session. How important is public legitimacy for police effectiveness and public safety? How can the support of the public be maintained while police take advantage of powerful new technologies that may decrease interaction with them?

Conclusion

In the United States and other developed democracies, changes are occurring that may undermine the monopoly of state-based policing as well as its community-based paradigm. In pointing out these changes between 1985 and 2008, we are not making value judgments about them. These changes may have made the police more effective at providing public safety without infringing human rights in unacceptable ways. We call attention to these changes because their potential effects are enormous and largely unappreciated. They constitute an invisible agenda as consequential as the problems discussed in the 1980s.

Twenty years ago, policing was in the throes of what is now regarded as a revolution in its operating approach. It shifted from a philosophy of "give us the resources and we can do the job" to realizing the importance of enlisting the public in the coproduction of public safety. Policing today faces much less obvious challenges. Current strategies and technologies seem to be sufficient to deal with foreseeable threats to public safety, with the possible exception of terrorism. If this is so, then policing will develop in an evolutionary way, fine-tuning operational techniques according to experience, particularly the findings of evidence-based evaluations. If, however, changes in the environment are reshaping the structure and hence the governance of policing, and adaptations within the police are weakening the connection between police and public, then we may be entering a period of evolutionary discontinuity that could be greater than that of the 1980s, perhaps even of 1829. Both the role of police in relation to other security providers and the soul of the police in terms of how it goes about its work may be in play today in more profound ways than are being recognized.

References

Australian Bureau of Statistics. "2006 Census of Population and Housing, Australia, Occupation by Sex (Based on Place of Employment)." Accessed February 11, 2010, at www .censusdata.abs.gov.au.

Bayley, David H. *Police for the Future*. New York: Oxford University Press, 1994.

Bayley, David H. *Changing the Guard: Developing Democratic Police Abroad*. New York: Oxford University Press, 2006.

Bayley, David H. and Clifford Shearing. *The New Structure of Policing: Description, Conceptualization, and Research Agenda*. Final report. Washington, D.C.: U.S. Department of Justice, National Institute of Justice, July 2001. NCJ 187083.

Bayley, David H. and David Weisburd. "Cops and Spooks: The Role of the Police in Counterterrorism." In *To Protect and Serve: Policing in an Age of Terrorism*, ed. David Weisburd, Thomas E. Feucht, Idit Hakimi, Lois Felson Mock and Simon Perry. New York: Springer, 2009:81–100.

Bieck, William and David A. Kessler. *Response Time Analysis.*

Kansas City, Mo.: Board of Police Commissioners, 1977.

Bratton, William and Peter Knobler. *Turnaround: How America's Top Cop Reversed the Crime Epidemic*. New York: Random House, 1998.

Burrows, John. *Investigating Burglary: The Measurement of Police Performance*. Research Study 88. London: Home Office, 1986.

Cunningham, William C. and Todd H. Taylor. *The Hallcrest Report: Private Security and Police in America*. Portland, Ore.: Chancellor Press, 1985.

Eck, John E. *Solving Crimes: The Investigation of Burglary and Robbery*. Washington, D.C.: Police Executive Research Forum, 1982.

Eck, John E. and Edward Maguire. "Have Changes in Policing Reduced Violent Crime? An Assessment of the Evidence." In *The Crime Drop in America*, ed. Alfred Blumstein and Joel Wallman. New York: Cambridge University Press, 2000:207–265.

Emsley, Clive. *Policing and Its Context, 1750–1870*. London: Macmillan, 1983.

European Union. "Panoramic Overview of Private Security Industry in the 25 Member States of the European Union." Presentation at Fourth European Conference on Private Security Services, Brussels, Belgium. Confederation of European Security Services and UNI-Europa, 2004. Accessed February 11, 2010, at www .coess.org/pdf/panormal.pdf.

Fridell, Lori, Robert Lunney, Drew Diamond and Bruce Kubu. *Racially Biased Policing: A Principled Response*. Washington, D.C.: Police Executive Research Forum, 2001.

Gascón, George and Todd Foglesong. "How to Make Policing More Affordable: A Case Study of the Rising Costs of Policing in the United States." Draft paper submitted to the Second Harvard Executive Session on Policing and Public Safety, Cambridge, Mass., 2009.

Goldstein, Herman. *Problem Oriented Policing*. Philadelphia, Penn.: Temple University Press, 1990.

Greenwood, Peter W., Joan Petersilia and Jan Chaiken. *The Criminal Investigation Process*. Lexington, Mass.: D.C. Heath, 1977.

Gurr, Ted R. "On the History of Violent Crime in Europe and America." In *Violence in America: Historical and Comparative Perspectives,* ed. H.D. Graham and Ted R. Gurr. Beverly Hills, Calif.: Sage Publications, 1979:353–374.

International Association of Chiefs of Police. *Post 9-11 Policing: The Crime Control–Homeland Security Paradigm—Taking Command of New Realities*. Alexandria, Va.: IACP, 2005.

Joh, Elizabeth E. "The Paradox of Private Policing." *Journal of Criminal Law and Criminology* 95(1):(2004)49–131.

Johnston, Les. *The Rebirth of Private Policing*. London: Routledge, 1992.

Kelling, George L. "Order Maintenance, the Quality of Urban Life, and Police: A Different Line of Argument." *In Police Leadership in America,* ed. William A. Geller. New York: Praeger Publishers, 1985:309–321.

Kelling, George L. and Mark H. Moore. *The Evolving Strategy of Policing*. Harvard University, Kennedy School of Government,

Perspectives on Policing Series, No. 4. Washington, D.C.: National Institute of Justice, November 1988. NCJ 114213.

Kelling, George L., Antony M. Pate, Duane Dieckman and Charles Brown. *The Kansas City Preventive Patrol Experiment: Summary Report.* Washington, D.C.: Police Foundation, 1974.

Koenig, Daniel J. *Do Police Cause Crime? Police Activity, Police Strength and Crime Rates.* Ottawa, Ontario: Canadian Police College, 1991.

Krahn, Harvey and Leslie Kennedy. "Producing Personal Safety: The Effects of Crime Rates, Police Force Size, and Fear of Crime." *Criminology* 23 (1985): 697–710.

Kroeker, Mark. Informal presentation to biannual meeting of the International Police Advisory Commission, Abuja, Nigeria, January 2007.

Lane, Roger. "Urban Police and Crime in Nineteenth-Century America." In *Crime and justice,* ed. N. Morris and Michael Tonry. Chicago: University of Chicago Press, 1980.

Laurie, Peter. *Scotland Yard.* New York: Holt, Rinehart & Winston, 1970.

Loftin, Colin and David McDowell. "The Police, Crime, and Economic Theory: An Assessment." *American Sociological Review* 47 (1982): 393–401.

Maguire, Kathleen and Ann L. Pastore, eds. *Sourcebook of Criminal Justice Statistics.* Years 2000–2007. Washington, D.C.: U.S. Department of Justice, Bureau of Justice Statistics. Accessed February 11, 2010, at www.albany.edu/sourcebook/about.html.

Morris, Pauline and Kevin Heal. *Crime Control and the Police: A Review of Research.* Research Study 67. London: Home Office, 1981.

Nadelman, Ethan A. "The Americanization of Global Law Enforcement: The Diffusion of American Tactics and Personnel." In *Crime and Law Enforcement in the Global Village*, ed. William F. McDonald. Cincinnati, Ohio: Anderson Publishing, 1997:123–138.

Nalla, Mahesh and Graeme Newman. "Public versus Private Control: A Reassessment." *Journal of Criminal Justice* 19 (1991): 537–549.

Police Foundation. *The Newark Foot Patrol Experiment.* Washington, D.C.: Police Foundation, 1981.

Prenzler, Tim and Rick Sarre. "Private and Public Security Agencies: Australia." In *Plural Policing: A Comparative Perspective,* ed. T. Jones and T. Newburn. London: Routledge, 2006:169–189.

President's Commission on Law Enforcement and the Administration of Justice. *The Challenge of Crime in a Free Society.* Washington, D.C.: U.S. Government Printing Office, 1967.

Reiner, Robert. *The Politics of the Police.* New York: St. Martin's Press, 1985.

Royal Commission on Criminal Procedure. Research Study 17. London: HMSO, 1981.

Shearing, Clifford D. "The Relation Between Public and Private Policing." In *Modern Policing*, ed. N. Morris and Michael Tonry. Chicago: University of Chicago Press, 1992.

Silberman, Charles. *Criminal Violence, Criminal Justice.* New York: Random House, 1978.

Singer, Peter W. *Corporate Warriors: The Rise of the Privatized Military Industry.* Cornell Studies in Security Affairs. Ithaca, N.Y.: Cornell University Press, 2003.

Skogan, Wesley and Kathleen Frydl. *Fairness and Effectiveness in Policing: The Evidence.* Washington, D.C.: National Academies Press, 2004.

Skolnick, Jerome H. and James Fyfe. *Beyond the Law.* New York: Free Press, 1993.

Snow, Thomas. "Competing National and Ethical Interests in the Fight Against Transnational Crime: A U.S. Practitioners Perspective." In *Crime and Law Enforcement in the Global Village,* ed. William F. McDonald. Cincinnati: Anderson Publishing, 1997:169–186.

Spelman, William and Dale K. Brown. *"Calling the Police": Citizen Reporting of Serious Crime.* Washington, D.C.: Police Executive Research Forum, 1981.

Stone, Christopher. "Strengthening Accountability in the New Global Police Culture." Presentation at conference on Crime and the Threat to Democratic Governance, Woodrow Wilson International Center for Scholars, Washington, D.C., 2003.

Tien, James M., James W. Simon and Richard C. Larson. *An Alternative Approach to Police Patrol: The Wilmington Split-Force Experiment.* Washington, D.C.: U.S. Government Printing Office, 1978.

Trojanowicz, Robert C. and Bonnie Bucqueroux. *Community Policing: A Contemporary Perspective.* Cincinnati: Anderson Publishing, 1990.

United Nations High Commissioner for Human Rights. *International Human Rights Standards for Law Enforcement: A Pocket Book on Human Rights for Police.* Geneva, Switzerland: UNHCHR, 1996.

U.S. Bureau of Labor Statistics, U.S. Department of Labor. "May 2005 Occupational Employment and Wage Estimates." Accessed February 11, 2010, at www.bls.gOv/oes/oes_dl/htm#2005_m.

U.S. Bureau of Labor Statistics, U.S. Department of Labor. "Security Guard Employment Before and After 2001." Summary 07–08 (August 2007). Accessed March 22, 2010, at www.bls.gov/opub/ils/pdf/opbils61.pdf.

Van Dijk, Jan. *The World of Crime.* Los Angeles: Sage Publications, 2008.

Walker, Samuel. "The New Paradigm of Police Accountability: The U.S. Justice Department 'Pattern or Practice' Suits in Context." *St. Louis University Public Law Review* 22(1) (2003):3–52.

Notes

1. The FBI, which provides the statistics on crimes known to the police, stopped calculating a rate for the entire Part I index after 2001. It did, however, continue to publish rates for both violent and property crime, from which a total rate for all Part I crime can be calculated.

2. Intelligence-led policing may be confused with evidence-based policing. Intelligence-led policing refers to the targeting of operations on the basis of specific information, whereas evidence-based policing refers to shaping of operational strategies on the basis of evaluations of their efficacy.

Critical Thinking

1. Why was community policing developed?
2. What factors are affecting the way policing is done today?
3. Does the increase of private policing present the possibility of problems?
4. What has been the public's reaction to the fact that crime has declined?

Create Central

www.mhhe.com/createcentral

Internet References

Law Enforcement Guide to the World Wide Web
http://leolinks.com

National Institute of Justice/National Criminal Justice Reference Service
www.ncjrs.gov/policing/man199.htm

DAVID H. BAYLEY is Distinguished Professor in the School of Criminal Justice at the State University of New York, Albany. **CHRISTINE NIXON** is APM Chair, Victorian Bushfire Reconstruction and Recovery Authority, and State Commissioner of Police, Victoria, Australia (Retired). The authors acknowledge valuable research assistance provided by Baillie Aaron, Research Assistant, in the Program in Criminal Justice and Police Management, John F. Kennedy School of Government, Harvard University.

From *New Perspectives in Policing*, http://goo.gl/dvnJ3 (September 2010). Copyright © by John F. Kennedy School of Government at Harvard University with funding by the National Institute of Justice. This article is available free of charge online at: http://cms.hks.harvard.edu/var/ezp_site/storage/fckeditor/file/pdfs/centers-programs/programs/criminal-justice/NPIP-The-Changing-Environment-for-Policing-1985–2008.pdf.

Article Prepared by: Joanne Naughton

A Year of Reckoning: Police Fatally Shoot Nearly 1,000

KIMBERLY KINDY ET AL.

Learning Outcomes

After reading this article, you will be able to:

- State what the percentage is of white police officers killing unarmed black men.

- Show that many encounters that end in police shootings began with minor infractions.

- Learn what the research shows about police shootings that involve mentally troubled people.

Nearly a thousand times this year, an American police officer has shot and killed a civilian. When the people hired to protect their communities end up killing someone, they can be called heroes or criminals—a judgment that has never come more quickly or searingly than in this era of viral video, body cameras, and dash cams. A single bullet fired at the adrenaline-charged apex of a chase can end a life, wreck a career, spark a riot, spike racial tensions and alter the politics of the nation.

In a year-long study, The *Washington Post* found that the kind of incidents that have ignited protests in many U.S. communities—most often, white police officers killing unarmed black men—represent less than 4 percent of fatal police shootings. Meanwhile, The Post found that the great majority of people who died at the hands of the police fit at least one of three categories: they were wielding weapons, they were suicidal or mentally troubled, or they ran when officers told them to halt.

The Post sought to compile a record of every fatal police shooting in the nation in 2015, something no government agency had done. The project began after a police officer shot and killed Michael Brown in Ferguson, Missouri, in August 2014, provoking several nights of fiery riots, weeks of protests and a national reckoning with the nexus of race, crime, and police use of force.

Race remains the most volatile flash point in any accounting of police shootings. Although black men make up only 6 percent of the U.S. population, they account for 40 percent of the unarmed men shot to death by police this year, The Post's database shows. In the majority of cases in which police shot and killed a person who had attacked someone with a weapon or brandished a gun, the person who was shot was white. But a hugely disproportionate number—three in five—of those killed after exhibiting less threatening behavior were black or Hispanic.

Regardless of race, in more than a quarter of cases, the fatal encounter involved officers pursuing someone on foot or by car—making chases one of the most common scenarios in the data. Some police chiefs and training experts say more restrictive rules on when to give chase could prevent unnecessary shootings.

Like a growing number of police shootings, the death of David Kassick on a snow-covered field near his sister's house in Hummelstown, Pennsylvania, was captured on video—a technological shift that has dramatically altered how Americans perceive officers' use of deadly force.

In 2 minutes and 10 seconds of harrowing footage, the Kassick video serves as an almost perfect Rorschach test in the national debate over when it is justifiable for an officer to take a life.

"Shots Fired"

Officer Lisa Mearkle has chased Kassick, first by car, then on foot. Now she's zapped him with her Taser and he's writhing on the ground, on snow, jammed up against a line of trees.

Viewed through the camera attached to the officer's Taser, Kassick reacts to each of three shocks from the stun gun.

Mearkle, screaming, orders Kassick, who is already involuntarily on the ground, to "Get on the ground! Get on the ground!"

"Okay, okay," he responds.

As the officer stands over Kassick, repeatedly ordering him to "Lie down" and "Show your hands," the 59-year-old does just that. He moans in pain, pulls his right hand out from under his head and stretches to display the hand.

But three times during the video, Kassick also does other things with his hands. As he says "Okay, okay" to the officer's command, he also reaches toward his jacket pocket. A little later, his left hand moves toward his front pants pocket. He appears to be trying to remove Taser wires from his clothing. Thirty seconds later, he uses his left hand to lift himself slightly from the snow.

At the 1:39 mark, there's a pop and Mearkle says, "Shots fired."

Within seconds, Kassick is flat on his stomach. He lifts his head. The officer, calm now, says, "Keep your hands where I can see them."

The video ends. Kassick is dead, shot twice in the back.

He was unarmed.

Mearkle had given chase after Kassick fled from her attempt to pull him over for having an expired inspection sticker on his car.

The Video Age

In today's tinderbox of public concern about police brutality, video of shootings can be damning evidence or a clear defense. Police chiefs and politicians like video because in most cases it absolves officers of allegations of wrongdoing. Civilians like video because when officers do act abusively, digital proof makes coverups unlikely.

In the Kassick case, some of Mearkle's defenders argue that intricate inspection of videos warps perceptions of the challenges police face. A system in which officers make split-second decisions—but in which their bosses, prosecutors, jurors and the public have the luxury of examining every frame of video—is unfair, said Les Neri, president of the Pennsylvania Fraternal Order of Police.

"We now microscopically evaluate for days and weeks what they only had a few seconds to act on," Neri said. "People always say, 'They shot an unarmed man,' but we know that only after the fact. We are criminalizing judgment errors."

The decisions police officers must make in a flash can have fatal consequences—for themselves as well as for suspects. Thirty-six officers have been shot and killed in the line of duty this year, according to the Officer Down Memorial Page.

The widespread availability of video of police shootings—from bystanders' smartphones as well as from police body and dashboard cameras—has been a primary factor in the rising number of indictments of officers.

Prosecutors cited video evidence against officers in 10 of the 18 felony cases filed against officers this year—twice as often as video played a role in prosecutions over the previous decade, The Post found.

"Thank God for technology," said the Rev. Ira Acree, pastor at Greater St. John Bible Church in Chicago, where Officer Jason Van Dyke faces a first-degree murder charge for shooting 16 rounds and killing Laquan McDonald, a 17-year-old who was walking down the middle of the street holding a three-inch knife. "Maybe it's finally helping us crack the blue code of silence."

After police dash-cam video of the 2014 incident was released last month, Mayor Rahm Emanuel (D) fired the city's police chief.

"In the past, an officer's word was not challenged," said Philip M. Stinson, a criminologist at Bowling Green State University who studies arrests of officers. "If anything has shifted this year, it's that. They are facing the kind of scrutiny the rest of us face when we kill someone."

But some officers' friends and attorneys attribute the uptick in prosecutions to rising political pressure. On a fundraising website, supporters of West Monroe, La., officer Jody Ledoux blamed his January felony negligent-homicide indictment on "our country's current climate towards police." Ledoux's attorney, Mickey DuBos, did not return calls seeking comment.

Ledoux killed Raymond Martinez, a homeless 51 year old, the day after a grand jury in New York City declined to bring criminal charges against Officer Daniel Pantaleo, who was recorded last year putting a fatal chokehold on Eric Garner, a Staten Island man who was stopped for selling loose cigarettes. The decision not to charge Pantaleo sparked nationwide protests.

Surveillance video in the Louisiana case shows Ledoux shot Martinez as he reached into a newspaper vending machine in front of a convenience store to retrieve his cellphone. Ledoux said he feared Martinez was reaching for a gun.

Although more officers were indicted in shooting cases this year, the outcome of such cases improved for officers. Five of the seven cases tried this year ended with the officer acquitted or with a mistrial. In two cases, charges were dismissed. Over the previous decade, one-third of officers charged in shooting cases were convicted of crimes ranging from misdemeanor reckless discharge of a firearm to felony murder.

This year, only one officer, Richard Combs, former chief of a small department in Eutawville, South Carolina, pleaded guilty. In September, following two mistrials on a murder charge, he pleaded to a misdemeanor charge of misconduct in office and was sentenced to one year of home detention after he fatally shot Bernard Bailey in a parking lot. Bailey had resisted arrest on a warrant in 2011.

As protests have increased pressure for transparency about fatal shootings, more departments have moved to equip officers with body cameras. Many chiefs say the cameras boost public confidence in the police, but most departments do not yet use them. About 6 percent of fatal shootings this year were captured by body cameras, according to The Post's database.

Where cameras are used, police often refuse to publicly release video. In more than half the cases in which body cam footage was available, police declined The Post's requests to make the video public. Officials said releasing footage before cases are closed could taint jury pools, making it difficult to win convictions.

Judging "Mind-set"

Officer Mearkle killed Kassick in February and was charged with third-degree murder, manslaughter and involuntary manslaughter. Eight months later, 12 jurors sat in judgment. Mearkle, 37, faced up to 40 years in prison and the end of her career.

Mearkle, who would later express regret for Kassick's death, testified that she had "no doubt" that Kassick—who was a heroin addict, though the officer didn't know that when she gave chase—was reaching for a weapon when he moved toward his jacket pocket as he squirmed in the snow. "There was no reason for him to reach into his frigging pocket!" she yelled in court.

She could not let Kassick escape, she said, because someone who runs from an officer might be a danger to the community. "Something is wrong here," she testified, recalling her thinking at the start of the chase. "This is not normal for someone to flee the police."

Last month, after 11 hours of deliberations, the jury acquitted Mearkle of all charges.

The jury foreman, Scot Benoit, says he would not have shot Kassick. After watching the video eight times, Benoit and some of his fellow jurors concluded it was not necessary to shoot the man on the ground. But that is not the question they were asked to consider.

"Our job was to look at her mind-set," Benoit said. "We had to determine if her fears were justified."

To figure that out, the jury had to look beyond the video. One fact weighed heavily on jurors: When the chase started, Kassick, trying to pull away from Mearkle, steered around another vehicle that was stopped at a red light.

"That escalated the situation in Officer Mearkle's mind," Benoit said. "Quite clearly, he was eluding the police and she didn't know why. The prosecutor kept saying this was just over an inspection sticker. But when Kassick went around the other vehicle, he's fleeing at a high rate of speed on a residential street and kids are coming home from school, so I could see where she's coming from."

Kassick's sister, Diane Fetters, says it was her brother who had reason to be afraid, not the officer. "He just panicked," she said. "He was afraid of going to jail because he was driving without a license. Her adrenaline kicked in and she wasn't able to deal with it. She had plenty of opportunity to back off.

"I mean, what she was pursuing him for, the expired sticker? She could have just sent him a summons in the mail."

A Lack of Data

The landscape of police shootings is surprisingly thinly explored. The FBI is charged with keeping statistics on such shootings, but The Post analysis of FBI data showed that fewer than half of the nation's 18,000 police departments report their incidents to the agency.

The Post documented well more than twice as many fatal shootings this year as the average annual tally reported by the FBI over the past decade. The FBI and the Federal Bureau of Justice Statistics now acknowledge that their data collection has been deeply flawed. FBI Director James B. Comey called his agency's database "unacceptable." Both agencies have launched efforts to create new systems for documenting fatalities.

The FBI will replace its current program with a "near real-time" database to be made public by 2017, said Stephen L. Morris, a senior FBI official whose division is responsible for collecting crime data.

"We are responding to a real human outcry," Morris said. "People want to know what police are doing, and they want to know why they are using force. It always fell to the bottom before. It is now the highest priority."

The Post's database, compiled from interviews, police reports, local news accounts and other sources, tracked more than a dozen details about each killing, including the events that led to the fatal encounter, whether the slain person was armed, and demographic data on each person. The Post will continue tracking fatal shootings by police in 2016.

The research also noted whether victims were mentally ill or experiencing an emotional crisis, a category that came to account for one-quarter of those killed. Officers fatally shot at least 243 people with mental health problems: 75 who were explicitly suicidal and 168 for whom police or family members confirmed a history of mental illness.

The analysis found that about 9 in 10 of the mentally troubled people were armed, usually with guns but also with knives or other sharp objects. But the analysis also found that most of them died at the hands of police officers who had not been trained to deal with the mentally ill.

"Often they have an edged weapon, like a knife, and when officers start yelling, 'Drop it! Drop it!' that will not calm them down," said Chuck Wexler, executive director of the Police Executive Research Forum, a Washington police think tank. "Instead, it increases their anxiety."

In most of those cases, police were called by a relative or a neighbor who was worried about a mentally fragile person's erratic behavior. Yvonne Mote of Alabama dialed 911 in March out of desperation, hoping police could help her brother, Shane Watkins, who suffered from schizophrenia. Instead, he wound up dead.

"A week after they killed my brother, there was an armed robbery," Mote said. "That guy had a gun, and they arrested him without killing him. Why did they have to kill my brother, who only had a box cutter? I still don't understand."

The prosecutor in the Mearkle case, Johnny Baer, still says it was right to charge the officer with murder. She was "out of control," he said.

In court, Baer told jurors that "anytime anyone involved in an encounter with a police officer doesn't show their hands, that isn't a reason to shoot. Ninety-nine point nine percent of police officers use extraordinary restraint in these situations."

But, Baer said weeks after the trial, "we had a conservative central-Pennsylvania jury and a female officer who is a mother and who was tearful and emotional in court."

It remains unusual for police to face criminal charges in fatal shootings, but the indictment rate in such cases more than tripled this year—a striking shift in the willingness of prosecutors to charge officers.

The Post found that an average of five officers per year have been indicted on felony charges over the previous decade; this year, 18 officers have been charged with felonies including murder, manslaughter and reckless discharge of a firearm.

Such accusations rarely stick, however. Only 11 of the 65 officers charged in fatal shootings over the past decade were convicted.

Guiding Principles

Aftershocks of the Mearkle case still reverberate in Hummelstown and beyond. Several thousand people signed an online petition asking that the town not reinstate Mearkle to her police job. No decision has been made on that.

Mearkle, whose criminal and civil attorneys did not return repeated calls from The Post, said at a news conference after the verdict that she is determined to return to her job and is sorry about the shooting.

"I truly wish it didn't happen, and I want [the family] to know that I never wanted to shoot anybody," she said.

Police departments design rules and training with the aim of resolving difficult situations without shooting anyone. But the rules vary enormously. About half of departments allow officers to give chase no matter what offense a suspect has committed, while the other half limits pursuits to certain kinds of offenses, according to a study by the International Association of Chiefs of Police.

The Post's database shows that nearly 1 in 3 shootings that result from a car chase start with a traffic stop for a minor infraction.

In recent years, pursuit policies have generally grown tighter. Old rules that left the decision to "officer judgment" have been replaced by sometimes complex matrixes requiring police to weigh the severity of the crime being committed before they decide whether to give chase.

After Las Vegas police in 2009 adopted a use-of-force policy requiring officers to put the highest premium on "the sanctity of human life," some other departments followed suit. Four years after the change in Las Vegas, the city's officer-involved shootings had fallen by nearly half.

"That is a real sign of the times, a new kind of language that changes police culture," said Wexler, whose organization recommends tighter pursuit policies. "The guiding principle has to be proportionality: Is my action proportional to the act being committed? We've recommended that the policy has to be ironclad, because if you say 'except if the officer fears for his life,' inevitably they will say they fear for their life."

When New York, Boston and other big cities tightened rules on pursuits, they saw a sharp decline in the number of officers who shot at vehicles.

"Good cops judge when they can hold back," said Geoffrey Alpert, a criminologist at the University of South Carolina who has studied pursuits for three decades. "So what if you get pushed in a volatile domestic situation? You're justified to use force, but you tactically withdraw, calm them down and move on."

More restrictive pursuit policies are no panacea, however. Although many experts support the change, a review by George Mason University criminologist Cynthia Lum of 33 studies of pursuit policies concluded that tightening the rules led to fewer police injuries—but also more crime.

Still, Rob Ord, a longtime instructor on defensive police tactics who now runs Falken Industries, a Virginia security company, said, "It's almost always better to back off and call for help."

When Ord was a police officer in Florida, he was directing traffic one day when a driver disobeyed his command to turn left. Instead, the driver gunned his engine and drove straight at Ord.

"I rolled onto his hood, firearm drawn," Ord recalled. "My finger was on the trigger, ready to pull."

"And I stopped. I did not fire," he said. "That person's alive and he was charged, and I'm alive and I have a house and a job and I wasn't sued. I'm happy."

Critical Thinking

1. Did Mearkle make a good argument in court for shooting Kassick?

2. Would you agree with Benoit's analysis?

3. Was the prosecutor correct to bring charges against Mearkle?

Internet References

991 People Shot Dead by Police in 2015
https://www.washingtonpost.com/graphics/national/police-shootings/

Man Shot, Killed by Greece Officer in Mall Lot
http://www.democratandchronicle.com/story/news/2015/06/01/police-investigate-near-sears-mall-greece-ridge/28314217/

Article

Prepared by: Joanne Naughton

Police Chiefs, Looking to Diversify Forces, Face Structural Hurdles

MATT APUZZO AND SARAH COHEN

Learning Outcomes

After reading this article, you will be able to:

- Explain why Inkster has such difficulty recruiting police officers.

- Show how state laws affect how local police departments hire police officers.

- Demonstrate that cities with large African American populations have wide gaps between the community's minority composition and that of local law enforcement.

Inkster, Michigan—When William T. Riley III became the police chief of this small city west of Detroit this summer, he found a department that bore little resemblance to the city it served.

Nearly three-fourths of Inkster's 25,000 residents are black. Its mayor and all six City Council members are, too. Yet in a newly released Justice Department survey, it was listed among the nation's least representative police forces, with 21 white officers and five black officers.

At first glance, the disparity made no sense.

"There's no doubt in my mind we have good police candidates in this city. No doubt," said Chief Riley, the first African-American to hold the city chief's post. "How hard can it be? You're telling me everybody here can't be a police officer?"

The gap was particularly jarring, because the chief had arrived from Selma, Ala., another largely African-American city, but one where the police force closely mirrors the community's makeup.

Though the history of discrimination and segregation looms large over American policing, many police chiefs are eager to hire minorities yet face structural hurdles that make it hard to diversify their departments. Those issues vary by state and city, making any single solution particularly elusive.

In many cities, well-intentioned policies that were not meant to discriminate have become obstacles to hiring a diverse police force. In Inkster, Chief Riley found, a significant problem was something that seemed mundane: how training is paid for.

Other cities face rigid hiring processes that were intended to prevent elected leaders from handing out police jobs as patronage, but that now make it harder to shape the force to mirror the population.

"Local police chiefs take the hit for this, but the truth is that states get what they ask for through legislation," said Edward F. Davis, a former Boston police commissioner. "That's the bottom line here."

In Massachusetts, for example, state law generally requires that officer hiring be based on a Civil Service test that is administered only once every two years. Military veterans who pass are given preference, a policy that exists in some form in many states.

Mr. Davis said that though he spent hundreds of thousands of dollars on minority recruitment and generated strong interest in police jobs, he could not significantly increase the number of minorities joining the force.

While there is no evidence that police departments with representative populations are less likely to face claims of excessive force or discrimination, civil rights activists and police executives alike say it is important for these forces to resemble their communities. In cities, such as Baltimore, Cleveland, and Philadelphia, the wide demographic gaps between the police departments the African-American populations have exacerbated tensions after racially charged protests over police actions.

"We must have police services that reflect the communities we serve," Chief Kathleen M. O'Toole of the Seattle Police

Department told thousands of police leaders from around the country at a conference last month.

The Justice Department collects national data on police demographics every few years, but the meaning of those numbers can depend on how they are viewed. Seen one way, there is no problem at all: African-Americans account for 12 percent of the population and 12 percent of officers in midsize and large departments surveyed, say figures from 2012 that were released in July.

But that statistic masks a stark disparity in cities with large African-American populations. The overwhelming majority of cities where blacks make up at least 35 percent of the population have wide gaps—20 percentage points or more— between the community's minority composition and that of local law enforcement.

Inkster is one such city.

Chief Riley was recruited here after a police brutality scandal in which a white officer was caught on video punching a black driver in the head during an arrest in January. Another video showed officers laughing and fist-bumping afterward. One officer was fired and prosecuted. The chief at that time resigned.

In his first weeks in Inkster, Chief Riley met a young black man who wanted to become a police officer. But the man said he did not have the $6,000 or more it would cost to attend a police academy and be certified.

The chief was taken aback. Traditionally, cities pay for training. Inkster does not. Like many Michigan cities, it prefers to hire only officers who are already certified. Hiring uncertified officers means paying not only the training expenses but also their salaries and benefits while they are at the academy.

That preference limits the pool of candidates to officers already working in other departments, or people who can afford their own training.

"That knocks out a whole swath of people that I know are eligible," said Chief Riley, the son of working-class parents, who got his start as an officer in Newport News, Va. "I'd never have been able to become a Newport News police officer if I had to pay to go to the academy."

It did not work that way in Selma. There, Chief Riley said, he recruited locally and attracted a talented, diverse pool of cadets. That is because Alabama reimburses cities for the cost of training new officers. Selma could afford to do what Inkster could not: look for young, local candidates regardless of their financial status.

Many other states, including Michigan, do not reimburse training costs. The majority of newly certified officers in Michigan pay their own way, said Hermina Kramp, the deputy director of the Michigan Commission on Law Enforcement Standards. That is good for local police budgets, she said, but not for "getting a diverse population in your police department."

"If you don't see yourself in the police department, you begin to think you can't get a fair shake," said Shawn L. Jones, an assistant police chief in Atlanta. Atlanta's is one of only a handful of very large police departments where the work force closely mirrors the city population.

Large cities have advantages, in that they tend to operate their own academies and can recruit nationally. "We have more flexibility to go wherever we need to go," the assistant chief said. But among the 50 largest departments, only three besides Atlanta's—in El Paso, Miami, and Washington—reflect the populations they serve. Most of the disparity in these departments comes from the agencies' failure to keep up with growing Hispanic populations.

It is also easier to recruit minorities into departments that already have reputations as diverse employers, said Patrick A. Burke, an assistant police chief in Washington. "Everybody knows they have a chance to succeed here," he said. The city's hiring process is more flexible and faster than procedures in other cities, which also helps.

But the push for more diversity comes at a time when many chiefs say they want to be more particular about whom they hire. College graduates, especially, are attractive candidates, as are people with language and problem-solving skills. Philadelphia recently began requiring 60 college credits and at least a C average for most new officers. Commissioner Charles H. Ramsey said the higher standards were good for the department.

At the same time, it is increasingly hard to fill police jobs in general. Philadelphia's academy is short 200 officers, he said. Officials in Fresno, California, are offering $1,000 signing bonuses to help fill vacancies. Police departments, typically slow to hire, face competition with private industries for many of the best candidates.

In Inkster, Chief Riley said that as police ranks have dwindled since the Justice Department survey, the diversity numbers have improved slightly. There are now 15 white officers and eight black officers, he said, a gap in representation that he said was still far too wide.

He said he would try to find the money to hire local recruits, if not from the budget then from elsewhere. Perhaps, the civil rights groups and civic organizations that have called for greater department diversity can help pay for training, he said.

"You don't have to lower standards," Chief Riley said. "You just have to be creative and fair."

If the money is there, he added, "I'm sure I can get candidates."

Correction: November 9, 2015

An earlier version of this article stated incorrectly a distinction for William T. Riley III, the police chief in Inkster, Michigan. He is not the first African American police chief in the city; Dick Humphrey was first.

Critical Thinking

1. What are some of the problems that municipalities face, making minority recruitment difficult?

2. How could they fix some of these problems?

3. Why is it important for police departments to reflect the communities they serve?

Internet References

Bureau of Justice Statistics
http://www.bjs.gov/index.cfm?ty=dcdetail&iid=248

PBS Newshour
http://www.pbs.org/newshour/rundown/ap-analysis-disparity-seen-number-hispanic-officers-police-departments/

Article   Prepared by: Joanne Naughton

Training Officers to Shoot First, and He Will Answer Questions Later

MATT APUZZO

Learning Outcomes

After reading this article, you will be able to:

- Describe William Lewinski's work and show why it is controversial.

- Report Arien Mack's criticism of Lewinski's use of "inattentional blindness" when discussing a police shooting.

Washington—The shooting looked bad. But that is when the professor is at his best. A black motorist, pulled to the side of the road for a turn-signal violation, had stuffed his hand into his pocket. The white officer yelled for him to take it out. When the driver started to comply, the officer shot him dead.

The driver was unarmed.

Taking the stand at a public inquest, William J. Lewinski, the psychology professor, explained that the officer had no choice but to act.

"In simple terms," the district attorney in Portland, Ore., asked, "if I see the gun, I'm dead?"

"In simple terms, that's it," Dr. Lewinski replied.

When police officers shoot people under questionable circumstances, Dr. Lewinski is often there to defend their actions. Among most influential voices on the subject, he has testified in or consulted in nearly 200 cases over the last decade or so and has helped justify countless shootings around the country.

His conclusions are consistent: The officer acted appropriately, even when shooting an unarmed person. Even when shooting someone in the back. Even when witness testimony, forensic evidence or video footage contradicts the officer's story.

He has appeared as an expert witness in criminal trials, civil cases and disciplinary hearings, and before grand juries, where such testimony is given in secret and goes unchallenged. In addition, his company, the Force Science Institute, has trained tens of thousands of police officers on how to think differently about police shootings that might appear excessive.

A string of deadly police encounters in Ferguson, Mo.; North Charleston, S.C.; and most recently in Cincinnati, have prompted a national reconsideration of how officers use force and provoked calls for them to slow down and defuse conflicts. But the debate has also left many police officers feeling unfairly maligned and suspicious of new policies that they say could put them at risk. Dr. Lewinski says his research clearly shows that officers often cannot wait to act.

"We're telling officers, 'Look for cover and then read the threat,'" he told a class of Los Angeles County deputy sheriffs recently. "Sorry, too damn late."

A former Minnesota State professor, he says his testimony and training are based on hard science, but his research has been roundly criticized by experts. An editor for *The American Journal of Psychology* called his work "pseudoscience." The Justice Department denounced his findings as "lacking in both foundation and reliability." Civil rights lawyers say he is selling dangerous ideas.

"People die because of this stuff," said John Burton, a California lawyer who specializes in police misconduct cases. "When they give these cops a pass, it just ripples through the system."

Many policing experts are for hire, but Dr. Lewinski is unique in that he conducts his own research, trains officers and internal investigators, and testifies at trial. In the protests that have followed police shootings, demonstrators have often asked why officers are so rarely punished for shootings that seem unwarranted. Dr. Lewinski is part of the answer.

An Expert on the Stand

While his testimony at times has proved insufficient to persuade a jury, his record includes many high-profile wins.

"He won't give an inch on cross-examination," said Elden Rosenthal, a lawyer who represented the family of James Jahar Perez, the man killed in the 2004 Portland shooting. In that case, Dr. Lewinski also testified before the grand jury, which brought no charges. Defense lawyers like Dr. Lewinski, Mr. Rosenthal said. "They know that he's battle-hardened in the courtroom, so you know exactly what you're getting."

Dr. Lewinski, 70, is affable and confident in his research, but not so polished as to sound like a salesman. In testimony on the stand, for which he charges nearly $1,000 an hour, he offers winding answers to questions and seldom appears flustered. He sprinkles scientific explanations with sports analogies.

"A batter can't wait for a ball to cross home plate before deciding whether that's something to swing at," he told the Los Angeles deputy sheriffs. "Make sense? Officers have to make a prediction based on cues."

Of course, it follows that batters will sometimes swing at bad pitches, and that officers will sometimes shoot unarmed people.

Much of the criticism of his work, Dr. Lewinski said, amounts to politics. In 2012, for example, just seven months after the Justice Department excoriated him and his methods, department officials paid him $55,000 to help defend a federal drug agent who shot and killed an unarmed 18-year-old in California. Then last year, as part of a settlement over excessive force in the Seattle Police Department, the Justice Department endorsed sending officers to Mr. Lewinski for training. And in January, he was paid $15,000 to train federal marshals.

If the science is there, Dr. Lewinski said, he does not shy away from offering opinions in controversial cases. He said he was working on behalf of one of two Albuquerque officers who face murder charges in last year's shooting death of a mentally ill homeless man. He has testified in many racially charged cases involving white officers who shot black suspects, such as the 2009 case in which a Bay Area transit officer shot and killed Oscar Grant, an unarmed black man, at close range.

Dr. Lewinski said he was not trying to explain away every shooting. But when he testifies, it is almost always in defense of police shootings. Officers are his target audience—he publishes a newsletter on police use of force that he says has nearly one million subscribers—and his research was devised for them. "The science is based on trying to keep officers safe," he said.

Dr. Lewinski, who grew up in Canada, got his doctorate in 1988 from the Union for Experimenting Colleges and Universities, an accredited but alternative Cincinnati school offering accelerated programs and flexible schedules. He designed his curriculum and named his program police psychology, a specialty not available elsewhere.

'Invalid and Unreliable'

In 1990, a police shooting in Minneapolis changed the course of his career. Dan May, a white police officer, shot and killed Tycel Nelson, a black 17-year-old. Officer May said he fired after the teenager turned toward him and raised a handgun. But an autopsy showed he was shot in the back.

Dr. Lewinski was intrigued by the apparent contradiction. "We really need to get into the dynamics of how this unfolds," he remembers thinking. "We need a lot better research."

He began by videotaping students as they raised handguns and then quickly turned their backs. On average, that move took about half a second. By the time an officer returned fire, Dr. Lewinski concluded, a suspect could have turned his back.

He summarized his findings in 1999 in *The Police Marksman,* a popular magazine for officers. The next year, it published an expanded study, in which Dr. Lewinski timed students as they fired while turning, running or sitting with a gun at their side, as if stashed in a car's console.

Suspects, he concluded, could reach, fire and move remarkably fast. But faster than an officer could react? In 2002, a third study concluded that it takes the average officer about a second and a half to draw from a holster, aim and fire.

Together, the studies appeared to support the idea that officers were at a serious disadvantage. The studies are the foundation for much of his work over the past decade.

Because he published in a police magazine and not a scientific journal, Dr. Lewinski was not subjected to the peer-review process. But in separate cases in 2011 and 2012, the Justice Department and a private lawyer asked Lisa Fournier, a Washington State University professor and an *American Journal of Psychology* editor, to review Dr. Lewinski's studies. She said they lacked basic elements of legitimate research, such as control groups, and drew conclusions that were unsupported by the data.

"In summary, this study is invalid and unreliable," she wrote in court documents in 2012. "In my opinion, this study questions the ability of Mr. Lewinski to apply relevant and reliable data to answer a question or support an argument."

Dr. Lewinski said he chose to publish his findings in the magazine because it reached so many officers who would never read a scientific journal. If he were doing it over, he said in an interview, he would have published his early studies in academic journals and summarized them elsewhere for officers. But he said it was unfair for Dr. Fournier to criticize his research based on summaries written for a general audience. While opposing lawyers and experts found his research controversial, they were particularly frustrated by Dr. Lewinski's tendency to get inside people's heads. Time and again, his reports to defense lawyers seem to make conclusive statements about what officers saw, what they did not, and what they cannot remember.

Often, these details are hotly disputed. For example, in a 2009 case that revolved around whether a Texas sheriff's deputy felt threatened by a car coming at him, Dr. Lewinski said that the officer was so focused on firing to stop the threat, he did not immediately recognize that the car had passed him.

Inattentional Blindness

Such gaps in observation and memory, he says, can be explained by a phenomenon called inattentional blindness, in which the brain is so focused on one task that it blocks out everything else. When an officer's version of events is disproved by video or forensic evidence, Dr. Lewinski says, inattentional blindness may be to blame. It is human nature, he says, to try to fill in the blanks.

"Whenever the cop says something that's helpful, it's as good as gold," said Mr. Burton, the California lawyer. "But when a cop says something that's inconvenient, it's a result of this memory loss."

Experts say Dr. Lewinski is too sure of himself on the subject. "I hate the fact that it's being used in this way," said Arien Mack, one of two psychologists who coined the term inattentional blindness. "When we work in a lab, we ask them if they saw something. They have no motivation to lie. A police officer involved in a shooting certainly has a reason to lie."

Dr. Lewinski acknowledged that there was no clear way to distinguish inattentional blindness from lying. He said he had tried to present it as a possibility, not a conclusion.

Almost as soon as his research was published, lawyers took notice and asked him to explain his work to juries.

In Los Angeles, he helped authorities explain the still-controversial fatal shooting of Anthony Dwain Lee, a Hollywood actor who was shot through a window by a police officer at a Halloween party in 2000. The actor carried a fake gun as part of his costume. Mr. Lee was shot several times in the back. The officer was not charged.

The city settled a lawsuit over the shooting for $225,000, but Mr. Lewinski still teaches the case as an example of a justified shooting that unfairly tarnished a good officer who "was shooting to save his own life."

In September 2001, a Cincinnati judge acquitted a police officer, Stephen Roach, in the shooting death of an unarmed black man after a chase. The officer said he believed the man, Timothy Thomas, 19, was reaching for a gun. Dr. Lewinski testified, and the judge said he found his analysis credible. The prosecutor, Stephen McIntosh, however, told *The Columbus Dispatch* that Dr. Lewinski's "radical" views could be used to justify nearly any police shooting.

"If that's the sort of direction we, as a society, are going," the prosecutor said, "I have a lot of disappointment." Since then, Dr. Lewinski has testified in many dozens of cases in state and federal court, becoming a hero to many officers who feel that politics, not science or safety, drives police policy. For example, departments often require officers to consider less-lethal options such as pepper spray, stun guns and beanbag guns before drawing their firearms.

"These have come about because of political pressure," said Les Robbins, the executive director of the Association for Los Angeles Deputy Sheriffs. In an interview, Mr. Robbins recalled how he used to keep his gun drawn and hidden behind his leg during most traffic stops. "We used to be able to use the baton and hit people where we felt necessary to get them to comply. Those days are gone."

Positions of Authority

Dr. Lewinski and his company have provided training for dozens of departments, including in Cincinnati, Las Vegas, Milwaukee and Seattle. His messages often conflict, in both substance and tone, with the training now recommended by the Justice Department and police organizations.

The Police Executive Research Forum, a group that counts most major city police chiefs as members, has called for greater restraint from officers and slower, better decision making. Chuck Wexler, its director, said he is troubled by Dr. Lewinski's teachings. He added that even as chiefs changed their use-of-force policies, many did not know what their officers were taught in academies and private sessions.

"It's not that chiefs don't care," he said. "It's rare that a chief has time to sit at the academy and see what's being taught."

Regardless of what, if any, policy changes emerge from the current national debate, civil right lawyers say one thing will not change: Jurors want to believe police officers, and Dr. Lewinski's research tells them that they can.

On a cold night in early 2003, for instance, Robert Murtha, an officer in Hartford, Conn., shot three times at the driver of a car. He said the vehicle had sped directly at him, knocking him to the ground as he fired. Video from a nearby police cruiser told another story. The officer had not been struck. He had fired through the driver's-side window as the car passed him.

Officer Murtha's story was so obviously incorrect that he was arrested on charges of assault and fabricating evidence. If officers can get away with shooting people and lying about it, the prosecutor declared, "the system is doomed."

"There was no way around it—Murtha was dead wrong," his lawyer, Hugh F. Keefe, recalled recently. But the officer was "bright, articulate and truthful," Mr. Keefe said. Jurors needed an explanation for how the officer could be so wrong and still be innocent.

Dr. Lewinski testified at trial. The jury deliberated less than one full day. The officer was acquitted of all charges.

Critical Thinking

1. Do you believe that it is appropriate for police chiefs not to know what their officers are being taught regarding use-of-force?

2. What effect do you think decisions like the one in *Murtha* have on the public's perception of law enforcement?

3. What's wrong with the fact that Lewinski's studies were not subject to peer-review?

Internet References

Force Science Institute Ltd
http://www.forcescience.org/biomachanics.html

Lisa Fournier
https://s3.amazonaws.com/pacer-documents/D.%20Or.%2008-cv-00950%20dckt%20000133_011%20filed%202012-06-28.pdf

Police Executive Research Forum
http://www.policeforum.org/assets/reengineeringtraining1.pdf

The Police Marksman
http://www.forcescience.org/articles/isyourshootingclean.pdf

Article   Prepared by: Joanne Naughton

Defining Moments for Police Chiefs

CHUCK WEXLER

Learning Outcomes

After reading this article, you will be able to:

- Understand the thinking of some police executives about critical situations.

- Show the importance of speaking to the media as soon as possible, with accurate information, after a serious police incident.

Introduction

The position of police chief has always been a demanding job. A police chief must know how to run a complex organization, in many cases a very large organization. Chiefs must have strong leadership skills and a vision for meeting the needs of the community. And the stakes are high, because police have unique power and authority over people. The consequences of a mistake by any member of the organization can be catastrophic. As a result, police departments undergo closer scrutiny than other types of organizations.

Since PERF's (Police Executive Research Forum) creation in 1976, one of our priorities has been to work with police chiefs to identify best practices and policies for meeting the challenges of the job. Our goal is to help police departments learn from each other about the critical issues they face.

And one thing we have seen is that even in a well-run department, a department with good policies, thorough training of officers, strong leaders, and solid management systems, things can go disastrously wrong at any moment. A single officer can make a bad decision in a split-second, or a natural disaster or large-scale criminal incident can overwhelm a department's capabilities.

A police chief who responds well in a crisis can mitigate the damage, and sometimes the storyline changes as a result. Instead of focusing on the disastrous incident, the community remembers how hard the police chief and the police department worked to handle it.

Unfortunately, in other cases, a slow or ill-considered response makes the situation worse.

In the summer of 2014, PERF decided to hold a national conference to address these issues. We decided to name the conference "Defining Moments for Police Chiefs." We wanted to ask leading police officials, "In your career, what was the one critical moment when you really felt tested? What did you do that worked well? And looking back, is there anything you wish you could do over and do differently?"

As we were planning the Defining Moments conference, the fatal shooting of Michael Brown by a police officer in Ferguson, Missouri on August 9, and the large-scale protest marches and riots that followed, brought international attention to many of the issues we were addressing.

For example, a key issue for a police department in any critical incident is how effectively it shares information with the public and the news media. Traditionally, police have often held back on releasing information, believing that they should exercise caution until they are certain of all of the facts, or that they should never release information that might be used later in a criminal case or lawsuit.

At our Defining Moments conference, police chiefs told us they are finding that that approach is no longer viable, because a narrative is created within a few hours of a critical incident happening, and the narrative is written whether or not the police contribute any information to the story. Too much damage can be done if police miss their chance to explain what happened and correct wrong information that can spread in the immediate aftermath of an incident.

So today's police leaders try to get out in front of the story, rather than being dragged into it against their will. They provide preliminary information with a strong cautionary note that as more information becomes available, the story may very well change. Chief David Brown of Dallas talked about the importance of getting this preliminary information out in the first news cycle.

Another critical aspect of "defining moments" for police chiefs is whether they have a reservoir of trust in the community that can help everyone to get through the difficult situation. Police chiefs must develop personal relationships with community leaders and people from all parts of their jurisdiction, well before any incident takes place. The work of building these relationships of mutual respect must be done constantly, and especially during "non-crisis" times. A critical incident is not the time to hold your first meeting with community leaders.

Many police chiefs believe that the Ferguson incident was a defining moment for the entire policing profession. As PERF President and Philadelphia Police Commissioner Charles Ramsey said at PERF's Defining Moments conference, "All of us have been in this business for a while, and we all have had incidents that fundamentally changed how we think about things. And sometimes there are incidents that occur outside our own jurisdictions that affect all of us."

At the request of PERF's Board of Directors, we extended the Defining Moments conference from one day to two days, in order to include a full discussion of the Ferguson incident, while maintaining our original plans to discuss a wide range of other defining moments.

The bulk of this document consists of quotations from police chiefs and other leaders who participated in our conference, and who offered valuable guidance about these issues.

I'd like to highlight one key issue that seems new to me; I haven't heard this discussed in previous PERF meetings. That is the question of whether we need police officers to take on a fundamentally different role than they have had in the past.

One central theme that grew out of the conference was the importance of developing a culture of policing that recognizes when officers should step in and when they should step back from encounters with the public. For example, in active shooter situations, we now expect officers to make split-second, life-or-death decisions when lives hang in the balance. (This goes against the pre-Columbine thinking, when officers were taught not to rush in but to assess the situation and get additional help.)

On the other hand, when the stakes are not high, when police are dealing with a relatively minor situation, we want police officers to recognize that stepping back from a contentious encounter and getting assistance from other officers is a sign of strength, not weakness. In these situations, slowing down the encounter and using de-escalation and crisis intervention skills can help prevent a relatively minor incident from cascading into a bad result that no one expected or wanted.

So there are times when we expect police to "step up," and times when we expect them to "step back," and knowing the difference may be as important a lesson as we can teach officers.

I believe you will find these discussions useful and interesting. The final chapter of this report summarizes the lessons we learned in this project.

Ferguson, Missouri: A National "Defining Moment" for Policing

The first day of PERF's conference on Defining Moments for Police Chiefs was devoted largely to a discussion of the issues raised by the August 9, 2014 shooting of Michael Brown in Ferguson, MO, and the handling of large-scale protests and riots that followed the shooting.

St. Louis County Police Chief Jon Belmar, whose department provided the bulk of the police officers responding to the incident, launched the discussion with a day-by-day summary of his thinking as he led the multi-agency response in the first few days of the protests.

Other chiefs then provided their analysis and perspectives.

St. Louis County Chief Jon Belmar: We Had 11 Days of Serious Rioting Without a Serious Injury to a Protester

I felt like I was pretty well positioned to understand how to deal with something like Ferguson. I was in tactical operations as a commander, and I was a patrolman back in the early '90s. I have good contacts in the communities. I go to the churches; I talk to my community leaders; I am engaged. I was from North St. Louis County, where Ferguson is located.

But when this happened, you have no idea how bad it can be, and how it can spin out of control unless you have gone through something like this before.

Taking this day by day, the Michael Brown shooting was on Saturday, August 9, at 12:02 P.M., and I got a call from Ferguson Police Chief Tom Jackson at about 12:25. He said he had a fatal officer-involved shooting and asked me to investigate it. I called my chief of the Tactical Operations Unit, who was down in South County at one of our hospitals, dealing with an armed invasion. I told him we had an officer-involved shooting up in Ferguson, and that he needed to get up there. I didn't hear anything until about 4:45 or 5 that afternoon, when the captain from Tactical Operations told me, "Boss, we have had a bad afternoon up here. We almost didn't get this crime scene processed. We had a lot of gun shots and people surrounding the body." He also told me that it took 4 ½ hours to process that crime scene.

I spent seven years as a lieutenant in robbery/homicide, and I believe that doing a crime scene the right way is an absolute. I also believe that if I had this one to do over again, I would have at least thought about moving Mr. Brown faster. But I don't think we could have done it much faster. It's easy to say, "Remove the body and go." But it's also easy to imagine people asking me later, "Why didn't you do a comprehensive investigation of the crime scene?"

The next day, on Sunday, August 10, I called my TAC commander Bryan Ludwig, who asked me, "Chief, what do you want down there today?"

I said, "Let me explain what I *don't* want." I said, "I don't want any trucks, I don't want anything other than the uniform of the day. I don't want any armor; I don't want any fatigues. And I want you guys staged way offside. Perhaps we will have a problem; let's hope we don't."

I got a call about 8:25 Sunday night from Ludwig's boss, Lt. Colonel Michael Dierkes, who's in charge of special operations. He was in Ludwig's Tahoe and he said, "Boss, we got a problem down here; we may have to go to gas."

I said, "Please don't do that," and then I thought about it for a second and said, "Mike, I'm not there; use your best judgment." What I didn't know was that while he was talking to me, a piece of a cinderblock was skipping off the Tahoe and into the windshield.

In 35 minutes I stepped down onto West Florissant Avenue, and there were probably 200 police cars parked all over the place, and the crowd was angry.

We made a conscious decision not to go into the crowd with night sticks and start locking people up. There was a lot of looting going on, but there were so many people, we really didn't understand the breadth of what was happening.

I really only did two things that night. I talked to each one of my police officers and told them to maintain their bearing. And I tried to calm people down. I saw ministers I knew, government people, activists that I knew, and I was telling them, "At some point, we are going to have to insist that everybody leave." But they told me, "We have no control. These young people aren't going to listen to us."

So obviously we were thinking at this point that we had a problem.

On Monday, August 11, there was shooting going on and reports of police cars getting rocked, and we had to use tear gas in West Florissant to disperse the crowd, but we weren't making a lot of arrests. On Tuesday, August 12, there were a lot of people on the corridor, a lot of activity. We left them alone, they left us alone, and they were able to demonstrate. A woman was shot in the head at Highmont in West Florissant about 11. And there were about 200 people at West Florissant and Chambers. They started breaking out some windows, so we went down there but we decided not to use tear gas.

Wednesday, August 13, was a nightmare. At the end of the day, I went back to the command post and met with the St. Louis City police commanders, my commanders, the Highway Patrol

commanders who had all been with me on this since Day One, and I said, "Ladies and gentlemen, we have got to do something different. We cannot sustain this night after night. We have to come up with a new strategy. Everybody go home tonight and I want you think about how we are going to do this differently tomorrow night."

But the next day, the Governor came in and relieved me, and put Captain Ron Johnson of the Highway Patrol in charge.

In the end, there were five shootings within the demonstration corridor over 11 days. But I would talk to the news media and ask, "Do you have any questions about the activity we are dealing with after nightfall?" But the media didn't want to talk what we were dealing with night after night. All they cared about was the criminal investigation into Mr. Brown's death, which I couldn't talk about.

I understand that the use of tear gas looks terrible on TV. My father is an 82-year-old Korean War veteran who loves his son, but on Day 4, he said to me, "Son, that tear gas didn't look good down there on West Florissant." I said, "Dad, I know, and it looks worse in person."

But I am unaware of a death attributed to CS tear gas in the United States. Police sometimes kill people with nightsticks, mace, police dogs, bullets, and everything else. But we didn't send anybody to the emergency room with a serious injury over 11 days of serious rioting.

St. Louis Chief Sam Dotson: Our Community Relationships Helped Us When We Had an OIS After the Brown Shooting

Chief Dotson discussed a fatal officer-involved shooting in St. Louis on August 19, 10 days after the Michael Brown shooting in Ferguson and not far from where the Ferguson shooting occurred. In the St. Louis incident, officers shot Kajieme Powell, who was holding a knife and behaving erratically. The shooting was captured on video by a bystander.[1]

We received a call about a person acting erratically with a knife who has just stolen some items from a convenience store. The young man went into the store, took a couple energy drinks and got no response from the clerks. A couple minutes later he went back in, stole a package of donuts, and it almost looked like he was looking for a response. He went outside and continued to pace around, talking to himself, until the shopkeeper finally came out and asked him to pay for the donuts. The officers arrived, and all they knew when they arrived was that a larceny had occurred and there was a subject armed with a knife.

When they stepped out of the car, the suspect immediately approached them with the knife, yelling, "Shoot me, kill me now." First he moved towards the officer who had been driving, then he backed up and walked toward the officer who had been on the passenger side. By this time, the officers were out of the vehicle, had their weapons drawn, and were repeatedly giving the verbal commands, "Stop, put the knife down, police, stop, put the knife down." The suspect was closing the distance between them, and both of the officers shot him.

This happened about a mile and a half from where the Michael Brown shooting happened, 10 days after that shooting. So no one would believe me if I said I wasn't thinking about Ferguson as I drove to this scene.

One of the lessons I had learned from Ferguson was that it's important to get your story out there as soon as you can. So I made a statement to the media at the scene of the shooting. I made several mistakes through all of this, but the one I want to talk about most was that I didn't put a large enough disclaimer in front of my comments in my initial briefing. I said something like, "This is what we know at this point; we'll provide more information as soon as it's available." That statement should have been stronger, because we all know that some of the first information we get about a critical incident can later turn out to be wrong.

At the time of the news briefing, we didn't know it, but there was a cell-phone video of the shooting. We found out about the video eight or nine hours later.

We had national media as well as local reporters at the briefing, and everyone was interested in linking the shooting to Ferguson. But there also was a sense of allowing us to tell the story, because we have some very strong relationships with the community, and we had two Aldermen with me there. In fact, one of the 911 callers was an Alderwoman who happened to be at the scene and had seen Kajieme Powell with the knife, so she called the police.

I found out about the cell phone video that evening. An attorney for the person who took the video was shopping it around and wouldn't give us a copy until 9 the next morning. So we were ready the next morning, and as soon as we received it, we reviewed it and decided that nobody could tell our story better than we could. So we put together the cell phone video, which caught the entire incident, and surveillance video from the convenience store, along with the 911 calls from the Alderwoman and the store owner, and the dispatch tapes, so everyone would know exactly what the officers knew as they were arriving on the scene.

Obviously if a man is walking up and down the street and says, "Shoot me now; kill me now," there will be questions about mental illness, but I wanted the public to know that the officers arrived only with the information they were provided by the 911 callers and the dispatchers. And it was only 15 seconds from the time the first officer's foot hits the pavement to the first shot that's fired. In 15 seconds they had to make decisions about the course of action they were going to use.

One of the lessons we learned from the police shooting of Kajieme Powell was that it's important to have your narrative heard. But in our rush to push information out, there were slight misstatements that were problematic. Witnesses told us that Mr. Powell made an overhand motion with the knife, and I repeated that to the media, but the video did not show that. So in retrospect, I should have made a larger disclaimer at the briefing, and said that this was just preliminary information that we received, and sometimes the early information turns out to be incorrect.

We were not completely without protests in St. Louis about the Powell shooting, but they were smaller, they didn't last as long, and the dynamic was different. We didn't see a large group of out-of-town people, the anarchists and others like that. The protesters we saw were local people whom we knew and had relationships with. Our community out-reach and our existing relationships with the community helped us.

Philadelphia Commissioner Chuck Ramsey: Ferguson Brought Attention to Issues That We All Should Be Addressing

Thank you both for the presentations. It was very enlightening and you made us aware of a lot of things that we didn't know about. What happened in Ferguson is the kind of incident that could have happened in many of our towns and cities in America. We can debate whether it would have had the same outcome, but it could have happened just about anywhere, I believe.

I hope we can focus on the larger issues that have surfaced as a result. For example, we've been hearing a lot about the "militarization" of police. As [Milwaukee Chief] Ed Flynn said, there is no real definition for it, but everybody visualizes for themselves what it means, and it's usually not positive as far as how policing is viewed as a profession.

So we need to talk about that, because there is a legitimate argument about the kind of equipment that we are getting into our inventory, and more importantly, the policies that we have about the circumstances under which equipment should be deployed. Do all departments need the kind of equipment that we see—MRAPs (Mine-Resistant Ambush Protected) and things of that nature? If you are going to have that kind of equipment available, especially in smaller jurisdictions, there should be a more regional approach, as opposed to individual agencies having all this equipment. I think that's a legitimate discussion that we need to have.

Another issue coming out of Ferguson—use of force—is one that we talk about all the time. We need to consider use of force not only from the standpoint of what officers deal with on an everyday basis, but also with regard to handling large demonstrations that include some violent elements. And it gets more complicated when you have multiple jurisdictions that are coming together because of a major incident. We need to discuss issues like whose authority do they fall under? Which agency's use-of-force policies control the response? What kind of equipment do you want them to bring, and what you do *not* want them to bring.

Another issue that has changed things is social media. Nearly everybody has a cell phone camera, so whenever something happens, I tend to assume there is a video somewhere. But one problem with videos is that often they don't capture the beginning of an incident—the events that started the whole thing. The camera typically is turned on sometime after the point where a situation has started to go bad, so often there is a lack of context.

We cannot ignore the fact that we have not achieved legitimacy in some of our more challenged neighborhoods. We have to go [to] back the drawing board and come up with different strategies to reach folks in these challenged neighborhoods. We can pat ourselves on the back and talk about how far we have come in reducing crime and establishing community policing, but we haven't come far enough. Ferguson isn't just about the shooting. It is about the tension and the issues that have been in existence for decades, and the reality of things that have happened to people over the years, some of which police have been very much responsible for.

So we have to recognize that and deal with it. We have got to take community policing to a different level. It's not one-size-fits-all; we must find a different way of reaching poor communities, communities of color, communities that are more challenged than others, if we really want to make progress.

It is not as simple as merely having diversity. When I was chief in DC, the MPD had 63 percent African-American police officers, but we still had tension and issues in our more challenged neighborhoods. Diversity is important, don't get me wrong, but we have to dig deeper. Having officers who look like the folks in the community in itself is not enough. We need to take a different look at community policing and what are we trying to achieve, or we will continue to have these incidents.

Note

1. https://www.youtube.com/watch?v5sEuZiTcbGCg

Critical Thinking

1. If a police officer steps back from a situation rather than taking immediate control, doesn't that convey weakness?

2. Chief Belmar said they had 11 days of rioting without a serious injury to a protester. What do you think about the fact that the rioting went on for 11 days?

3. What do you think about Commissioner Ramsey's comments about diversity?

Internet References

DOJ Report on Ferguson Police Department
http://www.justice.gov/sites/default/files/opa/press-releases/attachments/2015/03/04/ferguson_police_department_report.pdf

Police Executive Research Forum
http://www.policeforum.org/assets/definingmoments.pdf

Article   Prepared by: Joanne Naughton

The Supreme Court's Utah v. Strieff Decision and the Fourth Amendment

JOSHUA WAIMBERG

Learning Outcomes

After reading this article, you will be able to:

- Explain the Court's recent decision interpreting the exclusionary rule.

- Show how the decision will affect police work.

On Monday, the Supreme Court handed down a decision in *Utah v. Strieff*, involving the intricacies of the Fourth Amendment's search and seizure doctrine, and the accompanying exclusionary rule. In a 5-3 opinion written by Justice Clarence Thomas, the Court held that the evidence obtained from an unlawful police stop would not be excluded from court because the link between the stop and the evidence's discovery was "attenuated" by the discovery of an outstanding warrant during the stop.

The *Strieff* case arose from a 2006 incident where the police received an anonymous tip that drugs were being sold out of a Salt Lake City house. After observing the property for suspicious activity for the next week, Officer Douglas Fackrell stopped and detained Edward Strieff, Jr. as he was leaving the house. Officer Fackrell ran Strieff's identification, and discovered that Strieff had an outstanding arrest warrant for a traffic violation. When Strieff was searched incident to his arrest under the warrant, methamphetamines and drug paraphernalia was discovered in his pockets. Strieff was then charged with drug-related offenses.

Strieff argued that the evidence discovered on him should be suppressed because the police officer had no reasonable suspicion to stop him the first place. Under the exclusionary rule, when a police officer unlawfully stops an individual, the evidence obtained illegally is tainted and cannot be used in trial. Strieff argued that because the evidence was found during an illegal stop, the evidence was tainted and should be suppressed.

The state countered by arguing that the exclusionary rule should not apply because the existence of the warrant was an intervening event that broke the chain of causation between the illegal stop and the discovery of evidence during the search incident to arrest. The state said that because the arrest was based on the legal warrant, and not the illegal stop, the warrant was the proximate cause of the discovery.

The Utah Supreme Court sided with Strieff and ordered the evidence suppressed. They found that this incident did not fall within the attenuation exception to the exclusionary rule—an exception which allows for the use of evidence found unlawfully if the connection between the misconduct and the evidence's discovery is weak.

Justice Thomas, joined by Chief Justice John Roberts, Justice Anthony Kennedy, Justice Samuel Alito, and (surprisingly) Justice Stephen Breyer, reversed the Utah Supreme Court's decision. The majority wrote that if an officer makes an illegal stop and then discovers an arrest warrant, the stop and its fruit will not be excluded in court. However, if there was "flagrant police misconduct," which there wasn't in this case, then the exclusionary rule would apply.

Justice Thomas wrote, that,

> While Officer Fackrell's decision to initiate the stop was mistaken, his conduct thereafter was lawful. The officer's decision to run the warrant check was a 'negligibly burdensome precautio[n]' for officer safety . . . . And Officer Fackrell's actual search of Strieff was a lawful search incident to arrest . . .

> Moreover, there is no indication that this unlawful stop was part of any systemic or recurrent police misconduct. To the contrary, all the evidence suggests that the stop was an isolated instance of negligence that occurred in

connection with a bona-fide investigation of a suspected drug house . . .

Applying these factors, we hold that the evidence discovered on Strieff's person was admissible because the unlawful stop was sufficiently attenuated by the pre-existing arrest warrant. Although the illegal stop was close in time to Strieff's arrest, that consideration is outweighed by two factors supporting the State. The outstanding arrest warrant for Strieff's arrest is a critical intervening circumstance that is wholly independent of the illegal stop. The discovery of that warrant broke the causal chain between the unconstitutional stop and the discovery of evidence by compelling Officer Fackrell to arrest Strieff. And, it is especially significant that there is no evidence that Officer Fackrell's illegal stop reflected flagrantly unlawful police misconduct.

In a scathing dissent, Justice Sonia Sotomayor, joined in part by Justice Ruth Bader Ginsburg, concluded by writing:

By legitimizing the conduct that produces this double consciousness, this case tells everyone, white and black, guilty and innocent, that an officer can verify your legal status at any time. It says that your body is subject to invasion while courts excuse the violation of your rights. It implies that you are not a citizen of a democracy but the subject of a carceral state, just waiting to be cataloged.

We must not pretend that the countless people who are routinely targeted by police are "isolated." They are the canaries in the coal mine whose deaths, civil and literal, warn us that no one can breathe in this atmosphere. They are the ones who recognize that unlawful police stops corrode all our civil liberties and threaten all our lives. Until their voices matter too, our justice system will continue to be anything but.

Justice Elena Kagan also wrote a dissent of her own, and was also joined by Justice Ginsburg. She wrote that the majority's decision:

[C]reates unfortunate incentives for the police—indeed, practically invites them to do what Fackrell did here. Consider an officer who, like Fackrell, wishes to stop someone for investigative reasons, but does not have what a court would view as reasonable suspicion. If the officer believes that any evidence he discovers will be inadmissible, he is likely to think the unlawful stop not worth making—precisely the deterrence the exclusionary rule is meant to achieve. But when he is told of today's decision? Now the officer knows that the stop may well yield admissible evidence: So long as the target is one of the many millions of people in this country with an outstanding arrest warrant, anything the officer finds in a search is fair game for use in a criminal prosecution. The officer's incentive to violate the Constitution thus increases: From here on, he sees potential advantage in stopping individuals without reasonable suspicion—exactly the temptation the exclusionary rule is supposed to remove. Because the majority thus places Fourth Amendment protections at risk, I respectfully dissent.

Critical Thinking

1. Do you agree with Justice Thomas' reasoning?
2. Do you agree with Justice Sotomayor's criticism of the decision?
3. Do you agree with Justice Kagan's dissent?

Internet References

National Constitution Center
http://constitutioncenter.org/interactive-constitution/amendments/amendment-iv

Supreme Court of the United States
https://www.supremecourt.gov/opinions/15pdf/14-1373_83i7.pdf

JOSHUA WAIMBERG is a legal fellow at the National Constitution Center.

Article

Prepared by: Joanne Naughton

Excited Delirium and the Dual Response: Preventing In-Custody Deaths

BRIAN ROACH, KELSEY ECHOLS, AND AARON BURNETT

Learning Outcomes

After reading this article, you will be able to:

- Define excited delirium syndrome and show how it occurs.
- Specify the risk factors associated with ExDS.
- State the treatments to be used when the situation occurs.

Excited delirium syndrome (ExDS) is a serious and potentially deadly medical condition involving psychotic behavior, elevated temperature, and an extreme fight-or-flight response by the nervous system. Failure to recognize the symptoms and involve emergency medical services (EMS) to provide appropriate medical treatment may lead to death. Fatality rates of up to 10 percent in ExDS cases have been reported.[1] In addition to the significant morbidity and mortality associated with unrecognized ExDS, a substantial risk for litigation exists. These patients often die within 1 hour of police involvement. One study showed 75 percent of deaths from ExDS occurred at the scene or during transport.[2] Law enforcement organizations should take steps to increase officer awareness of ExDS and its symptoms and develop procedures to engage the medical community when identified. Without placing themselves or others at a greater risk for physical harm, officers must be able to rapidly detect symptoms of ExDS and immediately engage EMS for proper diagnosis and medical treatment. Failure to do so may prove fatal.

Historical Data and Cases Reviewed

Reports of presentations consistent with ExDS have occurred for more than 150 years. In 1849 Dr. Luther Bell, a psychiatrist

in Massachusetts, described an acute exhaustive mania (Bell's Mania) in which patients developed hallucinations, profound agitation, and fever, which often were followed by death.[3] A decrease in reports occurred in the 1950s that coincided with the advent of antipsychotic medications and then an increase again in the 1980s likely secondary to widespread cocaine use. At that time, there were several reports in which an intoxicated person or an individual with mental illness exhibited aggression, hallucinations, and insensitivity to pain; was physically restrained (often in a prone position); and then died in custody.

In the last 20 years, law enforcement officers have seen this syndrome repeatedly. Several cases were outlined by a special panel review on ExDS at Penn State.[4]

Excited delirium-associated death after handcuffing/ Hog-tying. In October 2005 a West Palm Beach, Florida, police officer found a shirtless and distraught man stumbling on the road and attempting to stop vehicles. Told to relax, the man kept gesticulating wildly with vehicles stopping to avoid him. After a struggle the officer placed the man in a prone position and handcuffed him. Other officers arrived, helped move the man out of the street, and further restrained him by hog-tying his legs and hands. The man later became unconscious. Responding paramedics failed to resuscitate him. The chief medical examiner for Palm Beach County determined the cause of death was "sudden respiratory arrest following physical struggling restraint due to cocaine-induced ExDS."

Excited delirium-associated death after major physical struggle. A panel member who also serves as a Vancouver Police Department sergeant related the case of officers responding to a male subject who had a knife in a street confrontation. A foot chase ensued with police grounding the subject and multiple officers restraining him. The sergeant stated,

"The subject was so resistive and so strong that he lifted five officers off of him at one point." After a protracted struggle, the subject suddenly was quiet, went into cardiac arrest, and died at the scene. The subject suffered from mental illness and had alcohol and marijuana in his system. An autopsy concluded the subject died from choking due to the officer's restraint, and the coroner ruled the death accidental.

Excited delirium-associated death after TASER use. According to press reports, Dallas, Texas, police found a 23-year-old male subject in his underwear, screaming and holding a knife on a neighbor's porch on April 24, 2006. The man refused English and Spanish instructions and came at the officers with the knife. One officer fired a TASER, which failed to connect. A second shot did, causing electrical shock. A third was reportedly fired. After being handcuffed on an ambulance backboard, the subject stopped breathing and was pronounced dead at a hospital. The Dallas County medical examiner attributed the death to "excited delirium."

Excited delirium-associated death with no police presence. Certainly, the cases cited in the 1849 paper by Dr. Luther Bell in the *Journal of Insanity* had no police presence. Most recently, a case occurred involving an Anderson University basketball player. An Anderson County, Indiana, coroner "said [the man] had complained of cramps and vision problems just before he collapsed on a campus basketball court September 30 and had an 'extremely elevated body temperature' when he was rushed to the emergency room of AnMed Health Medical Center. The man's death days later was caused by 'acute drug toxicity with ExDS that led to multiple organ failure.'"[5]

Further, an expert panel convened by the American College of Emergency Physicians recognized ExDS as a unique clinical syndrome amenable to early therapeutic interventions.[6] This article provides a scientific background for ExDS, outlines risk factors, clarifies identification of the syndrome based on common signs and symptoms, and discusses control and sedation of affected individuals.

Medical Background

The mechanism in which ExDS occurs is complex and not fully understood; however, recent research has provided greater insight. Although cocaine use is associated with ExDS, postmortem cocaine levels in those who have died after ExDS are similar to those of recreational cocaine users and lower than individuals who have died from heart attacks or other non-ExDS causes after cocaine use.[7] These findings suggest that cocaine intoxication alone does not cause ExDS. Further, a degree of cellular or genetic susceptibility may exist that leads some cocaine users to develop ExDS while others do not.

Researchers began to explore other mechanisms for ExDS, and the central dopamine theory emerged as a leading hypothesis.

Dopamine is a neurotransmitter with many functions. It plays a role in the brain's perception of reward and temperature regulation. Increased dopamine levels result in fast heart rates, feelings of euphoria, and hallucinations. Highly addictive drugs, specifically cocaine and methamphetamine, increase the level of dopamine in the brain. Schizophrenia also results in elevated levels of dopamine in the brain, and antipsychotics work to treat hallucinations by blocking dopamine on a cellular level. In chronic cocaine abusers who have died of ExDS, research has shown a loss of a crucial protein that eliminates dopamine from the brain. This loss results in increased dopamine levels and chaotic signaling in the brain. The elevated dopamine levels help explain some of the similarities between ExDS and schizophrenia (e.g., hallucinations, paranoia), but they do not account for the high rates of sudden cardiac arrest seen in the former but not the latter.

Clinical Presentation

The clinical presentation of excited delirium has distinct and recognizable features. Much of what is used to identify excited delirium both on the street and in the hospital is based on case reports that have identified common clinical features, patient behaviors, and historical factors. In 2009, the American College of Emergency Physicians Task Force on Excited Delirium established that both delirium (e.g., acute confusion, hallucinations, and disorientation that is rapid in onset and may fluctuate in intensity) and an excited or agitated state must be present to consider ExDS.[8] Previously published cases identified common sequences of events, typically involving "acute drug intoxication or a history of mental illness, a struggle with law enforcement, physical or noxious chemical control measures or electrical control device (ECD) application, sudden and unexpected death, and an autopsy which fails to reveal a definite cause of death from trauma or natural disease."[9]

ExDS subjects typically are males around the age of 30, and most have a history of psychostimulant use or mental illness (see Table 1). Law enforcement agents or EMS personnel often are called to the scene because of public disturbances, agitation, or bizarre behaviors. Subjects are usually violent and combative with hallucinations, paranoia, or fear. Additionally, subjects may demonstrate profound levels of strength, resist painful stimuli or physical restraint, and seem impervious to self-inflicted injuries. This information becomes particularly important to law enforcement personnel who may use techniques intended to gain control and custody of subjects through physical means, chemical agents, or ECDs. During initial assessment patients often are noted to have elevated body temperatures, fast heart rates, rapid breathing, elevated blood pressures, and sweaty skin.

Risk Factors Associated with Excited Delirium Syndrome

Males (average age 36)

Stimulant drug use
- Cocaine and to a lesser extent methamphetamine, PCP, and LSD

  Chronic users after an acute binge

  Preexisting psychiatric disorder
- Schizophrenia, bipolar disorder

Certain medical conditions have presented similarly to ExDS, including low blood sugar, thyroid abnormalities, and decompensated psychiatric illness. Methamphetamine, cocaine, PCP, and bath salt intoxication are associated with ExDS, but not every intoxicated individual develops it. Intoxication without ExDS will lack elevated body temperatures and certain laboratory abnormalities, such as metabolic acidosis. Severe sweating, a clue that a patient has an elevated temperature, combined with hallucinations always should prompt a consideration of ExDS. Differentiating ExDS from other medical causes or uncomplicated intoxication can prove difficult, but a prudent course is to assume the worst and bring patients to the hospital via EMS for evaluation by a physician.

Treatments

When subjects are identified as potentially exhibiting excited delirium, rapid control of the situation, and timely execution of medical evaluation are important. Protocols vary by region according to local EMS policies and in many cases are driven by consensus opinions. Subjects with excited delirium often do not respond to verbal redirection. Additionally, attempts at physical control may not be as effective given extreme levels of strength and resistance to painful stimuli. Ongoing physical struggle can worsen a subject's innate fight-or-flight system, which can raise a patient's temperature, cause changes in the body's acid-base balance, and increase the risk of sudden death.

Medications are required to sedate ExDS patients to expedite the medical evaluation, decrease their fight-or-flight response, and avoid further harm to both the subject and those involved in the patient's care. Several classes of medications are available, as well as different routes of administration, including intranasal, intramuscular, and intravenous. Advanced life support EMS personnel capable of cardiac monitoring, advanced airway management, and medical resuscitation should be present

at the time of administration. Common medications include benzodiazepines (e.g., lorazepam, midazolam, and diazepam), antipsychotics (e.g., haloperidol, droperidol, olanzapine, and ziprasidone), and the dissociative agent ketamine. Benzodiazepines are very safe but are limited by varying dose requirements from patient to patient, as well as variable time until adequate sedation. Antipsychotics often are more useful in subjects presenting with acute exacerbations of psychiatric illness but are plagued by warnings about potential cardiac side effects and prolonged time until onset.

Ketamine is a unique medication that may play a larger role in the initial treatment of patients with excited delirium. It is characterized by a rapid onset of action (less than 5 minutes), stable effects on blood pressure, consistent ability to provide adequate sedation, and, in general, it maintains the subject's ability to breathe. Potential side effects include hallucinations and confusion as the medication wears off (10 to 20 percent of adults 30 to 120 minutes after administration), vocal cord spasm, and increased salivation. A recent study published by Regions Hospital EMS in St. Paul, Minnesota, reviewed 13 cases between April and December 2011 where ketamine was administered prior to hospital arrival for excited delirium.[10] This review further supports ketamine as an effective prehospital treatment of the ExDS patient. Peak sedation was achieved in less than 5 minutes in 11 of 13 cases. Moderate or deeper sedation was achieved in 12 of 13 patients. However, ketamine is a powerful medication, and ExDS is a life-threatening condition. Three patients developed low oxygen saturations. Two required endotracheal intubation, and one was assisted with a bag-valve mask. Three patients experienced emergent reactions, two of which were successfully treated with low doses of benzodiazepines. There were no deaths.

Conclusion

In summary, excited delirium is becoming increasingly recognized as an important medical emergency encountered in the prehospital environment. Law enforcement agencies should undertake a concerted effort to increase awareness among officers of ExDS to include information to help identify symptoms and to establish protocols to engage the medical community. Armed with this information, officers will be in a better position to engage EMS for an urgent evaluation, treatment, and transport to the hospital. Using teamwork to safely and efficiently control these patients will lead to improved outcomes. Promising research is being conducted regarding the underlying mechanisms of this disease, as well as new methods of treatment, including ketamine, which may improve the ability to care for these patients.

Notes

1. M.D. Sztajnkrycer and A.A. Baez, "Cocaine, Excited Delirium, and Sudden Unexpected Death," *EMS World,* April 2005 (updated January 11, 2011), http://www.emsworld.com/article/article.jsp?id51863 (accessed April 30, 2014).

2. D.L. Ross, "Factors Associated with Excited Delirium Deaths in Police Custody," *Modern Pathology* 11 (1998): 1127–1137.

3. L. Bell, "Acute Exhaustive Mania," *American Journal of Psychiatry* (October 1849).

4. Information regarding these cases is derived from the National Institute of Justice Weapons and Protective Systems Technologies Center, "Special Panel Review of Excited Delirium, December 2011," https://www.justnet.org/pdf/ExDS-Panel-Report-FINAL.pdf (accessed April 14, 2014).

5. As reported by N. Mayo, *Independent Mail* (November 15, 2011).

6. American College of Emergency Physicians Excited Delirium Task Force, "White Paper Report on Excited Delirium Syndrome, September, 10, 2009: Report to the Council and Board of Directors on Excited Delirium at the Direction of Amended Resolution 21(08)," http://www.fmhac.net/Assets/Documents/2012/Presentations/KrelsteinExcitedDelirium.pdf (accessed April 14, 2014).

7. D.C. Mash, L. Duque, J. Pablo, Y. Qin, N. Adi, W. Hearn, B. Hyma, S. Karch, H. Druid, and C. Wetli, "Brain Biomarkers for Identifying Excited Delirium as a Cause of Sudden Death," *Forensic Science International* 190 (2009): e13-e19.

8. American College of Emergency Physicians Excited Delirium Task Force.

9. American College of Emergency Physicians Excited Delirium Task Force.

10. A.M. Burnett, J.G. Salzman, K.R. Griffith, B. Kroeger, and R.J. Frascone, "The Emergency Department Experience with Prehospital Ketamine: A Case Series of 13 Patients," *Prehospital Emergency Care* 16 (2012):1–7.

Critical Thinking

1. Are there other medical conditions that appear to be similar to ExDS?

2. What types of situations will often result in law enforcement or EMS being called?

3. How should law enforcement agencies treat this issue?

Internet References

American College of Emergency Physicians Excited Delirium Task Force

http://www.fmhac.net/Assets/Documents/2012/Presentations/KrelsteinExcitedDelirium.pdf (accessed April 14, 2014).

EMS World

http://www.emsworld.com/article/10324064/cocaine-excited-delirium-and-sudden-unexpected-death

Federal Bureau of Investigation, 2014.

Unit 4

UNIT

Prepared by: Joanne Naughton

The Judicial System

The courts are an equal partner in the American justice system. Just as the police have the responsibility of guarding our liberties by enforcing the laws, and prosecutors have the obligation to do justice rather than merely win cases, the courts play an important role in defending these liberties by applying and interpreting these laws, with the goal of attaining justice. The courts are the battlegrounds where civilized "wars" are fought without bloodshed, to protect individual rights and to settle disputes.

Courts must be vigilant to guard against the use of improper evidence obtained from violations of Constitutional rights, such as a suspect's right to remain silent, to be free from illegal searches, or to have legal counsel. Today, DNA testing of evidence seems almost routine, and in some cases it is capable of providing foolproof evidence of a suspect's guilt or innocence. But DNA testing in old cases too often highlights the tragedy of defendants having been convicted of crimes they didn't commit.

Our judicial process is an adversary system of justice, where the state is always represented by counsel, and the defendant's need for counsel is recognized in the Constitution.

Article   Prepared by: Joanne Naughton

Court Conundrum: Offenders Who Can't Pay, or Won't

SHAILA DEWAN

Learning Outcomes

After reading this article, you will be able to:

- See how Judge Diment explained his actions.
- State what the United States Supreme Court has held regarding the inability of poor people to pay a fine.
- Learn that the question of ability to pay can be difficult to determine.

Bowdon, Georgia—A few weeks ago, a courtroom cellphone video came to light in which Richard A. Diment, the longtime Municipal Court judge here, threatened to jail traffic offenders who failed to come up with enough money to apply to their fines. "Until you get $300 here tonight, you won't be able to leave," he told one defendant.

The response was swift and ugly. Judge Diment—he is white, while the defendants pictured were black and Hispanic—was called a good old boy, a racist, and worse. Threatening phone calls and emails rolled in. The furor was such that he briefly considered turning in his resignation.

Instead, he decided to explain himself. In an interview, the judge said he had never actually jailed anyone for failing to come up with money. The words were an empty threat intended to pressure people to pay their fines.

"I am not the ogre that that edited video is making me out to be," he said. "If they do not come up with any money, they're released. It's my way of determining whether they can pay or not."

It is rare for a municipal judge to submit to questions about his courtroom practices. But in granting an interview this month at his law office in nearby Carrollton, the judge delved into a relatively unexamined question about the legal system today: how to determine whether offenders are unable, or simply unwilling, to pay their penalties.

At a time when many jurisdictions are facing sharp questions about whether they are being overly aggressive in collecting court fines and fees from the poor, and sometimes jailing those who cannot pay, that question is hardly an idle one. The United States Supreme Court has held that the poor cannot be jailed solely for inability to pay a fine. But it has left somewhat open the question of how to determine if they can't, or won't.

Civil rights advocates envision a thorough consideration of income, assets, living expenses and debt, and say such hearings rarely occur. Judges, on the other hand, have been known to base their determinations on things like whether the defendant is wearing expensive shoes.

A test like Judge Diment's—if individuals can pay, they will once threatened with jail, he asserts—is not unheard-of. Nor, for that matter, is jailing those who cannot pay: A new report by the American Civil Liberties Union in New Hampshire found that the state's taxpayers paid $167,000 in 2013 to jail people who owed $76,000.

The question of ability to pay can be thorny, whether courts decline to consider it or try to do so. In Nashville, where millions in fines have gone uncollected, a special "indigency docket" has raised questions about whether waivers of court debt are too freely granted.

Sarah Geraghty, a lawyer with the Southern Center for Human Rights, which helped persuade Bowdon to change its practices after the video of Judge Diment came to light, said his test met neither the spirit nor the letter of the Supreme Court's rulings, even if no one was jailed.

"It's equally unacceptable to use deceit and trickery to coerce poor people to pay their last dollar to their city court traffic fines," she said.

The changes in Bowdon include advising defendants of a right to counsel before entering a plea, and abolishing the practice of requiring immediate payment under threat of jail. The city also agreed to stop requiring defendants to ask friends and family to pay their fines.

But Judge Diment said an examination of a defendant's income and expenses would be "a hollow sort of inquiry."

"It's well intentioned, but in my world—in the real world—that's an impractical endeavor in many cases, because experience has shown that the vast majority of these low-income people are still able to struggle and pay their fines in some form or another," he said. "Whereas if you were to look at them on the front end and determine whether they have the ability to pay, it would look like they don't."

Ordering community service is another option, but it can be a heavy burden for people who work or have family duties, the judge added.

Moreover, he said, waiving one poor defendant's fines would not be fair to others who managed to pay theirs.

"Many people are not going to do what they're supposed to do unless you apply pressure," Judge Diment said. He asserted that very few people he threatened with jail had failed to come up with at least part of the money.

Still, the judge said, he has often used his discretion to lower fines or convert them to community service. In the video, he lops $500 off one man's fine because the man had already spent a month in jail.

Judge Diment, 60, the father of four grown children, has served as judge in Bowdon for 22 years. He presides once a month, for which he receives $400, in a makeshift courtroom with three rows of folding chairs. After the video surfaced, many of his critics complained that as a real estate lawyer in private practice, with a passion for historical preservation, he had no business being a judge. When he was hired, he exceeded the qualifications for municipal judges in Georgia, who were not required at the time to have a law degree.

Coming to her father's defense in a lengthy email, Ellis Diment, a lawyer in Austin, Texas, described him as a proponent of civil rights, a lover of Carl Sagan and a supporter of President Obama.

"I have been with my father in public multiple times when someone has approached him to thank him for his leniency on her in court," she wrote.

In Bowdon, fines make up 3.8 percent of the budget, a figure much lower than the average for Georgia cities of similar size.

Judge Diment said he was well aware that most defendants in Bowdon are poor, and that many of their offenses, such as driving without insurance, "arise from their unfair economic circumstances."

"It weighs heavily on my heart every single time I go to court," he said. "I'm worried about being fair to everyone, and I'm exhausted when I go out."

The key United States Supreme Court ruling dealing with unpaid fines, in *Bearden v. Georgia* in 1983, written by Justice Sandra Day O'Connor, holds that a defendant must make bona fide efforts to seek employment or borrow the money, Judge Diment pointed out.

But the case does not address questions about whom defendants should ask for a loan and whether they should be forced to accept onerous terms.

Ideally, said Judith Resnik, a constitutional scholar at Yale Law School, the judiciary should develop standards for ability-to-pay hearings.

"I don't think you should read Justice O'Connor's opinion as saying, 'Implement this by threatening jail,' " Ms. Resnik said.

Judge Diment said he had other considerations when he pressured defendants to increase their initial payment, a practice he said he reserved for serious cases like driving on a suspended license or drunken driving. The more they pay right away, he said, the less time they spend on probation, and the less they spend on probation fees.

In Georgia, many defendants who are unable to pay the full amount of their fines are placed on probation as a means of collecting the debt; the monthly probation fee in Bowdon is $44.

"That's what I mean on the video by 'The more you come up with, the better it will be for you,' " the judge said. "I realize it takes grocery money away from them, but that's money that they are going to have to pay anyway."

In the video, taken in early 2014, the judge can be seen telling one defendant, "We're going to keep you in the jail until you come up with $150." That defendant was Leandro Gill, 40, who at the time was unemployed and now makes $8 an hour at a grocery store.

That night in court, Mr. Gill called his mother, who was sick with terminal cancer and living on disability checks. She agreed to mail in the $150. "That was her money to pay her bills with, but she sacrificed it to keep me from going to jail," he said. His mother died in April.

Once he told Judge Diment that the check would be in the mail, he said, he was permitted to leave.

Correction: September 30, 2015

An article on Sunday about Richard A. Diment, a municipal judge in Georgia who threatened to jail traffic offenders who failed to pay their fines, included outdated information about the qualifications for such judgeships. Georgia now requires all newly appointed municipal court judges to be lawyers, a change from the past when no law degree was necessary.

Critical Thinking

1. What do you think about Sarah Geraghty's statement regarding Judge Diment's test?

2. Do you agree with Judge Diment when he says an examination of a defendant's income and expenses would be "a hollow sort of inquiry?"

3. Should poor people who have violated traffic laws go into debt to pay fines?

Internet References

ACLU

http://aclu-nh.org/wp-content/uploads/2015/09/Final-ACLU-Debtors-Prisons-Report-9.23.15.pdf

Findlaw

http://caselaw.findlaw.com/us-supreme-court/461/660.html

WSMV

http://www.wsmv.com/story/29738597/waived-fines-in-nashville-totaled-62-million-in-2014

Youtube

https://www.youtube.com/watch?v=6bjzIXUpl_g

Article   Prepared by: Joanne Naughton

US Supreme Court to Police: To Search a Cell Phone, "Get a Warrant"

The US Supreme Court, ruling 9 to 0, invalidated the warrantless searches of cell phones, which hold "the privacies of life." Police have no right to "rummage at will," the justices said.

WARREN RICHEY

Learning Outcomes

After reading this article, you will be able to:

- State the relevant facts in *Wurie* and *Riley*.
- Present the Court's decisions in these cases.
- Explain the Court's reasoning.

Washington—In a major affirmation of privacy in the digital age, the US Supreme Court on Wednesday ruled that police must obtain a warrant before searching digital information on a cell phone seized from an individual who has been arrested.

The 9-to-0 decision marks a Fourth Amendment landmark of profound importance given the ubiquity of cell phones, tablets, and portable computers in public places throughout society.

"Modern cell phones are not just another technological convenience," Chief Justice John Roberts wrote for the court. "With all they contain and all they may reveal, they hold for many Americans the 'privacies of life,'" he said.

"The fact that technology now allows an individual to carry such information in his hand does not make the information any less worthy of the protection for which the Founders fought," the chief justice said.

"Our answer to the question of what police must do before searching a cell phone seized incident to an arrest is accordingly simple—get a warrant."

In an indication of how fundamental these protections are in the justices' view, the chief justice likened warrantless searches of cell phones to the "general warrants" and "writs of assistance" imposed during colonial America that allowed British troops to "rummage through homes in an unrestrained search for evidence of criminal activity."

"Opposition to such searches was in fact one of the driving forces behind the Revolution itself," Chief Justice Roberts said.

In reaching its decision, the justices rejected arguments by the Obama administration and the California attorney general that law enforcement officials must be able to immediately search the contents of a cell phone or other electronic device when the device was found on a person at the time of his or her lawful arrest.

The justices also rejected a suggested fallback position to allow police to conduct a limited search of a cell phone without a warrant whenever it was reasonable to believe the device contained evidence of the crime that prompted the arrest of the individual.

Roberts said that fallback position provided no practical limit because it would still give "police officers unbridled discretion to rummage at will among a person's private effects."

Instead, the court established a bright line rule that if police seize a cell phone during an arrest they must seek approval from a neutral judge before searching the phone for any evidence of crime.

Steps can be taken to secure the data on the phone to prevent destruction of potential evidence, he said. And the warrant process is becoming more efficient.

"We cannot deny that our decision today will have an impact on the ability of law enforcement to combat crime," Roberts said. "Cell phones have become important tools in facilitating coordination and communication among members of criminal enterprises, and can provide valuable incriminating information about dangerous criminals."

But the chief justice added: "Privacy comes at a cost."

Roberts said the court recognized that there might be instances when the government faces exigent circumstances that required swift and decisive action. In those cases, the courts have recognized an exception to the warrant requirement, an exception that must be later justified case by case to a judge.

The decision reflects a recognition by the high court of a growing threat to privacy in the digital age, with vast amounts of personal records, photos, video, and other intimate information readily accessible on smart phones and other electronic devices.

The government had argued that once an individual is placed under arrest, he or she has a diminished privacy interest and that diminished privacy protection does not extend to anything found in their pockets. Under this approach, searching the contents of a cell phone should be considered no different than searching inside a cigarette pack found in an arrestee's pocket, the government argued.

"This is like saying a ride on horseback is materially indistinguishable from a flight to the moon," Roberts said.

"Modern cell phones, as a category, implicate privacy concerns far beyond those implicated by the search of a cigarette pack, a wallet, or a purse," he said.

Cell phones are different, he said. Even the term cell phone doesn't accurately account for the full scope of their use.

"They could just as easily be called cameras, video players, rolodexes, calendars, tape recorders, libraries, diaries, albums, televisions, maps, or newspapers," Roberts said.

"Most people cannot lug around every piece of mail they have received for the past several months, every picture they have taken, or every book or article they have read—nor would they have reason to attempt to do so," he said.

He said to do so would require dragging a trunk around. The chief justice noted that under existing legal precedents, police would need a warrant to search such a trunk.

"Prior to the digital age, people did not typically carry a cache of sensitive personal information with them as they went about their day," he said. "Now it is the person who is not carrying a cell phone, with all that it contains, who is the exception."

Wednesday's decision stems from two cases in which police used information discovered during warrantless searches of cell phones being carried by individuals at the time of their arrest.

The phones contained images and other information that police used as evidence of criminal activity or to identify other evidence of crime.

One case involved a suspected drug dealer in Boston named Brima Wurie. Police used his cell phone to identify Mr. Wurie's home address. After obtaining a warrant they raided the home where they found drugs, cash, and a weapon.

Wurie was charged with possession with intent to distribute cocaine base, distributing cocaine base, and with being a felon in possession of a firearm.

Wurie's lawyers filed a motion to suppress the evidence that resulted from the warrantless search of his cell phone.

A federal judge denied the motion. At trial, Wurie was convicted and sentenced to nearly 22 years in prison.

On appeal, the First US Circuit Court of Appeals reversed the trial judge, ruling that the police should have obtained a warrant *before* accessing the information in Wurie's phone.

The other case involved a suspected criminal gang member in San Diego named David Riley.

Mr. Riley was pulled over in a traffic stop for driving with expired tags. After discovering that Riley's license had been suspended, the officer impounded Riley's car.

During a routine search of the car, police found two firearms under the car's hood. Riley was arrested.

As he was taken into custody, police seized Riley's smartphone. The arresting officer scrolled through the phone's text files and noticed notations that suggested that Riley was a gang member.

Two hours later, at the police department, the phone was turned over to a detective who specialized in gang crime investigations. The detective examined the contents of the phone and discovered images that allegedly linked the suspect to an earlier gang-related shooting. Police also used photos and video images found on the phone to connect the suspect to other gang-related activities.

Riley was charged with shooting at an occupied vehicle, use of a semiautomatic firearm, and attempted murder. He was also charged with involvement in a gang-related crime.

His lawyer argued that evidence obtained without a warrant from Riley's smartphone must be excluded from his trial. The judge rejected the motion, ruling that the action did not violate the Fourth Amendment.

Riley was convicted and sentenced to 15 years to life in prison. The California Court of Appeal upheld the conviction, noting that the California Supreme Court in 2011 had issued an opinion that police may search a smartphone without a warrant whenever the phone is being carried by an individual at the time of arrest.

In its ruling on Wednesday, the Supreme Court reversed the California Court of Appeal and affirmed the decision of the First Circuit in Boston.

The cases were *US v. Wurie* (13–212) and *Riley v. California* (13–132).

Critical Thinking

1. What were the "general warrants" and "writs of assistance" referred to in the Court's decision?

2. Why is searching a cell phone different from searching inside a cigarette pack found in an arrestee's pocket?

3. Is privacy worth the cost to law enforcement?

Internet References

Encyclopedia.com
http://www.encyclopedia.com/topic/Writs_of_assistance.aspx

Findlaw
http://criminal.findlaw.com/criminal-rights/search-and-seizure-and-the-fourth-amendment.html?DCMP5ADCCRIM_SearchSeizure-4thAmendment&& HBX_PK5fourth1amendment1regulation

The Christian Science Monitor
http://www.csmonitor.com/Innovation/2013/0718/FISA-101-10-key-dates-in-the-evolution-of-NSA-surveillance/Before-the-September-11-attacks

By Warren Richey. Reprinted with permission from the June 25, 2014 issue of The Christian Science Monitor. © 2014 The Christian Science Monitor (www.CSMonitor.com).

Article   Prepared by: Joanne Naughton

One Simple Way to Improve How Cops and Prosecutors Do Their Jobs

MIKE RIGGS

Learning Outcomes

After reading this article, you will be able to:

- Set forth what Byrne Grants are.
- Describe how the bulk of Byrne Grants are primarily used.

Every year, the U.S. Justice Department sends hundreds of millions of dollars to states and municipalities via the Edward Byrne Memorial Justice Assistance Grant. Named for 22-year-old NYPD Officer Edward Byrne, who was murdered in 1988 while he sat in his patrol car, the JAG program provides "critical funding necessary to support a range of program areas, including law enforcement; prosecution, courts, and indigent defense; crime prevention and education; corrections and community corrections; drug treatment and enforcement; program planning, evaluation, and technology improvement; and crime victim and witness initiatives."

Despite what that long list suggests, the bulk of JAG funding ends up going toward fighting the drug war. "Historically," the Drug Policy Alliance noted in 2010, "Byrne Grants have been used primarily to finance drug task forces, which have a record of racially disproportionate low level drug arrests and increased local and state costs with no measurable impact on public safety." At the time, the group suggested that JAG funding be reallocated in favor of more drug treatment programs, rather than enforcement.

As it stands, 60 percent of JAG funding over the last 3 years—totaling more than half a billion dollars—has gone to law enforcement activities. In a new report, titled "Reforming Funding to Reduce Mass Incarceration" [PDF], the Brennan Center for Justice explains why: Because law enforcement agencies can do whatever they want with this money, and most

of them think the best way to keep that money coming is to arrest as many people as possible.

This is no accident. The annual self-evaluation JAG recipients are required to complete measures performance in a way, says the Brennan Center report, that is "roughly analogous to a hospital counting the number of emergency room admissions, instead of considering the number of lives saved." Agencies are asked how many arrests they made, and prosecutors are asked how many cases they won. Not only is that data rather useless in terms of assessing the effectiveness of a given policy, it also says to the person answering the questions that their numbers should be really big.

JAG funding is only a slice of a law enforcement agency's budget, but it can still be a lot of money. Many cities receive JAG funding directly (L.A., New York, Chicago, Houston receive millions a year), and money also goes to states to dole out as they see fit. In 2013, Texas, California, Florida, New York, and Illinois received between $10 and $30 million in JAG grants. As a result of the perception that more arrests are better, the majority of JAG funding goes toward drug and gang enforcement. Programs that arguably should receive more funding in an age of overincarceration get far less: drug treatment programs receive only 5 percent of JAG funding, while on average .004 percent goes toward indigent defense.

Former and current law enforcement officials interviewed by the Brennan Center said that the DOJ's current JAG questionnaire encourages agencies to report "accomplishments that are easy to track but meaningless." To change that, says the Brennan Center, the Justice Department could do something awfully simple: ask a better set of questions when reviewing how agencies spent their grant money.

Is a new questionnaire going to "fix" over-policing of minor crimes and overincarceration of nonviolent offenders? No. But changing incentives is a first step in changing culture. "By signaling to recipients that effectiveness, proportionality, and fairness are DOJ priorities," the Brennan report suggests, "the proposed measures can help turn off the 'automatic pilot' of more punishment—and more incarceration."

Critical Thinking

1. What is the Brennan Center's main criticism of Byrne Grants?

2. Do you agree that too much emphasis is placed on enforcing drug and gang laws?

Internet References

Brennan Center for Justice
http://www.brennancenter.org/publication/reforming-funding-reduce-mass-incarceration

Bureau of Justice Assistance U.S. Department of Justice
https://www.bja.gov/Publications/JAG_LE_Grant_Activity_03-13.pdf

Drug Policy Alliance
http://www.drugpolicy.org/sites/default/files/FactSheet_ByrneJAG_Sept.%202010.pdf

Article   Prepared by: Joanne Naughton

Against His Better Judgment

In the meth corridor of Iowa, a federal judge comes face to face with the reality of congressionally mandated sentencing.

ELI SASLOW

Learning Outcomes

After reading this article, you will be able to:

- Explain how mandatory minimum sentences affect the ability of a judge to use discretion when imposing a sentence.

- Show that criminal defendants don't always know the sentences they are facing for their crimes.

- Discuss Judge Bennett's objections to mandatory minimum sentencing.

They filtered into the courtroom and waited for the arrival of the judge, anxious to hear what he would decide. The defendant's family knelt in the gallery to pray for a lenient sentence. A lawyer paced the entryway and rehearsed his final argument. The defendant reached into the pocket of his orange jumpsuit and pulled out a crumpled note he had written to the judge the night before: "Please, you have all the power," it read. "Just try and be merciful."

U.S. District Judge Mark Bennett entered and everyone stood. He sat and then they sat. "Another hard one," he said, and the room fell silent. He was one of 670 federal district judges in the United States, appointed for life by a president and confirmed by the Senate, and he had taken an oath to "administer justice" in each case he heard. Now he read the sentencing documents at his bench and punched numbers into an oversize calculator. When he finally looked up, he raised his hands together in the air as if his wrists were handcuffed, and then he repeated the conclusion that had come to define so much about his career.

"My hands are tied on your sentence," he said. "I'm sorry. This isn't up to me."

How many times had he issued judgments that were not his own? How often had he apologized to defendants who had come to apologize to him? For more than two decades as a federal judge, Bennett had often viewed his job as less about presiding than abiding by dozens of mandatory minimum sentences established by Congress in the late 1980s for federal offenses. Those mandatory penalties, many of which require at least a decade in prison for drug offenses, took discretion away from judges and fueled an unprecedented rise in prison populations, from 24,000 federal inmates in 1980 to more than 208,000 last year. Half of those inmates are nonviolent drug offenders. Federal prisons are overcrowded by 37 percent. The Justice Department recently called mass imprisonment a "budgetary nightmare" and a "growing and historic crisis."

Politicians as disparate as President Obama and Sen. Rand Paul (R-Ky.) are pushing new legislation in Congress to weaken mandatory minimums, but neither has persuaded Sen. Charles E. Grassley (R-Iowa), who chairs the Senate Judiciary Committee that is responsible for holding initial votes on sentencing laws. Even as Obama has begun granting clemency to a small number of drug offenders, calling their sentences "outdated," Grassley continues to credit strict sentencing with helping reduce violent crime by half in the past 25 years, and he has denounced the new proposals in a succession of speeches to Congress. "Mandatory minimum sentences play a vital role," he told Congress again last month.

But back in Grassley's home state, in Iowa's busiest federal court, the judge who has handed down so many of those sentences has concluded something else about the legacy of his work. "Unjust and ineffective," he wrote in one sentencing opinion. "Gut-wrenching," he wrote in another. "Prisons filled, families divided, communities devastated," he wrote in a third.

And now it was another Tuesday in Sioux City—five hearings listed on his docket, five more nonviolent offenders whose cases involved mandatory minimums of anywhere from 5 to 20 years without the possibility of release. Here in the methamphetamine corridor of middle America, Bennett averaged seven times as many cases each year as a federal judge in New York City or Washington. He had sentenced two convicted murderers to death and several drug cartel bosses to life in prison, but many of his defendants were addicts who had become middling dealers, people who sometimes sounded to him less like perpetrators than victims in the case reports now piled high on his bench. "History of family addiction." "Mild mental retardation." "PTSD after suffering multiple rapes." "Victim of sexual abuse." "Temporarily homeless." "Heavy user since age 14."

Bennett tried to forget the details of each case as soon as he issued a sentence. "You either drain the bathtub, or the guilt and sadness just overwhelms you," he said once, in his chambers, but what he couldn't forget was the total, more than 1,100 nonviolent offenders and counting to whom he had given mandatory minimum sentences he often considered unjust. That meant more than $200 million in taxpayer money he thought had been misspent. It meant a generation of rural Iowa drug addicts he had institutionalized. So he had begun traveling to dozens of prisons across the country to visit people he had sentenced, answering their legal questions and accompanying them to drug treatment classes, because if he couldn't always fulfill his intention of justice from the bench, then at least he could offer empathy. He could look at defendants during their sentencing hearings and give them the dignity of saying exactly what he thought.

"Congress has tied my hands," he told one defendant now.

"We are just going to be warehousing you," he told another.

"I have to uphold the law whether I agree with it or not," he said a few minutes later.

The courtroom emptied and then filled, emptied and then filled, until Bennett's back stiffened and his robe twisted around his blue jeans. He was 65 years old, with uncombed hair, a relaxed posture and a midwestern unpretentiousness. "Let's keep moving," he said, and then in came his fourth case of the day, another methamphetamine addict facing his first federal drug charge, a defendant Bennett had been thinking about all week.

His name was Mark Weller. He was 28 years old. He had pleaded guilty to two counts of distributing methamphetamine in his home town of Denison, Iowa, which meant his mandatory minimum sentence as established by Congress was 10 years in prison. His maximum sentence was life without parole. For four months, he had been awaiting his hearing while locked in a cell at the Fort Dodge Correctional Facility, where there was nothing to do but watch Fox News on TV, think over his life and write letters to people who usually didn't write back.

"I can't tell you how many times I've asked myself, 'How did I get into the situation I'm in today?'" he had written.

Marijuana starting at age 12. Whiskey at 14. Cocaine at 16, and methamphetamine a few months later. "Always hooked on something" was how some family members described him in the pre-sentencing report, but for a while he had managed to hold his life together. He graduated from high school, married, had a daughter and worked for six years at a pork slaughterhouse, becoming a union steward and earning $18 an hour. He bought a doublewide trailer and a Harley, and he tattooed the names of his wife and daughter onto his shoulder. But then his wife met a man on the Internet and moved with their daughter to Missouri, and Weller started drinking some mornings before work. Soon he had lost his job, lost custody of his daughter and, in his own accounting, lost his "morals along with all self control." He started spending as much as $200 each day on meth, selling off his Harley, his trailer and then selling meth, too. He traded meth to pay for his sister's rent, for a used car, for gas money and then for an unregistered rifle, which was still in his car when he was pulled over with 223 grams of methamphetamine last year.

He was arrested and charged with a federal offense because he had been trafficking methamphetamine across state lines. Then he met for the first time with his public defender, considered one of the state's best, Brad Hansen.

"How much is my bond?" Weller remembered asking that day.

"There is no bond in federal court," Hansen told him.

"Then how many days until I get out?" Weller asked.

"We're not just talking about days," Hansen said, and so he began to explain the severity of a criminal charge in the federal system, in which all offenders are required to serve at least 85 percent of whatever sentence they receive. Weller didn't yet know that a series of witnesses, hoping to escape their own mandatory minimum drug sentences, had informed the government that Weller had dealt 2.5 kilograms of methamphetamine over the course of eight months. He didn't yet know that 2.5 kilograms was just barely enough for a mandatory minimum of 10 years, even for a first offense. He didn't know that, after he pleaded guilty, the judge would receive a pre-sentencing report in which his case would be reduced to a series of calculations in the controversial math of federal sentencing.

"Victim impact: There is no identifiable victim."

"Criminal history: Minimal."

"Cost of imprisonment: $2,440.97 per month."

"Guideline sentence: 151 to 188 months."

What Weller knew—the only thing he knew—was the version of sentencing he had seen so many times on prime-time TV. He would have a legal right to speak in court. The court would have an obligation to listen. He asked his family to send testimonials about his character to the courthouse, believing his sentence would depend not only on Congress or on a calculator but also on another person, a judge.

The night before Weller's hearing, Bennett returned to a home overlooking Sioux City and carried the presentencing report to a recliner in his living room. He already had been through it twice, but he wanted to read it again. He put on glasses, poured a glass of wine and began with the letters.

"He was doing fine with his life, it seems, until his wife met another man on-line," Weller's father had written.

"After she left, the life was sucked out of him," his sister had written.

"Broken is the only word," his brother had written. "Meth sunk its dirty little fingers into him."

"I hope this can explain how a child was set up for a fall in his life," his mother had written, in the last letter and the longest one of all. "Growing up, all he pretty much had was an alcoholic mother who was manic depressive and schizophrenic. When I wasn't cutting myself, I was getting drunk and beating the hell out of him in the middle of the night. When I wasn't doing all that I was trying to kill myself and ending up in a mental hospital. Can you imagine being a four year old and getting beat up one day and having to go visit that same person in a mental hospital the next? No heat in the house, no lights, nothing. That was his starting point."

Bennett set down the report, stood from his chair and paced across a room decorated with photos of his own daughter, in the house that had been her starting point. There were scrapbooks made to commemorate each year of her life. There were videotapes of her high school tennis matches and photos of her recent graduation from a private college near Chicago.

He had decided to become a judge just a few months after her birth, in the early 1990s. His wife had been expecting twins, a boy and a girl, and had gone into labor several months prematurely. Their daughter had survived, but their son had died when he was eight hours old, and the capriciousness of that tragedy had left him searching for order, for a life of deliberation and fairness. He had quit private practice and devoted himself to the judges' oath of providing justice, first as a magistrate judge and then as a Bill Clinton appointee to the federal bench, going into his chambers to work six days each week.

Since then he had sent more than 4,000 people to federal prison, and he thought most of them had deserved at least some time in jail. There were meth addicts who promised to seek treatment but then showed up again in court as robbers or dealers. There were rapists and child pornographers that expressed little or no remorse. He had installed chains and bolts on the courtroom floor to restrain the most violent defendants. One of those had threatened to murder his family, which meant his daughter had spent her first three months of high school being shadowed by a U.S. marshal. "It is a view of humanity that can become disillusioning," he said, and sometimes he thought that it required work to retain a sense of compassion.

Once, on the way to a family vacation, he had dropped his wife and daughter off at a shopping mall and detoured by himself to visit the prison in Marion, Ill., then the highest-security penitentiary in the country. He scheduled a tour with the warden, and at the end of the tour Bennett asked for a favor. Was there an empty cell where he could spend a few minutes alone? The warden led him to solitary confinement, where prisoners spent 23 hours each day in their cells, and he locked Bennett inside a unit about the size of a walk-in closet. Bennett sat on the concrete bed, ran his hands against the walls and listened to the hum of the fluorescent light. He imagined the minutes stretching into days and the days extending into years, and by the time the warden returned with the key Bennett's mouth was dry and his hands were clammy, and he couldn't wait to be back at the mall.

"Hell on earth," he said, explaining what just five minutes as a visitor in a federal penitentiary could feel like, and he tried to recall those minutes each time he delivered a sentence. He often gave violent offenders more prison time than the government recommended. He had a reputation for harsh sentencing on white-collar crime. But much of his docket consisted of methamphetamine cases, 87 percent of which required a mandatory minimum as established in the late 1980s by lawmakers who had hoped to send a message about being tough on crime.

By some measures, their strategy had worked: Homicides had fallen by 54 percent since the late 1980s, and property crimes had dropped by a third. Prosecutors and police officers had used the threat of mandatory sentences to entice low-level criminals into cooperating with the government, exchanging information about accomplices in order to earn a plea deal. But most mandatory sentences applied to drug charges, and according to police data, drug use had remained steady since the 1980s even as the number of drug offenders in federal prison increased by 2,200 percent.

"A draconian, ineffective policy" was how then-Attorney General Eric H. Holder Jr. had described it.

"A system that's overrun" was what Republican presidential candidate Mike Huckabee had said.

"Isn't there anything you can do?" asked Bennett's wife, joining him now in the living room. They rarely talked about his cases. But he had told her a little about Weller's, and now she wanted to know what would happen.

"Childhood trauma is a mitigating factor, right?" she said. "Shouldn't that impact his sentence?"

"Yes," he said. "Neglect and abuse are mitigating. Definitely."

"And addiction?"

"Yes."

"Remorse?"

"Yes."

"No history of violence?"

"Yes. Of course," he said, standing up. "It's all mitigating. His whole life is basically mitigating, but there still isn't much I can do."

The first people into the courtroom were Weller's mother, his sister and then his father, who had driven 600 miles from Kansas to sit in the front row, where he was having trouble catching his breath. He gasped for air and rocked in his seat until two court marshals turned to stare. "Look away," he told them. "Have a little respect on the worst day of our lives. Look the hell away."

In came Weller. In came the judge. "This is United States of America versus Mark Paul Weller," the court clerk said.

And then there was only so much left for the court to discuss. Hansen, the defense attorney, could only ask for the mandatory minimum sentence of 10 years, rather than the guideline sentence of 13 years or the maximum of life. The state prosecutor could only agree that 10 years was probably sufficient, because Weller had a "number of mitigating factors," he said. Bennett could only delay the inevitable as the court played out a script written by Congress 30 years earlier.

"This is one of those cases where I wish the court could do more," said Hansen, the defense attorney.

"He's certainly not a drug kingpin," the government prosecutor consented.

"He could use a wake-up call," Hansen said. "But, come on, I mean . . ."

"He doesn't need a 10-year wake-up call," Bennett said.

"Ten years is not a wake-up call," Hansen said. "It's more like a sledgehammer to the face."

"We talk about incremental punishment," Bennett said. "This is not incremental."

They stared at each other for a few more minutes until it was time for Weller to address the court. He leaned into a microphone and read a speech he had written in his holding cell the night before, a speech he now realized would do him no good. He apologized to his family. He apologized to the addicts who had bought his drugs. "There is no excuse for what I did," he said. "I was a hardworking family man dedicated to my family. I turned to drugs, and that was the beginning of the end for me. I hope I get the chance to better my life in the future and put this behind me."

"Thank you, Mr. Weller. Very thoughtful," Bennett said, making a point to look him in the eye. "Very, very thoughtful," he said again, and then he issued the sentence. "You are hereby committed to the custody of the bureau of prisons to be imprisoned for 120 months." He lowered his gavel and walked out, and then the court marshal took Weller to his holding cell for a five-minute visitation with his family. He looked at them through a glass wall and tried to take measure of 10 years. His grandmother would probably be dead. His daughter would be in high school. He would be nearing 40, with half of his life behind him. "It's weird to know that even the judge basically said it wasn't fair," he said.

Down the hall in his chambers, Bennett was also considering the weight of 10 years: one more nonviolent offender packed into an overcrowded prison; another $300,000 in government money spent. "I would have given him a year in rehab if I could," he told his assistant. "How does 10 years make anything better? What good are we doing?"

But already his assistant was handing him another case file, the fifth of the day, and the courtroom was beginning to fill again. "I need five minutes," he said. He went into his office, removed his robe and closed his eyes. He thought about the offer he had received a few weeks earlier from an old partner, who wanted him to return to private practice in Des Moines. No more sentencing hearings. No more bathtub of guilt to drain. "I'm going to think seriously about doing that," Bennett had said, and he was still trying to make up his mind. Now he cleared Weller's sentencing report from his desk and added it to a stack in the corner. He washed his face and changed back into his robe.

"Ready to go?" his assistant asked.

"Ready," he said.

Critical Thinking

1. Do you believe that imprisoning drug law violators has helped alleviate the nation's drug problem?

2. Is a trial judge in a good position to have a realistic idea of the appropriate punishments that should be given to the defendants who appear before the court?

3. Does justice require that everyone who commits a crime get the same sentence, regardless of any other circumstances?

Internet References

The Hill

http://thehill.com/blogs/blog-briefing-room/231775-rand-paul-revives-mandatory-sentencing-reform-bill

The Nation

http://www.thenation.com/article/how-mandatory-minimums-forced-me-send-more-1000-nonviolent-drug-offenders-federal-pri/

US Sentencing Commission

http://www.ussc.gov/news/congressional-testimony-and-reports/mandatory-minimum-penalties/report-congress-mandatory-minimum-penalties-federal-criminal-justice-system

Article   Prepared by: Joanne Naughton

Does an Innocent Man Have the Right to Be Exonerated?

In the 1980s, Larry Youngblood was wrongfully imprisoned for raping a 10-year-old boy. The way the Supreme Court handled his case had lasting consequences.

MARC BOOKMAN

Learning Outcomes

After reading this article, you will be able to:

- Relate the facts of *Arizona v. Youngblood*.

- State the percentage of convictions that are ultimately overturned because of mistaken eyewitness identification, according to the Innocence Project.

- Explain the Supreme Court's decision in *Youngblood*.

In the early morning hours of June 16, 2004, a 31-year-old man named David Leon was killed by a train just west of Estavan Park in Tucson. The *Arizona Daily Star* ran a brief item on the accident but never mentioned Leon's background; the press seemed unaware that he had been in the middle of Tucson's biggest legal scandal for the past two decades.

There was a good reason the media hadn't recognized Leon's name: Over the years, he'd been referred to vaguely as "the victim" or under the pseudonym "Paul"; the U.S. Supreme Court had called him "David L." But concealing his identity hadn't prevented the young man from suffering untold damage. Weeks after the train accident, the autopsy revealed that he had been drunk at the time of his death, a fact that surely surprised no one who knew him. And so the story ended almost exactly where it began: within a stone's throw of Interstate 10.

By the time David Leon was in the fifth grade, he was already struggling with emotional problems. At the age of 4, he had been referred for therapy because he was acting out in his preschool and was unable to get along with the other children; a counselor later characterized him as hyperactive. But in at least one way he was like just about every other 10-year-old boy: He preferred carnivals to church. Such was the choice he faced when he accompanied his mother to the Southgate Shopping Center on the night of October 29, 1983. His mother's church, called The Door, was hosting a music concert that night, but there was a carnival in the parking lot, and naturally David wanted to go. Toward the end of the service, when everyone stood to pray, she noticed that he had slipped out. She circled the carnival grounds a number of times, but he was nowhere to be found.

The pastor's wife called David's mother later that night. The boy had come back, shaken up, with his clothes torn and inside-out. He had been abducted, raped, and dropped back at the church. His mother took him to Kino Community Hospital and the facts of the crime began to emerge. A black man with a bad eye had asked David if he'd give him a hand transporting a tent in his car—there was $5 in it for him if he would help. David initially hesitated—he wasn't supposed to get into cars with strangers—but the man was persistent, and eventually he got the boy to follow along behind his car. One thing led to another, and eventually David was thrown into the man's car, driven out to the desert, and raped twice. Just before he was returned to the church, the man told him that he had a go-cart at home and maybe he could see David again.

The police did what police do in these situations. First one officer talked to David, then another. A composite artist worked with him to get an accurate portrait of the perpetrator. They photographed him to document any injuries and collected his clothing. Finally, the doctor at the hospital brought out a rape kit—using swabs, he collected samples from the boy's mouth and rectum, as well as samples of the boy's blood, saliva, and hair. All that was left was to catch the black man with the bad eye.

It is a common complaint that media coverage of crime spotlights the perpetrator while ignoring the victim. Certainly this was true in the Leon case, or at least partly true. As it turned out, there were two victims, and the second one, Larry Youngblood, received a great deal of unwanted attention. This is because for 17 years he was seen as the perpetrator.

Nine days after the crime, a detective in the Tucson Police Department assembled a collection of photographs, six in all, of black men—each of them had an eye randomly blotted out. When detectives make a photo lineup—instead of having the eyewitness look through books of mugshots—it means they already have a suspect in mind, what the police call a "prime." In this case, the prime was Larry Youngblood. He'd been convicted of a robbery 10 years earlier and had some subsequent minor brushes with the police—and he was a black man living in Tucson with one bad eye. As the detective put it in law-enforcement speak, "Officers had suspicions that the subject in this case may have been Mr. Youngblood."

David was in his fifth grade classroom at the Irene Erickson Elementary School when Detective Joyce Lingel came to see him with the photo spread. David held the lineup very close to his face, prompting Detective Lingel to ask if he was having trouble seeing. He said that he had left his glasses in the classroom, and she sent him back to get them. When he returned, he again looked carefully at the photos and announced with certainty that Number Three was the guy. Larry Youngblood.

That was all they needed. Youngblood was arrested a month later, and not long after that he made arrangements to use his home as equity for bail. But he was still in custody five days before Christmas, when his preliminary hearing was scheduled. David came to court that morning with a member of the Victim Witness Program, and Detective Lingel joined him on a bench outside the courtroom while they waited for the case to begin. Larry Youngblood emerged from an elevator, escorted by a deputy sheriff, wearing prison issue and with his hands cuffed behind him. It was then that David looked him over, turned to the detective, and asked, "Is that him?"

According to the Innocence Project, eyewitness misidentification is responsible for 72 percent of the convictions ultimately overturned through DNA evidence. It's easy to understand why—just think of the last time you saw an old friend reading a book in the airport, tapped him on the shoulder, and then stumbled over the apology when it turned out not to be him. And that was an old friend, not a complete stranger. But not every identification is mistaken, and as the prosecutor told the jury, David had "ample time to observe the person who did it." What she didn't say, and maybe didn't have to say, was that

Youngblood was a black man with a bad eye living in Tucson. How many could there be?

From the beginning, though, David's description wasn't a perfect match for the suspect: He'd told his mother that the car he'd been kidnapped in was a two-door, when Youngblood's was a four-door, and that the man's hair had some gray running through it, although it was confirmed at trial by a professional hair dresser that Youngblood's hair had never been dyed and had never been gray. David hadn't described a man who limped, and one of Youngblood's legs was shorter than the other. There was even the issue of musical taste: David insisted the driver of the car had been playing country music, and everyone who knew Larry Youngblood knew he hated country music.

But there is no rule that a case gets stronger for the accused when the defense begins calling its witnesses. Although Youngblood's attorney told the jury that he always wore dark glasses to hide his bad eye—a fact that had gone unmentioned by the young victim—a defense witness and neighbor testified that he only wore those glasses about half the time. An eye doctor who was called to establish David Leon's bad eyesight, and thus his inability to correctly identify the perpetrator, ended up explaining to the jury that David's eyesight was actually good enough to enable him to obtain an Arizona driver's license one day. Perhaps just as harmful were the testimonies of Youngblood himself and his on-again, off-again girlfriend. Both insisted that they remembered the specific, thoroughly uneventful details of the evening in question. That was his alibi: that he was sleeping on a couch the night of the crime.

There was one other witness for the defense, a scientist from California named Keith Inman. His testimony filled 28 pages of the transcript, but after all the evidence about left eyes and right eyes, four-door cars and hair color, and whether the rapist limped or not, it seemed almost like an afterthought. Inman discussed blood types and spermatozoa and P-30 molecules and acid phosphatase and secretors versus non-secretors, all to one end: to show that if David Leon's underwear had been refrigerated by the police, which it had not been, scientific tests of the semen stains might have exculpated Larry Youngblood. The prosecutor spent her time getting the scientist to concede that those same tests might not have exculpated Youngblood. Such were the limitations of forensic science before the era of DNA testing.

David looked Youngblood over, turned to the detective, and asked, "Is that him?"

Although the state's failure to preserve the evidence proved critically important over the next 15 years as the case traveled up and down the appellate ladder, it turned out not to be important at all to the jurors; they took only 40 minutes to convict Young-blood of child molestation, sexual assault, and kidnapping. Right up to the moment of sentencing, Youngblood insisted on his innocence. "Any black man with a bad eye would have been found guilty," he told his pre-sentence investigator, who nonetheless recommended that he get therapy "geared toward his sexually deviant behavior" upon his eventual release. Larry Youngblood was going to prison.

To what lengths must the state go to ensure that the accused gets a fair trial? Not a perfect trial—the courts are very clear that no one is entitled to that. But the contours of a fair trial have been open to debate since the Constitution was written. For Youngblood the question was an easy one: How in the world could the police get away with not refrigerating the evidence that might have shown that he was innocent?

That is exactly how the Arizona Court of Appeals saw it. Reversing Youngblood's conviction, the opinion made clear that the court was not accusing the state of bad faith in failing to preserve the evidence; rather, the dismissal was necessary to avoid an unfair trial. Quoting a similar California case, the court held that when the police recover a semen sample of the assailant, "the authorities must take reasonable measures to adequately preserve this evidence." Youngblood had won, for the time being.

The appellate ladder had one last major rung, though. Rarely does a case get the attention of the United States Supreme Court—the Court denies 99 percent of the petitions asking for its review—but it was Larry Youngblood's continued misfortune to be in that 1 percent. In the late fall of 1988, only two years after he had won in the Arizona Court of Appeals, six justices led by Chief Justice William Rehnquist reinstated Youngblood's conviction. Seizing on the lower court's finding that the police had not acted in bad faith when they failed to refrigerate David Leon's underwear, the chief justice wrote that the state was under no obligation to preserve potentially useful evidence. In short, unless the state purposely set out to destroy evidence, you were out of luck.

The normally perspicacious Justice Stevens did not agree with the majority's opinion, but ruled against Youngblood using a different line of reasoning. He did not think that the state's good or bad faith was the deciding factor; rather, he noted that he might have voted the other way "in a case involving a closer question as to guilt or innocence . . . [T]his, however, is not such a case."

Justice Harry Blackmun, joined by the liberal lions William Brennan and Thurgood Marshall, dissented: "The Constitution requires that criminal defendants be provided with a fair trial, not merely a 'good faith' try at a fair trial," he wrote. Quoting the maxim that it's far worse to convict an innocent man than to let a guilty man go free, Blackmun drew the opposite conclusion from Stevens, stating that the evidence was "far from

conclusive," and the possibility that Youngblood might have been exonerated "was not remote." Perhaps not, but given that Blackmun was writing for the minority, it hardly mattered. The case was sent back to the Arizona courts with instructions that they proceed according to the majority opinion.

But the pendulum had not yet come to rest in the Youngblood case. While the United States Supreme Court has the last word on the meaning of the federal Constitution, each state can interpret its own constitution as it sees fit. Although the language of the Arizona Due Process Clause and the United States Due Process Clause are practically identical ("No person shall be deprived of life, liberty, or property without due process of law"), the Arizona Court of Appeals now ruled in Youngblood's favor again, finding that its constitution provided greater protection to the accused, at least under these facts, than the United States Constitution did. Once again, Youngblood's convictions were dismissed.

One can only imagine what was running through Youngblood's mind when yet another appeal was taken. The losing side never complains about endless litigation, and certainly the state of Arizona was happy to have one last chance to uphold its jury verdict—this time in the Arizona Supreme Court, which had chosen not to hear the case the first time around. Following the "bad faith" analysis set forth by Rehnquist, its opinion determined once and for all that Youngblood had not suffered a denial of due process no matter what constitution was applied; his convictions were reinstated. He had been sentenced to 10 ½ years in prison for sexually molesting David Leon, and the time had come to serve it.

As for David Leon, he never returned to the carnival. The effects of sexual assault on young victims are well-documented, and given the emotional difficulties he was already having before the night of the crime, it is not surprising that his life after it was one of struggle. The immediate impact was obvious in his mood swings—his mother testified that he had gone from being a "real tough type kid" to one who cried at the slightest thing—and his behavior at school became so violent that the administrators regularly had to send him home. David's mother told Youngblood's pre-sentence investigator that the incident had been "devastating to the family and a trauma to my son," and that David had become distant with the family, fearful, and unable to concentrate on his schoolwork. He spoke of taking revenge on his abuser, but his fear of being attacked again caused him to sleep in his mother's bed.

And it got worse from there. In 1993, the same year Youngblood finally went to prison after his long string of appeals had concluded, David was arrested for choking and kicking his girlfriend in front of her 2-year-old son. That put him behind bars, and when he came out, now a full-grown man, he started in with cocaine and alcohol. He went to live with his father, from whom he had been estranged since his parents' divorce when he was a child, but his father accused him of stealing money for drugs and threw him out. In 1999, David beat up another girlfriend, and that sent him to prison again. A probation officer wrote that David was "a very angry person. He is angry at the whole, entire world." How angry must he have been when, only a few weeks after his second incarceration, he learned that Larry Youngblood, the man at whom he had directed his rage for more than 15 years, the man he thought had altered the course of his life through the most intimate and brutal violation imaginable, was innocent?

In 1998, after serving more than five years in prison for sexually molesting David Leon, Larry Youngblood went home. But he didn't stay there. In the summer of 1999, his on-again off-again girlfriend had him removed from her house, and five months later he was arrested for failing to register a new address as a sex offender. By the late 1990s DNA testing had improved by quantum leaps, and Youngblood's new arrest prompted his lawyer to ask that the small amount of semen left unspoiled 16 years ago be tested again. The state agreed, and on August 9, 2000, prosecutors returned to court and announced that Larry Youngblood had been innocent all along. His lawyer, pointing out that it had taken 16 years to exonerate her client, proclaimed, "This is another example for the public on why we shouldn't have the death penalty."

But if Larry Youngblood was innocent, who was guilty? The crime against David Leon was reclassified as unsolved, and the DNA profile of the perpetrator was entered into a national database. The Tucson police chief announced that there were no suspects, and the case remained that way for 16 months, until the evidence was matched to Walter Calvin Cruise, who was serving time for a cocaine conviction in Texas. The prosecutors must have suspected right away that they had finally arrested the right man. Cruise was a black man who had two prior convictions for sexual abuse of children in Houston, and even an arrest for similar conduct in Tucson. And there was one other thing—he had a bad left eye.

When they brought him from a Texas prison into a Tucson courtroom in August 2002, Cruise was sentenced to 24 years in prison for sexually assaulting David Leon, who by that time was 29 years old. Cruise, for his part, said he didn't know that another man had served a prison sentence for a crime he had committed. He told the court he suffered from alcoholic blackouts, and said he was "sorry for everything I've done to hurt anybody in my life."

This was more than the state of Arizona would ever say to Larry Youngblood. Before he was even authorized to have the DNA retested, Youngblood had to sign releases agreeing not to sue the County Attorney's Office, the Police Department, or the state Department of Corrections, which ultimately assured that he would not be compensated for his years of wrongful incarceration. Indeed, the prosecution emphasized that it had done nothing wrong even when it moved to have Youngblood's conviction set aside:

> By virtue of this motion, the State is not conceding that the defendant was wrongly arrested in this matter. On the contrary, the State sought the prosecution and conviction of the defendant on these charges on the best evidence available at the time. A jury duly convicted Defendant of the charges.

But something had in fact gone very wrong. An innocent man had been convicted and gone to prison. A guilty man had avoided arrest for almost two decades even after being arrested for similar conduct in the same town, at practically the same time. Evidence that would have prevented both wrongs had been mishandled. And the courts, finding no bad faith by the government, had condoned it all.

The United States Supreme Court does not apologize for mistakes. In September 2014, Henry Lee McCollum was released from North Carolina's death row after serving 30 years there for the rape and murder of an 11-year-old girl. DNA evidence from a nearby cigarette butt had eventually implicated another man who had been overlooked by law enforcement, even though he lived only a block from where the victim's body was found and had confessed to a similar rape and murder occurring around the same time.

What made this story even more remarkable was an opinion Justice Antonin Scalia had made in 1994, when the Court refused to hear an appeal from a Texas death row prisoner. In his dissenting opinion, Justice Blackmun famously renounced capital punishment and vowed to no longer "tinker with the machinery of death." Justice Scalia, concurring with the majority, practically mocked his fellow justice, citing the awful facts of the McCollum case: "Justice Blackmun did not select as the vehicle for his announcement . . . the case of the 11-year-old girl raped by four men and then killed by stuffing her panties down her throat," wrote Scalia, describing the crime for which McCollum had been convicted. "How enviable a quiet death by lethal injection compared with that!"

And yet, when Henry Lee McCollum walked free, Justice Scalia never said a word.

Because Larry Youngblood was ultimately vindicated by scientific evidence, the *Youngblood* decision now reads like the discarded ending to an epic story—as if the writers of *Jaws* had drafted an earlier version of the script in which the shark devoured Sheriff Brody. The Supreme Court reached its conclusion at a time when Youngblood seemed guilty and modern DNA testing wasn't yet available. Its justices were pondering purely hypothetical questions—whether the evidentiary material *could* have been subjected to tests and the results *might* have exonerated Youngblood. Today's science makes their reasoning seem quaint and anachronistic. At the very least, one would have expected Justice Stevens—who agreed with the result but never signed on to the majority's reliance on the good faith of the government—to rethink his conclusion that there was little room to wonder about Youngblood's "guilt or innocence."

The *Youngblood* decision now reads like the discarded ending to an epic story.

And yet in the years since Youngblood's exoneration and Cruise's conviction, the United States Supreme Court has cited the opinion favorably three times. In 2009, in the case of *District Attorney's Office of the Third Judicial District v. Osborne,* a very divided Court decided that an Alaskan man named William Osborne, who was serving prison time for kidnapping and sexual assault, did not have the constitutional right to post-conviction DNA testing, even though he was willing "to test the evidence at his own expense and to thereby ascertain the truth once and for all." The majority cited the *Youngblood* opinion, arguing that DNA testing could lead down a slippery slope:

> We would soon have to decide if there is a constitutional obligation to preserve forensic evidence that might later be tested. Cf. *Arizona* v. *Youngblood*, 488 U. S. 51, 56–58 (1988). If so, for how long? Would it be different for different types of evidence? Would the State also have some obligation to gather such evidence in the first place? How much, and when?

These questions seemed worth pondering, especially given how Youngblood's story turned out. But Chief Justice John Roberts—writing for himself and fellow conservative Justices Scalia, Thomas, Kennedy, and Alito—determined that the Court did not want to answer them. He refused to "leap ahead" into a more scientific age, to fundamentally change the trial system by making DNA testing into a constitutional right. Even so, Roberts acknowledged that criminal justice, "like any human endeavor, cannot be perfect. DNA evidence shows that it has not been." That brief admission of fallibility was as close as the United States Supreme Court ever came to acknowledging Youngblood's innocence.

Two years later, in *Connick v. Thompson,* the Court reversed a $14 million damage reward against the New Orleans District Attorney's Office for the 14 years John Thompson wrongfully spent on death row: The state had failed to turn over test results on blood evidence that later led him to be acquitted of capital murder. The Court ruled against Thompson, refusing to set

a precedent that might open the way for wrongly convicted inmates to sue the state for misconduct by its prosecutors. Justices Scalia and Alito concurred in the result and used the *Youngblood* case to support their opinion that the state had had no obligation to provide the evidence to the defense in the first place. After that decision, Youngblood's lawyer told an *L.A. Times* reporter that she found it "astounding" that the Court was still relying on her client's case: "It was a horrible decision then, and I can't believe they are still citing it, since so many people have been cleared with DNA evidence since then."

Perhaps even more astounding was a concurring opinion in the virtually forgotten 2004 case of *Illinois v. Fisher.* Gregory Fisher had been arrested for cocaine possession, made bail, and then skipped trial for the next 10 years. By the time he was caught, the cocaine had been tested four times, found to be real, and then destroyed by the state; however, it had never been tested for his DNA. All of the justices, in an unsigned opinion, readily affirmed the *Youngblood* decision and law enforcement's right to destroy the cocaine under those circumstances. All of the justices but one, that is. Justice Stevens concurred but once again refused to join the reasoning of *Youngblood.* He maintained that there were some cases in which a piece of evidence was so critical that destroying it might make a trial fundamentally unfair, even if the state acted in good faith. Then, remarkably, he wrote: "This, like *Youngblood,* is not such a case." Was it possible he hadn't heard that Larry Youngblood was innocent?

The Supreme Court may remain attached to the *Youngblood* decision, but in academic circles the opinion has always been the subject of considerable condemnation. A 1989 article in the *Harvard Civil Rights-Civil Liberties Law Review* declared the Court's analysis "theoretically unsound and a serious erosion of protections for criminal defendants"; another, in 1990 in the *Virginia Law Review,* called the opinion "inherently flawed"; a third, in 1995 in the *Harvard Law Review* said that the bad faith test "needlessly weakened" the defendant's constitutional protection against unjust prosecution. All of this was long before Youngblood's misfortune became known. Once that truth became clear, no one captured the irony better than Peter Neufeld, co-founder of the Innocence Project, who wrote in a 2001 issue of the *New England Law Review:*

> In law school, we have been taught that, absent bad faith, the destruction of critical evidence will not be deemed prejudicial. As a result, there has been no requirement that law enforcement agencies use due diligence to preserve evidence. This doctrine rested for more than a decade on the shoulders of an innocent man.

But did the Court's decision have widespread consequences, beyond the years Youngblood himself spent in prison? Apparently so. In 2007, the *Denver Post* ran a series of articles detailing lost and destroyed evidence that left thousands of accused and victims alike without recourse to scientific testing. In 1992, the NYPD destroyed massive amounts of evidence to make room in its warehouse, which was nearing 100 percent capacity; the same space limitations caused Houston's police force to destroy rape kits through the 1990s; and between 1991 and 2001, New Orleans purged evidence for 2,500 rape cases.

In each of these purges, the lack of storage space may have seemed like a plausible rationale, but the timing was often suspect. The NYPD's decision came only a few months after New York's first DNA exoneration. In Houston, the rape kits were thrown out shortly after then-Governor George W. Bush pardoned a man based on DNA results. "If the implication is that they threw out the evidence because they thought it might produce further exonerations," then-United States Attorney General Janet Reno told the *Denver Post*, "that is cause for great concern." Yet not a single appeal concerning lost evidence in Houston, New York City, or New Orleans prompted a "bad faith" finding by a court.

This doctrine rested for more than a decade on the shoulders of an innocent man.

Indeed, the *Youngblood* standard has even protected the state in situations where evidence was pointedly destroyed—with life-or-death consequences. In Virginia, Robin Lovitt came within a day of execution after the Fourth Circuit Court of Appeals rejected his claim that bloody scissors had been thrown out by a chief deputy clerk, even though two of the clerk's subordinates, advising him that Lovitt was on death row, urged that the scissors and other exhibits be kept. In fact, the destruction of those scissors occurred shortly after a new statute had required that such evidence be preserved until after an inmate's execution. All of this was presented in the Virginia state and federal courts, but to no avail. The clerk "made a serious error in judgment in destroying the evidence," the Fourth Circuit concluded. But "the error cannot be attributed to the police or prosecution . . . and there existed no evidence of bad faith on anyone's part."

When the courts refused to act, then-Governor Mark Warner stepped into the breach, commuting Lovitt's death sentence to life without parole. "In this case, the actions of an agent of the Commonwealth, in a manner contrary to the express direction of the law, comes at the expense of a defendant facing society's most severe and final sanction," wrote Warner. "The Commonwealth must ensure that every time this ultimate sanction is carried out, it is done fairly." Still, Robin Lovitt will spend the rest of his life in prison. Hundreds of other inmates, without recourse to lost, mishandled, or destroyed DNA evidence, will do so as well.

Victims suffer, too, when evidence goes missing. The *Denver Post* series told the story of Janette Bodden, whose daughter had been raped and murdered in 1989. No one had ever been arrested, and 14 years later, she learned that it was unlikely anyone ever would: The evidence from the case had been destroyed. "That was almost like if they had murdered her all over again, when I found out about that," she said. "You lose your child, your baby, you want justice, truth."

There was never any question David Leon would suffer permanent damage from the sexual abuse he endured at the age of 10. The prosecutor told Youngblood's jury, "Unfortunately for David, he's not going to forget. He's not going to forget. He'll never forget." After obtaining a conviction, the same prosecutor argued for an aggravated sentence for Youngblood: "There is a lifelong impact on this child as a result of this act, of this violation that was committed on him by this defendant. It's not only an impact on that child but on his entire family." David's mother, speaking to the pre-sentence investigator, said that her son needed therapy and an explanation as to why he should not feel "dirty and useless in the eyes of society."

Fifteen years later, when Youngblood turned out to be innocent and the actual perpetrator was still unknown—when the only one in jail was her own son David—Patricia Leon said that she did not accept the DNA test as proof that Youngblood was innocent. "The only infallible thing is God," she told Mark Kimble of the *Tucson Citizen.* But two years after that, when Walter Cruise pled guilty to molesting David and apologized for everything he had done, there was little choice but to believe him.

Larry Youngblood was not in the courtroom when the justice system finally got around to Walter Cruise; his lawyer invited him to the sentencing, but he decided not to come. As he told the *New York Times,* "For 17 years, I knew I was innocent. They tried to get me to plea for less time, but I would never confess, especially to something like that. I am angry. They took the best years of my life."

Youngblood spent his last years panhandling on the streets of Tucson. In a grimly ironic twist, he was arrested in 2003 for pulling a knife on a Subway employee, but only after police first detained an innocent man a block south of the sandwich shop—forcing him to his knees, pointing a gun at him, and keeping him handcuffed for 10 minutes until a Subway employee told the officer he had made a mistake. The man on his knees was Julian Kunnie, the University of Arizona's director of Africana studies. "Never before have I experienced such humiliation and degradation," he said. "My human and civil rights were violated solely on the basis of my skin color." Youngblood remained homeless until he died of a drug overdose in 2007.

"I wasted most of my life hating Larry Youngblood. We've never been the same."

The other victim of the 1983 crime fared no better. Learning that he had identified the wrong man only fueled David's rage toward the true perpetrator. "I was raped repeatedly, brutally. I was 10 years old," he said. "It was bad. He should have killed me." Had the mistaken conviction of an innocent man made the pain worse? David's sister certainly thought so. "I spent most of my life and wasted most of my life hating Larry Youngblood," she told the judge at Cruise's trial. "We've never been the same. We, without option, were given life sentences . . . This is something we will deal with forever."

David Leon dealt with it for two more years. The day after he died, the local newspaper offered no explanation for the accident—the rails were straight in that area, and the night had been clear. A police sergeant speculated that he might have been attempting to cross the tracks. If so, was there a moment when he saw the glimmer of the headlight and thought that maybe, just maybe, it might be easier not to get out of the way? Or was his brain so fuzzy with alcohol that he didn't even see it coming? It's impossible to know. What we do know is that the four-mile stretch of Interstate 10, from the carnival to the train, represented a world of anguish for the young man who had been twice victimized—first by the abuser himself, and then by a justice system more committed to convictions than truth. "I figured that society wasn't fair. I give myself credit. I survived," Leon said at the Cruise sentencing. Surely he deserved more than that.

Critical Thinking

1. What was the difference between the Arizona Court of Appeals' decision and the US Supreme Court's decision?

2. What do you think about the idea that whether someone received a fair trial could depend on whether a police officer did something wrong, but did it accidentally and not in bad faith?

Internet References

CaseBriefs
http://www.casebriefs.com/blog/law/civil-procedure/civil-procedure-keyed-to-cound/trial/arizona-v-youngblood/
FindLaw
http://caselaw.findlaw.com/nc-court-of-appeals/1038742.html
New England Law Review Vol. 35:3
http://www.nesl.edu/userfiles/file/lawreview/vol35/3/neufeld.pdf
New Republic
http://www.newrepublic.com/article/119319/scalia-death-penalty-defense-cited-murder-case-it-was-just-overturned

Article Prepared by: Joanne Naughton

Anatomy of a Snitch Scandal

How Orange County Prosecutors Covered Up Rampant Misuse of Jailhouse Informants

JORDAN SMITH

Learning Outcomes

After reading this article, you will be able to:

- Show how Orange County D.A. Rackauckas reacted to the scandal.
- Observe how corruption in Orange County became routine.
- Relate the Supreme Court's holding in *Massiah v. United States*.

Prosecutorial Misconduct and the misuse of jailhouse informants are persistent problems in the criminal justice system. According to the National Registry of Exonerations, since 1989, there have been 923 exonerations tied to official misconduct by prosecutors, police, or other government officials, 89 of them in cases involving the use of jailhouse snitches. Over the last two years, a scandal involving both has engulfed Orange County, California, exposing systemic violation of defendants' constitutional rights and calling into question the legality of the prosecution of a number of violent felony cases.

What makes the Orange County situation particularly troubling is its eerie similarity to another such scandal that unfolded just miles to the north, in Los Angeles County, starting in the late 1970s, and culminated in an exhaustive grand jury report that detailed widespread misuse and abuse of criminal informants and revealed questionable prosecutorial tactics, potentially in more than 200 cases.

Alexandra Natapoff, a law professor at Loyola Law School in Los Angeles and the nation's leading expert on the use of snitches, said the fact that Orange County officials engaged in unconstitutional behavior similar to what made headlines years earlier in Los Angeles County reveals the "entrenched" nature of the practice of using snitches in questionable ways. "We see it from the outside as a scandal that should not be repeated. But apparently Orange County officials didn't see it that way," she said. "They saw it as business as usual."

The case of Luis Francisco Vega illustrates just how routine the corruption became in Orange County—and how devastating its consequences can be.

On a February Evening in 2009, three teenage friends were hanging out next to a parked car on a residential street in Santa Ana, California, when an SUV pulled up next to them. A group of Latino men sat inside the SUV. One of them, sitting just behind the driver, got out of the vehicle and approached the three friends.

"Where are you from?" he asked, a coded inquiry into their gang affiliation. "Nowhere," one of the teenagers replied, according to an account he later gave police. The man then raised his right arm, pointed a gun at the teenagers, and fired. At least five shots rang out. One of the friends bolted and was hit in the forearm; a second, sitting inside the parked car, was hit multiple times, including in the torso and thigh; a third escaped injury. All three survived. As the SUV pulled away with the shooter inside, the teens said they heard a passenger yell a single word: "Delhi"—the name of a Santa Ana street gang.

Speaking to police afterward, none of the teenagers could identify the gunman—they did not recognize him, nor could they provide a physical description. Yet, in an interview with Santa Ana Police Detective Andy Alvarez of the department's gang homicide unit, two of the shooting victims said they could identify one of the passengers in the SUV. He was a 14-year-old kid named Luis Francisco Vega—a former fellow student at nearby Saddleback High School. According to the teens, Vega had "jumped" one of them and beat him up a couple of months prior to the shooting. Notably, Alvarez was told, during that attack Vega had shouted the word "Delhi."

There were plenty of reasons for police to be skeptical. For starters, the victims had a hostile relationship with Vega, giving them a motive to implicate him. Plus the notion that both teens could have recognized a person seated on the far side of the car—in a matter of seconds, while being shot at—seemed farfetched. Neither could describe their attacker, who stood just feet away, nor could they agree on the kind of gun he used, or even the make or color of the SUV. Indeed, while each said Vega was seated on the right side of the car, one witness put him in the front passenger seat, while the other said he was in the rear of the vehicle.

Then there was the fact that the Santa Ana Police Department, which took pains to document the actions and affiliations of local gang members, possessed no records linking Vega to any gang—let alone Delhi. Alvarez couldn't prove that Vega was even in Santa Ana at the time of the shooting. Vega's lawyer argued that he was more than 120 miles from the scene, in Riverside County, where he had been living with an aunt since mid-January.

Still, that "Delhi" was allegedly yelled in the earlier incident was apparently too coincidental for Alvarez. The detective went out to Riverside County to question Vega in early March 2009. In the course of a 40-minute interview, the 14-year-old insisted he was not a gang member and had nothing to do with the shooting. But it didn't matter; even if Vega was not the shooter, he was still good for an attempted murder charge, which could send him to prison for life. Vega was arrested, brought back to Orange County, and locked up on a $1 million bond.

In the meantime, the cops kept looking for the shooter. Two weeks after Vega's interview, while the teenager sat in jail, Alvarez's supervisor, Cpl. David Rondou, sat down with an older youth, 17-year-old Alvaro Sanchez. Sanchez said he'd been "kicking it" with members of the Delhi gang for a couple of months—and admitted that he'd been present on the night of the shooting. That night, he said, he was sitting in the back of the SUV, a stolen Jeep Liberty, when the crew came upon the three teens. Sanchez said he got out of the car, because he thought the crews were going to fight. But he claimed he wasn't the shooter—and refused to provide the names of his companions that night. Sanchez was also charged with attempted murder.

Despite the relatively weak evidence against Vega, following a preliminary hearing in October 2009, an Orange County judge gave the state the go-ahead to try him for attempted murder.

Less than two weeks later, a jailhouse informant named Juan Calderon came forward with important information. Sanchez had admitted to him that he was guilty of the shooting, Calderon told Santa Ana police and a prosecutor with the Orange County District Attorney's Office, and Vega had nothing to do with the crime.

Calderon's claims, if confirmed, would exonerate Vega and thus were required by law to be turned over to his defense attorney. But the prosecutor assigned to Vega's case, Deputy District Attorney Steven Schriver, declined to do so. Calderon was an informant in a separate case the district attorney's office was handling; the prosecutor on that case did not want to tip his hand as to Calderon's activities because to do so might put the inmate at risk for retaliation. Schriver said he didn't want to release the information unless Calderon was placed in protective custody, but admitted he failed to take any steps to make sure that occurred.

It wasn't until December 2010, nearly two years after Luis Vega was arrested, that Schriver finally dismissed the charges against him. Orange County prosecutors never took Alvaro Sanchez to trial, instead pleading him out for 16 years on the attempted murder charge. Nor was it acknowledged that the state had held on to the information provided by Calderon for months, knowingly keeping an innocent kid locked up and separated from his school, family, and friends.

Vega's case might be just another example of the dysfunction that plagues the nation's prisons and jails. But there is growing evidence to show that he was one of many criminal defendants affected by prosecutors' malfeasance—part of a much bigger, unfolding scandal pointing to systemic misconduct inside Orange County, involving not just the DA's office, but also the Orange County Sheriff's Department (OCSD) and various local police departments. To date, more than a dozen felony cases involving murder or violent attack have unraveled as a result of the scandal, with charges dismissed or reduced or new trials granted.

Prosecutors routinely failed to disclose evidence favorable to defendants—so-called *Brady* material, named for the landmark U.S. Supreme Court case *Brady v. Maryland*—including thousands of pages of notes related to various jailhouse informants. There is also evidence that the OCSD, which runs the county's jails, employed jailhouse snitches in illegal schemes to compel other detainees to confess their crimes.

In Vega's case, for example, not only did the government delay disclosing the information from Calderon, but it also was holding information from a different jailhouse snitch, Oscar Moriel, which it *never* disclosed to Vega's attorney. Specifically, Moriel had documented a detailed conversation with Alvaro Sanchez wherein the Delhi gang member explained how the Santa Ana shooting went down and confessed that he was one of two shooters. Sanchez expressed bewilderment that Vega had been charged in connection with the crime, according to notes taken by Moriel, saying, "It's kind of fucked up because this guy [Luis Vega] get's popped for this case while the three other people who were actually there . . . were still out there."

If this fact didn't seem to trouble the DA's office, it was devastating for Vega and his family. Vega's mother, Maria Ruiz, said that what happened to her son has been emotionally shattering and "broke" their family. "This has been really hard on him. I am still at this point trying to get him to speak about it," she wrote in an email to *The Intercept* last fall. "It was really hard on our family."

"I never knew how corrupted Orange County was [until] now," she added. "Orange County law enforcement ruined my child's life."

The Details of Vega's case would never have come to light if it weren't for a public defender named Scott Sanders. At the end of 2011, Sanders was at work on two high-profile death penalty cases. One was against Daniel Wozniak, accused of killing two people (and dismembering one of them). The second was against Scott Dekraai, responsible for Orange County's worst-ever mass shooting.

As Sanders prepared for Dekraai's trial, he sought access to files held by prosecutors, including records on a jailhouse informant named Fernando Perez, to whom Dekraai had apparently confessed details about his crime. As it turned out, Perez had also collected a confession from Sanders's other client, Wozniak. It was an interesting coincidence, Sanders thought, that both of his clients had divulged incriminating information to the same man.

Prosecutors fought Sanders's request for the Perez records, but eventually Judge Thomas Goethals ordered the state to produce them. Upon receiving the file, Sanders and his team were stunned to receive a trove of information—approximately 5,000 pages of discovery materials connected to nine cases in which Perez worked as a snitch for the government.

As Sanders pored over the documents, he discovered that Perez had been used as an informant in a number of prominent gang-related cases. The same was true of another inmate whose name appeared in the records—the prolific Oscar Moriel. Both men were also members of the Mexican Mafia gang. Most damning were notes from Moriel to his government handlers that suggested Orange County sheriff's deputies had worked with the jail to orchestrate contact between Moriel and other detainees for the purpose of producing inculpating statements.

The arrangement, if true, would run afoul of a decades-old Supreme Court ruling, *Massiah v. United States*, which prohibits government agents, including informants, from questioning or coercing statements from defendants who have already been charged and are represented by counsel. As Sanders looked more closely at the records, he began to wonder: Had law enforcement agents used the same tactics to get Dekraai or Wozniak talking?

Sanders also noticed that the amount of material prosecutors disclosed to defense attorneys varied wildly from case to case.

In one case involving Perez, just four pages of records related to the snitch had been turned over; in another, some 200 pages had been released. The same was true for cases involving Moriel. "That was a stunner for me," Sanders told *The Intercept*.

The situation strongly suggested that some Orange County prosecutors had deliberately withheld critical information from defense attorneys that could have potentially helped their clients—either by calling into question the tactics that led to confessions or by suggesting that the two informants, each facing serious charges of his own, were working as snitches for personal benefit. That in turn would undermine their credibility, along with the information they claimed to have obtained. Or, as in the case of Luis Vega, the withheld information could demonstrate that a defendant was innocent.

No one argued that Sanders's client Dekraai was innocent, however. In October 2011, in the midst of a custody battle with his ex-wife, Dekraai walked into the salon where she worked in Seal Beach, California, and opened fire, hitting eight people, seven of whom died. Dekraai then killed an eighth person sitting in a parked car outside the salon. He was quickly captured and arrested. Two days later, Tony Rackauckas, the elected Orange County district attorney, announced that his office would seek the death penalty.

Exactly what Dekraai said to Perez has not been made public. But, according to court testimony, in more than 100 hours of recordings that prosecutors and sheriff's deputies made of the two men talking between their cells, Perez probed for details of Dekraai's crime. He questioned Dekraai's state of mind and even asked about what he'd told his lawyers about his case. Dekraai had actually confessed his crime to police just hours after his arrest—though he initially pleaded not guilty in court.

Why local officials, including prosecutors, would feel the need to employ a snitch in what would almost certainly be a slam-dunk death case in conservative, law-and-order Orange County is particularly confounding. To Sanders, it points directly to a "win-at-all-costs mentality" that has pervaded the Orange County District Attorney's Office.

In January 2014, after nearly a year spent scrutinizing records and transcripts related to a number of Orange County prosecutions—Sanders filed a whopping 505-page motion arguing that the death penalty should be taken off the table in Dekraai's case. In separate motions, he went further, arguing that his client's statements were obtained in violation of law and should be suppressed, and that the government's conduct was so corrupt that the OCDA should be recused from prosecuting the case. (In 2015, Sanders filed a similar 754-page motion in the Wozniak case.)

"The right to a fair trial is only meaningful when those who prosecute and investigate crimes are committed to both honoring defendants' constitutional rights and disclosing evidence that is favorable and material, as mandated by state and federal law," Sanders wrote in the Dekraai motion. "The Court-ordered discovery reveals investigative and discovery practices by the Dekraai prosecution team that are rooted in deception and concealment; an unchecked and lawless . . . informant program overseen by the OCDA; and a string of prosecutions which confirm a culture that confuses winning with justice—prosecutions marked by repeated and stunning *Brady* violations, suborned perjury, and a myriad of other misconduct."

Over the objections of prosecutors, Judge Goethals ordered a hearing. He was "anxious" to hear the evidence and determine "where the truth lies," he said.

To say that the OCDA's office was displeased would be an understatement. Veteran reporter R. Scott Moxley, who has covered criminal justice for the *OC Weekly* for two decades, has doggedly pursued the unfolding snitch scandal. He described standing next to a prosecutor when the "bombshell" Dekraai motion arrived in the DA's office. "He was livid," Moxley recalled. "The prosecutors, if I summarized it, you know, their position was up front: 'This is all bullshit.'"

The unprecedented hearing, which explored allegations of prosecutorial misconduct to a degree rarely seen, began in March 2014 and stretched into the summer. "As we proceeded, two things were happening in a general view," Moxley said. "One was that [Sanders] was scoring points in court." The testimony and evidence were consistently backing up his accusations and the attitude among the prosecutors started to shift. "At first they were really angry," Moxley said. "And then they were like, 'Well, OK, some of [the allegations are] right—but our intentions!'" he continued, with mock indignation. "He's impugning our intentions—and our intentions are noble. It's all accidental errors."

Over the course of the hearing, Sanders called to testify some 28 prosecutors and law enforcement officers, along with snitches like Perez and Moriel. Much of the testimony was simply incredible.

Prosecutors called to the stand consistently shifted their stories and minimized their infractions. Sure, there may have been instances of failure to turn over evidence to the defense, they argued, but that's because they were carrying a heavy caseload. Or because they didn't fully understand the requirements of the laws they're bound to uphold—namely *Brady* and *Massiah*, among the most basic laws governing due process for criminal defendants. At least one prosecutor repeatedly insisted he simply couldn't recall why he'd failed to turn over *Brady* materials.

In another turn, prosecutors and at least one sheriff's deputy attempted to shift blame to the feds—in particular, a former assistant U.S. attorney (and current Orange County judge) who they claimed had forced them to withhold *Brady* evidence related to informants who were also being used in federal cases.

But when the former federal attorney, Terri Flynn-Peister, took the stand that summer, she roundly refuted the accusation. Erik Petersen, a veteran gang prosecutor, also testified that in one case he'd actually been given "an order" not to turn over discovery. When asked who gave the order, Petersen responded, "I don't know."

At times, prosecutors' own files belied their insistence that they did not independently withhold important evidence. One memo extracted by Sanders showed an OCDA investigator telling Petersen that information provided by Fernando Perez would "likely greatly enhance" the prosecution of Dekraai; the investigator requested that Petersen not reveal Perez's name, noting that nothing about the snitch or his work had been revealed to Sanders.

With such shifty behavior exposed in court, the prosecutors' testimony came across as hardly more believable than that of the informants Perez and Moriel. Although the two men both faced charges that could send them to prison for life, the pair professed to be working as informants not for any personal benefit—like a potential sentence reduction—but simply, because it was the right thing to do.

On the stand, Perez recalled sitting in a jail cell and thinking about his life. "I . . . just felt that I was done, done with the [gang] life," he recalled. So he reached out to deputies with the OCSD's Special Handling Unit, in charge of the county's jailhouse informants. Since that day in 2010, Perez said, he's only told the truth about everything he's done and heard as an informant. "You know, I'm a changed man," he explained. "I changed my life around and I did the right thing."

But under intense questioning over three days, Perez's story unraveled. Although he portrayed himself on the stand as having begun his work with the government in 2010, he ultimately conceded that, yes, he'd acted as an informant prior to his supposed epiphany, and he'd also previously floated the story about being a changed man. Dekraai's attorneys noted a previous sentence reduction Perez had received as a result of his informant work, a detail Perez claimed not to remember. Still, notes he wrote to his law enforcement handlers after starting his latest stint as an informant were titled "Operation Daylight"— apparently a reference to his hope that his snitch work would result in his freedom.

Other elements of Perez's "work" proved even more troubling. Although he testified that he never cozied up to inmates or tried to get them to open up about their cases (conduct *Massiah* forbids), a recorded interview revealed Perez specifically telling prosecutors about asking Dekraai questions in an attempt to get him talking. In correspondence with Orange County law enforcement, Perez mentioned working on his "assignment" and expressed how much he loved "this little job I got." Another note opened with the line "My mission is complete."

Perez also wrote to deputies suggesting they move an inmate closer to his cell—apparently to gain a better opportunity to speak with him. Moriel, too, engaged in such strategizing; in at least one note to deputies, he invoked a plan to transfer a specific inmate close to him. The plan, which Moriel referred to as the "dis-iso" scam, was simple: Provide a snitch a particular housing classification—in this instance, a disciplinary-isolation placement—to bolster his credibility with other inmates. Because inmates assume snitches would not be placed in disciplinary housing, the move would help to mask his identity as an informant. Then, house the targeted inmate in the same block—within chatting distance of the snitch.

Proof of such maneuvers lent credence to allegations Sanders made about his clients' cases. That Perez had extracted confessions from both Wozniak and Dekraai indicated that he had been housed near them deliberately, he said. The state denied this charge.

Taken together, the months of testimony painted a shocking picture of collusion between Orange County law enforcement officers and the informants they employed to violate the constitutional rights of jail inmates awaiting trial—in particular, the right to have an attorney present for questioning by the government or its agents.

In August 2014, Judge Goethals made his ruling. He found that while there had clearly been some inexcusable discovery problems and questionable witness testimony, there was not enough evidence to suggest that the Dekraai case had been tainted by systemic corruption. As a sanction for the violations he did find, Goethals banned Orange County prosecutors from using any of Dekraai's incriminating snitch-collected statements at trial.

Sanders was "tremendously appreciative" that Goethals spent so much time on the hearing, he told *The Intercept*, but disappointed that the ruling was limited to suppressing the statements. "Judge Goethals had his reasons—and how could we not be respectful of his reasons?"

Nevertheless, Sanders kept probing for additional discovery. That September, he uncovered evidence that the Orange County Sheriff's Department—going back more than 20 years—had been documenting and concealing its justification for moving jail inmates. In Dekraai's case, the documents—known as TRED records—suggested that Perez's placement next to Dekraai was intentional.

The existence of the records also revealed that at least two witnesses lied at the 2014 hearing: sheriff's deputies Seth Tunstall and Ben Garcia, both with the Special Handling Unit. On the stand, Tunstall claimed it was not his responsibility to cultivate or manage informants. Both deputies professed to know hardly anything about inmates being moved to facilitate conversations, aside from a few isolated cases, and both denied the existence of records that might confirm Sanders's allegations.

The TRED records revelation persuaded Goethals to reopen the hearing. This time, Tunstall and Garcia had little choice but to change their tune. Tunstall tried claiming he'd simply forgotten about the TRED records during his previous testimony—despite estimating that he'd penned tens of thousands of them over his time with the department. Later, he testified that TRED records are considered confidential, but that he would have answered had he been asked specifically about them.

For his part, Garcia testified that he had reviewed TRED records prior to taking the stand in 2014—they helped determine "who moved who and why"—but, echoing Tunstall, said he failed to mention the records because "that's the way we were trained."

At the close of the hearing, Goethals was so disturbed by the new evidence that he concluded the entire OCDA should be recused from prosecuting Dekraai's pending death penalty case. On March 12, 2015, he amended his previous ruling—this time agreeing that there were "serious, ongoing discovery violations" in the case. The judge called out Tunstall and Garcia by name for having "either intentionally lied or willfully withheld information," as well as Petersen, the veteran gang prosecutor, whom he "did not believe." He also faulted District Attorney Tony Rackauckas for failing to ensure that defendants' constitutional rights were upheld not only by prosecutors but also by the law enforcement personnel with whom they work in tandem. "Certain aspects of the district attorney's performance in this case might be described as a comedy of errors but for the fact that it has been so sadly deficient," Goethals wrote. "There is nothing funny about that."

With the OCDA off the Dekraai trial, Goethals sent the case to the office of California Attorney General Kamala Harris for prosecution. Harris quickly appealed, arguing that the OCDA was unaware the TRED system existed and couldn't be blamed for problems inside the sheriff's office. Harris's office maintained there was no reason to believe the OCDA couldn't competently handle the case. This claim was particularly notable considering that Theodore Cropley, the deputy attorney general who wrote the appeal, was present in Goethals's courtroom throughout almost all of the months-long Dekraai hearing, sitting behind OCDA prosecutors, and was certainly aware of the troubling evidence of misconduct in that office. Yet, none of that information was included in the appeal.

Since Goethals's Ruling, Rackauckas and his prosecutors have remained defiant. Instead of expressing dismay that ethical or legal lapses may have violated the due process rights of countless defendants, those who have spoken publicly have mainly attacked Sanders, both personally and professionally. One prosecutor called him an "imbecile"; another said his legal thinking was daft. A third, Mark Geller, told the *Orange County*

Register that "Sanders shouldn't even be a lawyer based on the tactics he's engaged."

Prosecutors have also sought to undermine Goethals, who was once a prosecutor in the OCDA as well as a defense attorney. As the *Los Angeles Times* reported, since the start of the Dekraai hearings in early 2014, Orange County prosecutors have repeatedly sought to remove their cases from Goethals's court. Between February 2014 and March 2015, they sought to disqualify Goethals 57 times based on alleged prejudice—a marked contrast to previous years. Prosecutors sought disqualification only twice in 2013, and not at all in 2012.

In March, the scandal even took a violent turn when a local defense attorney, who recently succeeded in overturning a client's conviction based on misconduct, was beaten up in the courthouse by an OCDA investigator. The two had exchanged a short but heated set of accusations about who was more "sleazy," defense lawyers who exposed law enforcement cheating or the county officials responsible for it.

Amid the petty sniping (and blows to the defense attorney's face), fallout from the hearing continues. Even as officials insist that all is right in the house of Rackauckas, at least 15 serious felony cases have so far been directly affected, according to Sanders. Part of the problem is that the cops have gone quiet. In one case, Tunstall and Garcia, the deputies called out for lying in the Dekraai case, refused to testify, invoking their Fifth Amendment rights and thus avoiding cross-examination by defense attorneys.

And yet, more than a year after the deceptive testimony was exposed, neither the attorney general nor the OCDA has filed criminal charges against either deputy—or anyone else connected to the snitch scandal. To date, only Petersen, the prosecutor Goethals singled out for lacking integrity, has resigned his position.

The refusal to hold anyone accountable for the corruption is not just a matter of DA Rackauckas's nonchalance. Other officials implicated in the scandal have displayed a similar attitude. Sheriff Sandra Hutchens publicly shrugged off the allegations in an extensive interview with a local TV news anchor posted to YouTube in October 2015. Regarding the TRED system, she said the DA's office had known about those records for years, and the system wasn't meant to be secret. The deputies who said that were just mistaken—or "unclear" about what they could reveal. She added that judges have said the TRED record itself should be private, but not necessarily the information it contains. In other words, it's all just a big misunderstanding. "You know, there's this whole talk of a conspiracy that this is secret information. It's totally false," she said.

While denying every allegation leveled at her department, Hutchens also admitted that she hasn't conducted any actual investigation into the matter or addressed the potential perjury by Tunstall and Garcia. She has portrayed herself as being hamstrung while awaiting any comprehensive outside inquiry that might occur. "I can't do an administrative investigation until that is done. I can't even get a statement from my deputies," she lamented. "If they did something wrong, I'll deal with that. But we don't know that, to this day."

At the Dekraai hearing, Dan Wagner, who oversees the OCDA's homicide division, said that he and other attorneys looked into the allegations made against the office (an inquiry that was not officially documented) and found nothing amiss—aside from honest *Brady* mistakes. Rackauckas, for his part, initially said those errors were the result of an overworked staff, and then four months after the ruling, announced that he would seat a hand-picked panel of lawyers—dubbed the Informant Policies & Practices Evaluation Committee—to review the situation.

In an email to *The Intercept*, a California AG spokesperson said the office was conducting an "independent investigation," but only "specifically regarding" the Dekraai case. An OCSD spokesperson said the department's internal inquiry would proceed once the state investigation was completed.

In November 2015, almost two years after Sanders first stumbled upon the evidence that exposed the informant scandal, more than 30 individuals and interested groups joined Erwin Chemerinksy, dean of the law school at the University of California, Irvine, and former California attorney general John Van de Kamp in signing a letter requesting a Department of Justice investigation. "The unwillingness of the OCSD and OCDA to acknowledge the due process implications of the alleged misconduct has become only more entrenched as attention to the situation has grown," they wrote. "It is our firm belief that the Department of Justice is the only entity equipped to conduct this investigation and restore public confidence in the criminal justice system in Orange County."

The DOJ has not revealed whether it will undertake any investigation. (The department did not respond to *The Intercept*'s requests for comment.) But in familiar fashion, rather than consider Chemerinsky's concerns, Rackauckas's office lashed out at the respected legal scholar. In a press release, the OCDA parsed portions of a law review article Chemerinsky coauthored in 1996—in the wake of the O.J. Simpson trial—on the subject of legal commentators' ethical responsibilities. The OCDA essentially took the position that, since he hadn't been present during the entirety of the Dekraai hearing and hadn't ordered a full set of transcripts, Chemerinsky should not be speaking out. The DA said the concerns expressed in the letter were based on "factually incorrect media accounts of the circumstances of the case."

Chemerinsky, who spoke to *The Intercept* last year about the implications of the snitch scandal, recently declined further comment, noting that he is now representing Orange County's superior court system, which is fighting the OCDA over its retaliatory actions against Goethals. In a court filing, the county's supervising felony judge wrote that the DA's conduct toward Goethels has jeopardized "all felony cases" in Orange County by bottlenecking the system.

If Rackauckas hoped his informant committee would clear the DA's office, its investigation did no such thing. The committee completed its report in December, noting that where the use of informants is concerned, confidence in the criminal justice system in Orange County "has eroded." The report criticized the "win-at-all-costs mentality" among some prosecutors, describing the office as a "ship without a rudder." Among the recommendations: The OCDA should revise its policies for using informants and ensure better supervision of related cases; provide more robust training for prosecutors; and establish a conviction integrity unit to review post-conviction innocence claims.

But the committee also emphasized that its review was incomplete. Lacking subpoena power, it had access only to whatever materials officials voluntarily turned over, and it could not force anyone to talk. The review should be considered an "evaluation," not an "investigation," the committee wrote, and concluded that an outside "entity with document subpoena power and the ability to compel witnesses to be questioned under oath" should conduct a full inquiry. In short, the committee had come to nearly the same conclusion as Chemerinsky, whose opinion the DA had flatly dismissed.

In the wake of the report, Rackauckas finally submitted his own investigation request to the DOJ, although his appearance at a press conference around the same time suggested that he remains unconvinced it is actually needed. "We know there is no evidence whatsoever of any of this sensational wrongdoing that's been alleged," Rackauckas said bluntly. "There's been some mistakes made," particularly with meeting evidence discovery obligations, but there were "no innocent people" convicted as a result and "no injustice," he added. "We know that doesn't exist."

How exactly Rackauckas can be so sure is a mystery. With a scandal of such proportions, it's impossible to draw conclusions about possible miscarriage of justice absent a concerted effort to identify and review every case that may have been tainted by violations of due process. Orange County is littered with victims of the scandal—from the grieving families of Dekraai's victims, who have yet to see justice of any kind, to Luis Vega, now 22, who was locked up at 14 for a crime he almost certainly did not commit.

It might be one thing if the law enforcement officials involved had never navigated a scandal of such scope. But Rackauckas and Sheriff Hutchens should be more familiar with the process than most. Both were working in the criminal justice system in Southern California when the last big snitch controversy, in Los Angeles County, erupted in the state. Rackauckas had joined the OCDA and Hutchens was working in the L.A. County jail system—ground zero for the scandal. According to a sheriff's department spokesperson, Hutchens was a junior jailer at the time and didn't work at the men's jail where the scandal unfolded. The OCDA declined to comment.

The corruption in L.A. County was uncovered after a career criminal named Leslie White explained to the press and local sheriff's department how he cooked up detailed false confessions that he then peddled to jailers as having come from fellow inmates. The ensuing grand jury investigation involved testimony from more than 100 witnesses and thousands of documents. In its report, the 1989–1990 grand jury concluded, in part, that a number of informants had committed perjury, the DA's office had deliberately failed to curtail misuse of informants, and the sheriff's office had violated defendants' rights. The report estimated that over a 10-year period, as many as 250 cases involving informants were affected.

The grand jury report noted that convicted defendants could raise wrongful conviction claims based on the county's use of jailhouse informants—but it isn't clear how many claims were ever raised on those grounds. Today, the number of cases that may have been tainted by Orange County's scandal is similarly unclear. Whether such a figure will ever be known—or whether affected defendants will have a meaningful chance to challenge their convictions—will depend on a thorough and independent investigation.

Responding to questions about the scandal, an OCDA spokesperson declined to provide any answers, stating that *The Intercept* was requesting an "exorbitant amount of information" that would "require a lot of time and resources" to address. "Your questions show a slanted bias and our participation appears to solely serve as a filler. We don't believe you're interested in being fair," the response reads. "We respectfully decline to participate in your article." Indeed, the OCDA has consistently argued that the media have overblown resolvable discovery problems and that any systemic issues resided in the sheriff's department.

Still, it doesn't appear the scandal will recede into the background any time soon. In a court hearing last week related to Sanders's other capital client, Daniel Wozniak, sheriff's department officials testified that they'd found yet another trove of documents—computer notes related to jailhouse informants that were taken by Ben Garcia and other deputies—that has never been turned over to the defense, or, apparently, to prosecutors. According to the *Orange County Register*, officials testified that the OCSD administration had no idea deputies were keeping the notes, which span at least a five-year period beginning in 2008. The OCDA quickly issued a press release condemning the sheriff's department.

"Our criminal justice system is much better at looking forward than backward," Laura Fernandez, a lawyer and fellow at

Yale researching prosecutorial misconduct, wrote to *The Intercept*. Fernandez, who signed Chemerinsky's letter to the DOJ, said that outside of death penalty cases (which have built-in layers of post-conviction review), legislation and the expansion of certain legal doctrines have made "reviewing cases progressively more difficult." Yet the kind of misconduct that's surfaced in Orange County shows precisely why identifying and reviewing all potentially impacted cases is so crucial. "Where there is substantial evidence of concealment, distortion, and even outright deception on the part of the state, as there is here, reevaluating tainted cases is not only possible, but critically important."

What is abundantly clear about the situation in Orange County is that if it weren't for a handful of people—chiefly, public defender Sanders, Judge Goethals, and reporter Moxley—the snitch scandal probably would not have made news outside the courthouse in Santa Ana.

Indeed, as the scandal began to unfold, Moxley recalls being pulled aside in the courthouse by a veteran Orange County prosecutor, who suggested that he back off the story. "He goes, 'You know, if you turn away from this, this goes away,'" Moxley said. "And he wasn't saying that as a compliment. He was saying, 'You're inflating this. If you leave it, then it's just Sanders barking in a courtroom.' And it stunned me, because it was early on, and I thought, wow, this is how they're viewing it."

For Maria Ruiz, the mother of Luis Vega, who at 14, was jailed for nearly two years for a crime that county law enforcement knew he did not commit, that sort of flippancy isn't new.

Indeed, it wasn't until last year that Ruiz learned police and prosecutors had evidence in hand that her son was actually innocent months before the attempted murder charge against him was finally dropped. "I was so emotional" after finding out, she said. "I was crying for the whole month." She always knew her son was innocent—and early on, she told the prosecutor just that. "I told the DA, 'Look, you have the wrong person.' And he just shook his head at me."

Critical Thinking

1. What's wrong with Prosecutors withholding *Brady* material from defense attorneys?

2. Was anyone punished for having wrongly sent 14-year-old Vega to jail?

3. Aren't prosecutors supposed to do whatever they can to win their cases?

Internet References

Brady v. Maryland Turns 50, But Defense Attorneys Aren't Celebrating

http://www.huffingtonpost.com/2013/05/13/brady-v-maryland-50_n_3268000.html

Justia

https://supreme.justia.com/cases/federal/us/373/83/case.html

Quimbee

https://www.quimbee.com/cases/massiah-v-united-states

Article   Prepared by: Joanne Naughton

Stanford Sexual Assault: Records Show Judge's Logic Behind Light Sentence

Judge who oversaw Brock Turner's case says positive character reference, absence of criminal convictions, and media scrutiny swayed his decision.

JULIA CARRIE WONG

Learning Outcomes

After reading this article, you will be able to:

- Understand the judge's rationale for the sentence he imposed.
- See the importance the judge placed on the character letter from the Turner's classmate.

The judge who sentenced Brock Turner, the former Stanford swimmer convicted of sexually assaulting an unconscious woman, said at the sentencing hearing that a positive character reference submitted by Turner's childhood friend "just rings true", according to a newly released court transcript.

Specifically, Judge Aaron Persky drew attention to the character letter from Leslie Rasmussen, a classmate of Turner's since elementary school, whom he quoted as saying, "If I had to choose one kid I graduated with to be in the position Brock is, it would never have been him."

Perskey added: "To me, that just rings true as to–it sort of corroborates the evidence of his character up until the night of this incident, which has been positive."

The transcript provides the most comprehensive view yet of the reasoning of Persky, who has come under intense scrutiny and criticism as a result of his lenient ruling in the wake of the publication of the victim's personal impact statement.

Rasmussen's letter, which she has since apologized for, was widely criticized for seeming to place the blame for the sexual assault on the victim. "But where do we draw the line and stop worrying about being politically correct every second of the day and see that rape on campuses aren't always because people are rapists," she wrote.

After hearing statements from the victim, the prosecutor, Turner, Turner's father, and the defense attorney, Persky prefaced his remarks by quoting the victim's words: "As she writes, 'the damage is done,' " adding that it was his role to "follow the roadmap our system of criminal justice sets out for the court in sentencing decisions."

Persky sentenced Turner to probation rather than a state prison sentence, despite the judge's own admission that "this is a case where probation is prohibited except in unusual cases where the interest of justice would best be served."

Though he appeared to agree with the idea that Turner's intoxication at the time of the sexual assault reduced the degree of "moral culpability" for his crime, he said that he was not relying on that factor to meet the standard of allowing probation:

> Some weight should be given to the fact that a defendant who is, albeit voluntarily, intoxicated versus a defendant who commits an assault with intent to commit rape, a completely sober defendant, there is less moral culpability attached to the defendant who is legally intoxicated. That's a comparative measure. But I don't attach very much weight to that.

Instead, the judge stated, he was relying on guidelines that allowed him to consider probation "where a defendant is youthful and has no significant record of prior criminal offenses."

The judge also said that he was aware of evidence provided by the prosecution that pointed to a pending "minor-in-possession" of alcohol charge, and of "communications involving recreational drug use, even a video showing recreational drug use", but seemed to dismiss them based on the fact that they did not result in criminal convictions:

"On balance, I don't find that enough to negate the absence of any criminal convictions," he said.

The absence of drug convictions for Turner, who is white, speaks to a degree of privilege that the victim raised in her statement. Studies have found that black Americans are more likely to be arrested for drug crimes than white Americans, despite both groups using drugs at similar rates.

In her statement, the victim raised the issue, stating: "If a first time offender from an underprivileged background was accused of three felonies and displayed no accountability for his actions other than drinking, what would his sentence be?"

But Persky's remarks at the sentencing seem to indicate that Turner's privileged upbringing should, if anything, count in his favor, because it increased the amount of "adverse collateral consequences" he faced–in other words, Turner had more to lose.

"I think [the victim] made a good point, which is, well, if you had someone who wasn't in the fortunate circumstances that Mr Turner had found himself in his youth, that they shouldn't– it shouldn't count against them. But the–I–I think you have to take the whole picture in terms of what impact imprisonment has on a specific individual's life. And the . . . character letters that have been submitted do show a huge collateral consequence for Mr Turner based on the conviction."

Persky also suggested that the amount of media coverage attached to the case was a kind of punishment in its own right, saying: "Where, in certain cases, there is no publicity, then the collateral consequence of those on the defendant's life can be minimized. And so here, we have, I think, significant collateral consequences that have to be considered."

Critical Thinking

1. Do you think it is fair to call Turner a rapist since both he and the woman were drunk?

2. Do you think it is likely that a defendant who was a first time offender from an underprivileged background, now convicted of three felonies including rape, and who displayed no accountability for the rape would receive probation?

3. Do you think the judge may have identified with Turner in some way?

Internet References

RAINN
https://www.rainn.org/statistics/campus-sexual-violence

Sexual Assault on Campus
https://www.publicintegrity.org/accountability/education/sexual-assault-campus

Sexual Assault on College Campuses: A Culture of Indifference
http://invw.org/sexual-assault/

Unit 5

UNIT

Prepared by: Joanne Naughton

Juvenile Justice

Although there were variations within specific offense categories, the overall arrest rate for juvenile violent crime remained relatively constant for several decades. Then, in the late 1980s, something changed: more and more juveniles charged with violent offenses were brought into the justice system. The juvenile justice system is a 20th-century response to the problems of dealing with children in trouble with the law, or children who need society's protection.

Juvenile court procedure differs from the procedure in adult courts because juvenile courts are based on the philosophy that their function is to treat and help, not to punish and abandon the offender. Recently, operations of juvenile courts have received criticism, and a number of significant Supreme Court decisions have changed the way that the courts must approach the rights of children. Despite a trend toward dealing more punitively with children who commit serious crimes, by treating them as if they were adults, the major thrust of the juvenile justice system remains one of diversion and treatment, rather than adjudication and incarceration.

Article Prepared by: Joanne Naughton

Juveniles Facing Lifelong Terms Despite Rulings

ERIK ECKHOLM

Learning Outcomes

After reading this article, you will be able to:

- Relate the Supreme Court's decisions in *Miller* and *Graham.*

- Show how some states are responding to the Court's decisions regarding the use of mandatory life sentences for juveniles.

Jacksonville, FL—In decisions widely hailed as milestones, the United States Supreme Court in 2010 and 2012 acted to curtail the use of mandatory life sentences for juveniles, accepting the argument that children, even those who are convicted of murder, are less culpable than adults and usually deserve a chance at redemption.

But most states have taken half measures, at best, to carry out the rulings, which could affect more than 2,000 current inmates and countless more in years to come, according to many youth advocates and legal experts.

"States are going through the motions of compliance," said Cara H. Drinan, an associate professor of law at the Catholic University of America, "but in an anemic or hyper-technical way that flouts the spirit of the decisions."

Lawsuits now before Florida's highest court are among many across the country that demand more robust changes in juvenile justice. One of the Florida suits accuses the state of skirting the ban on life without parole in nonhomicide cases by meting out sentences so staggering that they amount to the same thing.

Other suits, such as one argued last week before the Illinois Supreme Court, ask for new sentencing hearings, at least, for inmates who received automatic life terms for murder before 2012—a retroactive application that several states have resisted.

The plaintiff in one of the Florida lawsuits, Shimeek Gridine, was 14 when he and a 12-year-old partner made a clumsy attempt to rob a man in 2009 here in Jacksonville. As the disbelieving victim turned away, Shimeek fired a shotgun, pelting the side of the man's head and shoulder.

The man was not seriously wounded, but Shimeek was prosecuted as an adult. He pleaded guilty to attempted murder and robbery, hoping for leniency as a young offender with no record of violence. The judge called his conduct "heinous" and sentenced him to 70 years without parole.

Under Florida law, he cannot be released until he turns 77, at least, several years beyond the life expectancy for a black man his age, noted his public defender, who called the sentence "de facto life without parole" in an appeal to Florida's high court.

"They sentenced him to death, that's how I see it," Shimeek's grandmother Wonona Graham said.

The Supreme Court decisions built on a 2005 ruling that banned the death penalty for juvenile offenders as cruel and unusual punishment, stating that offenders younger than 18 must be treated differently from adults.

The 2010 decision, *Graham v. Florida*, forbade sentences of life without parole for juveniles not convicted of murder and said offenders must be offered a "meaningful opportunity for release based on demonstrated maturity and rehabilitation." The ruling applied to those who had been previously sentenced.

Cases like Shimeek's aim to show that sentences of 70 years, 90 years or more violate that decision. Florida's defense was that Shimeek's sentence was not literally "life without parole" and that the life span of a young inmate could not be predicted.

Probably no more than 200 prisoners were affected nationally by the 2010 decision, and they were concentrated in Florida. So far, of 115 inmates in the state who had been sentenced to life for nonhomicide convictions, 75 have had new hearings, according to the Youth Defense Institute at the Barry University School of Law in Orlando. In 30 cases, the new sentences have been for 50 years or more. One inmate who had been convicted of gun robbery and rape has received consecutive sentences totaling 170 years.

In its 2012 decision, *Miller v. Alabama,* the Supreme Court declared that juveniles convicted of murder may not automatically be given life sentences. Life terms remain a possibility, but judges and juries must tailor the punishment to individual circumstances and consider mitigating factors.

The Supreme Court did not make it clear whether the 2012 ruling applied retroactively, and state courts have been divided, suggesting that this issue, as well as the question of de facto life sentences, may eventually return to the Supreme Court.

Advocates for victims have argued strongly against revisiting pre-2012 murder sentences or holding parole hearings for the convicts, saying it would inflict new suffering on the victims' families.

Pennsylvania has the most inmates serving automatic life sentences for murders committed when they were juveniles: more than 450, according to the Juvenile Law Center in Philadelphia. In October, the State Supreme Court found that the Miller ruling did not apply to these prior murder convictions, creating what the law center, a private advocacy group, called an "appallingly unjust situation" with radically different punishments depending on the timing of the trial.

Likewise, courts in Louisiana, with about 230 inmates serving mandatory life sentences for juvenile murders, refused to make the law retroactive. In Florida, with 198 such inmates, the issue is under consideration by the State Supreme Court, and on Wednesday it was argued before the top court of Illinois, where 100 inmates could be affected.

Misgivings about the federal Supreme Court decisions and efforts to restrict their application have come from some victim groups and legal scholars around the country.

"The Supreme Court has seriously overgeneralized about under-18 offenders," said Kent S. Scheidegger, the legal director of the Criminal Justice Legal Foundation, a conservative group in Sacramento, Calif. "There are some under 18 who are thoroughly incorrigible criminals."

Some legal experts who are otherwise sympathetic have suggested that the Supreme Court overreached, with decisions that "represent a dramatic judicial challenge to legislative authority," according to a new article in the *Missouri Law Review* by Frank O. Bowman III of the University of Missouri School of Law.

Among the handful of states with large numbers of juvenile offenders serving life terms, California is singled out by advocates for acting in the spirit of the Supreme Court rules.

"California has led the way in scaling back some of the extreme sentencing policies it imposed on children," said Jody Kent Lavy, the director of the Campaign for the Fair Sentencing of Youth, which has campaigned against juvenile life sentences and called on states to reconsider mandatory terms dispensed before the Miller ruling. Too many states, she said, are "reacting with knee-jerk, narrow efforts at compliance."

California is allowing juvenile offenders who were condemned to life without parole to seek a resentencing hearing. The State Supreme Court also addressed the issue of de facto life sentences, voiding a 110-year sentence that had been imposed for attempted murder.

Whether they alter past sentences or not, some states have adapted by imposing minimum mandatory terms for juvenile murderers of 25 or 35 years before parole can even be considered—far more flexible than mandatory life, but an approach that some experts say still fails to consider individual circumstances.

As Ms. Drinan of Catholic University wrote in a coming article in the Washington University Law Review, largely ignored is the mandate to offer young inmates a chance to "demonstrate growth and maturity," raising their chances of eventual release.

To give young offenders a real chance to mature and prepare for life outside prison, Ms. Drinan said, "states must overhaul juvenile incarceration altogether," rather than letting them languish for decades in adult prisons.

Shimeek Gridine, meanwhile, is pursuing a high school equivalency diploma in prison while awaiting a decision by the Florida Supreme Court that could alter his bleak prospects.

He has a supportive family: A dozen relatives, including his mother and grandparents and several aunts and uncles, testified at his sentencing in 2010, urging clemency for a child who played Pop Warner football and talked of becoming a merchant seaman, like his grandfather.

But the judge said the fact that Shimeek had a good family, and decent grades, only underscored that the boy knew right from wrong, and he issued a sentence 30 years longer than even the prosecution had asked for.

Now Florida's top court is pondering whether his sentence violates the federal Constitution.

"A 70-year sentence imposed upon a 14-year-old is just as cruel and unusual as a sentence of life without parole," Shimeek's public defender, Gail Anderson, argued before the Florida court in September. "Mr. Gridine will most likely die in prison."

Critical Thinking

1. Should juveniles be prosecuted as adults, even though they aren't adults?

2. Do the advocates for victims have a valid argument against making *Miller* retroactive?

3. Do you believe Shimeek Gridine's sentence violates the Supreme Court's decision in *Graham*?

Internet References

Sentencing Law and Policy
   http://sentencing.typepad.com/sentencing_law_and_policy/assessing-graham-and-its-aftermath/

Social Science Research Network
   http://papers.ssrn.com/sol3/papers.cfm?abstract_id52350316

The Campaign for the Fair Sentencing of Youth
   http://fairsentencingofyouth.org/2014/10/01/american-correctional-association-opposes-jlwop/

Article   Prepared by: Joanne Naughton

Old Laws Collide with Digital Reality in Colorado Teen Sexting Case

Laws intended to protect youth from sexual predators have put schools in a Catch-22.

P. Solomon Banda and Colleen Slevin

Learning Outcomes

After reading this article, you will be able to:

- Explain how laws across the country, intended to punish adult sexual predators, are causing young people to face criminal prosecution.
- Discuss the case in Pennsylvania brought by the ACLU.

Canon City, Colorado—Educators in a small Colorado town say they had no choice but alert police when they discovered that many high schoolers were using a cellphone app to collect and hide hundreds of naked photos of themselves.

The law in Colorado and many other states classifies any explicit photos of minors as child pornography, and requires school employees to bring in police the moment they learn of it.

Prosecutors are looking for evidence of coercion and to see if any adults were involved, saying they don't intend to file criminal charges against everyone.

Meanwhile, the teachers can't even counsel the students involved, because doing so would require their confidential conversations to be reported to police as well.

"You see the mess we're in, you know?" Canon City Schools Superintendent George Welsh said. "We have to watch out for the mental health needs of our children, yet we've kind of got a structure whereby they would be nuts to come and talk to us about it."

This kind of bind is increasingly common across the country as laws from the pre-smartphone era that were intended to protect children from sexual predators collide with the digitally saturated reality of today's teens.

Last year in Fayetteville, North Carolina, a boyfriend and girlfriend who exchanged nude selfies at 16 were charged as adults, with felony sexual exploitation of a minor. Their charges were reduced to misdemeanors following an uproar.

This week, two 14-year-old boys on New York's Long Island were arrested on felony child porn charges after one was accused of recording the other having sex with a girl. As many as 20 students at another school were suspended for either sending or watching the video.

And last week, 16 students in Greenbrier, Tennessee, were charged with sexual exploitation of a minor after exchanging explicit photos on their cellphones.

Canon City, a town of 16,000 in Southern Colorado, is home to several state and federal prisons. Many of its students are children of prison guards.

Authorities say the students involved hid the photos in an application that appears to be a calculator, punching in a sequence of numbers to reveal them.

The case became a national story after the school forfeited the final game of its football season, saying too many players had violated ethical standards for athletes.

Some students think the school overreacted, since older teens can legally have sex in many circumstances, even if sending and receiving explicit photos is illegal.

More than a dozen states have reduced the penalties for sexting teens in recent years, but most still treat teens as adults when it comes to possessing child pornography, possibly even labeling them as sex offenders.

Teens will continue to share explicit images on their smart phones no matter what authorities do, said Canon City high school student Elizabeth Ellis, 18.

"We're not the only high school that does it and we're not going to be the only one that gets found out," she said.

Indeed, in Denver's western suburbs, District Attorney Pete Weir's office has handled more than 100 sexting cases in the past two years, most of them referred by schools or parents, usually after the images are shared beyond the intended recipient.

Even if it turns out that teens sent the images consensually, Weir's office requires them to take self-esteem and relationship classes to avoid prosecution. Parents must attend the first and last session, and are coached on monitoring their children's phones.

This strategy can backfire: In Pennsylvania, the ACLU won a $33,000 settlement in 2010 against a school district for violating the privacy of a girl whose principal confiscated her phone, found nude photos she had taken of herself, and alerted authorities. That prosecutor required sexting girls to attend his "re-education" program to avoid prosecution on child porn charges until an appellate court ruled it unconstitutional.

Some teens, parents, and legal experts say law enforcement should adapt to the reality that sexting is increasingly common among teens—about 28 percent, according to a recent study.

Jeff Temple, an associate professor and psychologist at the University of Texas Medical Branch at Galveston who did the study, sees sexting as a new form of flirting and said it mostly happens between teens who are in a relationship or want to be. This behavior is best addressed by parents talking to their children about healthy relationships and boundaries, he said.

Distributing photographs to others or coercing people to share explicit photos of themselves is more serious and could merit a tougher response, he said.

Potentially allowing the entire world to see your most intimate photos is a real danger, but not one that should be punished criminally, said Marsha Levick, deputy director and chief counsel for the Juvenile Law Center in Philadelphia.

"Sexting is a pretty dumb thing to do, but so is having sex at 14 in your parents' basement," she said.

Critical Thinking

1. Was there a benefit to society in prosecuting the 16-year-old boyfriend and girlfriend in Fayetteville?

2. What is wrong with teens sexting?

3. Is punishing teens criminally the best way to handle teen sexting?

Internet References

American Academy of Pediatrics Gateway
http://pediatrics.aappublications.org/content/early/2014/09/30/peds.2014-1974.abstract

Drexel Now
http://drexel.edu/now/archive/2014/June/Sexting-Study/

Article   Prepared by: Joanne Naughton

Not a Lock: Youth Who Stay Closer to Home Do Better than Those in Detention, Texas Study Shows

Lynne Anderson

Learning Outcomes

After reading this article, you will be able to:

- Recount some of the findings of a study of reforms in the Texas Juvenile Justice Department.

- Explain how Texas reacted after abuses within the system came to light in 2007.

A broad study of reforms in the Texas Juvenile Justice Department "puts a nail in the coffin" of the strategy of youth prisons as a public safety option, said the director of the Juvenile Justice Strategy Group of the Annie E. Casey Foundation, which funded the report.

Most strikingly, said Nate Balis of Casey, the report shows that youth released from a juvenile correction facility were 21 percent more likely to be rearrested than a youth under supervision of a local juvenile probation department. Also, youth released from a state facility who reoffended were almost three times more likely to be rearrested for a felony.

The study, called "Closer to Home," was conducted by the Council of State Governments Justice Center in conjunction with Texas A&M University. It provides a detailed look at how reforms in the Texas system actually affected youth.

"I think this is really important for the field," Balis said. "Its value will go far beyond the borders of Texas. It bolsters what academic reports already have suggested, but this looks at actual experience. This will raise serious questions about youth prisons: It is a model that is destined to fail."

A Broken System, a Commitment to Change

Juvenile justice reform has been underway in many states for two decades. Reports and studies during that time have shown the futility of programs of youth jails, Balis said. What sets this report apart from previous studies, he said, is the breadth of its findings, collected from 165 counties in Texas over a three-year period, and the fact that the state was so transparent in sharing its numbers.

"The report and the study behind it are a huge contribution to the field," Balis said. "All parties involved deserve a huge amount of credit. . . . This isn't just an academic study but one that will lead to key actions."

After abuses within the Texas system came to light in 2007, Texas leaders moved to reduce the number of incarcerated youth. They particularly aimed to move youth closer to home.

To measure how the state was doing and how young people were affected, Texas began using an information system that let it track youth referred to the juvenile justice system, whether they were incarcerated or on probation locally.

State officials collected 1.3 million records for about 466,000 youth.

Crime, Reincarceration Drop

A key finding was that the number of young people incarcerated between 2007 and 2012 dropped more than 60 percent, from 4,305 to 1,481. During that time, juvenile crime, as measured by arrests, dropped more than 30 percent, from 136,206 to 91,873.

While no causal connection can be established, the authors of the report cite the drop as evidence that Texans' safety was not compromised by changes in the law.

Another important finding was that the number of youth under the supervision of a local juvenile justice probation office declined 30 percent.

Youth who were under probation supervision were rearrested three years later less frequently (64 percent) than those released from a youth prison (77 percent), the report shows.

And, youth under supervision were far less likely to be reincarcerated. The three-year reincarceration rate for these youth was 13 percent for juveniles beginning probation supervision and 44 percent for juveniles released from a state-run juvenile correctional facility.

The numbers from the report are so striking, Balis said, that it "bolsters the already overwhelming evidence that confining juveniles in large correctional facilities far from their homes is a failed strategy."

The study also shows the importance of a data-driven approach to solving issues within the juvenile justice system, said Tony Fabelo of the Council of State Governments, the lead author of the report. With more detailed data, it is easier to see areas of concern, he said. That, in turn, can address where resources might need to be directed.

In Texas, for example, 80 percent of the funding for county juvenile probation offices comes from the county, while 20 percent comes from the state. The data reveal where counties might need more state resources or a rechanneling of the resources they already have, Fabelo said.

And while the report revealed good news, it also showed some areas that need continued attention, he said. Differences in outcomes between white and minority youth were apparent, and those merit deeper study. And, the study suggested that what works in the case of one youth will not necessarily work in another.

"There's a lot of room for improvement," Fabelo said. "There's no one size fits all. But hopefully, there will be conversations in the Legislature, the counties themselves and juvenile justice professionals working for their own plans in improving outcomes."

Critical Thinking

1. Why is incarcerating juveniles in large correctional facilities far from their homes a failed strategy?

2. What are the benefits of a data-driven approach to solving issues within the juvenile justice system?

Internet References

Juvenile Justice Information Exchange
   http://jjie.org/hub/community-based-alternatives/
The Council of State Governments
   http://csgjusticecenter.org
The Council of State Governments
   http://csgjusticecenter.org/youth/publications/closer-to-home/

Article Prepared by: Joanne Naughton

Juvenile Injustice: Truants Face Courts, Jailing without Legal Counsel to Aid Them

Tennessee court procedures highlight national debate over minor offenders' rights.

SUSAN FERRISS

Learning Outcomes

After reading this article, you will be able to:

- Describe "status offenses."

- Show the value of having legal counsel at a court appearance.

- State what the 1974 federal law provides, and what the 1980 amendment allows.

K noxville, TN—She was barely 15 and scared at the prospect of being in court. She agreed to plead guilty to truancy. But when Judge Tim Irwin announced what he planned to do with her, the girl known as A.G. screamed in disbelief.

Guards forced the sobbing teen out of the Knox County Juvenile Court and clapped shackles on her legs. She had been struggling with crippling anxiety and what she said was relentless bullying at school. Now she was being led through a county juvenile detention center to a cell with a sliver of a window and a concrete slab with a mattress. For truancy.

"I cried all night long," A.G. said. "It seemed like everyone was against us in court."

Like tens of thousands of kids every year, A.G. was in court to answer for a noncriminal infraction that only a minor can

commit. These infractions are called "status offenses," and they can include skipping school, running away, underage drinking or smoking or violating curfews. But since status offenses aren't technically crimes, indigent minors don't benefit from the constitutional right to the appointment of defense counsel before they plead guilty.

That meant A.G. whose family couldn't afford to hire a lawyer, was left with no trained defense counsel to argue that there might be justifiable reasons why she was having so much trouble going to school.

It also meant the girl had no counsel to object to her abrupt jailing in April 2008—a jailing that lawyers who reviewed A.G.'s file argue exceeded the court's statutory power during the teen's first appearance in court.

"A.G.'s incarceration immediately following her guilty plea for truancy, a status offense, was illegal under state and federal law," asserted Dean Rivkin, a law professor at the University of Tennessee who later represented A.G. and oversees the Knoxville campus' Education Law Practicum.

Due to litigation that's pending, Irwin declined repeated request to comment on A.G.'s case or those of other prosecuted truants, some of whom were also jailed.

A.G.'s lockup has never been investigated or reviewed on appeal. But it's the type of allegation that's put Tennessee at the center of a national debate over whether status offenders should be guaranteed immediate legal counsel once in court—to ensure minors' basic rights are respected—and under what conditions they can be incarcerated.

In late February, the nation's top juvenile justice official quietly asked the Justice Department's civil rights division to investigate whether Tennessee status offenders were wrongly deprived of legal counsel.

A.G., who was already in counseling, was so shattered by her shackling and detention that when she was released at 7 A.M. the next day her parents took her to a doctor rather than straight to school, as they said they were ordered to do. Their daughter had become suicidal, and she spent the next week in a psychiatric hospital.

Unraveling the Rules

Forty years ago, a federal law—the Juvenile Justice and Delinquency Prevention Act—actually *barred* states that receive federal juvenile-justice funds from sending status offenders into detention, reflecting the widespread belief that incarcerating these minors exposes them to danger and bad influences. In 1980, though, Congress amended the 1974 federal Act to allow judges a significant federal exception to the lockup ban. It's called the "valid court order" exception.

The exception permits jailing as a last resort to try to control status offenders once they've pleaded guilty and gone on to violate *instructions* from the court: the valid court order. But if states want federal funds, lockup as a punitive response is only supposed to occur after courts hold multiple formal proceedings, give children time to comply with instructions, consider alternatives to jail—and take great care to ensure kids benefit from full due process rights, including right to appointment of defense counsel for indigent children.

This chance to obtain defense counsel must be afforded *before* status offenders face formal accusations that they've disobeyed valid court orders and could potentially face jailing or removal from parents' custody.

This same federal law *does* allow status offenders to be held in detention before trial for less than 24 hours or over a weekend, but only under limited circumstances—such as credible concern that minors might not appear at a scheduled hearing or because police have found kids wandering on streets and no non-jail shelter space is available, or because parents are not immediately available to pick them up.

If states don't ensure courts follow these requirements to provide legal counsel and limits on detention, they can get their federal delinquency-prevention grants pulled.

In A.G.'s case, "nobody said anything about an attorney," said A.G.'s mother, who had no idea what her daughter's rights were before A.G. pleaded guilty and was taken away and put into detention.

The Knox County District Attorney's office, which prosecutes truants, said children's privacy rights prohibit staff from commenting on specific cases like A.G.'s.

A Continuing Controversy in Knox County

Since late last year, the Center for Public Integrity has been reviewing previously sealed documents that suggest a vigorous pattern of locking up status offenders in Knox County. Families and attorneys here have also alleged that accused truants with diagnosed mental-health and other difficulties were shackled and jailed straight from court.

Children whose only infraction was struggling with a loathing for school were pulled into the criminal-justice system, branded with permanent delinquency records and jailed with kids who had actually committed crimes, parents complained. All this happened without their kids having lawyers, some parents said, and some children dropped out rather than getting back to an education.

Patricia Puritz, executive director of the nonprofit National Juvenile Defender Center in Washington, DC, said that across the country there is a disturbing shortage of timely legal representation to ensure kids' rights are respected when they're pulled into courts for crimes and for status offenses.

"Little people, little justice," Puritz said.

In Knox County, a behind-the-scenes disagreement over providing access to counsel continues.

Judge Irwin, the county's elected and sole juvenile court judge, has refused to allow volunteer lawyers to set up a project at the courthouse to offer free counsel to accused truants as they arrive with their parents for hearings, according to Harry Ogden, a Knoxville business attorney who wants to participate in such pro bono representation.

"This project can be a 'win-win' for the court, the school system, the D.A.'s office . . . and—most of all—at-risk children and youth," wrote Rivkin, the University of Tennessee law professor, in a December 2012 letter to Judge Irwin.

Irwin did not respond to Rivkin's plea, and has also declined to speak to the Center about his decision not to endorse the pro bono idea, which remains in limbo.

On the court's behalf, Knox County Law Director Richard Armstrong sent a letter to the Center for Public Integrity that said: "Children and their families are welcomed and encouraged to retain counsel in all matters brought before the juvenile courts of this state."

But in March of last year, "know your rights" brochures that the volunteer lawyers had left in the court lobby for families of accused truants were removed, according to an email that Rivkin wrote to Irwin and sent to him via the judge's administrative assistant.

"Needless to say," Rivkin wrote, "we were surprised to learn that the brochures had been removed from the rack shortly after they were placed there." Irwin did not respond to Rivkin's email and an offer to meet to talk about the brochures.

In February, Rivkin also requested that the Tennessee Supreme Court review an appeal of one truant's conviction; for the last 2 years, as part of a series of appeals, Rivkin has also been trying, so far in vain, to convince a state court to issue an opinion that would guarantee faster appointment of defense for accused truants.

Heavy Penalties, Confusing Courts

Whether all kids in courts, including status offenders, should automatically benefit from defense counsel is part of a broader national debate over just what legal rights children have, and whether the country's confusing patchwork of state and local regulations is enough to ensure children are treated fairly.

The National Juvenile Defender Center is leading an ongoing project that dispatches observers to juvenile courts, so they can recommend, state by state, measures to improve proceedings that are supposed to be primarily rehabilitative.

Puritz said observers have witnessed kids facing serious repercussions with no lawyers to advise them, either because they were not afforded counsel, or because they waived rights with a casual shrug that belied their confusion over what was at stake. In 2006, observers reported that half the kids they saw in Indiana courts waived counsel even though the minors were accused of misdemeanors or felonies.

Agitated parents, Puritz added, sometimes hope a rough court experience will scare a kid straight. But parents often fail to grasp, Puritz said, how pleading guilty even to a status offense can lead to penalties that could bedevil minors for years.

In Texas, teen Elizabeth Diaz spent 18 days in an adult county jail when a judge in Hidalgo County began a campaign in 2009 to collect old truancy fines. The judge issued warrants to arrest minors once they turned 17 and force them to pay—or get thrown in jail.

Elizabeth's $1,600 in fines had been imposed in a court where she had no counsel. She missed her high school exit exam while jailed, the American Civil Liberties Union said, and was traumatized by harassment in jail. A federal court in 2012 ruled that her detention for failing to pay fines she couldn't afford was an unconstitutional violation of due process.

In Knox County, A.G. was required to return to court a month after being jailed and hospitalized, but she was still not afforded an attorney. Another five months went by before, on her third court appearance, as was then the practice, A.G. was appointed a public defender, for a fee of $100. After several more months, with A.G. continuing to miss school and warned she'd be jailed again, the family was referred to Rivkin at the University of Tennessee campus in Knoxville.

Rivkin was able to put a hold on the teen's ongoing prosecution and began representing her in negotiations with her school.

A.G.'s case, her lawyers said, illustrates why they believe timely, trained counsel is in the child's best interest: In spite of increasing difficulties at school, A.G. was not tested for special needs or offered an alternative education plan before her name was turned over for truancy prosecution. Instead, A.G.'s parents said, school staff advised them to ask police to force A.G. out of the house and into the school building. Reluctantly, they followed that advice, but it only deepened the family's crisis.

School district staff said privacy rules prohibit them from discussing students' histories. But Melissa Massie, executive director of student support services for the Knox County School District, said that she had not heard of staff advising parents to call police. She did say, though, that she was critical of some past antitruancy efforts.

In 2010, approximately 137,000 status offenders like A.G. were "petitioned," or sent into courts nationwide, more than a third for truancy, according to statistics cited by the Vera Institute of Justice. In Tennessee alone in 2012, more than 9,600 minors were taken to court for truancy.

The Education Law Practicum Rivkin supervises offers pro bono help to Knoxville area families seeking special-education services. Like the Vera Institute, Rivkin favors a "counter-narrative" on truancy: When counselors take the time, they find that most chronic truants are struggling with learning disabilities, emotional distress or mental-health illness, bullying, violence, or financial or other crises.

Few of these kids or their parents, Rivkin said, can be expected to understand that kids have more options than just pleading guilty in court.

In Tennessee, as in many states, statutes theoretically limit juvenile courts to initially responding to truants who plead guilty by issuing them monetary fines, ordering them to perform community service and putting them on probation, with instructions to follow, and initiating the valid court order process.

States are also expected to conduct audits to monitor how well courts are complying with the limits on putting status offenders in detention. Periodically, federal justice authorities review these state audits to look for patterns of violations.

Last November, Rivkin wrote to Robert Listenbee, the head of the Justice Department's Office of Juvenile Justice and Delinquency Prevention, suggesting a hard look at the lockups of status offenders in Knox County and the rest of Tennessee.

He suspected federal officials—while signing off on grants to the state—were not getting the full story.

In a reply to Rivkin dated Feb. 28 of this year, Listenbee explained that he had asked the Justice Department's Civil Rights Division for an "investigation."

Failure to provide counsel to kids potentially facing incarceration, Listenbee wrote to Rivkin, if true, "would be of great concern to all of us here . . . and is not in keeping with the best practices outlined by this office."

Appealing to Higher Courts

In 2011, Rivkin began a prolonged and complex attempt to overturn convictions of four students' truancy convictions, in an attempt to clarify some of these issues.

He first lost before Irwin, then before the state's Fourth Circuit and then before a state Court of Appeals panel. He submitted a final appeal this year to the Tennessee Supreme Court on behalf of only one plaintiff. As of May, his review request was still pending.

Along the way, the battle has revealed that judges, lawyers and other officers of juvenile courts can have strikingly different interpretations of laws that can end up critical to a child's life: Do indigent status offenders have a right to appointed counsel before valid court orders are issued to them, or only after they are accused of violating orders and are thus vulnerable to judges legally jailing them or removing them from their parents' custody?

In essence, Rivkin has argued that accused truants have the constitutional right of appointment of counsel if not before pleading guilty, then before judges begin imposing court orders that could pave the way to incarceration.

"There may be compelling reasons why the [valid court order] is not warranted due to the juvenile's mental health condition, due to educational disabilities, due to family circumstances such as lack of transportation, etc.," Rivkin wrote in his appeal to the Fourth Circuit.

"Without an attorney it is unrealistic to expect a juvenile to make these arguments," he wrote. Waiting to afford children attorneys until they face imminent potential jailing, Rivkin wrote, is "too little, too late."

The four original plaintiffs were Knox County students who, like A.G., suffered from significant mental-health stress and had no legal counsel at their side when they pleaded guilty. None could afford to hire attorneys, and some parents said they didn't dream they would need legal counsel.

None were jailed the same day they pleaded guilty, but they were threatened with jailing, Rivkin's appeal alleged, if they violated any of a litany of instructions given to them under the label of probation or, in some cases, valid court orders.

The plaintiffs were admonished not to miss another day of school, unexcused, or face jail. They were also told not to get into any trouble at school, and to pay for and attend court-selected counseling programs. They were also ordered to submit to and pay for random, mandatory drug testing, although none faced drug charges.

One plaintiff, a 13-year-old middle school student identified as T.W., was jailed twice, without the benefit of legal counsel first appointed to represent him, according to the appeal.

On a February 2009 mandatory return to court after pleading guilty, T.W. was jailed overnight directly from court because his school reported he had accumulated more unexcused absences after pleading guilty. During another return to court in January 2010, T.W. was given a drug screen that registered positive for marijuana and he was immediately taken into juvenile detention again for several days.

Some kids Rivkin eventually represented at the Practicum were appointed public defenders during their third visit to court.

But Rivkin argued that there was nothing in T.W. or the other plaintiffs' files proving in writing, as required by state regulation, that they'd agreed to waive the right to defense. Like other parents, T.W.'s mother, Debbie Jones, submitted an affidavit declaring that her son was not informed of his full rights to counsel.

As his appeal moved through courts, Rivkin submitted an affidavit signed by Knox County Public Defender Mark Stephens in 2012 noting that the public defender's office had no record of a single request from the court between 2010 and fall of 2012 to represent a truant before valid court orders were imposed.

In some cases, including T.W.'s, the court assigned truants lawyers known as guardians ad litem, who advise judges on what they believe is best for children, including removal from the home. But these lawyers are distinct from defense counsel. Minors interviewed by the Center said that their guardians ad litem didn't object to them being jailed or drug tested, and didn't raise questions about their schools' responsibility to evaluate them for special needs—issues Rivkin later raised for truants after he began representing them.

Setbacks

In 2011, in his rejection of Rivkin's appeal, Judge Irwin upheld his own convictions. In a written order, he said that the four truants entered court and after being advised of "the right to remain silent, the right to confront witnesses against them, and the right to an attorney, chose to enter a plea immediately, without the advice of counsel and offered no justification for . . . excessive absences."

But, again, while truants in Tennessee must be informed of the rights that Irwin recited, indigent status offenders don't have the right to the *appointment* of a defense attorney if they decide not to plead guilty and want a trial.

After Irwin's initial ruling, the state of Tennessee and the Knox County D.A.'s office took on the defense of the juvenile court's practices.

As part of that defense, the state argued that the juvenile court had adhered to proper procedure, including by jailing T.W., and that T.W. had missed a 10-day deadline for appealing his 2009 detention order. The state's lawyers submitted forms identified as court notes with identical language on them declaring that T.W., during each of his court appearances, was "advised of rights."

But as Rivkin noted in a filing, the state didn't challenge the argument that there were no signed waivers in the files of his plaintiffs.

In 2012, in a second rejection for Rivkin, Judge Bill Swann of the Fourth Circuit found that the juvenile court's actions were generally proper. He didn't opine on whether he thought T.W. had been appropriately afforded an opportunity for appointed counsel before he was jailed. But Swann did reject Rivkin's interpretation of federal law, arguing that existing law requires appointment of counsel only *after* indigent truants have already violated valid court orders and face possible incarceration.

"The constitutional right to counsel only attaches at that point, and not before," Swann wrote. But he added that the plaintiffs "laudably urge the advancement of a social policy" that only the state's legislators could change.

Last December, when a Court of Appeals panel also rejected Rivkin's arguments, the judges found that the plaintiffs didn't meet the burden of new evidence to justify a review of their convictions.

Knox County District Attorney Special Counsel John Gill told the Center for Public Integrity that the D.A.'s office acknowledges that state and federal law do not permit jailing truants except when valid court orders are issued and kids are informed that they have a right to the appointment of an attorney.

Asked about general allegations that kids were put into detention frequently in recent past years perhaps without understanding their rights, Gill did say: "There were some practices that hadn't been scrutinized."

"I'm not saying it hasn't happened," Gill said, referring to truants being jailed.

He said that he doesn't believe that valid court orders are currently being issued in the court to handle truants or that they are being jailed. The D.A.'s interest, he said, is "getting kids back to school, not convictions and not in locking them up."

How Many Were Shackled, Handcuffed, and Jailed?

In his appeal filings, Rivkin noted that by Knox County's own count, more than 600 accused truants were called to the juvenile court between 2008 and 2012. But it's hard to determine who among them was locked up because the court refuses to release detailed detention data that could include reasons for jailing, and whether detention was pretrial or posttrial and if the kids had counsel.

Without transparent data, Rivkin said, "there is no way of knowing how many children and youth have suffered the consequences our clients did before we began representing them."

In 2011, Rivkin filed public record act requests asking for lockup information, with juveniles' names redacted. Irwin declined the request. The judge retained a lawyer for himself, Robert Watson of Knoxville, who has since died. Watson argued in a letter that the records were "confidential and inspection is allowed only if the judge so chooses."

A Center associate in Tennessee filed a request for redacted juvenile detention records and was told in January that she would have to provide $17,500 in processing costs to Knox County first.

In the meantime, Rivkin was able to obtain, though an unofficial channel, an internal Knox court compilation tracing status offender histories over several years; the document contains no information about whether lawyers were appointed. But it is illuminating nonetheless.

The Center reviewed the compilation, which was submitted to the Fourth Circuit Court. The review found that in 2009 alone more than 50 status offenders identified only by "client" numbers were put into detention. The only charge listed in connection with some lockups was truancy. Most followed a succession of prior appearances and prior detentions for a mix of infractions no greater than truancy, running away, cigarette possession, curfew violation and probation revocation or valid court order violations.

One minor, the records show, appeared in court twice for truancy in 2006 and 2007, and then had probation revoked in 2008 and was put into detention that same year. The same minor was back in court again for tobacco possession in 2008, followed by revocation of probation again and detention again. In 2009, the minor was in court again for revocation of probation and again put into detention.

A young woman who asked to be identified as K.P. also has a history of cycling through court in Knox County during this time frame.

In February 2008, when she was 15, she pleaded guilty to truancy, without the benefit of an attorney. She was arrested twice later that year and put into detention both times. She was accused of disobeying truancy probation, but she had no valid court order in her file, lawyers at the Practicum who later represented her said.

In September 2008, K.P. was held for several days in detention. There was nothing in her file to indicate that she was being held to ensure she would appear for a court hearing that had been scheduled. In December 2008, K.P. was arrested by police again, this time in front of classmates, while she was attending classes at the same school she was accused of failing to attend.

"Defendant was picked up at [redacted] High School on an outstanding petition for revocation of probation. She was transported to Knox County Juvenile Center," an arrest report says.

In an interview, K.P. said that being put into handcuffs, shackles and prison garb "only made me want to rebel more."

She said she originally began refusing to go to classes because of sexual harassment—she was attacked on the school bus she rode daily—and because she had developed anxiety and bladder problems at school. She said her complaints were not addressed at school, and she was not offered an alternative learning option.

"These are not all kids with chains hanging off their belts, in gangs," said attorney Brenda McGee, who is Rivkin's wife and collaborates with the Education Practicum, and much later represented K.P.

State Proposal to Ensure Truants Get Counsel Fails

In 2012, a fledgling attempt to pass state legislation establishing an immediate right to appointment of counsel for truants quickly died.

The measure failed to get out of a subcommittee after it was estimated the state indigent defense fund would require an additional half a million dollars a year; that sounds modest, said its sponsor, former Sen. Andy Berke, now mayor of Chattanooga. But the increase was too much for some legislators, Berke said, given that less than $2 million out $37 million spent from the fund in 2010 went to juvenile defense.

Because of this failure, Rivkin believes it's more important than ever to provide pro bono counsel to accused truants.

States' rules and statutes all vary, and there's virtually no formal data on the issue, but Rivkin estimates based on his own research that 33 states now ensure a relatively early right to counsel for truants during court proceedings.

In some states, such as Pennsylvania, counsel is automatic and can only be waived after multiple steps to ensure children grasp what they are doing. Pennsylvania was rocked by a scandal a couple of years ago when two juvenile court judges in Wilkes-Barre were found guilty of taking bribes for sending kids who had waived counsel to do time at private detention camps.

Puritz of the National Juvenile Defender Center remains concerned that minors, who are being processed through crowded courts, too frequently waive rights even in states with expansive rights to counsel on paper.

The idea to offer pro bono counsel to accused truants in Knox County is modeled after a similar project in Atlanta. Judge Irwin privately confided to lawyers that he didn't think accused truants had extensive unmet legal needs, according to Harry Ogden of Knoxville's prominent Baker Donelson firm, one of those attorneys who tried to personally persuade the judge to support the project.

"He's a great guy," Ogden said of the judge, "but when you're 14 years old, and standing in front of the juvenile judge, then you are probably about as tongue-tied as I was as a third-year law student in front of a judge."

Unnecessary Drug Rehab, Diagnoses Ignored

Irwin, 55, is a 6-foot-7 former University of Tennessee football hero who went on to a more than 14-year-pro-football career, 13 of those years as a tackle for the Minnesota Vikings. He has plenty of fans in Knoxville who admire his strong support for the local Boys and Girls Club, and gestures like passing out stuffed animals to small kids in court who could be taken from parents due to neglect.

But A.G. and other truants said that the judge, who's been on the bench since 2005, was intimidating. A.G. said that when she returned to court after her stay in a psychiatric hospital, she tried to tell him about a diagnosis she was given of "school phobia" and bipolar disorder.

"He said, 'I have a phobia, too. It's a phobia of kids not going to school,'" according to A.G.

K.P. and her mother today believe that a hostile court environment forced the family into a decision they regret and believe could have been avoided if they'd had legal counsel.

When K.P. tested positive for marijuana while on truancy probation, her mother feared the court would take her child into state custody and foster care. The mother panicked, and scrambled to find space in a secure drug and behavior rehab facility—for nine months—even though she didn't believe K.P. required such treatment. The move satisfied the court, K.P.'s mother said, but "nearly tore us apart."

"They walked all over us because we didn't have a representative," said K.P.'s mom.

K.P. said, "I lost a year of my life. Being at that rehab center didn't help at all. It was awful. I felt like I didn't belong there."

Debbie Jones, T.W.'s mom and a daycare worker, has stuck with Rivkin's appeal because she feels the court's treatment of her son made his problems worse.

Jones told the Center that T.W. loved school as a young boy. "I couldn't pay him to stay home when he was sick," she said. But at 13, he became reclusive, and struggled with classroom learning. He pretended to board his school bus and hid out instead of going to classes.

"He said he felt smothered at school," Jones said.

For all the punitive treatment he received, T.W. never graduated and now he's too old to be prosecuted. Rivkin is looking for a suitable adult school for T.W., whose phobias make it difficult for him to sit among large groups.

John Gill, the D.A.'s special counsel, said that office has been working more diligently with educators and social workers to address roots of truancy and avoid putting kids into court.

About 80 percent of initial truancy complaints the D.A. gets are resolved now, he said, after families attend the mass meetings warning them to straighten out problems. New petitions—not including ongoing petitions—to prosecute these kids declined to 65 in 2012 compared to 76 in 2011.

Knox County Assistant Public Defender Christina Kleiser said the court's reaction to truancy seems to have softened. But not long ago, when police were referring to truancy as a "gateway crime," Kleiser said many truants were getting locked up over weekends to show toughness.

Massie, who leads the school district's student support services, admits to inconsistent intervention in the past to help struggling students who were frequently absent. Educators, she said, are now required to follow an intervention checklist and convene meetings more promptly with parents so specialists can evaluate students and plan targeted support.

"I think the truancy program is much better than it was before," she said.

But she said that by statute, the district is still required to provide the D.A.'s office with names of students when they reach more than 10 unexcused absences.

Although his pro bono services remain little known, Rivkin said, two parents did contact him this year complaining that children with emotional problems were threatened at school with jailing if they missed more school. Last fall, Rivkin also met, by chance, Carla Staley, a mom who received a warning letter from the D.A. accusing her son Lowell, 13, who has cerebral palsy, with excessive absences that could land them in court.

National Trends, Federal Teeth

Knox County isn't the only region where truancy has galvanized community crackdowns.

Communities want to increase graduation rates, boost collection of attendance-based funding schools lose when kids are absent, and keep kids off the streets. But aggressive campaigns involving prosecution are attracting scrutiny, especially when minors are not afforded counsel.

In Washington state, another lawsuit over truants' right to counsel led—briefly—to expansion of that right. In the state's Bellevue School District, a 13-year-old girl, a Bosnian refugee, appeared at an initial truancy hearing in 2006 with no counsel and signed a promise to attend school or face penalties ranging from community service to "house arrest, work crew and possibly detention," according to the American Civil Liberties Union.

The girl was appointed an attorney only when found in contempt because her absences continued and she then faced imminent punishment.

Asked to weigh in, that state's Courts of Appeals found that all accused truants had a constitutional right to counsel from the onset of hearings that could lead to penalties. The Washington State Supreme Court overturned that ruling in 2011, favoring the state's argument that truancy statutes protect a child's right to education, so no counsel is initially required.

Last December, the board of trustees of the National Council of Juvenile and Family Court Judges took another approach by urging Congress to eliminate the valid court order exception as part of a long-overdue reauthorization of the 1974 federal juvenile justice act. Back in 1980, it was this same judges' group that urged Congress to include the valid court order exception.

In 2009, Sen. Patrick Leahy, D-Vt., proposed eliminating this exception in the reauthorization of the act—which Congress has still failed to do. And in March of this year, Rep. Tony Cardenas, Democrat from California's San Fernando Valley, also introduced legislation to get rid of the valid court order.

Federal official Listenbee, a former defense attorney, is also starting to speak out more in his new role as the nation's top juvenile-justice official.

In a speech he gave last August, he warned that detention should not be taken lightly. "Research has . . . shown," Listenbee said, "that the minute a youth sets foot in detention or lockup, he or she has a 50 percent chance of entering the criminal justice system as an adult."

In March, Listenbee responded to Center for Public Integrity's inquiries about when his office believes status offenders' right to appointment of counsel begins.

Language in the federal regulations does not specifically address whether judges must afford appointment of counsel to kids before they are issued valid court orders, Listenbee acknowledged. But he believes that this is the intent. He also said he doesn't believe states can claim they're following the rules unless they ensure that courts provide counsel before valid court orders are meted out.

"Attorneys should be appointed in advance so they can have an opportunity to meet with their clients and properly prepare for the hearings," Listenbee said. "We make this clear in our training [for state officials] and do our best to emphasize this expectation in communicating with states around compliance matters."

In January, auditors on a visit from Listenbee's office found that Tennessee must "prioritize training and technical assistance" to ensure respect for due process and the valid court order process. But auditors only examined 2012 data.

As for A.G. and K.P., they're both 20 now. It was only last summer, after both young women turned 19, that Rivkin and McGee were legally able to request that Irwin expunge delinquency records the young women said they didn't even know the judge had given them back when they were teens. The judge granted the requests to expunge the records.

Delinquency records equate status offenders with kids who've committed crimes. And they remain on file, if they aren't expunged. A delinquency record can follow a youth, surfacing to jeopardize job, college, and other applications, lawyers warn.

After the Practicum began to represent A.G., more than a year after she was jailed, A.G.'s school finally designed a learning plan that shielded her from crowds of students and bullying and enabled her to graduate in 2011.

Looking back, K.P. said the adults who ultimately helped her finish high school in 2011 were the lawyers at the Practicum, who pushed for the school district to evaluate her for special needs and provide her a special-education plan—after she was twice jailed and put into unnecessary rehab for nine months.

With lawyers' help, she said, "I actually graduated a year early. So much for being the bad kid."

Critical Thinking

1. Should minors be able to waive their rights in court without a lawyer to advise them about what, exactly, those rights are?

2. Should Congress eliminate the "valid court order exception" to the 1974 federal juvenile justice act?

3. Does incarcerating young people have risks for their future adult lives?

Internet References

Center for Public Integrity
   https://www.documentcloud.org/documents/1156538-knox-truant-found-guilty-jailed-same-day.html
Create Central
   www.mhhe.com/createcentral
National Juvenile Defender Center
   http://www.njdc.info/pdf/Indiana%20Assessment.pdf

Reprinted by permission of The Center for Public Integrity.

Article

Prepared by: Joanne Naughton

Level 14

How a Home for Troubled Children Came Undone and What It Means for California's Chance at Reform

This story was co-published with the California Sunday Magazine.

JOAQUIN SAPIEN

Learning Outcomes

After reading this article, you will be able to:

- Describe some of the problems suffered by children entering FamiliesFirst.

- Compare group homes and wraparound care.

- Relate some of the problems faced by the staff of such facilities.

On the morning of June 6, 2013, Davis Police Department squad cars rolled up to the group home at 2100 Fifth Street. More than a dozen officers in bulletproof vests made their way past the facility's memorial planter bearing painted handprints of children. They were no strangers to the location.

For more than a year, officers had been grappling with problems at the home, one of California's largest residential facilities for emotionally damaged kids. They had repeatedly returned runaways. They had coaxed suicidal teens off rooftops. There were reports of fights, drug use, children having sex with adults. In a single week in the spring, Davis police responded to 74 calls. On May 29, though, there had been a report of a different order: An 11-year-old girl at the home claimed that boys from the facility had raped her. Two boys had been arrested. After months of unraveling, the home had come undone.

Over the next several days, the campus began to empty out as parents turned up, searching for their children and for answers about what had happened to them. Social workers scrambled to find alternate placements, sending some kids to emergency shelters. Others remained in dormitory rooms, where police tracked them down to ask a long-overdue question: Do you feel safe? State officials opened the inevitable investigation, interrogating the staff and combing through records.

In the months leading up to the raid, neither the police nor the Department of Social Services, the state agency responsible for regulating group homes, had prevented the disaster at FamiliesFirst. They didn't step in that spring when there were reports of children living in a homeless encampment in a nearby park. They didn't intervene when a 9-year-old girl, new to the home, wound up half naked on the doorstep of a house in Davis and was later detoxed in a hospital emergency room. A Department of Social Services investigator visited the campus repeatedly in the weeks before the police raid, but the agency never curbed the turmoil.

The breakdown at FamiliesFirst has helped spur California to rethink how it cares for its most troubled children, a question that for decades has confounded not just the state but the country. A panel of experts, officials, care providers, and families has generated a raft of reforms it hopes will soon become law. Over the years, the places that used to be repositories for such children—state psychiatric hospitals and juvenile detention centers—have been shuttered or scaled back, usually in the wake of their own scandals. Group homes, too, have increasingly been deemed a failed model, yet year after year vulnerable and volatile California children remain housed in them for lack of a better option.

The Davis facility, one of California's roughly 1,000 group homes, closed for good in September 2013. Spelled out in police records and Department of Social Services files, in budgets and in the recollections of staffers, is the story of negligent stewardship and a state agency's flawed oversight. It's a story that continues to haunt those it touched.

The Child

Alex Barschat-Li spent the first days of his life in the neonatal intensive care unit at Hoag Hospital in Newport Beach, California. Born on March 12, 1999, he experienced such severe breathing difficulties that his mother, Wendy, worried that he might not survive. She was 29, supporting herself and her husband on a medical assistant's salary.

Two months after Alex came home, his parents split up. When Alex was 3, Wendy fell into such a deep depression that she checked herself into a psychiatric ward, sending him to his grandmother's. Upon her release, an aunt proposed that Wendy to marry an undocumented Chinese national in exchange for $10,000 in cash. Wendy married Peter Li on the day she met him, and ten years later, they're still together. "No one's ever treated me the way he does," she says. The family eventually moved to Roseville, half an hour north of Sacramento, where Wendy and Peter bought a floor-and-tile-installation business.

According to Wendy, Alex was an easy child the first years of his life. But after he turned 5, she became concerned about his behavior. He'd sit on the brick stoop and sing and wave at cars for hours. At 6, he would grab knives out of the kitchen cabinets and hold them against his neck. At 7, he spent hours underneath his bed, hoarding food and clothing. He obsessed over seemingly insignificant details, refusing to go to school unless his mother gave him a certain kind of pencil or allowed him to wear a particular pair of socks.

Wendy sought help from Child Protective Services, which arranged for counselors and therapists to come to the home. Alex's behavior, though, grew increasingly violent. He smashed furniture and windows. To protect themselves, Wendy and Peter installed a deadbolt on their bedroom door. Alex's food hoarding became so extreme that they secured the refrigerator and cabinets with padlocks. By the time Alex was 11, the police had come to the home at least 11 times, and he had been held for psychiatric evaluation seven times. He was diagnosed with a handful of disorders—attention deficit, anxiety, bipolar, oppositional defiant—requiring a complicated set of prescriptions, many of which had side effects.

Alex broke Wendy's resolve the afternoon he beat her bedroom door down with a kitchen chair. Peter barely managed to restrain Alex until the police arrived. "I was in a panic," she says. "I knew in my heart that if I didn't do something extreme he was going to be one of those kids I saw on TV for raping someone or making a bomb."

Wendy's options were limited. Only 11 of California's 58 counties have hospitals that provide psychiatric care, and those that do have few beds. Psychiatrists had suggested that Wendy get Alex placed in a residential treatment facility. California's system for group homes is arcane, shaped by decades of litigation and legislation. The homes are classified by levels that range from 1 through 14. The top two levels serve the most troubled children and are required by law to provide intensive psychiatric services.

A child "graduates" from a Level 14 home when it is deemed he or she can function either in a lower-level group home or a foster home, or with a relative or a biological parent. The goal is to get the child to something that most closely resembles a family.

When Alex was 11, he was sent to Compass Rose, a Level 12 group home in Loomis, California. Three months in, on a cold winter morning, he and a friend were found walking alongside the I-80 freeway in shorts and T-shirts. Alex soon ran away again, showing up at a nearby church, where he told a couple that his parents had abandoned him. After police took Alex back to Compass Rose, administrators told Wendy they'd had enough. Alex, they said, needed to be in a more restrictive group home with more intensive therapeutic services.

Alex's social worker identified two homes: Milhous Treatment Center in Nevada City and FamiliesFirst in Davis. Wendy visited both. The 6.5-acre FamiliesFirst campus, she says, was by far the more impressive. It included a school, a gym, an arts center, and eight to nine-bedroom dormitories—with names likes Pioneer House and Sapphire House—that looked out onto a large playground and an expanse of lawn.

Alex entered FamiliesFirst on April 7, 2011. He was now among the roughly 750 children in California living in a Level 14 facility.

FamiliesFirst was founded in 1974 by a 26-year-old University of California at Davis graduate named Evelyn Praul. She started with a single foster home, two employees, and three emotionally disturbed boys. Over the next two decades, Praul opened six more group homes for boys in Davis and expanded throughout Northern California. In 1994, Praul decided to build a campus at 2100 Fifth Street in the southwest corner of town. Centralizing the Davis homes, she concluded, would help the organization serve more children and make it easier for staff to respond to emergencies.

Building the campus, though, proved costly, and by the mid-2000s, the facility was running a deficit. The home's ability to meet its obligations depended on the number of children counties referred to the facility. (The current rate for Level 14 homes is $9,669 per child per month.) As a rule, group homes budget for 90 percent capacity, but the referral stream can dip and surge from month to month. If the population falls below 90 percent over an extended period of time, a home can quickly go into the red, a situation that the Davis campus found itself in.

There was an additional factor working against the facility. In the mid-1990s, just as FamiliesFirst decided to build the Davis campus, California and many other states were beginning to question the value of group homes. Concentrating troubled children in a residence, many had come to believe, tended to exacerbate their problems and make their disorders more difficult to address. Instead the state was considering a model of treatment known as wraparound care, which involves bringing therapists and counselors into the homes where children reside. Focused attention on the child within a household was viewed as a less disruptive approach that could also closely examine family dynamics.

Deciding it could not make it on its own, in 2009 FamiliesFirst merged with a larger nonprofit called Eastfield Ming Quong, or EMQ, which functioned mostly in the Bay Area and surrounding counties. The deal offered obvious advantages to both organizations. FamiliesFirst worked in regions where EMQ had almost no presence, giving the newly constituted company, EMQ FamiliesFirst, a bigger share of the social-service market. In turn, the more financially secure EMQ could provide stability to the FamiliesFirst operations it absorbed.

When Alex came to the Davis campus, the facility employed more than 130 full- and part-time staff who could look after as many as 72 children. Like many such institutions, the home accommodated a dizzying assortment of children. They ranged from 6 to 18 years old. They came from all over the state, from wealthy families as well as poor. They were white, black, Latino, and Asian. Most had passed through countless sets of foster parents and group homes. Some had been sent by school districts that lacked the resources to respond to their needs. Some had been sent by courts as part of a sentence for a minor criminal offense.

"At any given time about 20 percent of our youth have a diagnosable disorder," says Dr. Gary Blau of the U.S. Department of Health and Human Services, "and 10 percent have a serious emotional disturbance, which means their disorder impairs their ability to function at home or in the community. The rarer occasion is that they are a danger to themselves, that they warrant hospitalization or residential treatment."

The children at FamiliesFirst, as in all Level 14 homes, suffered from a spectrum of psychiatric disorders: Asperger's, autism, attention deficit, bipolar, chronic depression, obsessive compulsive, and schizophrenia. Many were suicidal, nearly all assaultive, and some self-injurious. Many were confused about their sexuality and gender orientation. Many arrived with medical problems caused by malnourishment and neglect. Some had stunted growth. Some had Type 2 diabetes. Several had spent a portion of their lives living in closets, basements, or other confined spaces. One set of twins were said to have been forced by a relative to have sex with each other inside a locked cage. A 6-year-old boy, known at the home as Cowboy Dan, was said to have stolen at least three cars by the time he arrived.

The regimen was strict: out of bed at 7:00, breakfast at 7:30, classes at 8:00. At 2:00, the children retired to the dorms, had a snack, and broke up into small groups. They'd rotate through a treatment program made up of three separate sessions: art, recreation, and life skills. In the life-skills session, children were instructed in mastering the mundane: how to clean one's feet, for example, or how to figure out what size batteries to buy, or how to board a bus. Each child was expected to have a behavioral goal, usually simple, like saying something nice to someone twice a day.

Just 12 years old when he arrived, Alex was big for his age—five foot two and 163 pounds—with short brown hair and high cheekbones. He was used to imposing himself physically and didn't take well to the structure. Early on, he got into a fight with a smaller boy and ended up in one of the campus's many "quiet rooms," which were meant to give a child in the throes of a tantrum a safe place to "de-escalate." For Alex, the experience seemed to have the opposite effect. "I got thrown in there all the time," he says. "I hated it because I would catastrophize. I thought I was being treated like an animal."

Alternately affectionate and sullen, Alex was prone to radical mood swings, speaking in a rapid staccato one minute, turning almost monosyllabic the next. According to an evaluation report sent to Wendy six months into his stay, he suffered from "an inability to build or maintain satisfactory interpersonal relationships with peers and teachers." A minor annoyance or a denial of a privilege could set him off, and he would hurl himself at whoever irked him.

In time, though, he began to show signs of progress. In the fall of 2012, he moved into a dorm called Adventurer, which was led by a group of experienced staffers who connected with him. He was still easily distracted and easily angered, but the extremes had leveled off. Where once he threw tantrums during chores, he would now take a break in his room, gather his composure, and get back to the task at hand. He was less confrontational, less violent—happier.

Toward the end of 2012, Alex noticed that there were fewer counselors on campus—he had heard there had been layoffs—and that they seemed to be under more stress than usual. They also had become more lenient. He could now walk off the campus without anyone stopping him, and whenever someone had a manic episode, the staff was less likely to employ restraints, the term for the physical holds staff are allowed to use to prevent children from harming themselves or others.

At first, Alex left campus by himself, often hanging out at a bicycle shop where the employees liked him. He went to a Dairy Queen and moped until an employee gave him an order of fries on the house. Soon he was tagging along with a group of eight to twelve children from the home who stole food and clothing from stores around Davis. They started staying out all night, drinking alcohol, smoking pot, and having sex in parks. Before long he and others were hitchhiking out of town. Alex got as far as Sacramento.

"We had different jobs for different kids," says Alex, whose task was to shoplift. "Kids who begged, kids who found bikes for us, kids who went back to campus to get blankets and stuff. We'd be gone for days."

Early in the spring of 2013, Alex and his friends took over a homeless encampment on the outskirts of a park, a tangle of blankets and mattresses, abandoned furniture and trash, all jammed into a thicket dense enough to obstruct the view of passersby. It was one of several places where the children began to sleep at night. Another favorite, which Alex calls Plan B, was behind a Comcast building alongside Interstate 80.

The staff rarely told Wendy when Alex wasn't on campus. Her most reliable way to find out his whereabouts was through his Facebook posts. Alex would go to a library and send her messages or she would see photos on his page that showed him in town. She says she drove to Davis many times looking for him. On June 3, she pleaded with him on Facebook: PLEASE ALEX PLEASE GO BACK TO THE GROUP HOME WHERE YOU ARE SAFE AND SURROUNDED BY PEOPLE THAT CARE ABOUT YOU.

He did return, but on June 6, Wendy found out he'd gone missing again, this time for two days. She drove to Davis and searched all his usual spots. Around 1:00 P.M., she called FamiliesFirst and a staffer told her Alex had turned up and was taking a shower. But when she arrived, she was told it had been a mistake: No one knew where Alex was. Furious, Wendy went looking for him again. At 3:00, staff told her that Alex had been picked up by his social worker and removed from the home. They wouldn't say where. All they said was that police and reporters had been at the campus.

The Social Worker

After the merger in 2009, executives at EMQ FamiliesFirst faced a serious challenge: The Davis campus had lost nearly $1.5 million in the previous two years. According to a former financial officer at FamiliesFirst, making payroll every two weeks could be a "real white-knuckle" experience. In early 2010, executives turned to FamiliesFirst's longtime intake coordinator, Ron Fader, and asked if there was a population of underserved children that could keep the beds filled. Warily, Fader said yes: teenage girls.

For years, county social workers had been pleading with the Davis campus to accept girls. More recently, staffers at Community Care Licensing, the division of the Department of Social Services that oversees group homes, had pushed for the campus to go coed; the Sacramento region, they said, desperately needed a Level 14 facility for girls. FamiliesFirst, though, had always resisted. It wasn't just that girls with mental health needs acute enough to warrant Level 14 care are difficult to treat. They demand a different approach than boys. They would require hiring new staff and retraining old.

"I said, 'Look, I can fill the beds, no problem, but these girls present some extreme challenges,'" Fader says. "They are cutters. Many have a diagnosis of borderline personality disorder. They're sexually promiscuous. They're runners. Their behaviors are very intense, and they could possibly upset the milieu here."

Despite Fader's concerns, EMQ FamiliesFirst decided to go ahead, and in the summer of 2010 the Davis home opened its first dormitory for girls. The administration, though, hadn't established a policy on what boundaries should be set. Should the boys and girls be in the same classrooms? Could they walk to school together? Should relationships be forbidden? Essentially, it was an experiment: mixing highly volatile girls and highly volatile boys, many in the grip of changing hormones.

To Andrea Guthrie, who was a social worker at the Davis campus, it was a dangerous experiment. "Since the merger happened," Guthrie says, "there was this constant need to put the plane together in the middle of the sky."

Guthrie had been on staff since June 2000, a year after she graduated from the University of California at Davis. Her first job was as a counselor, for which she was paid $8.35 an hour. She took it mostly to pay her bills while she busied herself with Peace Corps applications. She was hoping to go to West Africa. But the reward of making progress with troubled kids hooked her, and she soon dropped her plans, deciding there was no sense in traveling across the world to make a difference when she could do it 25 minutes from where she grew up. She attended graduate school, earned her master's in counseling, and, in 2005, was promoted to clinical social worker at the home. Her new salary was $37,500.

The girls filled two dorms, and Guthrie's colleague Kim Rowerdink, who had some experience counseling girls, was named supervisor of one of them. Guthrie and Rowerdink often discussed how the girls mimicked one another. Outside of a group home, this wouldn't necessarily be alarming: It could mean girls dyeing their hair the same color or wearing the same clothes. But in an institutional environment it meant an abrupt surge in cutting, running away, or violence. Rowerdink once caught three girls trying to slash their arms at the same time. As part of their daily rounds, Guthrie helped her scour the dorm for any object that could be used to inflict injury—bobby pins, broken CDs, loose screws, and cracked light fixtures. If a girl with a history of harming herself ran off the campus, they'd try to stop her.

"I can tell you that my staff had no specific training whatsoever to address self-injury, suicidality, or anything like that," Rowerdink says. "It would just be one crisis after the next.

A girl would cut herself, we'd take her to the hospital, bring her back, and then she'd do it again. It was like Groundhog Day."

Rowerdink and others say this was the daily environment for the next two years. During one psychotic episode, a girl tried eating a light bulb. During another, a girl inserted shards of glass into her vagina and anus. Unlike Guthrie and Rowerdink, the vast majority of the staff who interacted with the kids did not have degrees in education, psychology, or social work. Most had received no more than seven days of classroom training, the standard for all employees, which offered an overview of children in Level 14 facilities and instruction in how to restrain them safely.

In the fall of 2012, Audrie Meyer, the home's director, announced a change in policy. From now on, she said, physically preventing children from leaving campus should occur only when they were in "immediate danger." If that was not the case, the counselors were instructed to shadow them. The directives perplexed and angered the staff. What did "immediate danger" mean? Did a girl have to be cutting herself or merely reaching for a sharp object? Did a child need to be standing in the middle of the freeway or walking toward it? The staff had always trusted some children to leave the campus and not others. Now what were they supposed to do? Sit back and let any kid take off?

No California law directly addresses whether a child is allowed to leave the grounds of a group home. Nor is there a law that says whether a group home is responsible for the actions of the child once the child crosses the property line. Group-home administrators develop their own policies on how to handle runaways based on their interpretation of three statutes: that a group home is responsible for providing care and supervision for every child it has taken in, that a group home cannot be locked, and that restraints can't be administered unless children pose an immediate danger to themselves or others.

The act of leaving the campus doesn't constitute an immediate danger, which means that a group-home counselor is not supposed to prevent a child from leaving. "It's extremely ambiguous," says Carroll Schroeder, the executive director for a trade group called the California Alliance of Child and Family Services. "Our experience has been that folks get caught between the protection of a child's personal rights and requirements to assure a child's safety."

Michael Weston, spokesman for the Department of Social Services, says that if a child is suicidal or has a reputation for leaving the campus and inflicting harm on herself or others, it's within a group administrator's authority to prevent that child from leaving. But group-home administrators say it's not as clear-cut as that. The department can cite a home for restraining a child from leaving campus if it believes the action was unnecessary, and it can cite a home for failing to supervise children who leave the campus and harm themselves or someone else.

"It's such a Catch-22 for our kind of program," says Steven Elson, the chief executive officer of Casa Pacifica, a group-care company in Southern California. "If we knew that a child had a plan to leave the campus and drink near a park with a 25-year-old friend, we would very likely contain the child. But you don't know about those things in advance."

In late January 2013, Guthrie was given an assignment she dreaded. She would be directly responsible for the girls' care in a dorm called Jade House. To her surprise, though, Guthrie found the girls endearing. They got excited about things that held no appeal for boys. The walls of the dorm were decorated in purple and pink and covered in Hello Kitty stickers, glitter, and posters of pop stars. A trip to Walmart to buy socks sent the girls over the moon. Early on, there were indications she was making inroads. One girl, schizophrenic and violent, no longer exhibited sudden aggressive episodes. Three girls graduated, their behaviors deemed stable enough for them to move in with a relative or into a lower-level home.

As the year went on, though, the victories became less frequent. That winter, EMQ FamiliesFirst had laid off the on-call workers the home relied on to fill in for sick or injured employees, and the staff immediately felt the pinch. "It was a budgeting decision," says Ron Fader. "Everyone knew it was going to create a house of cards." When staff became injured or burnt out, no one was now available to replace them. Social workers, therapists, and sometimes management had to supervise the children, an assignment usually designated for counselors, causing paperwork, group therapy, and other duties to slip. Guthrie began putting in 60 hours or more a week. Each morning, she woke up to an email inbox filled with urgent messages requesting that she follow up with children about violent events or disappearances from campus.

"We would dread the on-call rotations," Guthrie says, "because it was sheer hell—an entire week of not sleeping on top of already being completely exhausted."

The children began to realize how much they could get away with now that the facility was understaffed and the counselors had all but stopped employing restraints. One child ripped off large pieces of a metal gutter from a dormitory roof and hurled them at the staffers beneath. Others smashed windows and vandalized staff-owned vehicles. By April, Guthrie and other staff could no longer contain their frustration. They worried that it would be only a matter of time before a child was raped, or killed, or kidnapped.

At an all-staff meeting on April 24, Guthrie and others confronted Meyer, the home's director. They told her that several girls were coming back to campus with stories of having sex, sometimes with boys from the home, sometimes with adults in the community. Meyer's response was not what the staff expected. The children, she said, were going to have to learn to avoid such trouble on their own. Guthrie remembers looking around the room and seeing aghast expressions on the faces of her colleagues. "These kids are here because they cannot think like that," Guthrie says.

That day, a wisp of a girl arrived at Jade House. She was about four and a half feet tall, 75 pounds, and wore her unwashed blond hair at shoulder length. She tried to flirt and sit in the laps of staff. She spoke often of wanting a boyfriend. She adored a pair of high heels she said her mother had given her. She was 9 years old.

"She came in right before s—hit the fan," Guthrie says. "I was livid. I was like, 'Really? We can't even handle what we have right now, and you think that's an OK environment to bring this young of a kid into a teenage-girl house?' No."

Soon the girl was leaving overnight with children several years her senior. She told the campus nurse that she hitchhiked to nearby Woodland. She told a counselor that she performed oral sex on an older boy in a park; she said the boy urinated in her mouth. Early on a Saturday morning in late May, Guthrie was asleep in her studio apartment when her phone rang. The girl had been gone since Thursday. The counselor on the line said the police had located her and she was now in the emergency room, where she was being detoxed.

When Guthrie returned to work on Monday, she learned that the girl had been found partially naked after she had banged on the door of a house in a quiet residential neighborhood in Davis, begging for help. The girl couldn't recall much. She said she'd been with a group of older kids in an abandoned freight car near the railroad tracks alongside I-80. One of the older boys panhandled for some money to buy dresses for the girls at a Rite Aid and shoplifted some liquor. The crew met a homeless man who joined them for the freight-car party. The girl described him as "really nice." She said the last thing she remembered was taking a single swig from a bottle of alcohol the kids had passed around.

Guthrie told Meyer the story later that day. Meyer tried to remain calm, but Guthrie could see she was panicked.

The Police Officer

Jeff Beasley stood in the parking lot of Harrison Self-Storage. The facility shared a cinder-block wall with a corner of the campus. A police officer for 12 years, Beasley was the department's liaison to the group home. On this day in spring 2013, he was attempting to persuade yet another teenager from FamiliesFirst to come down off the storage roof. Beasley did what he'd always done. He asked the boy his name, where he was from, and why he was up there.

"F—you. You're a f—ing cop!" the boy shouted. "I don't have to listen to you."

Beasley took a deep breath and shook his head. "Yeah, yeah, that's fine," he replied. "But you know, we're not going

anywhere. You want to stay up there all day? You want to climb down? Or you want us to haul you down?"

"No," the boy said. "It's getting hot. I'll come down."

As he drove the boy back to campus, Beasley thought about the past two years. His fellow officers had talked the same boy off the same roof several times in the previous week. He'd talked at least three kids down off rooftops around Davis over the course of 18 months. The place was falling apart. The staff should know how to do such things on their own. Would the administration ever address the problems? Couldn't they, at a minimum, put up a barrier along the back wall to prevent children from reaching the storage facility?

For the first five months of 2013, the Davis Police Department received more than 500 calls involving FamiliesFirst. Most of the calls came from staff who were asking for assistance on campus. But many came from town: the Taco Bell on G Street, when children from the home terrorized employees and customers; the Sudwerk Brewery, around the corner from campus, where girls were often found bleeding after cutting themselves with broken bottles. Residents complained about kids harassing pedestrians. Store owners complained about kids shoplifting. Sometimes the kids themselves would call or show up at the station, demanding that the police take them to a psychiatric hospital.

For Beasley and his fellow officers, the calls raised large questions. Was defusing one more ugly and dangerous incident enough? Did the volume of problems at the facility constitute a threat to the welfare of the children and to Davis? Most of the time, in Beasley's judgment, the children weren't doing anything that warranted an arrest. They were already in the social welfare system. Some had done stints in juvenile detention. Sending them back into custody probably wasn't going to improve their situation, but bringing them back to the campus wasn't working, either.

Beasley was singularly qualified to be the department's liaison. He had graduated from Pacific Union College with a bachelor's degree in theology and had served as a pastor at an evangelical church in his 20s and 30s. He later earned a master's in counseling at the University of San Francisco, and, in 1991, accepted a job as a residential social worker in one of FamiliesFirst's three-bedroom homes in Davis. The place was special to him. It was where he met his wife—she was an office manager—and, in his four years there, he and other staffers developed a deep camaraderie, maybe because the work could be so draining.

One day, a 12-year-old boy asked for permission to spend time in a quiet room. When Beasley looked in several minutes later, the boy had smeared feces on the walls and was lying naked. He had blindfolded and gagged himself and was bleeding from his gums. He had torn his clothes and run the shreds through his teeth.

Beasley wanted to know more about where such troubled children came from, to see if he could do something at the problem's root. In 1996, he took a job as an investigator with Yolo County's Child Protective Services Department. He has no doubt that he saved lives—he removed countless children from deplorable conditions—but after four years, the job wore him out. At 47, he joined the Davis Police Department.

For a police officer, Davis is enticing. Magazines often cite the city as "one of the best places to live" in the United States. More than half of its 66,000 residents are either employees or students at the University of California, which dominates the south end of town. The violent-crime rate is less than half that of the average American city. Five murders have occurred in the past ten years. The work of police mostly involves traffic stops, burglary investigations, and breaking up the odd bar fight or raucous college party. As Beasley points out, "there is no wrong side of the tracks in Davis."

When Beasley was assigned as the department's liaison to the group home in November 2012, the two institutions were at an impasse. The home's administrators wanted officers to escort children back onto the campus when they ran away and help subdue them if they became unruly once they arrived. Beasley and another officer named Tony Dias explained that they were not private security guards. Beasley and Dias met with administrators once a month. They tried to come up with a way to handle the increase in calls to the police, a disproportionate number of which involved a group of about 12 children who routinely ran away and slept in parks around town—the group that Alex hung out with.

Beasley was well liked on campus. Fifty-eight years old, with short white hair and a neatly trimmed mustache, he still had a preacher's way, shifting easily from impassioned to contemplative. The children occasionally confided in him about another resident or staff member. He'd mentor some of the counselors in how to defuse situations or calm a disruptive child. Officers learned the backgrounds of many of the children who were leaving the campus regularly and tried to adjust their approaches when they picked them up so as not to retraumatize them. One officer played basketball with the kids on campus; another went on jogs with the kids and counselors. Still, a huge divide existed between how the home approached the children and how the police did. In general, staff thought the officers were too aggressive, and the officers thought the staff were too lenient.

By April 2013, five months after Beasley had become liaison, the relationship between officers and staff had become contentious. Police threatened to arrest staff for allowing children off campus. Counselors explained that policy prohibited them from preventing children from leaving. Beasley and Dias decided that the agency might take the department more seriously if top brass got involved. They turned to their supervisor,

Assistant Chief Darren Pytel. He had been concerned about the home since the fall of 2011, when emergency calls from the facility jumped almost threefold from the previous year. But the explosion of calls that began to occur in January 2013 had no precedent.

"Entire shifts were spent chasing around runaway kids," Pytel says. "The staff, even when they knew where the kids were, refused to come out and pick them up. They wanted us to drive them back, as if we were a taxicab service. Eventually, I couldn't walk into my office without one of my patrol officers saying, 'Hey, we've got to do something about this place.'"

In late April and then in early May, Pytel and several of his deputies met with administrators from the home. The first time was with Audrie Meyer. According to Pytel, the conversation devolved quickly. He told Meyer that the calls had exhausted his department's resources. Meyer explained that it was EMQ FamiliesFirst policy not to prevent children from leaving the campus and that doing so would constitute a violation of state guidelines. Pytel asked to meet with her superiors.

At the second meeting, EMQ FamiliesFirst regional director Gordon Richardson and a lawyer for the agency joined Meyer. They told Pytel that the home would revisit the runaway policy and consider transferring some children. Pytel came away convinced the agency's leadership was hopelessly lost.

"It was really clear that nothing was being done to change what was becoming significant criminal behavior," Pytel says. "What was so disturbing to me was that this facility was full of social workers and people whose job it was to help these minors, but that was not happening. These minors were not being protected. They were being victimized to a point that was just absolutely shocking."

Days after the second meeting, Pytel reached out to the Department of Social Services, imploring it to intervene. The department, Pytel says, didn't seem "to take great interest." (Department of Social Services spokesman Michael Weston says no record of any discussion was kept, but that the agency was "responsive to law enforcement.")

In late May, Beasley was assigned to investigate the alleged rape of an 11-year-old girl. She had been at the home just over a month and had fallen in with the children who were leaving the campus for days at a time. She came back one morning, after being out all night, and told counselors that she'd been drinking and smoking in a park with two boys, 13 and 14 years old, from the home. She said they took turns raping her while two other kids pinned her down.

After the staff reported the allegation, Beasley and a colleague spent hours talking to the alleged perpetrators and witnesses. (Another officer interviewed the victim.) The prime suspect drew diagrams for Beasley that showed who was having sex with whom on campus. He told him that adults in the community were providing them with alcohol and pot. He admitted to shoplifting. But he vehemently denied having sex with the 11-year-old. Beasley concluded that if anything sexual had occurred that night, it didn't rise to the level of criminal behavior. His partner came to the same conclusion about the second alleged perpetrator.

Beasley says he expressed his doubts, but that Pytel was adamant: He wanted an arrest. Beasley came away convinced that the assistant chief intended to use the charges to shut down the home. Beasley sympathized with Pytel's exasperation but was furious at his willingness to charge children erroneously.

Pytel denies Beasley's accusations. He notes that the local prosecutor wound up pursuing the case. One of the boys pleaded guilty to two felony counts of unlawful sexual battery, and the other was acquitted. He says his intention was never to close the home. "What we wanted," he says, "was for everything to go back to the way it was before."

To Beasley, the boys' arrest was a political move. The police could solve the problem of the home and look like saviors. "When children fleeing a dangerous environment and needing help came to Davis," he says, "Davis said, 'Get the f—out.' Whether it was the police department, FamiliesFirst, licensing, the judicial system, nobody asked, 'What can we do to help?' Instead it was, 'How fast can we get rid of them?'"

The Director

When EMQ FamiliesFirst asked Audrie Meyer to lead the Davis home in July 2012, she was surprised. By her own admission, she was not an obvious candidate. Meyer, who is 58 years old, had spent most of her professional life working as a tech consultant. Holding a master's in business administration, she helped build information systems for Pepsi and advised the French computer firm Groupe Bull on strategic planning.

She decided to change her career, and in 2008 she earned a master's degree in counseling and took a job as a social worker at a group home northeast of Sacramento. She left to join EMQ FamiliesFirst in 2011 as an associate director for the Davis facility's day-treatment program. She had been on the job for seven months when the head of the home resigned and she was asked to serve as interim director. She had been a licensed therapist for just two years.

Meyer was taking over the home at a particularly fraught moment. EMQ FamiliesFirst was beginning to question whether the Davis campus should remain open. Despite the addition of girls, the home continued to operate at a deficit. It was essential, she was told, that expenses be brought in line. Just as worrisome, the use of restraints on campus was unacceptably high, which was arousing concerns at the Department of Social Services. In 2011, staff employed restraints more than 800 times. In the first six months of 2012, they had already employed restraints more than 500 times.

Meyer enacted policy changes at a furious pace. In November, she lowered the campus's maximum to 63 children, laying off at least six full-time employees. By December she had eliminated all the part-time workers the home had relied on to fill in for staff absences. According to Meyer, several were made full-time, ensuring adequate supervision of the children.

Meyer also quickly zeroed in on restraints. Her supervisor was Gordon Richardson, who oversaw EMQ FamiliesFirst's operations in and around Sacramento. Meyer says he asked her to reduce the use of restraints by 25 percent from the previous year. (Like all current employees of EMQ FamiliesFirst, Richardson declined to be interviewed for this story. According to an EMQ FamiliesFirst spokesperson, "Due both to privacy concerns and pending litigation, we have been advised by legal counsel not to engage in further public comments regarding this past matter.") In October 2012, a staffer broke a child's arm in a restraint, drawing more scrutiny from the Department of Social Services. During the fall, Meyer met several times with Ashley Sinclaire, the department inspector assigned to the home, who warned her that the facility was in danger of losing its license if restraints weren't decreased substantially.

"For good or bad I got restraints down by 40 percent," Meyer says. "The downside for the program was it made the staff feel unsafe. When the staff feels unsafe, the children feel unsafe. At the same time that we are dropping restraints, licensing shows up and starts hammering me to drop them further, and the Davis Police Department starts threatening to arrest staff for letting kids off the campus."

People who work in the field agree that restraints ought to be used as infrequently as possible—as a last resort. The act can be necessary to maintain safety and order but can also be emotionally unsettling and physically dangerous for both the adult and the child. Overuse of restraints, most authorities say, is almost always an indication of deeper problems at a facility.

Leslie Morrison, an attorney for the nonprofit advocacy group Disability Rights California, is an opponent of restraints and believes that they can be avoided in all but the most extreme circumstances. But she said it's common for a group home to set a hard and fast goal to reduce restraints without properly teaching staff other means of calming children. "Senior management does this thing," she says, "where they used to go hands-on quite a lot and then, suddenly, they want no hands-on. What you have to do is give your staff a lot of training on alternatives. If you don't, you are going to have problems."

Meyer acknowledges that all the policy changes were too much too fast, but she also said the staff fought every attempt to reform the campus, even her efforts to have them learn alternatives to restraints.

Staff members insist that what was happening on the ground was much different from what Meyer saw from her office—that the workforce cuts, the belated training, and the new restraint policy had dangerously reduced the quality of care. From their point of view, it was a question of trust. They didn't believe that EMQ was committed to keeping the facility open. Just look at its history, they said: This was a company that had downsized its two group homes after it had decided that wraparound care was the future. For many of the staff, every budget cut that Meyer enacted was a precursor to EMQ shuttering the place; every policy change was setting them up to fail. According to Meyer, the staff's fears were not entirely off base. EMQ's executives never said so outright, but it was clear to her they were considering closing the campus.

Some staff were sympathetic toward Meyer. "I liked her," says Vivienne Roseby, a consulting psychologist at FamiliesFirst from 2000 until November 2012. "I think she was trying hard to do what EMQ wanted her to do, which was to get it tightened up, more efficient, more coherent. I do think that the pressure that she was under and the speed that she was being asked to make these changes made it difficult, if not impossible."

Roseby's, though, was a minority view. Most of the staff came to regard Meyer as distant and negligent, and the flash point was her policy on children leaving the campus. At staff meetings, Meyer repeated the message she'd been trying to get through from almost the moment she had arrived: The children, young and vulnerable as they were, were going to have to examine their own decisions about why they were leaving and what they were doing while they were gone. What happened to the children outside its walls was not the home's responsibility. California law, she said, was clear on this. Meyer assured the staff there was a logic to her thinking. If the children came to harm, the home could document the problem and perhaps get the children placed elsewhere. "Failing up," she called it.

"There is something wrong with this woman," says Kim Rowerdink, the dorm supervisor. "The police kept asking us, 'What is Audrie doing?' And we'd say, 'They keep telling us we're not responsible for what the kids do off campus. We can let them go.'"

Meyer, for her part, came to regard the staff as too emotionally involved. "It seemed completely foreign to them," she says, "that any program would not be able to stop a child from leaving the program. But you can't. I think the staff felt like it was the program's fault if the girls put themselves in harm's way, and I just don't think that's a fair statement."

Michael Weston of the Department of Social Services says Meyer's view amounts to a misguided understanding of a home's role. "The group home," he says, "is responsible for care and supervision, regardless whether the children are on campus or not." Referring to FamiliesFirst's policy guidelines, he says, "Read it right here. It talks about when a child goes off campus, we are responsible for their care and supervision."

In truth, that's not quite what the home's guidelines say. Rather, it states that staff will shadow children who leave the campus and will try to persuade them to return, employing restraints or calling police if they begin to harm themselves or someone else. The problem for the Davis home was that if its staff shadowed all the children who were leaving in the winter and spring of 2013, there would not be enough staff to supervise the children who remained on campus.

Between October 2012 and the beginning of May 2013, records show that Sinclaire and other licensing investigators visited the facility on at least 15 occasions. In late February, Sinclaire did bring up with Meyer the number of children leaving campus and the police's involvement in returning them. But Meyer says Sinclaire told her that she couldn't prevent children from leaving the campus by restraining them. (Michael Weston says that the Department of Social Services has no record of Sinclaire giving this directive. Sinclaire declined to comment, saying that she'd been instructed not to talk.)

Every group home in California must file a report to the Department of Social Services for a range of incidents, accidental or deliberate, alleged or substantiated. The roughly 500 reports that the home filed during the first four months of 2013 paint a picture of a facility whose staff and administration were overmatched. Meyer says that by April and May there were likely hundreds more reports that were never filed, in violation of state rules. "The volume went from 300 a month to 1,000 a month," she says, "and we didn't have enough trained people to file them."

From February to May, at least six counselors, therapists, and social workers resigned. "They were quitting faster than we could fill the jobs," Meyer says. According to people who had worked at the home for years, there'd never been a time when so many staff quit or took stress leave within such a short period. In May, the police received 252 calls, five times as many as they had received in January.

When Meyer made her superiors at EMQ FamiliesFirst aware of the problems on campus, she says, they were "very slow to grasp the seriousness of what was going on." She recalls several disconcerting conversations with Gordon Richardson: "When I relayed staff concerns about not having enough people, his reflection was, 'Well, maybe that's why restraints were down, and that's a good thing.'"

By late spring, Meyer says she became convinced the situation was hopeless. "I was very, very impacted by what was going on with these kids," she says. "I was not OK. I saw that it was horrible. When I realized the police weren't going to respond, and the staff was not getting support, and the kids were getting free rein—that was a horrible situation. I couldn't see a way to recover at that point."

Meyer was right. On the morning of June 6, she was sitting in the conference room once again listening to her staff express their frustration when she took a phone call. It was the front desk. Fifteen Davis police officers in bulletproof vests were in the lobby.

Epilogue

On January 9, 2015, California's Department of Social Services issued a 56-page report to the legislature outlining what needed to be done to care for the kinds of children who lived and suffered at the Davis home. The report called for increased minimum qualifications and training for group-care workers; more-varied therapeutic services; and better screening of children to more appropriately determine their needs and where they should be placed.

Most dramatically, the report called for group homes to be eliminated, or at least limited to offering short-term stays. "It is well-documented," the report states, "that residing long-term in group homes with shift-based care is not in the best interest of children and youth. Not only is it developmentally inappropriate, it frequently creates lifelong institutionalized behaviors and contributes to higher levels of involvement with the juvenile justice system and to poor educational outcomes."

As long as group homes exist, they will still present challenges of oversight. The Department of Social Services report says little about improving its own performance in inspecting and investigating the homes. To many, the department has long been poorly positioned or equipped to monitor Level 14 group homes. Inspections are required only once every five years, and records show they are perfunctory, mostly involving a review of physical conditions, food supplies, and water temperatures. The inspections typically do not include interviews with residents and staff or extensive examinations of records. The department employees charged with performing the inspections are not required to have backgrounds in social work, even though they are often called to look into what for an experienced police officer are the most sensitive kinds of cases—sex crimes and battery involving minors.

The state attorney general's office appears to recognize the responsibility for better protecting these children. In February, California attorney general Kamala Harris set up the Bureau of Children's Justice, a new division of the Department of Justice that will focus on holding counties and state government agencies accountable for crimes that concern child welfare.

When it comes to taking care of the state's most damaged children, the California legislature has too often been slow to act and reluctant to spend money. But Carroll Schroeder, the executive director of the California Alliance of Child and Family Services, thinks this time it could be different. "I feel much more optimistic [about it] than anything else I have seen," he says. "This is a once-in-a-generation opportunity to get it right." The report's proposals have been drafted into a formal bill that is expected to move through several legislative committees. It could be signed into law as early as July 1.

Today, the Davis campus is a ghost town. Its classrooms are empty, its hallways silent. For months food rotted in the refrigerators, bedding was piled up in the dorm rooms, and rules on restraints were still tacked on the walls.

EMQ FamiliesFirst, accused by the state of having failed to safeguard the children at the home, signed a stipulation conceding widespread violations. It continues to be one of the largest providers of social services in California. Gordon Richardson, who insisted to the state that he was not aware of the depth of the home's problems, remains a senior executive at the nonprofit.

Audrie Meyer was asked to resign in July 2013. Two months later, she signed a stipulation with the Department of Social Services. Without admitting to any of the allegations against her, she agreed never to work for another entity overseen by the department "for the balance of [her]life." She now runs a private therapy practice in Sacramento.

Andrea Guthrie was laid off in early August 2013. She now has her own family-therapy practice, working primarily with older teens, young adults, and couples. After more than 10 years working at the Davis campus, she's reluctant to work with children.

Jeff Beasley retired in August 2013, two months after the police raid.

Alex Barschat-Li was sent to another Level 14 facility after the raid. He was soon kicked out and moved to still another Level 14 residence. He graduated to a Level 12 facility. This past February, he returned home, and he now attends public high school, where he has joined the wrestling team. Wendy says she feels hopeful, but she's felt that way before.

Critical Thinking

1. What effect did layoffs of staff seem to have on the children?
2. What changes in the way troubled children are cared for would you recommend?

Internet References

Pro Publica

http://www.propublica.org/documents/item/1698895-families-first-davis-program-statement

Pro Publica

http://www.propublica.org/documents/item/1203114-2013-24-hour-ccl-reports-pbs-final-copy-redacted

Pro Publica

http://www.propublica.org/documents/item/1698860-ccr-legislativereport

Pro Publica

http://www.propublica.org/documents/item/1698848-ccl-familiesfirst-visits-october-2012-through

---

JOAQUIN SAPIEN has covered criminal justice, military healthcare, and environmental issues for ProPublica since 2008.

Article   Prepared by: Joanne Naughton

Arrest of Tennessee Children Exposes Flawed Juvenile Justice

SHEILA BURKE

Learning Outcomes

After reading this article, you will be able to:

- Discuss the report prepared by Police Chief Durr's committee.
- Relate some details about the alleged bullying.

Nashville, Tennessee (AP)—A Tennessee police officer tried to prevent the arrests that would embroil his department in a national furor over policing in schools, but his colleagues and supervisors refused to change course.

They insisted on arresting children as young as 9 years old at their elementary school and took them away—two in handcuffs—in view of waiting parents to a juvenile detention center as the school day came to an end.

What followed in Murfreesboro, about 30 miles southeast of Nashville, was an unusually public examination of how police handle children suspected of wrongdoing. Amid protests from parents and community leaders, the incident put the new police chief, Karl Durr—who had come from Oregon less than two weeks earlier—in a tough spot.

The chief formed a committee with a mandate to examine the situation. It found a series of internal conflicts and miscommunications between police and school authorities leading up to the arrests on April 15. The committee's report, though partially redacted, lays bare a reality that frustrates many parents in communities across the nation: officers assigned to schools often have wide leeway when handling juveniles, and the interests of children don't always come first.

Ten children, all African Americans 9- to 12-years-old, were taken to the juvenile detention center that day. Their alleged crime: taking part in some off-campus neighborhood bullying

weeks earlier. Some kids had recorded the bullying on their smartphones. An excerpt posted online shows a group of kids following and taunting a boy who shakes off some punches from smaller children.

The report says Officer Chris Williams wasn't aware of the planned arrests at Hobgood Elementary when he arrived. He later was told the students would be pulled out of class just before the afternoon bell. Bad idea, he thought.

The school's principal, Tammy Garrett, also tried to intervene, texting another officer to ask why the children couldn't be arrested at their homes, to avoid a spectacle during the school's afternoon dismissal.

But the text went unanswered, and two other officers who had concerns remained silent. And as Williams went up the chain of command, he was told to follow orders.

The bullying episode took place off school grounds, and was posted on YouTube on March 20. It's not clear exactly when it happened, and why officers waited for weeks to make the arrests at school. Murfreesboro Police spokesman Kyle Evans said in an email that state law prohibits him from answering these questions. Juvenile court petitions show 10 children—mostly boys—were charged with "criminal responsibility for the actions of another."

The report recommends 16 areas for improvement, including "establish protocol for juvenile operations in schools," and seeing that police supervisors are "proactively and fully addressing concerns of other officers." A group of local ministers is involved, recommending firmer standards and lines that shouldn't be crossed.

The officer who obtained the petition against the children has since been transferred, and a supervisor is on paid leave while under investigation.

The report places no blame on Williams, who did not respond to a request from The Associated Press for comment.

But he apologized to his congregation and others during a public meeting at the First Baptist Church of Murfreesboro, with Chief Durr in the audience.

Williams told the crowd his wife had only seen him cry twice: when his grandfather died and after the children were arrested, according to a report from WKRN.

"The principal shed tears, the vice principal shed tears, and the office staff shed tears," Williams added.

His pastor, the Rev. James McCarroll, said he thinks the new chief and other local officials want juvenile justice reforms that could create "a model for the rest of the country."

This goes way beyond Rutherford County, he said: "The school-to-prison pipeline is a problem around the country."

Lawyers and juvenile justice experts say it shows what can go awry when adults don't consider what's best for the children.

Nationwide, their treatment in criminal justice situations varies widely. Some states, counties, and cities allow even young children to be arrested; others don't. Some bar the shackling and handcuffing of kids; others make no exceptions. Some allow police to issue citations to juveniles rather than arrest them. Some require parents to be present when children are interrogated.

Whether to arrest a child at school for a minor offense committed off campus is a decision that varies by police agency, said Mo Canady, executive director of the National Association of School Resource Officers. The organization's guidelines for restraining or arresting kids is focused on children with special needs, he added.

Unlike some other states, Tennessee doesn't have a minimum age for when a child can be arrested. And under Rutherford County's rules, children must be brought to the juvenile detention center for even the most minor infractions, unless an officer decides to issue a verbal warning.

"I can't understand why we would treat a juvenile more harshly then we are treating adults who are accused of a crime," said Tom Castelli, legal director of the American Civil Liberties Union of Tennessee.

There is no clear national data showing how often children are handcuffed like adult criminals for relatively minor offenses, said Terry Maroney, a law professor at Vanderbilt University.

"It's safe to think this happens less frequently than you fear, but more than what you would like," Maroney said.

Copyright 2016 the Associated Press

Copyright Associated Press. All rights reserved. This material may not be published, broadcast, rewritten, or redistributed.

Critical Thinking

1. Do you think there should be a minimum age for when a child can be arrested?
2. Can you think of a better way the bullying incident could have been handled?

Internet References

NEA Today
http://neatoday.org/2015/01/05/school-prison-pipeline-time-shut/
Power U Center for Social Change
http://www.njjn.org/uploads/digital-library/Telling%20it%20Like%20it%20Is,%20STPP,%20Advancement%20Project,%208.24.11.pdf

Article   Prepared by: Joanne Naughton

Tribal Youth in the Juvenile Justice System

OFFICE OF JUVENILE JUSTICE AND DELINQUENCY PREVENTION

Learning Outcomes

After reading this article, you will be able to:

- Describe some of the problems faced by American Indian (AI) and Alaska Native (AN) young people who come in contact with the juvenile justice system.

- State how jurisdiction for crimes committed in Indian country is determined.

- Discuss some of the risk factors faced by AI/AN youth.

Research has examined the juvenile justice system's disparate treatment of racial and ethnic minorities. This research includes studies of the disproportionate representation of American Indian and Alaska Native (AI/AN) youth[1] across the contact points in the juvenile justice system; the lack of access to treatment, services, and other resources that AI/AN youth can obtain; and the risk factors that may increase AI/AN youth's contact with the justice system (Lindquist et al. 2014; Rodriguez 2008; Mmari et al. 2009; Rountree 2015).

Defining AI and AN Populations

AI/AN individuals are generally defined as people who identify as having some degree of tribal heritage and are recognized as members of these groups either by a tribe or the U.S. government (Dorgan et al. 2014). According to the 2010 census, the U.S. population comprises 308.7 million people, of which 5.2 million (1.7 percent) identified as AI/AN, either alone or in combination with another race category (Norris, Vines, and Hoeffel 2012).

The U.S. government recognizes 566[2] AI/AN tribes, most of which have their own distinct language and culture (Lindquist

et al. 2014; Indian Health Service 2015). The contemporary AI/AN population is also markedly diverse in terms of geographic distribution; roughly half of AI/AN populations live on reservations or tribal lands (federal or state reservations, AN areas, or designated tribal statistical areas). The other half live outside of designated AI/AN areas, particularly in urban areas (Beauvais, Jumper-Thurman, and Burnside 2008). Moreover, the AI/AN population is relatively young. The 2000 census showed that about 33 percent of this group was under age 18, compared with 26 percent of the total population, and that the median age for this group (29 years) was less than the median age (35 years) for the general U.S. population (Ogunwole 2006; Lindquist et al. 2014).

Jurisdictional Issues Faced by Tribal Youth

Crimes committed in Indian country (which is defined as all Indian lands and communities within the borders of the United States) can fall under the jurisdiction of the federal, state, or tribal justice systems (Dorgan et al. 2014; Adams et al. 2011). Jurisdiction depends on the following four factors: the location of the crime, type of crime, status of the perpetrator, and status of the victim.

In general, the federal government has jurisdiction over all federal crimes (including bank robbery and drug trafficking) committed in Indian country, regardless of whether the perpetrator or the victim is AI/AN (Adams et al. 2011; Motivans and Snyder 2011; Rountree 2015).

If the offense is not a federal crime, jurisdiction in Indian country depends on whether the state is designated a Public Law 280 (PL 280) state. In 1953, the federal government greatly expanded six states' jurisdiction over tribal matters under PL 280, which allows both the state and the tribe to have jurisdiction over the tribe (Tribal Law and Policy Institute n.d.). This means that even if a state decides to pursue a case against a tribal youth, this does not prevent the tribe from prosecuting the same case; in addition, the double jeopardy rule does not apply because tribes have inherent sovereign powers that are not derived from the federal government. If an AI/AN juvenile commits a crime in a PL 280 state, jurisdiction is shared by both the state and the tribe. Alternatively, if a non-AI/AN juvenile commits a crime, jurisdiction rests solely with the state (Adams et al. 2011; Tribal Law and Policy Institute n.d.).

Conversely, in other states, jurisdiction depends on whether the defendant is AI/AN, the victim is AI/AN, and whether the crime is considered a "major crime," as defined by the Major Crimes Act. The Major Crimes Act lists 15 offenses as major crimes such as murder and manslaughter. If a non-AI/AN individual committed the offense and the victim is AI/AN, jurisdiction rests with the federal government. Alternatively, if the case involves a non-AI/AN defendant against a non- AI/AN victim, the state has jurisdiction. Thus, at a minimum, for a tribal court to have jurisdiction, the defendant must be AI/AN (Adams et al. 2011).

This complex arrangement among the three jurisdictions (tribal, state, and federal) determines which justice system will handle the processing of tribal youth (Rountree 2015). This is not a situation which most youths, including those in other minority groups, must face; most juvenile cases are handled in state courts (Hockenberry and Puzzanchera 2014). In addition, determining which system will handle tribal youth cases depends on available resources, because tribal justice systems are often underfunded and unable to handle the processing (Dorgan et al. 2014).

Overrepresentation of Tribal Youth in the Justice System

Research suggests that tribal youths are more likely than their white peers to be arrested, adjudicated, and incarcerated in juvenile justice systems across the United States. For example, tribal youths are 50 percent more likely than white youths to receive the most punitive sanctions such as out-of-home placement after adjudication or a waiver to adult court.[3] One of the clearest examples of overrepresentation of tribal youth in the justice system can be found in the federal system: 60 percent of the federal juvenile justice population comprises tribal youth (Hartney 2008).

Only a small number of tribal youths are held in tribal facilities. For example, in 2007, only 13 percent of all detained tribal youths were held in jails or facilities on tribal lands. Such statistics show that not only are tribal youths disproportionally represented in the juvenile justice system, but they are also mostly housed in detention and long-term state and federal facilities that are far from tribal lands. This can negatively impact their ability to successfully reintegrate back into society (Lindquist et al. 2014).

A review of research conducted between 2002 and 2010 on racial disparities in the juvenile justice system uncovered 11 studies that examined the effect of being AI/AN on juvenile justice processing (Cohen et al. 2009). Across the 11 studies, the negative impact of race was found in over half of the case outcomes.

For example, 1 of the 11 studies was an analysis of referrals to juvenile court in Arizona. In this study, Rodriguez (2008) found that AI/AN youths were more likely than white youths to be detained, even when controlling for factors such as prior record and offense type. In another study of racial disparities in Alaska, it was found that AI/AN youths were less likely than white youths to be diverted from the juvenile justice system (Leiber, Johnson, and Fox 2006).

Overall, the review by Cohen and colleagues (2013) found that even when controlling for important factors—such as prior record, offense type, gender, and age—tribal youths still experience disparate treatment in the juvenile justice system, when compared with white youths. In addition, the review also found that, compared with other minority youth, there is a lack of research on AI/AN youth. The review located 56 studies on black youth and 30 studies on Hispanic/Latino youth, but only 11 studies on AI/AN youth (Cohen et al. 2013).

Risk Factors
Historical Trauma

Historical trauma in the lives of tribal youth is generally traced back to the erosion of tribal sovereignty in the late nineteenth and early twentieth centuries (Litt and Singleton n.d.; Eid et al. 2013; Rountree 2015). During this time, youths were sent to boarding schools, which forbade native languages and customs, causing generations of AI/AN people to lose connection with their tribal culture. Research also suggests that tribal youth are also still negatively impacted by the historical trauma that was caused by forced relocations, cultural assimilation, and broken treaties with the U.S. government (Litt and Singleton n.d.; Eid et al. 2013; Rountree 2015).

Violence

The exposure to violence is one of the most troubling problems facing tribal youth (Dorgan et al. 2014). In a study of the self-reported results from the Youth Risk Behavior Surveillance Survey, Pavkov and colleagues (2010) found that tribal youths were more likely than White youth to have carried a gun in the past 30 days, been involved in a physical fight in the last 12 months, been injured in a physical fight in the last 12 months, and been involved in a fight at school in the last 12 months. Tribal youth were also more likely than Hispanic/Latino youth to have carried a gun in the past 30 days and been injured in a fight in the last 12 months.

Tribal youths are also more likely than their peers to be the victims of serious violence or simple assault (Litt and Singleton n.d.). According to the Indian Law and Order Commission, the rate of posttraumatic stress disorder (PTSD) among tribal youths matches or exceeds the rate of PTSD in military personnel who have served in the Afghanistan, Iraq, and Persian Gulf Wars (Litt and Singleton n.d.; Eid et al. 2013).

Suicide

The Centers for Disease Control and Prevention found that between 1999 and 2009, tribal youths experienced suicide rates that were 50 percent higher than nontribal youths (Litt and Singleton n.d.). More recent research shows that tribal youths are 2.5 times more likely to die by suicide than nonnative youths (Eid et al. 2013). Moreover, some tribal leaders have indicated that approximately 20 percent of their youths have attempted suicide (Eid et al. 2013).

Substance Use

Alcohol use disorders are among the most severe health problems for AI/AN people (SAMHSA 2013). This chronic exposure to high substance use has negatively affected the younger generation and continued this vicious cycle. For instance, tribal youths use cigarettes, engage in binge drinking, and use illegal substances at greater rates than the general population (Litt and Singleton n.d.; Eid et al. 2013). Moreover, the Indian Law and Order Commission found that binge drinking is more common among tribal youths than any other racial or ethnic group, and that tribal youths up through the age of 24 are more than twice as likely to die as a result of binge drinking than non-tribal youths (Eid et al. 2013).

Lack of Cultural Instruction

Most tribal youths attend public schools operated by the town or city near their home, even if they live on reservations (Pavkov et al. 2010). However, Mmari and colleagues (2010) found that attending school outside of the reservation can be a risk factor. For example, Arizona passed English-only laws, which replaced previous bilingual laws in schools. As a result, cultural instruction has been limited—if not discontinued—and even AI/AN teachers can no longer teach the tribal language. Tribal youths who attend schools outside the reservations feel a loss of language and cultural identity, and ultimately experience family separation (Mmari et al. 2010).

Overall, these risk factors, in combination with poverty rates and tribal communities' frequent lack of funding for mental health and other services, make tribal youths more susceptible to coming into contact with the juvenile justice system.

Protective Factors

Protective factors are those characteristics of the child, family, and wider environment that can increase resiliency and reduce the likelihood of adversity leading to negative child outcomes and behaviors, such as contact with the juvenile justice system (Development Services Group, Inc. 2013).

Family

The presence and support of family can be an especially important protective factor for tribal youth. For example, Mmari and colleagues (2010) conducted focus groups with tribal community members and found that family, especially parents, can have a protective presence in the lives of tribal youth. Parental support and having a close relationship with parents was one of the most frequently cited protective factors among tribal members. A study by LaFromboise and colleagues (2006) surveyed AI adolescents in grades 5–8 to examine protective factors that impact resilience. They found that maternal warmth (a measure of parenting behavior) significantly increased the odds of a youth being resilient. As measures of maternal warmth increased, the measures of a youth's resilience also increased. Pu and colleagues (2013) studied protective factors for violence among AI students in grades 6–12. They found that perceived parental monitoring was a significant protective factor for violence among female tribal adolescents (although not among male adolescents). Female adolescents who perceived greater parental monitoring were more confident they could avoid getting involved in violence.

Culture

Culture (which includes traditional values, customs, activities, and ceremonies in AI/AN communities) can play an important, protective role in the lives of tribal youth. For example, one protective factor that Mmari and colleagues (2010) found to be particular to tribal youths was their knowledge of tribal language. Tribal language was seen as a way to teach youths about cultural values and customs. For some youths, this gave them a sense of purpose and guidance. However, this factor was not as important to all tribal youths who were interviewed. While some felt that their communities taught them the importance of learning the tribal language and cultural heritage, others did not feel it was as important to learn the language (Mmari et al. 2010). This particular finding emphasizes how tribal communities differ from each other, and how protective factors may be distinctive to particular tribes and tribal settings. Additionally,

LaFromboise and colleagues (2006) examined the impact of enculturation—which is the process of learning about one's native culture—on the resilience of AI adolescents. They found that the more enculturated the youths were, the greater their resilience. As measures of enculturation increased, youths were 1.8 times more likely to be resilient. Further, Whitbeck and colleagues (2001) found that enculturation was positively associated with school success, meaning that the more enculturated youths had higher class grades and more positive school attitudes. The results show the important and positive influence of traditional culture in the development of tribal youths.

Outcome Evidence

Few evidence-based programs target tribal youths and the particular problems they face. Below are examples of evidence-based programs that seek to address problems such as suicide and substance use, which are prevalent among tribal youths.

American Indian Life Skills Development.

Also known as Zuni Life Skills Development, this is a school-based, culturally sensitive, suicide-prevention program for AI/AN adolescents. Tailored to AI/AN norms and values, the curriculum was designed to reduce behavioral and cognitive factors associated with suicidal thinking and behavior. For the Zuni people, suicide is especially distressing because it is forbidden in their traditional culture (LaFromboise and Howard-Pitney 1995). Zuni leaders initiated the development of a suicide prevention program for students in grades 9 and 11, with the goal of reducing the risk factors related to suicidal behavior.

LaFromboise and Howard-Pitney (1995) found mixed results regarding the curriculum's impact on AI/AN students. The intervention group showed significantly fewer feelings of hopelessness and demonstrated a significantly higher level of suicide intervention skills than the no-intervention group. Intervention students also demonstrated significantly higher levels of problem-solving skills, but only in the more mild suicide scenario, and not in the more serious suicide scenario. But there were no significant effects on measures of suicide probability and depression.

Cherokee Talking Circle (CTC).

CTC is a culturally based intervention targeting substance use among AI/AN adolescents. The program was designed for students who were part of the United Keetoowah Band of Cherokee Indians, the eighth largest tribe in Oklahoma. The goal of CTC is to reduce substance use, with abstinence as the ideal outcome. CTC integrates Keetoowah–Cherokee values into the intervention and is based on the Cherokee concept of self-reliance. The Keetoowah–Cherokee use self-reliance as part of their overall worldview that all things come together to form a whole. Keetoowah–Cherokee leaders note that self-reliance is a way of life that directly affects health and helps maintain balance (Lowe et al. 2012).

An evaluation by Lowe and colleagues (2012) found that CTC was significantly more effective overall in reducing substance use and other related problem behaviors among AI/AN adolescents, compared with non-cultural, standard substance abuse education programs.

Bicultural Competence Skills Approach.

This is an intervention designed to prevent abuse of tobacco, alcohol, and other drugs by AI/AN adolescents by teaching them social skills. Intervention groups are led by two AI/AN counselors and include 10 to 15 sessions, of 50 minutes each. Through cognitive and behavioral methods tailored to the cultural prerogatives and reality of the lives of AI/AN youths, participants are instructed in and practice communication, coping, and discrimination skills. All sessions include discussion of AI/AN values, legends, and stories.

Schinke and colleagues (1988) found that at the 6-month follow up, program students were significantly more knowledgeable about substance use and abuse and held less favorable attitudes about substance use in the AI/AN culture; scored higher on measures of knowledge of substance abuse, self-control, alternative suggestions, and assertiveness; and reported less use of smoked tobacco, smokeless tobacco, alcohol, marijuana, and inhalants in the previous 14 days than their control group counterparts. At the 3-year follow-up, Schinke, Tepavac, and Cole (2000) found that rates of smokeless tobacco, alcohol, and marijuana use were lower by 43 percent, 24 percent, and 53 percent, respectively, for those who received the life skills training, as compared with the control group.

Project Venture.

This is an outdoor/experiential program that targets at-risk AI/AN youths. The program concentrates on AI/AN cultural values—such as learning from the natural world, spiritual awareness, family, and respect—to promote healthy, prosocial development. The goals of Project Venture are to help youths develop a positive self-concept, effective social and communication skills, a community service ethic, decision-making and problem-solving skills, and self-efficacy. By fostering these skills, the program aims to build generalized resilience; increase youths' resistance to alcohol, tobacco, and other drugs; and prevent other problem behaviors.

At the 18-month follow up, Carter, Straits, and Hall (2007) found mixed results; however, overall the program had a significant effect on alcohol use. Treatment youths demonstrated less growth in substance use, as measured by the four outcome measures (cigarettes, marijuana, alcohol, and other illicit substances) taken together. However, looking at the outcome measures separately, there was a significant effect found only for alcohol use. The other substances followed trends similar to alcohol use, but were not significant.

Outcome Evidence Limitations

Unfortunately, the impact of evidence-based programs for AI/AN youths is limited for reasons other than the often-cited lack of funding for tribal communities. First, although there are some studies that analyze the effectiveness of evidence-based programs on tribal populations (such as those described above), most evaluation research does not include AI/AN youths in study samples. Similarly, if AI/AN youths are included as part of the sample, the study does not usually include a subgroup analysis that could show how the program impacts AI/AN youths differently than other minority or non-minority youths. Second, even when tribal communities are interested in evidence-based programming, their concerns about whether the program aligns with tribal values can hinder widespread implementation (Walker et al. 2015). Third, not only are there differences between tribes and other minority groups, but there are also differences among the various tribes. As a result, a program that works in one tribal community may not work in others with different cultures, values, and philosophies (Melton 2004). For example, although the evaluation of Project Venture showed positive impacts on youths from the United Keetoowah Band of Cherokee Indians, the study noted that there were limitations to the generalizability of the program to other tribes in other communities (Lowe et al. 2012). Finally, evaluation studies of evidence-based programs in tribal communities are often cited as having study limitations, such as small sample size, short follow-up period, and the use of self-report measures instead of official measures of delinquency (Carter et al. 2007).

Recommendations from the Attorney General's Advisory Committee

The Attorney General's Advisory Committee on American Indian and Alaska Native Children Exposed to Violence was tasked with examining issues related to tribal youths' exposure to violence, and developing recommendations to address these problems. A number of recommendations put forth by the Committee focused on providing needed funding to tribal communities, and improving the federal- and state-level responses

to the violence-related issues that plague a large number of tribal communities and tribal youth (Dorgan et al. 2014). For instance, in 2013, as a result of sequestration, there was $85 billion in federal cuts to programmatic funding for populations throughout Indian Country, including for education and child welfare programs that assist tribal youth (Center for Native American Youth 2013).

With regard to the juvenile justice system, the Committee made a number of recommendations to improve the processing and rehabilitation of tribal youths, such as (1) providing publically funded legal representation, to ensure the protection of tribal youths' rights and minimize the harm that the justice system may cause; (2) only using detention when youths pose a danger to themselves or the community, and providing individually tailored services (such as reentry services) when detention is necessary; and (3) providing trauma-informed, culturally appropriate screening, assessment, and care throughout the federal, state, and tribal justice systems (Dorgan et al. 2014).

Conclusion

Advocates say that more must be done for tribal youth, particularly those involved in the juvenile justice system. An understanding of the unique cultural differences of tribal youth, and the different risk and protective factors they face, compared with nontribal youth, is an important step in developing comprehensive and culturally appropriate prevention and treatment services. More research is needed to gain a better understanding of the complicated issues that face tribal youth in today's society, along with additional evaluations on interventions that target tribal youth, and how these interventions can be better implemented in tribal communities (Morsette et al. 2012; Walker et al. 2015). According to Arya and Rolnick (2009), federal and state government agencies, in cooperation with tribal communities, should sort out the "tangled web of justice" that tribal youths encounter if they come into contact with the juvenile justice system. In addition, juvenile justice staff, service providers, and others who work directly with youth should be trained in culturally appropriate and trauma-informed approaches to treatment (Dorgan et al. 2014).

[1] For the purposes of this literature review, Tribal Youth is defined as American Indian and Alaska Native (AI/AN) Youth.

[2] This number is current as of April 1, 2016. However, this number will soon increase to 567. http://www.bia.gov/cs/groups/public/documents/text/idc1-030829.pdf

[3] The published study did not offer comparisons to other racial or ethnic categories.

References

Adams, William, Julie Samuels, Janeen Buck Willison, Hannah Dodd, Meredith Dank, Barbara Parthasarathy, Kamala Mallik-Kane, Jessica Kelly, Sybil Mendonca, and KiDeuk Kim. 2011. *Tribal Youth in the Federal Justice System*. Washington, D.C.: Urban Institute.

Arya, Neelum, and Addie Rolnick. 2009. "A Tangled Web of Justice: American Indian and Alaska Native Youth in Federal, State, and Tribal Justice Systems." *Campaign for Youth Justice Policy Brief* 5: 1–25.

Beauvais, F., P. Jumper-Thurman, and M. Burnside. 2008. "The Changing Patterns of Drug Use Among American Indian Students Over the Past 30 Years." *American Indian & Alaska Native Mental Health Research: Journal of the National Center* 15(2):15–24. http://eric.ed.gov/?id=EJ822990

Carter, Susan L., Kee J.E. Straits, and McClellan Hall. 2007. *Project Venture: Evaluation of a Positive, Culture-Based Approach to Substance Abuse Prevention with American Indian Youth.* Technical Report. Gallup, N.M.: National Indian Youth Leadership Project.

Cohen, Marcia, William Feyerherm, Elizabeth Spinney, Rachel Stephenson, and Martha Yeide. *Disproportionate Minority Contact in the U.S. Juvenile Justice System: A Review of the DMC Literature, 2001–2010.* Submitted to OJJDP May 31, 2013. Bethesda, Md.: Development Services Group, Inc.

Center for Native American Youth. 2013. *Sequestration: The Impact on the Most At-Risk Population–Native Youth*. Washington, D.C.: The Aspen Institute, Center for Native American Youth. http://www.aspeninstitute.org/sites/default/files/content/upload/Sequestration%20Paper_FINAL.pdf

Development Services Group, Inc. 2013. *Protective Factors for Populations Served by the Administration on Children, Youth and Families: A Literature Review and Theoretical Framework.* Bethesda, Md.: Development Services Group, Inc.

Dorgan, Bryon L., Joanne Shenandoah, Dolores Subia Bigfoot, Eric Broderick, Eddie F. Brown, Valerie Davidson, Anita Fineday, Matthew L.M. Fletcher, Jefferson Keel, Ron Whitener, and Marilyn J. Bruguier Zimmerman. 2014. *Attorney General's Advisory Committee on American Indian and Alaska Native Children Exposed to Violence: Ending Violence So Children Can Thrive.* Washington, D.C.: Office of Juvenile Justice and Delinquency Prevention.

Eid, Troy A., Affie Ellis, Tom Gede, Carole Goldberg, Stephnaie Herseth Sandlin, Jefferson Keel, Ted Quasula, Earl Ralph Pomeroy III, and Theresa Pouley. 2013. *A Roadmap for Making Native America Safer: Report to the President and Congress of the United States*. Washington, D.C.: Indian Law & Order Commission.

Hartney, Christopher. 2008. "Native American Youth and the Juvenile Justice System." *Focus: Views from the National Council on Crime and Delinquency.* Oakland, Calif.: National Council on Crime & Delinquency.

Hockenberry, Sarah, and Charles Puzzanchera. 2014. *Juvenile Court Statistics 2011.* Pittsburgh, Pa.: National Center for Juvenile Justice.

Indian Health Service. 2015. *Year 2015 Profile*. Washington, D.C.: U.S. Department of Health and Human Services. http://www.ihs.gov/newsroom/includes/themes/newihstheme/display_objects/documents/factsheets/Profile.pdf

LaFromboise, Teresa D., and Beth Howard–Pitney. 1995. "The Zuni Life Skills Development Curriculum: Description and Evaluation of a Suicide Prevention Program." *Journal of Consulting Psychology* 42(4):479–86.

LaFromboise, Teresa D., Dan R. Hoyt, Lisa Oliver, and Les B. Whitbeck. 2006. "Family, Community, and School Influences on Resilience among American Indian Adolescents in the Upper Midwest." *Journal of Community Psychology* 34(2):193–209.

Leiber, Michael J., Joseph Johnson, and Kristan Fox. 2006. *An Examination of the Factors that Influence Justice Decision Making in Anchorage and Fairbanks, Alaska: An Assessment Study.* Technical Report, prepared for the State of Alaska, Department of Health and Social Services, Division of Juvenile Justice.

Lindquist, Christine, Tasseli McKay, Mindy Herman Stahl, Ada Pecos Melton, Rita Martinez, and David J. Melton. 2014. *Cross-Site Evaluation of the Office of Juvenile Justice and Delinquency Prevention Tribal Green Reentry Program.* Research Triangle Park: N.C.: RTI International.

Listenbee, Robert L., Joe Torre, Gregory Boyle. Sharon W. Cooper, Sarah Deer, Deanne Tilton Durfee, Thea James, Alicia Lieberman, Robert Macy, Steven Marans, Jim McDonnell, Georgina Mendoza, and Antonio Taguba. 2012. *Report of the Attorney General's National Task Force on Children Exposed to Violence.* Washington, D.C.: Office of Juvenile Justice and Delinquency Prevention.

Litt, Jonathan, and Heather Valdez Singleton. (n.d.). *American Indian/Alaska Native Youth & Status Offense Disparities: A Call for Tribal Initiative, Coordination & Federal Funding.* Washington, D.C.: Coalition for Juvenile Justice.

Lowe, John, Huigang Liang, Cheryl Riggs, and Jim Henson. 2012. "Community Partnership to Affect Substance Abuse among Native American Adolescents." *The American Journal of Drug and Alcohol Abuse* 38(5):450–55.

Melton, Ada Pecos. 2004. *Building Culturally Relevant Youth Courts in Tribal Communities.* Washington, D.C.: Office of Juvenile Justice and Delinquency Prevention.

Mmari, Kristin N., Robert Wm. Blum, and Nicolette Teugel-Shone. 2010. "What Increases Risk and Protection for Delinquent Behaviors among American Indian Youth?" *Youth & Society* 41(3):382–413.

Morsette, Aaron, Gyda Swaney, Darrell Stolle, David Schuldberg, Richard van den Pol, Melissa Young. 2009. "Cognitive Behavioral Intervention for Trauma in Schools (CBITS): School-Based Treatment on a Rural American Indian

Reservation." *Journal of Behavior Therapy and Experimental Psychiatry* 40(1):169–78.

Motivans, Mark, and Howard Snyder. 2011. *Summary: Tribal Youth in the Federal Justice System.* Washington, D.C.: U.S. Department of Justice, Office of Justice Programs, Bureau of Justice Statistics.

Norris, T., Vines, P. L., & Hoeffel, E. M. 2012. *The American Indian and Alaska Native Population: 2010.* Washington, D.C.: U.S. Department of Commerce, Economics and Statistics Administration. http://www.census.gov/prod/cen2010/briefs/c2010br-10.pdf

Ogunwole, S. U. 2006. *We the People: American Indians and Alaska Natives in the United States* (CENSR–28). Washington, D.C.: U.S. Census Bureau, U.S. Department of Commerce. http://www.census.gov/prod/2006pubs/censr-28.pdf

Pavkov, Thomas, Leah Travis, Kathleen A. Fox, Connie Bear King, and Terry L. Cross. 2010. "Tribal Youth Victimization and Delinquency: Analysis of Youth Risk Behavior Surveillance Survey Data." *Cultural Diversity and Ethnic Minority Psychology* 14(2):123–134.

Pu, Jia, Better Chewning, Iyekiyapiwin Darlene St. Clair, Patricia K. Kokotailo, Jeanne Lacourt, and Dale Wilson. 2013. "Protective Factors in American Indian Communities and Adolescent Violence." *Maternal and Child Health Journal* 17(7):1199–1207.

Rodriguez, N. 2008. *A Multilevel Analysis of Juvenile Court Processes: The Importance of Community Characteristics.* Report submitted to the National Institute of Justice. https://www.ncjrs.gov/pdffiles1/nij/grants/223465.pdf

Rountree, Jen. 2015. *American Indian and Alaska Native Youth in the Juvenile Justice System.* Baltimore, Md.: The Technical Assistance Network for Children's Behavioral Health.

Substance Abuse and Mental Health Services Administration. 2013. "Addressing Substance Use in Tribal Communities." *SAMHSA News* 21(1). http://media.samhsa.gov/samhsaNewsletter/Volume_21_Number_1/tribal_communities.aspx

Schinke, Steven P., Gilbert J. Botvin, Joseph E. Trimble, Mario A. Orlandi, Lewayne D. Gilchrist, and Von S. Locklear. 1988. "Preventing Substance Abuse among American–Indian Adolescents: A Bicultural Competence Skills Approach." *Journal of Consulting Psychology* 35(1):87–90.

Schinke, Steven P., Lela Tepavac, and Kristin C. Cole. 2000. "Preventing Substance Use among Native American Youth: Three-Year Results." *Addictive Behaviors* 25(3):387–97.

Tribal Law and Policy Institute. (n.d.). *General Guide to Criminal Jurisdiction in Indian Country.* Accessed on October 20, 2015, http://www.tribal-institute.org/lists/jurisdiction.htm

Walker, Sarah Cusworth, Rob Whitener, Eric W. Trupin, and Natalie Migliarini. 2015. "American Indian Perspectives on Evidence-Based Practice Implementation: Results from a Statewide Tribal Mental Health Gathering." *Administration and Policy in Mental Health and Mental Health Services Research* 42: 29–39.

Whitbeck, Les B., Dan R. Hoyt, Herry D. Stubben, and Teresa LaFromboise. 2001. "Traditional Culture and Academic Success among American Indian Children in the Upper Midwest." *Journal of American Indian Education* 40(2):48–60.

Last Update: April 2016

Suggested Reference: Development Services Group, Inc. 2016. "Tribal Youth in the Juvenile Justice System." Literature Review. Washington, D.C.: Office of Juvenile Justice and Delinquency Prevention. http://www.ojjdp.gov/mpg/litreviews/Tribal-youth-in-the-Juvenile-Justice-System

Critical Thinking

1. Is it fair to treat tribal youth differently from other American juveniles who are charged with a crime?

2. How important is it that the Attorney General's Advisory Committee recommendations be followed?

Internet References

Campaign for Youth Justice
http://www.campaignforyouthjustice.org/documents/CFYJPB_TangledJustice.pdf

Education Resource Information Center
http://files.eric.ed.gov/fulltext/EJ822990.pdf

Indian Health Service
https://search.usa.gov/search?utf8=✓&affiliate=indianhealthservice&query=juvenile+justice&commit= [insert website title and URL]

Unit 6

UNIT

Prepared by: Joanne Naughton

Punishment and Corrections

In the 1950s and 1960s the term *corrections* came to replace *penology,* reflecting a new philosophy that emphasized rehabilitation. But this philosophical view of offenders' treatment took an opposite turn in the 1980s when today's "get tough" policies were instituted. Corrections refers to programs and agencies that have legal authority over the custody or supervision of people who have been convicted of violating criminal law.

The correctional process begins with the sentencing of the convicted offender. The predominant sentencing pattern in the United States encourages maximum judicial discretion and offers a range of alternatives, from probation—supervised, conditional freedom within the community—through imprisonment, to the death penalty.

The current condition of the American penal system and the effects that sentencing, probation, imprisonment, and parole have on the convicted offender should receive serious consideration, because most people who have been sentenced to incarceration are eventually released back into their communities.

Article   Prepared by: Joanne Naughton

The Archipelago of Pain

DAVID BROOKS

Learning Outcomes

After reading this article, you will be able to:

- Discuss studies done on the effect of isolation on animals.
- Relate what Grassian concluded from his work on the effects of solitary confinement on prisoners.
- Compare prison officials' arguments about the need for solitary confinement with what research shows.

W e don't flog people in our prison system, or put them in thumbscrews or stretch them on the rack. We do, however, lock prisoners away in social isolation for 23 hours a day, often for months, years or decades at a time.

We prohibit the former and permit the latter because we make a distinction between physical and social pain. But, at the level of the brain where pain really resides, this is a distinction without a difference. Matthew Lieberman of the University of California, Los Angeles, compared the brain activities of people suffering physical pain with people suffering from social pain. As he writes in his book, "Social," "Looking at the screens side by side . . . you wouldn't have been able to tell the difference."

The brain processes both kinds of pain in similar ways. Moreover, at the level of human experience, social pain is, if anything, more traumatic, more destabilizing and inflicts more cruel and long-lasting effects than physical pain. What we're doing to prisoners in extreme isolation, in other words, is arguably more inhumane than flogging.

Yet inflicting extreme social pain is more or less standard procedure in America's prisons. Something like 80,000 prisoners are put in solitary confinement every year. Prisoners isolated in supermaximum facilities are often locked away in a 6-by-9-foot or 8-by-10-foot barren room. They may be completely isolated in that room for two days a week. For the remaining five, they may be locked away for 23 hours a day and permitted an hour of solitary exercise in a fenced-in area.

If there is communication with the prison staff, it might take place through an intercom. Communication with the world beyond is minimal. If there are visitors, conversation may be conducted through a video screen. Prisoners may go years without affectionately touching another human being. Their only physical contact will be brushing up against a guard as he puts on shackles for trips to the exercise yard.

In general, mammals do not do well in isolation. In the 1950s, Harry Harlow studied monkeys who had been isolated. The ones who were isolated for longer periods went into emotional shock, rocking back and forth. One in six refused to eat after being reintegrated and died within five days. Most of the rest were permanently withdrawn.

Studies on birds, rats and mice consistently show that isolated animals suffer from impoverished neural growth compared with socially engaged animals, especially in areas where short-term memory and threat perception are processed. Studies on Yugoslav prisoners of war in 1992 found that those who had suffered blunt blows to the head and those who had been socially isolated suffered the greatest damage to brain functioning.

Some prisoners who've been in solitary confinement are scarcely affected by it. But this is not typical. The majority of prisoners in solitary suffer severely—from headaches, an oversensitivity to stimuli, digestion problems, loss of appetite, self-mutilation, chronic dizziness, loss of the ability to concentrate, hallucinations, illusions, or paranoid ideas.

The psychiatrist Stuart Grassian conducted in-depth interviews with more than 200 prisoners in solitary and concluded that about a third developed acute psychosis with hallucinations. Many people just disintegrate. According to rough estimates, as many as half the suicides in prison take place in solitary, even though isolated prisoners make up only about 5 percent of the population.

Prison officials argue that they need isolation to preserve order. That's a view to be taken seriously because these are the people who work in the prisons. But the research on the effectiveness of solitary confinement programs is ambiguous at best. There's a fair bit of evidence to suggest that prison violence is not produced mainly by a few bad individuals who can be removed from the mainstream. Rather, violence is caused by conditions and prison culture. If there's crowding, tension, a culture of violence, and anarchic or arbitrary power, then the context itself is going to create violence no matter how many "bad seeds" are segregated away.

Fortunately, we seem to be at a moment when public opinion is turning. Last month, the executive director of the Colorado prisons, Rick Raemisch, wrote a moving first-person Op-Ed article in *The Times* about his short and voluntary stay in solitary. Colorado will no longer send prisoners with severe mental illnesses into solitary. New York officials recently agreed to new guidelines limiting the time prisoners can spend in isolation. Before long, one suspects, extreme isolation will be considered morally unacceptable.

The larger point is we need to obliterate the assumption that inflicting any amount of social pain is O.K. because it's not real pain.

When you put people in prison, you are imposing pain on them. But that doesn't mean you have to gouge out the nourishment that humans need for health, which is social, emotional and relational.

Critical Thinking

1. Isn't a prison sentence supposed to be harsh?
2. Based on the evidence from animals and people, does solitary confinement help a prisoner become a functioning member of society upon release?
3. Is it more humane to subject prisoners to solitary confinement for rules infractions than to beat them?

Internet References

American Psychological Association
http://www.apa.org/monitor/2012/05/solitary.aspx

The New York Times
http://www.nytimes.com/2014/02/21/opinion/my-night-in-solitary.html

Article   Prepared by: Joanne Naughton

Meet the Ungers

JASON FAGONE

Learning Outcomes

After reading this article, you will be able to:

- Explain *Unger v. State* and how jury instructions in Maryland have changed since 1976.

- Describe the experiment that has been taking place in Maryland for the past three years.

- Relate what the outcome has been for the 143 Ungers who have been released, regarding new crimes and reimprisonment.

Several decades ago, when they were young, 230 men and 1 woman were convicted of terrible crimes—murders, rapes, robberies. They thought they were going to die in prison. They were supposed to. But then, just a few years back, Merle Unger Jr., one of the most notorious escape artists of our time, discovered an ingenious (and legal) way to get them out. It was an unimagined second chance for them—and a nerve-wracking experiment for everyone else.

He was a 72-year-old man with a messed-up back and he knew he shouldn't be lifting this stuff, but he was here to help a friend move, and so were some other old guys who had their own issues with bad knees and arthritic joints, so Hercules Williams Jr. plucked a small wooden end table from the back of a U-Haul truck and carried it down the sidewalk, slowly.

"That's the Herc I always knew. Lifting that thing like it was nothing," shouted 64-year-old Larry Owens, who sometimes walks with a cane. "You're gonna feel that tomorrow."

"I feel it now," Williams said, setting the table down and placing a hand on his back. "I feel it *now*."

Donald Shakir, the beneficiary of all this labor, saw that Williams was having trouble and grabbed the table from his hands, pulling it up the steps and into the living room. Shakir is a muscular 63-year-old with thick black glasses and a bright-orange beard. He's legally blind and can't see at all out of his

left eye, even with the glasses. He also suffers from arthritis in his knees, but if the pain was bothering him that afternoon, he didn't let on.

He had been leading the operation, telling the guys where to put a chair or a couch, insisting on lifting the heavier objects, pausing every so often to look around at his new neighborhood.

He didn't want to call attention to himself, but this was a big day for him, a setting down of roots after a period of upheaval and wandering. Three years earlier, he had met a woman named Nzinga Amon and fell in love. They moved in together. At first, they slept on a couch in Shakir's sister's basement; they had to spoon each other to keep from falling off. "Hoooooo," Amon says now. "It was hilarious. But what do they say: love is blind?" After that, they moved to a cramped one-bedroom apartment. This new place, though—a house instead of an apartment, with a Formstone facade, on a quiet block in southwest Baltimore? "It means stability," Amon told me.

After the men unpacked the first load of boxes and furniture, they drove the empty U-Haul back to the old place to load up again, passing fans and flower pots through an open first-floor window. Inside, a TV was tuned to the Orioles' first game of the season.

"The Orioles ain't won nothing since I've been home," Hercules Williams said, shaking his head. He was dressed in an Orioles raincoat and a white Orioles cap. He told me that he went to his first game at Camden Yards three years ago and couldn't believe the size of it; he'd only ever seen a game at the far smaller Memorial Stadium, which the team abandoned in 1991. "I thought I was in New York City. The crowds, you know? And the *gaiety* of it all?" he said. "That was the first big positive crowd I saw since I got out."

Every so often these guys let slip a phrase that reveals how long they spent in prison. Forty-one years and four months for Williams. Nearly 44 years for Owens; 41 and change for Shakir. They were all convicted of murder in the early 1970s. Shakir was 19 when he shot and killed a 77-year-old confectioner during a stickup. He wanted money to buy drugs. Owens had just turned 20 when he gunned down a dry cleaner, also during a robbery to fuel a drug habit. The circumstances around Williams' conviction are murkier. He maintained his innocence and had a strong alibi, but his alleged accomplice testified against him in exchange for immunity, sticking him with the same sentence Shakir and Owens got: life in prison.

Back then, lifers who demonstrated good behavior and personal growth could get paroled after 20 or 25 years. But in the following decades, the state's prison system became more punitive. Maryland is one of three states where the governor can overturn the parole board's decision to release a prisoner. In 1995, after a lifer named Rodney Stokes committed a brutal murder while on work release, Governor Parris Glendening, a Democrat, said the parole board shouldn't bother sending him any more applications from lifers, because "life means life." Every governor since has followed his lead. So by the time Williams and Shakir and Owens had put in their 25 years, it didn't matter what they had done with their time. They weren't getting out. They were going to die in prison, with their loved ones far away. But then a fellow inmate named Merle Unger Jr. discovered an unexpected kind of door.

Merle Unger escaped from jail for the first time in 1967, when he was an 18-year-old dropout with an interest in petty crime. People in his native Greencastle, Pennsylvania, saw him as a harmless character—a scrawny kid who figured out how to tie his bedsheets together and climb out of the nearby jail at night so he could see his girlfriend and play bingo at the Catholic Church before climbing back into his cell in time for roll call. He did this until a sheriff's deputy went to play bingo, saw Unger sitting there and was like, *wait a minute.*

Whenever jail officials increased security, Unger found another route out. A local radio station started a Merle Unger Fan Club. His public defender made T-shirts that said, "Merle, baby, where are you?"

In 1975, after more escapes and arrests, he found himself locked up in Carlisle, Pennsylvania, fixating on a skylight in the lunchroom, 45 feet up. Early one morning he tied a piece of rope to a 5- or 10-pound dumbbell and wrapped the other end of the rope around his neck. He piled up some tables, put a small step ladder on top of the pile, climbed atop a beam, pulled up the ladder, set it up again, reached higher, hurled the dumbbell through the skylight's glass, and climbed through the broken window into the December cold, wearing a short-sleeved shirt. "I mean, I'm not proud of that," Unger told me last month. "I just wanted my freedom."

On the run, Unger made it to Hagerstown, Maryland, where he robbed a grocery store at gunpoint. An off-duty cop, Donald Kline, happened to be shopping at the time and shouted, "Halt, police officer!" When Unger ran, Kline chased him into an alley. Unger opened fire. Kline was hit three times and died in the hospital.

Later that night, police found Unger hiding in a house, bleeding from one of Kline's bullets. But before he could be tried, Unger escaped again, using a hacksaw slipped to him during a visit. He cut the bars of his cell and crawled out through an air duct. His public defender opened the mail one day to find a poem from Unger: "Some say I am un-cool or even a fool/ because I escaped again./But tell me true/What would you do/If your life was at an end?"

He fled to Florida and got caught in Orlando. Brought to Talbot County, Maryland, in 1976 to stand trial for the Kline murder, he was convicted and sentenced to life plus 40 years. But Unger had a strong preference for staying in Florida, a preference he expressed in 1981 by escaping a maximum-security prison in Maryland at the wheel of a hijacked dump truck. The FBI led a national manhunt after that episode. He was captured a month later while breaking into a gun store in Clearwater, Florida, and convicted of armed burglary, beginning a tug-of-war between Florida and Maryland for the right to incarcerate him.

In the middle of all this, in the '80s, Unger happened to meet a woman. A fellow inmate in Florida had put a personal ad in *Mother Earth* magazine, and he got so many responses that he sold the extras to other prisoners for a dollar apiece. Unger bought a few, sent letters and a woman from Illinois came to visit. They ended up getting married in 1988 and had two children, both conceived in prison. He says his life changed when he held his infant son for the first time: "I didn't want to commit no crimes anymore."

In Unger's telling, this is the moment he developed an obsessive interest in the American legal system. Another friend worked in the prison's law library and told him about a case in which a federal inmate earned his freedom by challenging the constitutionality of the jury instructions in his trial. Unger spent hours studying the case. It was all he could talk about. And the more he read, the more he thought he might have a shot at winning a new trial on the murder charge if he came back to Maryland to fight it.

Today in Maryland, juries are told to decide cases solely by evaluating the facts. But this isn't what they were told before 1980. As the judge in one 1976 murder trial put it to the jury, "It is your responsibility in this case to determine the facts, as you do in every case, but also it is your responsibility to determine for yourselves what the law is." The practice was a holdover from the 1700s, when colonists, fearing that tyrannical British judges would run roughshod over their rights, gave juries the power to nullify unjust prosecutions. Over the centuries, though, states moved away from these instructions, because they encouraged juries to second-guess fundamental rights of defendants, like the presumption of innocence and the standard of reasonable doubt. "These are all fragile rights," says Michael Millemann, a law professor at the University of Maryland. "It's hard enough to get jurors to enforce when you tell them, 'That's the law, you have to do it.' And when you tell them, 'You have to decide what the law is,' it just invites gross injustice."

For decades, the state's higher courts blocked attempts by convicts to obtain new trials; reopening all those cases would have thrown the system into chaos. But by the time Unger returned to Maryland to file his petition, the makeup of the state's Court of Appeals had changed, and in 2012, the court ruled that Unger's constitutional rights had been violated. He was entitled to a new trial. And by the logic of the decision, so were the 230 other living prisoners—mostly first-degree murderers, and some rapists—convicted before Maryland changed its jury instructions.

Unger v. State doesn't say that these prisoners should be freed, only that they can ask to be retried. In practice, though, there's a strong incentive to settle cases where the defendant has a clean prison record. Retrying a case that's 30 or 40 years old can be tricky: the witnesses have moved away, the detectives are dead and the case file is skeletal, or missing, or destroyed. Since the decision came down, 142 of 231 prisoners have negotiated their freedom, almost all of them getting probation. One was acquitted at a new trial. Another eight have died behind bars before they could get a hearing. There are still about 70 prisoners with open cases, which means that even more may yet go free.

But Merle Unger Jr. is not one of them. In 2013, a Maryland prosecutor tried him a second time for the murder of Donald Kline, relying on the original 1976 trial transcript. A judge found Unger guilty once again and sentenced him to life. Now he lives alone in a five- by 10-foot cell, making fine-art cards that feature paintings and colored-pencil drawings of deer, elk and eagles. He sells them for around $10 apiece on Etsy. In a phone call from prison, Unger told me he's still fighting his case, filing appeals to win his freedom. "When you get old," he said, "you look back at all the things you did and you regret them. . . . I want to prove that I can do something good."

When I asked him how it felt to still be in prison after springing so many others, he tried to be gracious. "I'm happy for all them," he said, "because they all deserved a second chance. That's something the American prison system got away from: giving people second chances."

For the first time in a generation, American politicians actually agree that we put too many people in prison and that this is a bad thing. (The United States has the highest incarceration rate in the world, with 716 people per 100,000 behind bars; the comparable rate is 475 in Russia and 121 in China.) And yet the most commonly proposed solutions tend to focus on nonviolent federal drug offenders: relaxing sentences, rescheduling drugs, diverting addicts into treatment programs. These steps barely address the larger problem. The vast majority of U.S. prisoners are in state prisons, not federal, and the majority of those have been convicted of violent crimes (54 percent) as opposed to drug crimes (16 percent). To reduce the American prison population in a meaningful way, states will have to liberalize sentences and parole for some violent offenders—a terrifying prospect for politicians.

In Maryland, though, the politically impossible has been happening for three years now. *Unger v. State* is essentially a natural experiment in the controlled release of violent offenders. And because the experiment is so new, nobody knows how it will end up—not the lawyers, the judges, the social workers, the families of the ex-offenders, the families of the victims, the citizens of Maryland or the former prisoners themselves. Thanks to a legal lightning strike, almost 150 people who were supposed to disappear in prison are now living on the outside. Are they ready? Are we?

"It just sort of developed," Nzinga Amon told me of her relationship with Donald Shakir. We were sitting on a stoop across from their old place in West Baltimore, watching Shakir and the other guys lug desks and drawers into the U-Haul. She said she met her husband by chance in 2013—just two people waiting for a bus. She wasn't looking for a relationship at the time. She had a job as a reading tutor at an elementary school and was enjoying her independence.

Still, she was drawn to Shakir. She liked his calmness, his seriousness. She liked that he shared the poetry he had written in prison and that he talked to her about his regrets: the son he didn't raise, the mother who died while he was away. And she liked how he kept finding ways to surprise her. Shakir had this beautiful singing voice, a high, sweet falsetto that seemed unconnected to his big body. "We all change, we all grow up," she said. "I can appreciate the man he turned out to be."

It wasn't until they moved in together that Amon realized how hard it is for lifers to re-enter the world. These are not unskilled people; in prison they learned masonry and welding and other trades, and the ones approved for work release regularly earned promotions and even managed crews. But the only job Shakir could land at first was as a minimum-wage dishwasher at Pizza Hut. He felt as though his manager was constantly testing him, giving him all the crappy assignments, like cleaning the drains, to see if he could take it. He ultimately quit because his arthritis made it too painful to spend hours on his feet.

At home he seemed scared a lot of the time. He was afraid of the night. The kids on the street and the way they dressed and talked, the vacant blocks where people used to live when he was young—he didn't feel safe. "I've never seen so many drug users in my life," he told me. "I'll never get over seeing so many empty houses." When Amon has meetings after dark, Shakir calls repeatedly to make sure she's O.K. One time he waited for her on the stoop of their place, in his pajamas.

"We lived in a world that had rules," Shakir told me. "And we came out into a world without rules." For many of the released, it was unsettling to move through public space, a series of little jolts. They found roads where buildings used to be, buildings where parks used to be. Banks spewed money out of a wall, 24 hours a day; there were no ATMs in the early '70s. Crazy people walked down the street holding loud conversations with themselves; friends had to explain what Bluetooth was. The city had reconfigured itself while they were away. And in a lot of cases, so had their families, or what was left of them. Shakir's friend Larry Owens didn't have a spouse or a sibling or a child to come home to. The last time he saw any of his kin was in 1992. "I look at it like this," he told me. "They got their life to live." He ended up moving in with his 62-year-old cousin, Barbara Lotts. She and Owens were never close, but her reason for housing him was simple: "Wasn't nobody else," she said. "It is what it is."

He's still living in a spare bedroom in her house, and they basically get along. She accepts that he'll moan and talk to himself in the night and that he'll continue to wake up every day at 6 a.m. "Larry," she wants to say, "you're free, you can sleep in." Owens doesn't like to be a burden, so he takes out the trash and kicks in a little money when he can. "I love her," he says, "but I want my own."

Owens and Shakir are lucky in the sense that they have each other. They've been close since they were 9 or 10, having grown up in the same housing project in the neighborhood of Fairfield. They fell into drugs at the same time, and for the first year of their incarceration, they shared a cell at the Maryland Penitentiary. They're basically inseparable now. They get together every weekend and talk on the phone during the week, and they also hang out with other ex-lifers released thanks to *Unger v. State*, like Hercules Williams, and another friend, Kareem Hasan, who was locked up at 17 after a fatal neighborhood dispute. (His co-defendants testified against him in exchange for shortened sentences.) Now 57, Hasan has achieved a lot in the short time he has been out: a steady job with the city of Baltimore, a car, a marriage to a registered nurse named Annette, a business plan for a youth mentoring nonprofit. He functions as a constant positive presence in the group, a connector and a joker. Just before his release, he called Annette and said, "Mmm-hmm. Mmm-hmmm. I hope your shit is in order. I'm coming home." She was elated. "I'm at peace of mind with him, you know?" she says. "I never gave up on him."

The men seem to share a bond that's reflected in language. Often they refer to themselves as part of "the Unger family," or sometimes just as "Ungers." More than one of them told me, "I'm an Unger." They realize they're a part of something bigger than themselves.

And they are. Digging them out of prison took an unprecedented effort by the Maryland Office of the Public Defender, which worked with professors and students at the University of Maryland law school to help prisoners file petitions to reopen their cases. Early on, the attorneys also realized there needed to be a major social-work component: if the Ungers didn't have help adjusting to life on the outside, they were more likely to fail. So teams were mobilized to snag the Ungers in a safety net. These social workers still travel across the state to prepare prisoners for re-entry. They are there on the day of release to hand the client a personal hygiene kit, a binder of information on government programs, and a $20 bus pass. And in the weeks and months after release, they help Ungers with challenges large and small, everything from obtaining health care and I.D. cards to finding independent living situations.

One of the first Ungers to win his release was James Richardson, a stocky 71-year-old with cataracts in both eyes and two bum knees. He lived with his daughter for eight months until UMD social workers helped him get his own apartment in a Baltimore building that caters to seniors and sets the rent as a percentage of income. (UMD asked me not to name the building because there are only a few complexes that accept residents with criminal records and the school doesn't want to create "negative backlash" for the management company.) Five other Ungers live there, including Hercules Williams. They see each other in the elevators, check in, sit on their balconies, and talk. Williams described the building as "clean, laid-back. A man can chill. Some fresh old ladies. We got the run of them." Then he shook his head and added, "I'm an old man, I'm not trying to get with anyone." One afternoon Richardson showed me the panoramic view of the city from his upper-floor balcony. Life after prison has been "way more than I really expected," he said. "I was met with open arms, and people willing to help in any way they could help."

Maybe the most important strands of the safety net are the two monthly meetings in Baltimore where the men gather as a group—25 to 40 people saying hello, snacking on carrot sticks and pretzels. These aren't fancy events, but they give the guys a place to see their friends and get help if they need it. The social workers set up a presentation or two: a pitch by a nonprofit leader looking to train black men in computer programming, a class on nutrition and health benefits delivered as a "Jeopardy!"-style game show. ("Let's try Social Security for $1,000.") Often a man named Walter Lomax speaks about justice reform. Lomax spent 39 years in prison on a wrongful conviction, and since winning his freedom in 2006, he has been organizing on behalf of older prisoners. Another elder who speaks is a lanky Baltimorean named Karriem Saleem El-Amin, who did 42 years on a murder conviction. El-Amin told me he tries to get people to share their struggles by poking fun at his own. One time, he went to use a public toilet and couldn't find the flush lever; he started to panic, until the toilet sensed movement and flushed itself. He didn't know toilets could do that. "Don't nobody tell you these little *delicate* things that have changed," he explained.

There is only one woman in the Unger family. Her name is Etta Myers. She went to a few of the meetings, but people kept mistaking her for someone's spouse, so she stopped. Myers is attractive, with short yellow hair. She smokes cigarettes and sips tea from a mug that says "Woman of God." As tough as some of the men have had it, she has probably had it worse. The state locked her up in 1977, when she was 22 and struggling with a heroin addiction. Police said that Myers and her ex-boyfriend shot and killed a man during a robbery. The only evidence linking her to the scene was the testimony of three men who thought they saw her walk away and who admitted to being on drugs that day. She swore she was never there. The jury found her guilty of first-degree murder.

Myers spent 36 years in a women's prison. Over the decades she became a leader there, the cofounder of a therapy group and a manager in the sewing shop, a multimillion-dollar business that made flags and uniforms. The Maryland Parole Commission tried to release her twice, but governors blocked the commission both times. When she finally got out in 2013, she was given a bed in a Catholic halfway house for women. She now rents a small place in North Baltimore, which she shares with a white and orange cat named Ya-Ya.

When I met her there a few months ago, the TV was tuned to a children's station showing a cartoon about the Bible. Myers said she watches children's shows, because there are a lot of precocious kids at her church and she wants to understand them better. She's astonished by her great-niece Chloe, who is 3 years old. "She had a little bump on her head. And I said, 'How did you bump your head, Chloe?' And she said, 'Well, I don't think we have time for that, that's really irrelevant right now.' And I said, 'Who says irrelevant at 3 years old?'"

The last decades of her incarceration were marked by a spreading loneliness, her loved ones dying one after the other—her mother, her brother. "I was like, there's nothing else, there's nothing else for me." And then she came home and realized that for the first time in her life, she was finally in a position to have a healthy relationship. Before prison, her boyfriend beat her. After they were convicted, she didn't see him again until the day they were both released—36 years later. He used to be a specimen, a beautiful, muscular man, but he rolled into court in a wheelchair. Later, she saw him at an event and reached down to hug him. She didn't want to waste her time being angry.

What she wanted was to meet a "nice older man" and feel less alone. But the rules of courtship had changed since 1977. "Guys don't come after girls," she says. "That was amazing to me. And I guess it had to do with the fact that I was much older. And then the challenge was, O.K., well, where do you go to meet nice old men at? . . . I've been to several bingo places, and

it's usually a bunch of old biddies, and I don't consider myself an old biddie."

Grocery store? Church? "You don't find a whole lot of single men in church. You see them there, they have a wife right beside them. Then their wives are looking at you trying to make sure you're not trying to hit on them or something crazy."

After a while, she stopped trying to find a partner. She now spends her time volunteering at her church and with nonprofits that work on criminal justice issues. In March, after the Maryland legislature restored voting rights for ex-offenders, she registered to cast the first vote of her life, at 62. "I put my trust in the God that I worship, and believe He'll send me a companion if it's meant to be," she said. "And if not, I guess I just won't have one."

In 2013, when 89-year-old Shirley Rubin heard that her husband's killer was about to be released from prison, she felt physically sick. The couple had owned a small grocery store in southwest Baltimore until one day in 1972, when a teenager walked into their store and shot them both during a robbery attempt. Shirley's husband died; she survived. She ended up losing the store and struggled to raise the kids on the little money she had left. The gunman "ruined my life," she told the *Baltimore Sun*. "The only thing that kept me going in these last 41 years was the fact that [he] was in prison."

Antonio Gioia, as the deputy state's attorney for major crimes in Baltimore, has the unenviable task of calling people like Rubin and telling them that their loved one's killer may soon be walking around. He's been doing it for three years, and he still dreads it. "The most prominent emotion is one of disbelief. 'Why are you calling, Mr. Gioia?'" he told me. "They just cannot accept the fact that this very painful episode that's left a terrible hole in the lives of the family is being reopened."

In April, I went to see Kevin Magrogan, whose only sibling, Thomas Magrogan, was shot in the heart 45 years ago by a teenage drug addict named Bryant Lee Goodman. Magrogan now lives in the farm country west of Baltimore, where he works as a tax preparer. Sitting behind a desk piled with returns, he told me that his brother's murder made him "the new head of the household, because my father just never recovered." His father was a fleet superintendent for a linen company in Baltimore. Before the murder, he worked 12 or 14 hours a day, but afterward, he could only muster 4 or 5 hours, and Kevin had to help out after school to make sure the linen trucks got in at night. His father stopped going out in public because people were always talking to him about Tom. He stopped going to Irish dances with Kevin's mother. "He would just come home and sit," Magrogan said.

Family members of victims have a right to speak at Unger settlement hearings, and when Goodman's came up, Magrogan opposed his release, arguing that because Goodman had been given a drug infraction in prison, he was still potentially dangerous. "Where's he going to get the money for drugs when he goes back on them?" Magrogan told me. "He's going to revert back to crime. And if he gets in a pressure situation again— we know he's already killed once. Why not kill again? He's got nothing to lose." Goodman, who is now in his 60s, also exercised his right to speak during the hearing—one of the few Ungers to do so. He said he was "truly sorry" for what he had done, according to the Sun. He went free. The process left Magrogan feeling as if the state just wanted to save the cost of incarcerating elderly prisoners. "It was all show and tell," he said. "I'm sure that if I was very rich and powerful, he would have been retried."

This feeling that the system is rigged is common among the families of Unger victims. The sister of a Johns Hopkins medical student killed by a 16-year-old in 1979 told me she thinks the idea of a life sentence has been devalued. "What message are we sending to other possible criminals, that we're getting kind of soft?" she asked. She said she recently read a story about a former lifer eating a lobster with his family. How did that make her feel? "How would it make anybody feel? You know what I mean? What are you doing eating a lobster?"

Generally, the defense attorneys and social workers trying to ease the Ungers' transition into post-prison life don't dispute the damage their clients have done. "You can't ignore the tragedy of homicide," says UMD's Michael Millemann. "You can't escape from that." But when he receives an anonymous voicemail that says, "I hope one of these guys kills you," or when an Internet commenter assumes he must be a Communist, he thinks people aren't getting the full picture.

Millemann has been working with prisoners since the late '60s. A judge once called him "the LeBron James of lawyering for poor people." In 2013, he put together a team of law students and social workers to analyze the earliest Unger cases, and pretty soon, a familiar pattern emerged: poor black defendants convicted by all-white juries after paltry or nonexistent police investigations. A large number of the petitioners weren't murderers the way most people think of them. In Maryland, you don't have to pull the trigger to be charged with felony murder; the non-shooter in a fatal robbery is just as guilty of murder as the shooter. That was the situation with a significant number of the Ungers, including Karriem Saleem El-Amin. They were drunk and armed at 16 or 17 or 18 and robbed someone with a group of friends. They didn't shoot, but they got life. Meanwhile, in some cases, the actual gunmen cut deals with the state and went free after a few decades—so why was the non-shooter still in prison, still bearing the burden of society's judgment?

Even some of the social workers had been skeptical at first. But that changed quickly. Almost to a person, the prisoners spoke with insight about the people they used to be, expressed remorse for their crimes and described the programs they'd completed in prison to better themselves. They were like living remnants of an earlier, rehabilitative era in corrections, when Maryland lifers could go out on work release (ended in 1993) and take college classes through Pell Grants (ended by Congress in 1994). A forensic social work fellow named Elizabeth Smith interviewed dozens of men all over the state. She told me that she "would get pulled up by [corrections officers], and they'd say, 'Get this man out of here. He should die at home with his grandchildren.'"

It seems counterintuitive, but murderers can be good bets for parole. A study by the Stanford Criminal Justice Center found that between 1995 and 2010, 48.7 percent of all paroled prisoners in California went on to commit new crimes. But among murderers, the rate was a tiny 0.58 percent, "and none of them recidivated for life-term crimes." Data from New York shows similarly low recidivism rates for paroled murderers.

The likeliest reason for this is age. According to figures from the Bureau of Justice Statistics, people who murder, rape or rob tend to be in their late teens and early 20s. By the time murderers are eligible for release, they are usually way past their criminal primes. The average age of the freed Ungers is 64. I told Millemann that out of all these people, there had to be a few who still posed a threat. "If prosecutors think there are [Ungers] who are too dangerous to be released," he pointed out, "they've got an option: Re-try them and convict them." (Prosecutors took this route with Merle Unger and a man who killed his wife with a shotgun in 1972. In the case of a notorious petitioner who murdered an 11-year-old girl in 1969, Baltimore city prosecutors fought to keep him in prison, and he died behind bars this past December.)

For all these reasons, the people fighting for the prisoners feel they're doing the right thing. So far, the results have justified their faith. According to the Office of the Public Defender, of the 143 Ungers who have been released, not a single one has been convicted of anything more serious than a traffic offense. There has only been one probation violation, a technical infraction that resulted in a stern talking-to. Zero of the Ungers have violated parole. Zero have been sent back to prison.

These numbers didn't surprise me. After meeting a range of Ungers, and seeing them interact with their families and each other, and talking to them about the horrific things they saw in prison—guys losing it in weak moments and slashing their wrists with razor blades, hanging themselves in their cells, keeling over from sudden aneurysms—it seemed obvious that the last thing anyone wanted to do was go back. Although they didn't perform their remorse for me, sometimes falling back on cliché (Shakir: "Don't nobody have a right to take a life, period"), they also didn't evade questions about their original crimes and the people they used to be. They caused pain to other families and to their own, and now that they can sit on their balconies or go to an Orioles game or eat a meal with their wives, they would rather not blow it up, for themselves and for their friends who are still in prison, the 70 Ungers with pending cases.

The experiment is young and tenuous. The state of Maryland is looking to prevent future releases and recently filed the latest in a series of legal challenges to *Unger v. State* in appellate courts. If a single member of the Unger family fails in a big way—and even advocates recognize there's a risk of that—everyone could be affected. The guilt would be a lot to bear. "You don't mess up so you don't mess up the chances of the guy behind you comin' out," Kareem Hasan told me. "That's one of the things we stress when we get everybody together. That's why we try to grab them right when they come out the door."

Every month or two, a few more Unger petitioners are released. I went to Baltimore in February to see three of these men, all serving sentences for first-degree murder, sign settlement agreements. A crowd of about 30 family members, legal staff and social workers watched with me from the courtroom's wooden benches. Walter Lomax, wearing a black pinstripe suit and a scarf, sat right where the guys could see him. They're usually nervous when they walk in, Lomax explained, and he wanted them to recognize a friendly face. "Murphy's Law," he said. "Anything that can go wrong, will go wrong."

The prisoners wore blue Department of Corrections jumpsuits and were handcuffed with their arms in front, chains circling their waists. Antonio Gioia stood at the prosecutor's table and read their names one by one: Tyrone Toliver, Leroy Brunson, Carl Marine. They looked solemn, standing absolutely still, staring forward or at the ground. Eventually, each was asked some questions to ensure that he was competent to sign the deal. Was he currently under the influence of drugs or alcohol? Did he understand that he was forfeiting his right to a new trial under *Unger v. State*, along with all innocence claims, in exchange for a suspended sentence and probation? No victims' representatives were part of the proceedings; Gioia told the judge that in two of the cases, no surviving family members of the victim could be located, and in the third, the family member did not respond to a letter. After Marine signed his deal, Gioia said, "Your honor, that does conclude our business with the court," and the men were led downstairs to a holding cell while some final paperwork was processed. The whole thing took 31 minutes.

Following the hearing, the 30 supporters went to a Dunkin Donuts across the street to wait for the men to emerge from a side door of the courthouse. The guards always release the Ungers last, after the rest of the day's defendants are packed into vans and returned to prison. I tried to talk to Carl Marine's twin sister, but she smiled shyly and put her head down on the table. "I'm too excited," she said. Kareem Hasan had driven here from his job at the city's wastewater treatment plant, and

Donald Shakir and Larry Owens had arrived together. They all said they remembered going through this process themselves, and how strange it felt to be suddenly deposited on a sidewalk. "All these guys who are being released, we have history," Shakir told me. "They're family. They may be closer to us than our own family."

After two hours and many coffees, people got restless and went outside to stand on the sidewalk. The air grew colder. Hasan had to leave for a family function. Shakir started singing a Motown song to himself. It was fully dark outside when two of the three Unger men appeared across the street in civilian clothes—Brunson and Marine.

A cry went up from the sidewalk. "*My man!*" Marine's family rushed over. "Look at you, boy!" A guy mock-punched Marine in the chest and then threw his arms around him and burst into laughter. They grinned and said he was too skinny and needed to fatten up. "Believe me," he told them, "that won't be a problem." He whirled around, overwhelmed, trying to acknowledge all of his people. "Thank you and thank God," he said. "We gonna make y'all proud. I'm home now. This is my team."

Brunson's people were more subdued. They waited to the side as he spoke to three female social workers from UMD, who gave him their usual release packet—the binder, the hygiene kit, the bus pass and their business cards. Then the UMD team and the family of the third client, Toliver, went over to the courthouse door to ask a guard why he was being kept inside. The guard said that one of the clerks had gone home for the day before completing Toliver's paperwork. He would have to spend one more night behind bars. The guard said he was sorry.

While all this was happening, Owens and Shakir hung back, not wanting to get in the way. When it seemed as if Brunson was getting ready to leave, Shakir went over to embrace him. "Hey brother, we gotta hook up," Owens said. He and Shakir gave Brunson their numbers and made sure he knew he could call if he wanted to talk. Brunson nodded and thanked them. Over at the courthouse door, a set of metal gates spread open, and Toliver, still in chains, walked the couple of yards to the last blue van. It drove away, and Owens and Shakir walked off together, into the city.

Critical Thinking

1. Is it a reasonable response for a state governor to deny parole to all eligible prisoners after a parolee has committed a vicious crime?

2. Is it fair to release people who have been convicted of serious, violent crimes?

3. Is it safe to release prisoners who have committed murder?

Internet References

Alternatives to Violence Project—USA
http://avpusa.org/

Office of Justice Programs—Recidivism
http://www.nij.gov/topics/corrections/recidivism/pages/welcome.aspx

Stanford Law School
http://law.stanford.edu/wp-content/uploads/sites/default/files/child-page/164096/doc/slspublic/SCJC_report_Parole_Release_for_Lifers.pdf

JASON FAGONE is a contributing writer for *Highline*. His work has also appeared in *The New York Times*, *GQ*, *New York*, and *Wired*. He is currently working on a book, *The Cryptologists*, about U.S. women codebreakers in the world wars.

Article   Prepared by: Joanne Naughton

For Mentally Ill Inmates at Rikers Island, a Cycle of Jail and Hospitals

MICHAEL WINERIP AND MICHAEL SCHWIRTZ

Learning Outcomes

After reading this article, you will be able to:

- Report what percentage of the population at Rikers has been diagnosed with mental illness.
- Relate what happened when state mental hospitals were closed in the 1960s and 1970s.
- Describe how ACT teams operate.

It was not a particularly violent crime that sent Michael Megginson to Rikers Island. He was arrested for stealing a cellphone.

But in jail, Mr. Megginson, who is 25 and has been in and out of psychiatric hospitals since the age of 6, quickly deteriorated, becoming one of the most violent inmates on the island.

In his 18 months there, he was constantly involved in some kind of disturbance, his records show. He fought with other inmates and officers; spit and threw urine at them; smashed windows and furniture and once stabbed an officer in the back of the head with a piece of glass.

At least twice, his bones were broken in beatings by guards.

He also repeatedly hurt himself, cutting his body all over, banging his head against walls and tying sheets and clothing around his neck in apparent suicide attempts.

There were times he became severely psychotic. He once stripped naked and broke the toilet in his cell, causing a flood. "I'm trying to save everybody from the devil with holy water," he said, according to jail records.

For years, Rikers has been filling with people like Mr. Megginson, who have complicated psychiatric problems that are little understood and do not get resolved elsewhere: the unwashed man passed out in a public stairwell; the 16-year-old runaway; the drug addict; the belligerent panhandler screaming in a full subway car.

It is a problem that cuts two ways. At the jail, with its harsh conditions and violent culture, the mentally ill can deteriorate, their symptoms worsening in ways Rikers is unequipped to handle. As they get sicker, they strike out at guards and other correction employees, often provoking more violence.

Judges, prosecutors, police officers and correction leaders, as well as elected officials like Mayor Bill de Blasio, have grown increasingly vocal about the damage that incarceration can do to these men and women.

By now, Mr. Megginson's Legal Aid lawyer had expected him to be freed. But his volatile behavior has kept him behind bars, and recently he was transferred to a state psychiatric prison hospital for violent criminals with no set release date.

The New York Times spent 10 months examining Mr. Megginson's troubled life, conducting hours of interviews with him as well as his family members, doctors and lawyers. With his permission, *The Times* also reviewed thousands of pages of medical, disciplinary and legal records from his time at Rikers and in hospitals, community programs and supervised housing.

Though there may be a consensus that Michael Megginson does not belong in jail, there is no agreement about where else he could go. At times, he was just as violent in hospitals. He once jumped over a nurses' station at Kings County Hospital Center in Brooklyn, attacking clinicians; during a stay in St. Barnabas Hospital in the Bronx, he was placed in restraints 11 times.

But unlike jail, psychiatric hospitals treated his behavior as a symptom of illness. If he was out of control, he was often given an injection to knock him out and was placed in a quiet room until he was calm.

In interviews, members of Mr. Megginson's family said they believed that longer-term hospitalization would be best for him. But that option has all but disappeared. For the last four decades, the push in the mental health field has been to close these hospitals. Since a 1970s Supreme Court ruling that was meant to protect civil liberties, only the very sickest patients can be involuntarily held for an extended period.

Mr. Megginson was repeatedly released from state hospitals against his doctors' wishes because he did not meet legal requirements for involuntary commitment.

His treatment has cost millions of dollars in public funds. Outside of hospitals, he was enrolled in some of the most successful outpatient and community programs in the mental health field.

He failed out of all of them.

Which raises the question: Is there any place for Michael Megginson?

Over the last decade, the proportion of inmates with diagnosed mental illness has climbed dramatically. Today, they make up nearly 40 percent of the population at Rikers, a total of 4,000 men and women at any given time, more than all the adult patients in New York State psychiatric hospitals combined.

Several studies have shown that they are more likely than other inmates to be the victims as well as the perpetrators of violence.

In July, *The Times* documented 129 cases from 2013 in which inmates were beaten so severely during encounters with officers that they required emergency care. Seventy-seven percent of the inmates had a mental health diagnosis.

Mr. Megginson was one of the 129. In October 2013, a nurse found him facedown on a cellblock floor, beaten unconscious. Several bones in his face were broken, and his shoulder was dislocated.

When he returned from Elmhurst Hospital in Queens, he was punished with 127 days in solitary confinement.

National penal experts have been impressed by Mr. de Blasio's efforts to make Rikers a safer and more humane place. In the last year, the mayor has appropriated tens of millions of dollars to create specialized therapeutic units that reward improvements in behavior. He has also scaled back a punitive system that had kept some inmates locked away in solitary confinement for more than a year.

But individuals like Mr. Megginson burn through resources, requiring services that jails had never been expected to provide. Each Wednesday, the department's chief, two assistant chiefs and five wardens meet with the jail's top mental health officials to discuss what to do about a small number of the most disruptive inmates—a group that included Mr. Megginson.

His problems have been a long time in the making. Psychiatrists can't even agree on what's wrong with him. He has been confined in psychiatric hospitals at least 20 times and labeled with almost every diagnosis that could be applied to a person with a history of aggressive behavior: schizophrenia, bipolar disorder, polysubstance dependence, attention deficit disorder, impulse control disorder, antisocial personality disorder and intermittent explosive disorder.

From the time he was a little boy, growing up in the Kingsbridge section of the Bronx, he had uncontrollable rages. He bit teachers, fought with classmates, urinated on hospital staff and refused to go to school for weeks at a time. At age 6, he spent nearly a month at Bronx Children's Psychiatric Center, a state hospital.

His home life was often unstable. His father, who is also mentally ill, was in and out of prison. In 1990, shortly after his mother gave birth to him at age 16, she moved to Florida, leaving him with his great-grandmother for several years.

Many members of his extended family had mental illness and substance abuse problems. His paternal grandparents were both alcoholics, and his maternal grandfather died after falling out a window—or possibly jumping.

His mother, Shakima Smith-White, acknowledged that she was not always there for her son initially. But she said she re-entered his life full-time when he started school. She has been married now for 20 years, works two jobs and is studying to be a nurse practitioner.

"We weren't perfect, but we tried with Michael," she said.

When he was 5, she said, she took him to Miami on her honeymoon, to her husband's dismay. And when Michael was going through a bad stretch in his late teens, she said, her husband took their two daughters and moved out, worried it was too dangerous to stay. "He pretty much gave me an ultimatum, that it was him or Michael," she said. "And I chose my son."

"At the time he needed me more than the girls or my husband," she said.

When Mr. Megginson was doing well, she said, he was wonderful to be around—calm, affectionate, funny.

"Normally something would happen that would be like a great disappointment," she said. "Or someone would anger him and he would lash out, and from there he would just spiral downwards."

In an interview at Rikers, Mr. Megginson said his great-grandmother had been the most important person in his life. When he was 10 and she died, he said, it was devastating. "The way my mental illness led to an outbreak of getting worse was when my great-grandmother passed," he said. "It tore my insides out and gave me a lot of darkness."

By age 12, he had been admitted to Bronx Children's Psychiatric Center four times, according to medical records, and in his teens spent time at a Manhattan group home for young people with behavioral problems. Between hospital stays he often lived with his mother, and for a while, she said, she could calm him when he was upset. When he was 19, though, they got into a vicious fight. After he started swearing at her, she said, she struck him. He punched her back, knocking out two teeth, grabbed a knife and tried to stab her, she said.

She called 911 and he was arrested, spending three months at Rikers.

When he was released, she refused to allow him back into the house, insisting that he should complete a mental health program first.

For his part, Mr. Megginson said his mother was responsible for many of his problems. He complained that she had not been there for him and blamed her for refusing to put up the $5,000 to bail him out during his most recent incarceration.

"She says a lot of hurtful things, disrespectful things," he said, "like 'Oh I wish you wasn't my son,' or 'I wish I got, you know, I almost got an abortion when you was born, I should've did it.'"

His mother disputed this, saying she was thrilled when she found out she was having a boy.

Mr. Megginson came of age at a time when the public mental health system in New York was going through a major transformation.

By the 1960s and 1970s, state psychiatric hospitals were widely considered failures, inhumane places where patients were routinely neglected and abused. New medications had been developed that allowed patients to be stabilized and discharged, leading to widespread deinstitutionalization. But as the asylums were closed, the states provided little funding for community housing programs. The discharged patients often ended up homeless and, with their illness untreated, could become a danger to themselves and at times a risk to public safety.

On Jan. 3, 1999, Andrew Goldstein, a 29-year-old man with schizophrenia, was standing on a subway platform when he pushed a young woman, Kendra Webdale, in front of an N train, killing her instantly. When asked why he did it, he told the police, "I felt a sensation like something was entering me."

Mr. Goldstein knew he was sick. He kept asking for help. But there were long waiting lists for supervised housing and case management services, and often he was only given a slip of paper with a clinic's address. He is currently at a prison upstate, serving a 23-year sentence for manslaughter.

In the aftermath, legislators passed Kendra's Law, which allows authorities to order people with a history of violence who have repeatedly rejected treatment to take their medication and report regularly to a state-designated program. The state also appropriated millions of dollars for community mental health services.

While the system still suffers from serious shortages, today there are 40,500 state-funded supervised beds where mentally ill people have regular access to clinicians, twice as many as 15 years ago.

One of the most significant innovations available to Mr. Megginson is the Assertive Community Treatment program, or ACT, which is made up of a team that includes a psychiatrist, nurses, social workers and a substance abuse counselor. It is their job to make sure that even the most troubled individuals stick with their treatment. The idea is to avoid costly hospitalizations while enabling people to live safely in the community.

The state requires an ACT team to have a caseload of no more than 68 people and to see each client at least six times a month. There are 46 such teams in New York City, 82 statewide.

On a recent Tuesday, seven members of an East Harlem-based ACT team, who work for a nonprofit agency called the Bridge, met for several hours to discuss each of their 68 clients. Among their concerns: a man with a history of suicide attempts whose cousin had recently killed himself; three people with addiction problems who needed to provide urine samples; a man who was being lewd; and a new client with a history of assault who was acting belligerent toward staff members. "He might need another mood stabilizer," said Aneeza Ali, the team leader. "Or an attitude check."

Starting when he was 18 and after numerous hospitalizations, Mr. Megginson was assigned at least twice to ACT teams including the Bridge program. After he assaulted his mother in 2009, he was mandated under Kendra's Law to enroll with an ACT team as a condition of his probation.

His mother said her son seemed happier in the program because he could live on his own. "He always wanted to feel normal," she said, adding, "It gave him a sense of 'I'm O.K., I'm like everyone else.'"

ACT teams get high marks from activists. Susan Garrison, a social worker and a member of the Harlem chapter of the National Alliance on Mental Illness, said the program had made a big difference in her son's life. At 45, despite having severe schizophrenia, he has been able to stay out of the hospital, and at times he has even held a job, including recently working seven hours a week at a Rite Aid in Harlem.

But as good as ACT is, Ms. Garrison said, her constant involvement in her son's life has been crucial. Without an anchor—a parent, a spouse, a sibling—a person will often go off treatment and deteriorate, she said.

By the time Mr. Megginson reached his 20s, he had lost almost all contact with his mother and was mostly alone.

When his father was released from prison, they made an attempt to reconnect.

At one point, the father, also named Michael, found his son a job working for a storefront tax operation in Harlem. For $100 a week, he dressed in a Statue of Liberty costume and handed out fliers.

But in the fall of 2012, the two had a falling out. The son said his father stole his savings and lost it gambling. The father said he had permission to take the money.

Either way, that November, after a heated argument, the son pulled a chicken from the oven and hurled it at his father. He was committed soon after and remained hospitalized for the next five months.

In recent years, as jails and prisons have filled with the mentally ill, academics and clinicians have suggested that long-term hospitalization could be the best option for more individuals.

Observing a person during an extended hospitalization may improve a psychiatrist's chances of establishing a reliable diagnosis. It can also provide a safe environment, in which a variety of medications and dosages can be calibrated to the patient's needs.

In a hospital, Mr. Megginson would be compelled to take his medication, which would help curtail his aggression. At Rikers, clinicians say, inmates frequently go off their medication until they become uncontrollably violent.

Under state law, patients cannot be held against their will unless they are an immediate danger to themselves or others. During several hospitalizations, Mr. Megginson appeared before judges and successfully challenged his confinement. Though doctors disagreed, they had to release him.

His final hospital stay before Rikers lasted five months and ended on a hopeful note. A psychiatrist wrote that he was taking medication and attending substance abuse programs, that his grooming and hygiene had improved and that he was "free of psychotic features."

"He was very proud of his accomplishment," an April 22, 2013, progress note said, "and anxious to move on to independent living."

But after being discharged to a housing program, Mr. Megginson deteriorated rapidly. He stopped attending treatment sessions, according to medical records, and started drinking heavily and abusing marijuana. On June 12, he hit a counselor in the face with a cellphone charger and was kicked out of the program. Two months later, he stole a woman's cellphone and was sent to Rikers.

Several prosecutors, judges, police and correction officials said in interviews that they were frustrated by the lack of options for keeping people like Mr. Megginson out of jail.

Karen Friedman Agnifilo, the chief assistant district attorney in Manhattan, said she would like to have an alternative to jail for certain convicted offenders who are seriously mentally ill, such as a voluntary confinement that would provide treatment while keeping them off the streets.

"The problem is these individuals have typically been offered every service available," Ms. Friedman Agnifilo said. "As a result, we have no choice but to continue to cycle them through the system. We wish we could do something else, but we don't know what that something else is."

At this point few, if any, alternatives exist for offenders.

The Manhattan district attorney's office has joined several other prosecutors and judges in voicing support for a treatment model being proposed by Francis J. Greenburger, a Manhattan real estate developer whose mentally ill son is currently imprisoned. Under his plan, people with serious mental illness would plead guilty to certain felonies and avoid prison by agreeing to stay in a locked treatment center for up to two years. If at some point they failed to comply, they would be sent to prison.

For the last year and a half, Mr. Greenburger has been trying to get the state to license a pilot project, with limited progress.

At Rikers, Mr. Megginson became such a problem that at times he was transported in handcuffs and leg irons. He had to wear mittens to prevent him from grabbing things, and because he had a history of spitting at officers, was made to wear a mask.

In his 18 months in jail, he had 70 physical confrontations with officers, according to records, an extraordinary number given that most inmates never have one.

In nearly half the cases, guards used pepper spray to subdue him. Eleven times he was described in records as threatening to kill himself. The trouble often started when he ignored such routine orders from guards as to return to his cell, or to get out of the shower.

In the Rikers interview, he described how enraged it would make him to have no control over his daily life. He said it could turn a minor incident like being denied telephone privileges or getting cold food into a major frustration.

"I just get agitated and, you know, you can't do anything about it because you behind a magnetically confined door," Mr. Megginson said. "Mentally ill people should not be confined inside a box; it's not healthy for the mind."

"It makes us people we're not," he said.

Last year, Mr. Megginson was among a dozen particularly volatile inmates chosen for a new program run by the city's health department. A case worker visited him three times a week for therapy sessions that included meditation, breathing exercises and conflict resolution strategies.

Martin J. Murphy, the Correction Department's top uniformed officer, said the time spent working with Mr. Megginson and the inmates like him had resulted in a significant drop in the number of use-of-force cases involving them.

Correction officers, led by union leaders, have long called solitary confinement the most effective punishment for violent inmates. But Chief Murphy said in an interview that the intensive therapy had worked better.

Mr. Megginson spoke fondly of the therapist. He said she had taught him "just to use my thinking instead of using my fists. Like, if I get in an incident with an officer, instead of resolving it in a violent manner, rather just, you know, walk away sometimes. I try to think it out, think what I'm doing first and try to alleviate the situation."

In the weeks before leaving Rikers, he sounded optimistic, saying he hoped to get a job in building maintenance. "I'm just a one-time felon," he said, "and my felony is very light. If I had two felonies on my record or three, then it would be rough. I still got a chance. I believe in opportunity."

Two months ago, Mr. Megginson pleaded guilty to stealing the cellphone as well as to the assaults on the officers. He was given a one-to-three-year prison sentence and, because of his time served at Rikers, was immediately eligible for parole.

On Feb. 18, he was transferred to Downstate Correctional Facility in Fishkill for what was supposed to be a short stay. He had a parole hearing scheduled for mid-March and his lawyer, Jane Pucher, had started looking for a therapeutic program for him in the city.

But at the prison, he was unable to hold himself together. On Feb. 26, he was disciplined for threatening to cut an officer, according to state prison records. On March 4 and 6, he got into fights with inmates, and on March 7 he was written up for smashing a table against a door.

Then on March 15, according to records, he defecated on his cell floor, smeared his feces on the window as well as a security camera and jumped on the metal bed frame until it broke off the wall. When guards arrived, he threw his feces at them.

A few days later, he was transferred to Central New York Psychiatric Center, a state maximum-security forensic hospital, located in Marcy.

In an interview there on Wednesday, Mr. Megginson said he had lost control in prison because he had stopped receiving his medication. Other inmates repeatedly picked on him, he said.

But in the last three weeks at the hospital, he said, things are going well: He is back on his medication, working out and planning to attend church on Sunday.

He said that this time, when he was released, things would be different.

"I'm not going to do nothing bad or illegal," Mr. Megginson said.

Critical Thinking

1. Shouldn't all people who break the law be punished by the criminal justice system, regardless of their mental problems?

2. Do you think it is possible to keep people in psychiatric hospitals, against their will, without violating their Constitutional rights?

3. Do you have any suggestions for how to treat Mr. Megginson?

Internet References

National Alliance on Mental Illness
https://www.nami.org/About-NAMI/NAMI-News/Two-Major-Mental-Health-Bills-Introduced-in-US-Sen

The New York Times
http://topics.nytimes.com/top/reference/timestopics/organizations/r/rikers_island_prison_complex/index.html?inline=nyt-org

The New York Times
http://www.nytimes.com/2014/07/14/nyregion/rikers-study-finds-prisoners-injured-by-employees.html?_r=0

The New York Times
http://www.nytimes.com/2014/11/21/nyregion/rikers-needs-culture-change-mayor-de-blasio-says.html

Article Prepared by: Joanne Naughton

States Struggle with What to Do with Sex Offenders after Prison

MONICA DAVEY

Learning Outcomes

After reading this article, you will be able to:

- State how Minnesota's civil commitment program was intended to operate and how it worked in practice.

- Show how the civil commitment programs in the various states may violate rights protected by the Constitution.

- Describe the weight given to political considerations when changes are being considered.

Moose Lake, Minnesota—Behind razor wire and locked metal doors, hundreds of men waited on a recent morning to be counted, part of the daily routine inside a remote facility here that was built based on a design for a prison.

But this is not a prison, and most of these men—rapists, child abusers, and other sex offenders—have completed their sentences. They are being held here indefinitely under a policy known as civil commitment, having been deemed "sexually dangerous" or "sexual psychopathic personalities" by courts. The intent, the authorities say, is to provide treatment to the most dangerous sex offenders until it is safe for the public for them to go home.

Yet not one of the more than 700 sex offenders who have been civilly committed in Minnesota over the past two decades has actually gone home. And only a few men have been provisionally discharged to live outside of state facilities under strict supervision. "You knew you were going to die here," said Craig Bolte, a sex offender who has been held here nine years and who says he would rather be sent to prison, where "there is still hope."

But now Minnesota's civil commitment program—which detains more people per capita than any other state—is facing an overhaul. Earlier this year, a federal judge found it unconstitutional, calling it "a punitive system that segregates and indefinitely detains a class of potentially dangerous individuals without the safeguards of the criminal justice system."

The judge, Donovan W. Frank, of Federal District Court in St. Paul, on Thursday ordered the state to promptly conduct independent risk and treatment assessments on everyone being detained, to seek releases or ease restrictions in appropriate cases, and to begin conducting annual assessments to determine whether everyone here still meets the legal requirements for civil commitment.

Minnesota is not alone in revisiting its policies. In Missouri, a federal judge last month found that state's program violated people's right to due process, potentially imposing "lifetime detention on individuals who have completed their prison sentences and who no longer pose a danger to the public, no matter how heinous their past conduct." Of about 250 people held since Missouri began committing people in 1999, state officials say seven have been granted what the state considers release with court-ordered restrictions, though some of those men remain in a group-home-like setting behind razor wire at a state facility.

In Texas, which previously had a unique outpatient method for treating sex offenders civilly committed after their prison sentences, the Republican-dominated State Legislature this year revamped the program after a Houston Chronicle investigation found that none of the hundreds committed to the program had ever graduated from it. The investigation also found that nearly half of the men detained for treatment while living in halfway houses and other facilities were actually sent back to prison for breaking the program's rules.

"My sense was that we had to make changes or a federal court is going to strike down the whole program, and we need this program—some of these people would scare the hell out of you," said State Senator John Whitmire, a Democrat who helped push through the overhaul, which included opening a former prison in remote Littlefield to house the detainees. "The way it was, it just looked like incarceration with double jeopardy," Mr. Whitmire said. "This at least holds out a pathway to graduate."

Civil commitment gained support in the 1990s amid reports of heinous sex crimes by repeat offenders. Today, 20 states, along with the federal government, detain some sex criminals for treatment beyond their prison time. But not all have been as sharply criticized as Minnesota's program. In Wisconsin, 118 offenders have been fully discharged from commitment since 1994, and about 135 people have been given supervised release, according to Judge Frank. New York had sent home 30 people and moved 64 people out of secure facilities for the civilly committed and into strict supervision and treatment, Judge Frank wrote.

But the picture in Minnesota looks far different. Since the current program was created in the mid-1990s, civil commitments have soared. The abduction, rape and murder in 2003 of Dru Sjodin, a North Dakota college student, by a sex offender who had been released six months earlier enraged residents and set off a wave of efforts by county attorneys to call on judges to hold such offenders after prison.

Minnesota now has the highest population of civilly committed offenders per capita—nearly all men—in the nation, Judge Frank found, and the lowest rate of release. And costs have soared—to about $125,000 per resident per year, at least three times the cost of an ordinary prison inmate in Minnesota, the judge said.

Yet even in a state that is often seen as liberal-leaning, changing the policy is politically fraught. Gov. Mark Dayton, a Democrat, faced intense criticism before his last election over a plan, later dropped, to release from commitment—with strict conditions—a rapist who had admitted attacking at least 60 women. And proposals to pay for regular risk evaluations for committed people, and other changes, have stalled in the State Legislature.

"It's really a stalemate now because the House Republicans have made it clear that anybody who supports any kind of step forward is going to be castigated in the 2016 elections," Mr. Dayton said.

In his order on Thursday, Judge Frank said that "political sensitivities" had repeatedly hampered efforts to revamp the policy, and that state officials should urge the Legislature to provide money to make the changes he was requiring, including regular evaluations. The judge added that he was likely to require even more changes later. The state indicated that it would seek a stay in the judge's order as it appeals the case.

In an interview last week, Mr. Dayton said the state's program met constitutional requirements, and noted that more people than ever were permitted to leave the facilities under strict supervision. Six people have been granted provisional discharges by the courts, officials said. Three of them are living outside the facilities with close supervision. And though no one has ever been entirely released from the commitment system, Lucinda Jesson, the commissioner of the State Human Services Department, said more people than ever are in a final phase of treatment, a fact that she described as promising.

"I consider myself certainly as committed to improving our social service efforts on behalf of people who need help in our society," Mr. Dayton said. "But there's a line you need to draw for public safety—and these people, if you look at some of their case files, it's repeated, horrific crimes that put them in this situation."

"Minnesota's a compassionate state," he continued, "but there's a line you've got to draw. No one wants to take a risk with somebody who would rape or murder somebody's spouse or child, and look them in the eye and say, 'We put your family at risk in any way.' "

Linda Walker, the mother of Ms. Sjodin, the slain college student, said she was disheartened by the notion that hundreds of men might be reevaluated and considered for less restrictive settings. "Tragically, there are going to be people who have to live in fear that those who chose to perpetrate are quite possibly going to be released back into the society," Ms. Walker said. "The predators are driving the bus here. We need to focus more on the victims. What about the rights of the victims?"

But critics of Minnesota's civil commitment program say it is focused more on warehousing and punishing people than on treating them. They say that offenders receive no regular risk assessments to see whether they require more treatment or supervision, and that the treatment program itself has been revised and reinvented repeatedly over the years as new Human Services employees have come and gone, especially in Moose Lake, a small town where state officials acknowledge hiring is difficult.

Dan Gustafson, a lawyer for the plaintiffs in the class-action lawsuit, said the state's reports of more detainees making progress in the program arrived only recently, and appeared to be largely in response to the criticism by the court and other officials. At least 43 men have died while committed.

"There is a pervasive sense of hopelessness among everybody, knowing that there is no out date and knowing that there is no way to complete anything," said Mr. Bolte, who was sent here nine years ago, at age 19, after being convicted as a juvenile of sexually assaulting a family member and later acknowledging sexual contact with other minors during a troubled childhood.

Critics also complain that the program treats people like Mr. Bolte, whose crimes occurred when they were juveniles, largely the same as it treats adult sex offenders. Other offenders here are much older—one man is 93—and, some suggest, unlikely or even incapable of committing new offenses. More than 30 of the men are older than 70.

Dennis Steiner, a balding man who was civilly committed more than two decades ago in lieu of a prison sentence for molesting boys from ages 8 and 17, said he had done various versions of the state treatment program "about seven times." He lives in a second state complex in St. Peter, southwest of the Twin Cities, where offenders in the later phases of treatment are housed, and allowed increased privileges in a dormitory-like setting.

Mr. Steiner, who is 66 and wore a suit on a recent morning, clutched a thick binder with scores of documents from treatment over the years, including one that listed plans if he ever emerges from the program: "attend support groups," "follow rules of electronic monitoring," "go to outpatient treatment." Mr. Steiner, who wants to move in with his mother, 87, said he would never harm anyone else.

"When do you stop proving that to people?" he said. "If I can't get out on the street and prove it to people, I can't keep proving it to people in here over and over."

Critical Thinking

1. Should people who committed their crimes when they were juveniles be treated as if they had been adults at the time?

2. Is it fair to keep people locked up without any definite date of release?

3. How is it determined how dangerous a sex offender will be if released?

Internet References

Megan's Law
http://meganslaw.ca.gov/facts.htm

Stop It Now!
http://www.stopitnow.org/help-guidance/faqs/faqs-on-sex-offender-treatment

The Marshall Project—I Married a Sex Offender
https://www.themarshallproject.org/2016/02/18/i-married-a-sex-offender#.Ajoi7dq6n

Article   Prepared by: Joanne Naughton

The Painful Price of Aging in Prison

Even as harsh sentences are reconsidered, the financial—and human—tolls mount.

Sari Horwitz

Learning Outcomes

After reading this article, you will be able to:

- Understand some of the issues involved in incarcerating old, sick prisoners.
- Relate how six jurors felt about Bruce Harrison's case.

Inside Coleman Prison, Fla.

Twenty-one years into his nearly 50-year sentence, the graying man steps inside his stark cell in the largest federal prison complex in America. He wears special medical boots because of a foot condition that makes walking feel as if he's "stepping on a needle." He has undergone tests for a suspected heart condition and sometimes experiences vertigo.

"I get dizzy sometimes when I'm walking," says the 63-year-old inmate, Bruce Harrison. "One time, I just couldn't get up."

In 1994, Harrison and other members of the motorcycle group he belonged to were caught up in a drug sting by undercover federal agents, who asked them to move huge volumes of cocaine and marijuana. After taking the job, making several runs and each collecting $1,000, Harrison and the others were arrested and later convicted. When their sentences were handed down, however, jurors objected.

"I am sincerely disheartened by the fact that these defendants, who participated in the staged off-loads and transports . . . are looking at life in prison or decades at best," said one of several who wrote letters to the judge and prosecutor.

In recent years, federal sentencing guidelines have been revised, resulting in less severe prison terms for low-level drug offenders. But Harrison, a decorated Vietnam War veteran,

remains one of tens of thousands of inmates who were convicted in the "war on drugs" of the 1980s and 1990s and who are still behind bars.

Harsh sentencing policies, including mandatory minimums, continue to have lasting consequences for inmates and the nation's prison system. Today, prisoners 50 and older represent the fastest-growing population in crowded federal correctional facilities, their ranks having swelled by 25 percent to nearly 31,000 from 2009 to 2013.

Some prisons have needed to set up geriatric wards, while others have effectively been turned into convalescent homes. The aging of the prison population is driving health-care costs being borne by American taxpayers. The Bureau of Prisons saw health-care expenses for inmates increase 55 percent from 2006 to 2013, when it spent more than $1 billion. That figure is nearly equal to the entire budget of the U.S. Marshals Service or the Bureau of Alcohol, Tobacco, Firearms and Explosives, according to the Justice Department's inspector general, who is conducting a review of the impact of the aging inmate population on prison activities, housing and costs.

"Our federal prisons are starting to resemble nursing homes surrounded with razor wire," said Julie Stewart, president and founder of Families Against Mandatory Minimums. "It makes no sense fiscally, or from the perspective of human compassion, to incarcerate men and women who pose no threat to public safety and have long since paid for their crime. We need to repeal the absurd mandatory minimum sentences that keep them there."

The Obama administration is trying to overhaul the criminal justice system by allowing prisoners who meet certain criteria to be released early through clemency and urging prosecutors to reserve the most severe drug charges for serious, high-level offenders.

America's aging federal inmates

While the younger segment of the federal inmate population has shrunk in the past 15 years, groups age 35 and older all saw increases. In 2014, inmates 55 and older accounted for 10.6 percent of the population, an increase from 6.4 percent in 2000.

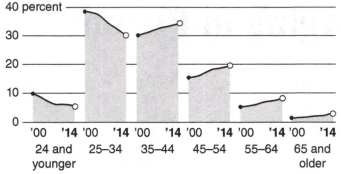

Source: Federal Bureau of Prisons

At the same time, the U.S. Sentencing Commission, an independent agency, has made tens of thousands of incarcerated drug offenders eligible for reduced sentences.

But until more elderly prisoners are discharged—either through compassionate release programs or the clemency initiative started by then-attorney general Eric H. Holder Jr. last year—the government will be forced to spend more to serve the population. Among other expenditures, that means hiring additional nurses and redesigning prisons—installing showers that can be used by the elderly, for instance, or ensuring that entryways are wheelchair-accessible.

"Prisons simply are not physically designed to accommodate the infirmities that come with age," said Jamie Fellner, a senior advisor at Human Rights Watch and an author of a report titled "Old Behind Bars."

"There are countless ways that the aging inmates, some with dementia, bump up against the prison culture," she said. "It is difficult to climb to the upper bunk, walk up stairs, wait outside for pills, take showers in facilities without bars and even hear the commands to stand up for count or sit down when you're told."

For years, state prisons followed the federal government's lead in enacting harsh sentencing laws. In 2010, there were some 246,000 prisoners age 50 and older in state and federal prisons combined, with nearly 90 percent of them held in state custody, the American Civil Liberties Union said in a report titled "At America's Expense: The Mass Incarceration of the Elderly."

On both the state and federal level, the spiraling costs are eating into funds that could be used to curtail violent crime, drug cartels, public corruption, financial fraud and human trafficking. The costs—as well as officials' concerns about racial disparities in sentencing—are also driving efforts to reduce the federal prison population.

For now, however, prison officials say there is little they can do about the costs.

Edmond Ross, a spokesman for the Bureau of Prisons, said: "We have to provide a certain level of medical care for whoever comes to us."

Except for the loud clang of heavy steel security doors that close behind a visitor, the Butner Federal Medical Center in North Carolina feels nothing like the prisons portrayed on television and in movies.

Elderly inmates dressed in khaki prison uniforms are not locked up during the day, but instead congregate with each other in their wheelchairs, wait for treatment in clinics and walk, sometimes with canes or walkers, through their living quarters.

Federal inmate population, 1980–2014

The population is more than 93 percent male. It costs the Department of Justice $6.5 billion annually to operate the federal prison system.

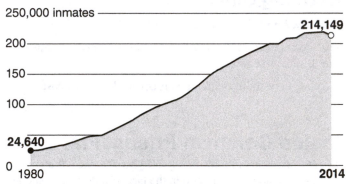

There were 208,859 federal inmates as of April 30, 2015.

Source: Federal Bureau of Prisons

Signs hang from the ceiling, directing prisoners to various units: "Urgent Care," "Mental Health," "Surgery," "Ambulatory Care, "Oncology."

"This facility mirrors a hospital more than a prison," said Kenneth McKoy, acting executive assistant to the warden at Butner, a prison about 20 minutes northeast of Durham. "We provide long-term care."

The facility is the largest medical complex in the Bureau of Prisons, which has 121 prisons, including six that have medical centers. With more than 900 inmates in need of medical care, Butner even provides hospice-like care for dying inmates.

In his "cell" on a recent day, Michael E. Hodge lay in a hospital-like bed where he spent his days mostly staring at the television. A prison official had just helped him get out of his wheelchair. A prison employee delivered his meals. He could hardly keep his eyes open.

In 2000, Hodge was convicted on charges of distribution and possession of marijuana and possessing a gun, and was sentenced to 20 years. When a *Washington Post* reporter visited Hodge in mid-April, he was dying of liver cancer. He died April 18, prison officials said.

"Tell my wife I love her," said Hodge, who said he was in great pain.

Many prisoners at Butner are as sick as Hodge was, McKoy says.

"Why are we keeping someone behind bars who is bedridden and needs assistance to get out of bed and feed and clothe himself?" asked Fellner, of Human Rights Watch. "What do we gain from keeping people behind bars at an enormous cost when they no longer pose any danger to the public if they were released?"

Hodge submitted at least four requests for compassionate release over the past few years, but none were approved by officials, according to his ex-wife Kim Hodge, whom he still referred to as his wife.

"The man is 51 and dying," Kim Hodge said in an interview last month. "He never killed nobody, he's not a child molester, he's not a bad person. Now he's going to die in there."

Taxpayers are increasingly picking up the tab for inmates who received lengthy mandatory sentences for drug offenses and have since aged and developed conditions that require around-the-clock medical care. The average cost of housing federal inmates nearly doubles for aging prisoners. While the cost of a prisoner in the general population is $27,549 a year, the price tag associated with an older inmate who needs more medical care, including expensive prescription drugs and treatments, is $58,956, Justice Department officials say.

At Federal Medical Center Devens, a prison near Boston, 115 aging inmates with kidney failure receive treatment inside a dialysis unit.

"Renal failure is driving our costs up," said Ted Eichel, the health-services administrator for Devens. "It costs $4 million to run this unit, not counting medications, which is half our budget." Devens also employs 60 nurses, along with social workers, dietitians, psychologists, dentists and physical therapists. They look like medical workers, except for the cluster of prison keys they're carrying.

Down the hallway, inmates in wheelchairs line up to receive their daily pills and insulin shots.

Although the prison houses about 1,000 low- to high-security inmates, they are not handcuffed or shackled, except when being transferred outside the facility. A golf cart has been redesigned into a mini-ambulance.

At prisons such as Devens, younger inmates are sometimes enlisted as "companion aides," helping older inmates get out of bed, wheeling them down the halls to medical appointments and helping them take care of themselves.

"The population here is getting older and sicker," said Michael Renshaw, a Devens clinical nurse and corrections officer who noted the differences between working as a nurse there and "on the outside."

"Inmates get very good care here," Renshaw said. "But on the outside, maybe you would give a patient a hug or he would hug you. Here, you have to be able to maintain your borders. It's a prison."

As with all prisons, fights occasionally break out. At Devens, it's sometimes between patients who are in wheelchairs or, in at least one case, between an inmate who climbed out of his wheelchair and onto another prisoner's bed to assault him.

John Thompson, a patient-care technician who works with Devens's dialysis patients, said he knows a number of people who "want no part of" providing medical care to prisoners.

"But I just feel like they're good people," Thompson said. "And they're doing their time. Some guys have an attitude, but I tell them, if you show me respect, I'll show you respect."

Jesse Owens, a dialysis patient serving about 12 years for cocaine charges, said he's grateful for the care. "They're keeping us alive," he said.

Harrison's crammed cell at the Federal Correctional Complex Coleman in Florida near Orlando is devoid of the clutter of life on the outside. The space he shares with another inmate has only a sink, a toilet, a bunk bed with cots, a steel cabinet, two plastic gray chairs, a desk and a bulletin board with a postcard of a Florida waterspout.

From a tiny window, he can see Spanish moss draped over trees in the distance.

Forty-five years ago, Harrison served with the Marines in Vietnam. A machine gunner, he was shot twice and was awarded two Purple Hearts. When he came back, he felt as though he had nowhere to turn. He later joined a motorcycle group known as the Outlaws.

Harrison was approached by an undercover agent who was part of a law enforcement team trying to bring down the group, which had been suspected of illegal activity. He and fellow members of the club were offered a kilogram of cocaine to offload and transport drugs. He declined, saying none of them wanted to be paid in drugs.

"I didn't want drugs, because I really wouldn't have known what to do with them," Harrison said in an interview. "We didn't sell them."

But Harrison and the others took the job because the agents offered cash, and they needed the money. Over a period of several months, they would move what they believed to be real drugs—more than 1,400 kilos of cocaine and about 3,200 pounds of marijuana.

Harrison carried a gun for protection during two of the offloads. He didn't use it, but after authorities arrested him and fellow members of his group, he was charged with possessing a firearm while committing a drug offense.

His 1995 trial in Tampa lasted four months. His lawyer at the time argued that "this was a government operation from beginning to end. . . . Everything was orchestrated by the government. . . . He was not a leader. The only leaders in this case, the only organizers in this case was the United States government."

The jury, nonetheless, found Harrison and the others guilty of transporting the drugs.

Harrison was sentenced to roughly 24 years for possessing cocaine and marijuana with the intent to distribute. The conviction on the firearms charge carried a 25-year penalty, meaning he is effectively serving a life sentence.

"There's no doubt that that's a harsh penalty," said U.S. District Judge Susan C. Bucklew during the sentencing hearing. "But that's what the statute says, and I don't think I have any alternative but to do that."

"I don't have a whole lot of discretion here," she said at another point.

After Harrison and the others were sentenced, several of the jurors expressed shock to learn how long those convicted were to spend behind bars.

"If I would have been given the right to not only judge the facts in this case, but also the law and the actions taken by the government, the prosecutor, local and federal law enforcement officers connected in this case would be in jail and not the defendants," juror Patrick L. McNeil wrote.

Six jurors signed a letter requesting a new trial be ordered, saying that if they had been told by the court that they could have found that the government had entrapped the defendants, they would have found them not guilty.

"Bruce Harrison had never been involved in unloading drugs," said his current lawyer, Tom Dawson. "He didn't arrange for any of these drugs. The government did."

Andrea Strong, a childhood friend of Harrison, said he doesn't claim to have been a saint.

"But, in a compassionate world, this man would not be less than halfway through a sentence for a drug offense that happened 20 years ago," Strong said. "He would've done his time, paid his debt to society, and be released to his network of supportive family and friends."

Along with tens of thousands of other inmates around the country, Harrison is applying for clemency under the Obama administration's program to release drug offenders who have been in prison for at least 10 years and whose cases meet certain criteria.

"If I got out, I'd go back home and be with my three grandkids and help them out," Harrison said.

Another aging inmate at Coleman, 58-year-old Luis Anthony Rivera of Miami, has also applied for clemency. He was convicted of conspiracy to import cocaine and has so far served 30 years.

When he was sentenced in 1985, it marked his first criminal offense.

While in Coleman's maximum-security penitentiary, Rivera began painting with oil and watercolors, trying to re-create the world outside bars. When he was moved to the medium-security prison on the same grounds, he wasn't allowed to bring his art supplies, and he can't afford to buy new ones.

But the move brought a new joy. He saw a tree for the first time in 10 years.

"It was amazing to see a tree," said Rivera, a former pilot who was in the National Guard and the Army and now spends his days working in the prison commissary stocking shelves and filling orders.

"I understand the system of putting people in prison. It works. No doubt," Rivera said. "But how much time you put them in for makes a determination. For the first five years, you suffer. You really do. They keep everything away from you—food, all your basics. So you long for them, watching a commercial on TV, seeing a product that you can't touch or have."

"But after that, you start to get hardened," Rivera said, his voice cracking.

If he does not receive clemency, how much time does he have to serve before getting out?

His lips quivered and his eyes filled with tears.

"I'm not," Rivera said. "I have life, plus 140 years."

Critical Thinking

1. Do you think harsh sentences and mandatory minimums have been successful in reducing drug use?
2. What is the purpose of a prison sentence?
3. Are old, sick prisoners likely to be a danger to society?

Internet References

The Clemency Report
http://clemencyreport.org/something-doesnt-love-wall/

Office of the Inspector General, US DOJ
https://oig.justice.gov/challenges/2014.htm

The Washington Post
https://www.washingtonpost.com/world/national-security/us-clemency-effort-slow-to-start-will-rely-on-an-army-of-pro-bono-lawyers/2015/02/28/2ba8c6bc-bc42-11e4-8668-4e7ba8439ca6_story.html

Article

Prepared by: Joanne Naughton

The Radical Humaneness of Norway's Halden Prison

The goal of the Norwegian penal system is to get inmates out of it.

JESSICA BENKO

Learning Outcomes

After reading this article, you will be able to:

- Discuss the concept of "dynamic security."
- Describe the 1967 report to President Johnson, "The Challenge of Crime in a Free Society."
- Show the effects of Robert Martinson's 1974 article.

Like everything else in Norway, the two-hour drive southeast from Oslo seemed impossibly civilized. The highways were perfectly maintained and painted, the signs clear and informative and the speed-monitoring cameras primly intolerant. My destination was the town of Halden, which is on the border with Sweden, straddling a narrow fjord guarded by a 17th-century fortress. I drove down winding roads flanked in midsummer by rich green fields of young barley and dense yellow carpets of rapeseed plants in full flower. Cows clustered in woodfenced pastures next to neat farmsteads in shades of rust and ocher. On the outskirts of town, across from a road parting dark pine forest, the turnoff to Norway's newest prison was marked by a modest sign that read, simply, HALDEN FENGSEL. There were no signs warning against picking up hitchhikers, no visible fences. Only the 25-foot-tall floodlights rising along the edges hinted that something other than grazing cows lay ahead.

Smooth, featureless concrete rose on the horizon like the wall of a dam as I approached; nearly four times as tall as a man, it snaked along the crests of the hills, its top curled toward me as if under pressure. This was the outer wall of Halden Fengsel, which

is often called the world's most humane maximum-security prison. I walked up the quiet driveway to the entrance and presented myself to a camera at the main door. There were no coils of razor wire in sight, no lethal electric fences, no towers manned by snipers—nothing violent, threatening or dangerous. And yet no prisoner has ever tried to escape. I rang the intercom, the lock disengaged with a click and I stepped inside.

To anyone familiar with the American correctional system, Halden seems alien. Its modern, cheerful and well-appointed facilities, the relative freedom of movement it offers, its quiet and peaceful atmosphere—these qualities are so out of sync with the forms of imprisonment found in the United States that you could be forgiven for doubting whether Halden is a prison at all. It is, of course, but it is also something more: the physical expression of an entire national philosophy about the relative merits of punishment and forgiveness. The treatment of inmates at Halden is wholly focused on helping to prepare them for a life after they get out. Not only is there no death penalty in Norway; there are no life sentences. The maximum sentence for most crimes is 21 years—even for Anders Behring Breivik, who is responsible for probably the deadliest recorded rampage in the world, in which he killed 77 people and injured hundreds more in 2011 by detonating a bomb at a government building in Oslo and then opening fire at a nearby summer camp. Because Breivik was sentenced to "preventive detention," however, his term can be extended indefinitely for five years at a time, if he is deemed a continuing threat to society by the court. "Better out than in" is an unofficial motto of the Norwegian Correctional Service, which makes a reintegration guarantee to all released inmates. It works with other government agencies to secure a home, a job and access to a supportive social network for each inmate before release; Norway's social safety net also provides health care, education and a pension to all citizens. With one of the highest per capita gross domestic products of any country in the world, thanks to the profits from oil production in the North Sea, Norway is in a good position to provide all of this, and spending on the Halden prison runs to more than $93,000 per inmate per year, compared with just $31,000 for prisoners in the United States, according to the Vera Institute of Justice, a nonprofit research and advocacy organization.

That might sound expensive. But if the United States incarcerated its citizens at the same low rate as the Norwegians do (75 per 100,000 residents, versus roughly 700), it could spend that much per inmate and still save more than $45 billion a year. At a time when the American correctional system is under scrutiny—over the harshness of its sentences, its overreliance on solitary confinement, its racial disparities—citizens might ask themselves what all that money is getting them, besides 2.2 million incarcerated people and the hardships that fall on the families they leave behind. The extravagant brutality of the American approach to prisons is not working, and so it might just be worth looking for lessons at the opposite extreme, here in a sea of *blabaerskog,* or blueberry forest.

"This punishment, taking away their freedom—the sign of that is the wall, of course," Gudrun Molden, one of the Halden prison's architects, said on a drizzly morning a few days after I arrived. As we stood on a ridge, along with Jan Stromnes, the assistant warden, it was silent but for the chirping of birds and insects and a hoarse fluttering of birch leaves disturbed by the breeze. The prison is secluded from the surrounding farmland by the blueberry woods, which are the native forest of southeastern Norway: blue-black spruce, slender Scotch pine with red-tinged trunks and silver-skinned birches over a dense understory of blueberry bushes, ferns and mosses in deep shade. It is an ecosystem that evokes deep nostalgia in Norway, where picking wild berries is a near-universal summer pastime for families, and where the right to do so on uncultivated land is protected by law.

Norway banned capital punishment for civilians in 1902, and life sentences were abolished in 1981. But Norwegian prisons operated much like their American counterparts until 1998. That was the year Norway's Ministry of Justice reassessed the Correctional Service's goals and methods, putting the explicit focus on rehabilitating prisoners through education, job training and therapy. A second wave of change in 2007 made a priority of reintegration, with a special emphasis on helping inmates find housing and work with a steady income before they are even released. Halden was the first prison built after this overhaul, and so rehabilitation became the underpinning of its design process. Every aspect of the

facility was designed to ease psychological pressures, mitigate conflict and minimize interpersonal friction. Hence the blueberry forest.

"Nature is a rehabilitation thing now," Molden said. Researchers are working to quantify the benefits of sunlight and fresh air in treating depression. But Molden viewed nature's importance for Norwegian inmates as far more personal. "We don't think of it as a rehabilitation," she said. "We think of it as a basic element in our growing up." She gestured to the knoll we stood on and the 12 acres of *blabaerskog* preserved on the prison grounds, echoing the canopy visible on the far side. Even elsewhere in Europe, most high-security prison plots are scraped completely flat and denuded of vegetation as security measures. "A lot of the staff when we started out came from other prisons in Norway," Stromnes said. "They were a little bit astonished by the trees and the number of them. Shouldn't they be taken away? And what if they climb up, the inmates? As we said, Well, if they climb up, then they can sit there until they get tired, and then they will come down." He laughed. "Never has anyone tried to hide inside. But if they should run in there, they won't get very far—they're still inside."

"Inside" meant inside the wall. The prison's defining feature, the wall is visible everywhere the inmates go, functioning as an inescapable reminder of their imprisonment. Because the prison buildings were purposely built to a human scale, with none more than two stories in height and all modest in breadth, the wall becomes an outsize presence; it looms everywhere, framed by the cell windows, shadowing the exercise yards, its pale horizontal spread emphasized by the dark vertical lines of the trees. The two primary responsibilities of the Correctional Service—detention and rehabilitation—are in perpetual tension with each other, and the architects felt that single wall could represent both. "We trusted the wall," Molden said, to serve as a symbol and an instrument of punishment.

When Molden and her collaborators visited the site in 2002, in preparing for the international competition to design the prison, they spent every minute they were allowed walking around it, trying to absorb the *genius loci,* the spirit of the place. They felt they should use as much of the site as possible, requiring inmates to walk outside to their daily commitments of school or work or therapy, over uneven ground, up and down hills, traveling to and from home, as they would in the world outside. They wound up arranging the prison's living quarters in a ring, which we could now see sloping down the hill on either side of us. In the choice of materials, the architects were inspired by the sober palette of the trees, mosses and bedrock all around; the primary building element is kiln-fired brick, blackened with some of the original red showing through. The architects used silvery galvanized-steel panels as a "hard" material to represent detention, and untreated larch wood, a low-maintenance species that weathers from taupe to soft gray, as a "soft" material associated with rehabilitation and growth.

The Correctional Service emphasizes what it calls "dynamic security," a philosophy that sees interpersonal relationships between the staff and the inmates as the primary factor in maintaining safety within the prison. They contrast this with the approach dominant in high-security prisons elsewhere in the world, which they call "static security." Static security relies on an environment designed to prevent an inmate with bad intentions from carrying them out. Inmates at those prisons are watched at a remove through cameras, contained by remote-controlled doors, prevented from vandalism or weapon-making by tamper-proof furniture, encumbered by shackles or officer escorts when moved. Corrections officers there are trained to control prisoners with as little interaction as possible, minimizing the risk of altercation.

Dynamic security focuses on preventing bad intentions from developing in the first place. Halden's officers are put in close quarters with the inmates as often as possible; the architects were instructed to make the guard stations tiny and cramped, to encourage officers to spend time in common rooms with the inmates instead. The guards socialize with the inmates every day, in casual conversation, often over tea or coffee or meals. Inmates can be monitored via surveillance cameras on the prison grounds, but they often move unaccompanied by guards, requiring a modest level of trust, which the administrators believe is crucial to their progress. Nor are there surveillance cameras in the classrooms or most of the workshops, or in the common rooms, the cell hallways or the cells themselves. The inmates have the opportunity to act out, but somehow they choose not to. In five years, the isolation cell furnished with a limb-restraining bed has never been used.

It is tempting to chalk up all this reasonableness to something peculiar in Norwegian socialization, some sort of civility driven coredeep into the inmates since birth, or perhaps attribute it to their racial and ethnic homogeneity as a group. But in actuality, only around three-fifths of the inmates are legal Norwegian citizens. The rest have come from more than 30 other countries (mostly in Eastern Europe, Africa and the Middle East) and speak little or no Norwegian; English is the lingua franca, a necessity for the officers to communicate with foreign prisoners.

Of the 251 inmates, nearly half are imprisoned for violent crimes like murder, assault or rape; a third are in for smuggling or selling drugs. Nevertheless, violent incidents and even threats are rare, and nearly all take place in Unit A. It is the prison's most restrictive unit, housing inmates who require close psychiatric or medical supervision or who committed crimes that would make them unpopular in Units B and C, the prison's more open "living" cell blocks, where the larger population of inmates mixes during the day for work, schooling and therapy programs.

I met some of the prisoners of Unit A one afternoon in the common room of an eight-man cell block. I was asked to respect the inmates' preferences for anonymity or naming, and for their choices in discussing their cases with me. The Norwegian news media does not often identify suspects or convicts by name, so confirming the details of their stories was not always possible. I sat on an orange vinyl couch next to a wooden shelving unit with a few haphazard piles of board games and magazines and legal books. On the other side of the room, near a window overlooking the unit's gravel yard, a couple of inmates were absorbed in a card game with a guard.

An inmate named Omar passed me a freshly pressed heart-shaped waffle over my shoulder on a paper plate, interrupting an intense monologue directed at me in excellent English by Chris Giske, a large man with a thick goatee and a shaved head who was wearing a heavy gold chain over a T-shirt that strained around his barrel-shaped torso.

"You have heard about the case? Sigrid?" Giske asked me. "It's one of the biggest cases in Norway."

In 2012, a 16-year-old girl named Sigrid Schjetne vanished while walking home one night, and her disappearance gripped the country. Her body was found a month later, and Giske's conviction in the case made him one of the most reviled killers in Norwegian history.

He explained to me that he asked to transfer out of Unit A, but that officials declined to move him. "They don't want me in prison," he said. "They want me in the psychiatric thing. I don't know why."

He was denied the transfer, I was later told, partly because of a desire not to outrage the other inmates, and partly because of significant concern over his mental health—and his history of unprovoked extreme violence against young women unfortunate enough to cross his path. Giske had previously spent two years in prison after attacking a woman with a crowbar. This time, there was disagreement among doctors over whether he belonged in a hospital or in prison. Until the question was settled, he was the responsibility of the staff at Halden. It was not the first, second or even third casual meal I had shared with a man convicted of murder since I arrived at the beginning of the week, but it was the first time I felt myself recoil on instinct. (After my visit, Giske was transferred to a psychiatric institution.)

Omar handed me a vacuum-sealed slice of what appeared to be flexible plastic, its wrapper decorated with a drawing of cheerful red dairy barns.

"It's fantastic!" he exclaimed. "When you are in Norway, you must try this! The first thing I learned, it was this. Brown cheese."

According to the packaging, brown cheese is one of the things that "make Norwegians Norwegians," a calorie-dense fuel of fat and sugar salvaged from whey discarded during the cheese-making process, which is cooked down for half a day until all that remains are caramelized milk sugars in a thick, sticky residue. With enthusiastic encouragement from the inmates, I peeled open the packaging and placed the glossy square on my limp waffle, following their instructions to fold the waffle as you would a taco, or a New York slice. To their great amusement, I winced as I tried to swallow what tasted to me like a paste of spray cheese mixed with fudge.

Another guard walked in and sat down next to me on the couch. "It's allowed to say you don't like it," she said.

Are Hoidal, the prison's warden, laughed from the doorway behind us and accepted his third waffle of the day. He had explained to me earlier, in response to my raised eyebrows, that in keeping with the prison's commitment to "normalcy," even the inmates in this block gather once a week to partake of waffles, which are a weekly ritual in most Norwegian homes.

At Halden, some inmates train for cooking certificates in the prison's professional-grade kitchen classroom, where I was treated to chocolate mousse presented in a wineglass, a delicate nest of orange zest curled on top. But most of the kitchen activity is more ordinary. I never entered a cell block without receiving offers of tea or coffee, an essential element of even the most basic Norwegian hospitality, and was always earnestly invited to share meals. The best meal I had in Norway—spicy lasagna, garlic bread and a salad with sun-dried tomatoes—was made by an inmate who had spent almost half of his 40 years in prison. "Every time, you make an improvement," he said of his cooking skills.

When I first met the inmates of C8, a special unit focused on addiction recovery, they were returning to their block laden with green nylon reusable bags filled with purchases from their weekly visit to the prison grocery shop, which is well stocked, carrying snacks and nonperishables but also a colorful assortment of produce, dairy products and meat. The men piled bags of food for communal suppers on the kitchen island on one side of their common room and headed back to their cells with personal items—fruit, soda, snacks, salami—to stash in their minifridges.

I met Tom, an inmate in his late 40s, as he was unpacking groceries on the counter: eggs, bacon, bread, cream, onions, tomato sauce, ground beef, lettuce, almonds, olives, frozen shrimp. Tom had a hoarse voice and a graying blond goatee, and his sleeveless basketball jersey exposed an assortment of tattoos decorating thick arms. His head was shaved smooth, with "F_____ the Police" inked in cursive along the right side of his skull; the left side said "RESPECT" in inch-tall letters. A small block of text under his right eye was blacked out, and under his left eye was "666." A long seam ran up the back of his

neck and scalp, a remnant of a high-speed motorcycle accident that left him in a coma the last time he was out of prison.

"You are alone now, yeah?" Tom nodded toward the room behind me. I turned around to look.

There were maybe eight inmates around—playing a soccer video game on the modular couch, folding laundry dried on a rack in the corner by large windows overlooking the exercise yard, dealing cards at the dining table—but no guards. Tom searched my face for signs of alarm. The convictions represented among this group included murder, weapons possession and assault.

I was a little surprised, but I stayed nonchalant. I might have expected a bit more supervision—perhaps a quick briefing on safety protocol and security guidelines—but the guards could see us through the long windows of their station, sandwiched between the common rooms of C7 and C8. It was the first of many times I would be left alone with inmates in a common room or in a cell at the end of a hallway, the staff retreating to make space for candid conversation. "It's O.K.," Tom assured me, with what I thought sounded like a hint of pride.

A man named Yassin, the uncontested pastry king of C8, politely motioned for me to move aside so he could get to the baking pans in the cabinet at my feet. When Halden opened, there was a wave of foreign news reports containing snarky, florid descriptions of the "posh," "luxurious" prison, comparing its furnishings to those of a "boutique hotel." In reality, the furniture is not dissimilar from what you might find in an American college dorm. The truly striking difference is that it is *normal* furniture, not specially designed to prevent it from being turned into shivs, arson fuel or other instruments of violence. The kitchen also provides ample weapons if a prisoner were so inclined. As one inmate pointed out to me, the cabinets on the wall contained ceramic plates and glass cups, the drawers held metal silverware and there were a couple of large kitchen knives tethered by lengths of rubber-coated wire.

"If you want to ask me something, come on, no problem," Tom said, throwing open his hands in invitation. "I'm not very good in English."

Yassin stood up, laughing. "You speak very nice, Tom! It is prison English!" Yassin speaks Arabic and English and is also fluent in Norwegian, a requirement for living in the drug-treatment block, where group and individual counseling is conducted in Norwegian. Like many in the prison, Tom never finished high school. He was raised in a boys' home and has been in and out of prison, where English is common, for more than 30 years. (Yassin's first prison sentence began at 15. Now 29 and close to finishing his sentence for selling drugs, he wants to make a change and thinks he might like to run a scared-straight-style program for teenagers. Before this most recent arrest, the background photo on his Facebook profile was the Facebook logo recreated in white powder on a blue background, with a straw coming in for the snort. He immigrated to Norway as a child with his Moroccan family by way of Dubai.)

"I don't leave Norway," Tom said. "I love my country." He extended his arm with his fist clenched, showing a forearm covered in a "NORGE" tattoo shaded in the colors of the Norwegian flag. But I couldn't detect any tension between Tom and Yassin in the kitchen. Tom was adamant that overcoming his substance-abuse problem was his responsibility alone. But he conceded that the environment at Halden, and the availability of therapists, made it easier. Compared with other prisons, "it's quiet," he said. "No fighting, no drugs, no problem," he added. "You're safe."

The officers try to head off any tensions that could lead to violence. If inmates are having problems with one another, an officer or prison chaplain brings them together for a mediation session that continues until they have agreed to maintain peace and have shaken hands. Even members of rival gangs agree not to fight inside, though the promise doesn't extend to after their release. The few incidents of violence at Halden have been almost exclusively in Unit A, among the inmates with more serious psychiatric illnesses.

If an inmate does violate the rules, the consequences are swift, consistent and evenly applied. Repeated misbehavior or rule violations can result in cell confinement during regular work hours, sometimes without TV. One inmate claimed that an intrepid prisoner from Eastern Europe somehow managed to hack his TV to connect to the Internet and had it taken away for five months. ("Five months!" the inmate marveled to me. "I don't understand how he survived.")

It is perhaps hard to believe that Halden, or Norway more broadly, could hold any lessons for the United States. With its 251 inmates, Halden is one of Norway's largest prisons, in a country with only 3,800 prisoners (according to the International Center for Prison Studies); by contrast, in the United States, the average number is around 1,300 at maximum-security prisons, with a total of 2.2 million incarcerated (according to the federal Bureau of Justice Statistics). Halden's rehabilitation programs seem logistically and financially out of reach for such a system to even contemplate.

And yet there was a brief historical moment in which the United States pondered a similar approach to criminal justice. As part of his "war on crime," Lyndon B. Johnson established the President's Commission on Law Enforcement and Administration of Justice, a body of 19 advisers appointed to study, among other things, the conditions and practices of catastrophically overstretched prisons. The resulting 1967 report, "The Challenge of Crime in a Free Society," expressed concern that many correctional institutions were detrimental to rehabilitation: "Life in many institutions is at best barren and futile, at worst unspeakably brutal and degrading . . . . The conditions in

which they live are the poorest possible preparation for their successful re-entry into society, and often merely reinforce in them a pattern of manipulation and destructiveness." And in its recommendations, the commission put forward a vision for prisons that would be surprisingly like Halden. "Architecturally, the model institution would resemble as much as possible a normal residential setting. Rooms, for example, would have doors rather than bars. Inmates would eat at small tables in an informal atmosphere. There would be classrooms, recreation facilities, day rooms, and perhaps a shop and library."

In the mid-1970s, the federal Bureau of Prisons completed three pretrial detention facilities that were designed to reflect those best practices. The three Metropolitan Correctional Centers, or M.C.C.s, were the first of what would come to be known as "new generation" institutions. The results, in both architecture and operation, were a radical departure from previous models. Groups of 44 prisoners populated self-contained units in which all of the single-inmate cells (with wooden doors meant to reduce both noise and cost) opened onto a day room, where they ate, socialized and met with visitors or counselors, minimizing the need for moving inmates outside the unit. All the prisoners spent the entire day outside their cells with a single unarmed correctional officer in an environment meant to diminish the sense of institutionalization and its attendant psychological stresses, with wooden and upholstered furniture, desks in the cells, porcelain toilets, exposed light fixtures, brightly colored walls, skylights and carpeted floors.

But by the time the centers opened, public and political commitment to rehabilitation programs in American prisons had shifted. Much of the backlash within penological circles can be traced to Robert Martinson, a sociology researcher at the City University of New York. In a 1974 article for the journal *Public Interest,* he summarized an analysis of data from 1945 to 1967 about the impact of rehabilitation programs on recidivism. Despite the fact that around half the individual programs did show evidence of effectiveness in reducing recidivism, Martinson's article concluded that no category of rehabilitation program (education or psychotherapy, for example) showed consistent results across prison systems. "With few and isolated exceptions," he wrote, "the rehabilitative efforts that have been reported so far have had no appreciable effect on recidivism." Martinson's paper was immediately seized upon by the news media and politicians, who latched on to the idea that "nothing works" in regard to prisoner rehabilitation. "It Doesn't Work" was the title of a "60 Minutes" segment on rehabilitation. "They don't rehabilitate, they don't deter, they don't punish and they don't protect," Jerry Brown, the governor of California, said in a 1975 speech. A top psychiatrist for the Bureau of Prisons resigned in disgust at what he perceived to be an abandonment of commitment to rehabilitation. At the dedication ceremony for the San Diego M.C.C. in 1974, one of the very structures designed with rehabilitation in mind, William Saxbe, the attorney general of the United States, declared that the ability of a correctional program to produce rehabilitation was a "myth" for all but the youngest offenders.

Martinson's paper was quickly challenged; a 1975 analysis of much of the same data by another sociologist criticized Martinson's choice to overlook the successful programs and their characteristics in favor of a broad conclusion devoid of context. By 1979, in light of new analyses, Martinson published another paper that unequivocally withdrew his previous conclusion, declaring that "contrary to my previous position, some treatment programs *do* have an appreciable effect on recidivism." But by then, the "nothing works" narrative was firmly entrenched. In 1984, a Senate report calling for more stringent sentencing guidelines cited Martinson's 1974 paper, without acknowledging his later reversal. The tough-on-crime policies that sprouted in Congress and state legislatures soon after included mandatory minimums, longer sentences, three-strikes laws, legislation allowing juveniles to be prosecuted as adults and an increase in prisoners' "maxing out," or being released without passing through reintegration programs or the parole system. Between 1975 and 2005, the rate of incarceration in the United States skyrocketed, from roughly 100 inmates per 100,000 citizens to more than 700—consistently one of the highest rates in the world. Though Americans make up about only 4.6 percent of the world's population, American prisons hold 22 percent of all incarcerated people.

Today, the M.C.C. model of incarceration, which is now known as "direct supervision," is not entirely dead. Around 350 facilities—making up less than 7 percent of the incarceration sites in the United States, mostly county-level jails, which are pretrial and short-stay institutions—have been built on the direct-supervision model and are, with greater and lesser fidelity to the ideal, run by the same principles of inmate management developed for the new-generation prisons of the 1970s. The body of data from those jails over the last 40 years has shown that they have lower levels of violence among inmates and against guards and reduced recidivism; some of these institutions, when directly compared with the older facilities they replaced, saw drops of 90 percent in violent incidents. But extrapolating from this tiny group of facilities to the entire nation, and in particular to its maximum-security prisons, is an impossible thought experiment. Much about the American culture of imprisonment today—the training of guards, the acculturation of prisoners, the incentives of politicians, the inattention of citizens—would have to change for the Norwegian approach to gain anything more than a minor foothold in the correctional system. The country has gone down a different road during the past half century, and that road does not lead to Halden Fengsel.

Even understanding how well the Norwegian approach works in Norway is a difficult business. On a Saturday

afternoon in Oslo, I met Ragnar Kristoffersen, an anthropologist who teaches at the Correctional Service of Norway Staff Academy, which trains correction officers. Kristoffersen published a research paper comparing recidivism rates in the Scandinavian countries. A survey of inmates who were released in 2005 put Norway's two-year recidivism rate at 20 percent, the lowest in Scandinavia, which was widely praised in the Norwegian and international press. For comparison, a 2014 recidivism report from the United States Bureau of Justice Statistics announced that an estimated 68 percent of prisoners released in 30 states in 2005 were arrested for a new crime within three years.

I asked Kristoffersen if he had spent time at Halden. He reached into his briefcase and pulled out a handful of printed sheets. "Have you seen this?" he asked while waving them at me. "It's preposterous!" They were printouts of English-language articles about the prison, the most offensive and misleading lines highlighted. He read a few quotes about the prison's architecture and furnishings to me with disgust. I acknowledged that the hyperbolic descriptions would catch the attention of American and British readers, for whom the cost of a prison like Halden would probably need to be justified by strong evidence of a significant reduction in recidivism.

Somewhat to my surprise, Kristoffersen went into a rant about the unreliability of recidivism statistics for evaluating corrections practices. From one local, state or national justice system to another, diverse and ever-changing policies and practices in sentencing—what kinds and lengths of sentences judges impose for what types of crimes, how likely they are to reincarcerate an offender for a technical violation of parole, how much emphasis they put on community sentences over prison terms and many other factors—make it nearly impossible to know if you're comparing apples to apples. Kristoffersen pointed out that in 2005, Norway was putting people in prison for traffic offenses like speeding, something that few other countries do. Speeders are at low risk for reoffending and receiving another prison sentence for that crime or any other. Excluding traffic offenders, Norway's recidivism rate would, per that survey, be around 25 percent after two years.

Then there was the question of what qualifies as "recidivism." Some countries and states count any new arrest as recidivism, while others count only new convictions or new prison sentences; still others include parole violations. The numbers most commonly cited in news reports about recidivism, like the 20 percent celebrated by Norway or the 68 percent lamented by the United States, begin to fall apart on closer inspection. That 68 percent, for example, is a three-year number, but digging into the report shows the more comparable two-year rate to be 60 percent. And that number reflects not reincarceration (the basis for the Norwegian statistic) but rearrest, a much wider net. Fifteen pages into the Bureau of Justice Statistics report,

I found a two-year reincarceration rate, probably the best available comparison to Norway's measures. Kristoffersen's caveat in mind, that translated to a much less drastic contrast: Norway, 25 percent; the United States, 28.8 percent.

What does that mean? Is the American prison system doing a better job than conventional wisdom would suggest? It is frustratingly hard to tell. I asked Kristoffersen if that low reincarceration rate might reflect the fact that long prison sentences mean that many prisoners become naturally less likely to reoffend because of advanced age. He agreed that was possible, along with many other more and less obvious variables. It turned out that measuring the effectiveness of Halden in particular was nearly impossible; Norway's recidivism statistics are broken down by prison of release, and almost no prisoners are released directly from maximum-security prisons, so Halden doesn't have a recidivism number.

After nearly an hour of talking about the finer points of statistics, though, Kristoffersen stopped and made a point that wasn't about statistics at all.

"You have to be aware—there's a logical type of error which is common in debating these things," he said. "That is, you shouldn't mix two kinds of principles. The one is about: How do you fight crimes? How do you reduce recidivism? And the other is: What are the principles of humanity that you want to build your system on? They are two different questions."

He leaned back in his chair and went on. "We like to think that treating inmates nicely, humanely, is good for the rehabilitation. And I'm not arguing against it. I'm saying two things. There are poor evidence saying that treating people nicely will keep them from committing new crimes. Very poor evidence."

He paused. "But then again, my second point would be," he said, "if you treat people badly, it's a reflection on yourself." In officer-training school, he explained, guards are taught that treating inmates humanely is something they should do not for the inmates but for themselves. The theory is that if officers are taught to be harsh, domineering and suspicious, it will ripple outward in their lives, affecting their selfimage, their families, even Norway as a whole. Kristoffersen cited a line that is usually attributed to Dostoyevsky: "The degree of civilization in a society can be judged by entering its prisons."

I heard the same quotation from Are Hoidal, Halden's warden, not long before I left Halden. He told me proudly that people wanted to work at the prison, and officers and teachers told me that they hoped to spend their whole careers at Halden, that they were proud of making a difference.

"They make big changes in here," Hoidal said as we made our way through the succession of doors that would return us to the world outside. There was, improbably, an actual rainbow stretching from the clouds above, landing somewhere outside the wall. Hoidal was quiet for a moment, then laughed. "I have the best job in the world!" He chuckled and shook his head. He sounded surprised.

Correction: April 26, 2015

An article on March 29 about Norway's Halden prison described incompletely the circumstances of Anders Breivik's 21-year sentence for a bombing-and-shooting attack. While the maximum sentence for most crimes is 21 years, the Norwegian penal code allows for preventive detention, which is the extension of a sentence in five-year increments if the convicted person is deemed to be a continued threat to society. Therefore, the maximum term for any crime is not 21 years.

Critical Thinking

1. How do you think the goal of the Norwegian penal system, to get inmates out of it, compares with the goal of the American system?

2. Do you believe forgiveness should be a part of the American correctional philosophy?

3. Could a Halden-like prison be effective in the US?

Internet References

Bureau of Justice Statistics
  http://www.bjs.gov/index.cfm?ty5pbdetail&iid54986
Euro Vista
  http://euro-vista.org/wp-content/uploads/2015/01/EuroVista-vol2-no3-6-Kristofferson-edit.pdf
International Centre for Prison Studies
  http://www.prisonstudies.org/country/norway
The New York Times
  http://www.nytimes.com/2012/08/25/world/europe/anders-behring-breivik-murder-trial.html?_r=1
Vera Institute for Justice
  http://www.vera.org/pubs/special/price-prisons-what-incarceration-costs-taxpayers

---

JESSICA BENKO is a print and radio journalist whose work has appeared in *National Geographic* and *Wired* and on "This American Life."

Article　　　　　　　　　　　　　　　　　　　　Prepared by: Joanne Naughton

Portugal Cut Addiction Rates in Half by Connecting Drug Users With Communities Instead of Jailing Them

Fifteen years ago, the Portuguese had one of the worst drug problems in Europe. So they decriminalized drugs, took money out of prisons, put it into holistic rehabilitation, and found that human connection is the antidote to addiction.

JOHANN HARI

Learning Outcomes

After reading this article, you will be able to:

- Describe the Rat Park experiment.
- Relate the findings of a study by the *British Journal of Criminology*.
- Explain what happened when Portugal decriminalized all drugs nearly 15 years ago.

It is now 100 years since drugs were first banned—and all through this long century of waging war on drugs, we have been told a story about addiction by our teachers and by our governments. This story is so deeply ingrained in our minds that we take it for granted: There are strong chemical hooks in these drugs, so if we stopped on day twenty-one, our bodies would need the chemical. We would have a ferocious craving. We would be addicted. That's what addiction means.

This theory was first established, in part, through rat experiments—ones that were injected into the American psyche in the 1980s, in a famous advertisement by the Partnership for a Drug-Free America. You may remember it. The experiment is simple. Put a rat in a cage, alone, with two water bottles. One is just water. The other is water laced with heroin or cocaine. Almost every time you run this experiment, the rat will become

obsessed with the drugged water, and keep coming back for more and more, until it kills itself.

The ad explains: "Only one drug is so addictive, nine out of ten laboratory rats will use it. And use it. And use it. Until dead. It's called cocaine. And it can do the same thing to you."

But in the 1970s, a professor of Psychology in Vancouver called Bruce Alexander noticed something odd about this experiment. The rat is put in the cage all alone. It has nothing to do but take the drugs. What would happen, he wondered, if we tried this differently?

So Professor Alexander built Rat Park. It is a lush cage where the rats would have colored balls and the best rat-food and tunnels to scamper down and plenty of friends: everything a rat about town could want. What, Alexander wanted to know, will happen then?

In Rat Park, all the rats obviously tried both water bottles, because they didn't know what was in them. But what happened next was startling.

The rats with good lives didn't like the drugged water. They mostly shunned it, consuming less than a quarter of the drugs the isolated rats used. None of them died. While all the rats who were alone and unhappy became heavy users, none of the rats who had a happy environment did.

At first, I thought this was merely a quirk of rats, until I discovered that there was—at the same time as the Rat Park experiment—a helpful human equivalent taking place. It was called the Vietnam War. *Time* magazine reported using heroin was "as common as chewing gum" among U.S. soldiers, and there is solid evidence to back this up: some 20 percent of U.S. soldiers had become addicted to heroin there, according to a study published in the *Archives of General Psychiatry.*

Many people were understandably terrified; they believed a huge number of addicts were about to head home when the war ended.

But in fact some 95 percent of the addicted soldiers—according to the same study—simply stopped. Very few had rehab. They shifted from a terrifying cage back to a pleasant one, so didn't want the drug any more.

Professor Alexander argues this discovery is a profound challenge both to the right-wing view that addiction is a moral failing caused by too much hedonistic partying, and the liberal view that addiction is a disease taking place in a chemically hijacked brain. In fact, he argues, addiction is an adaptation. It's not you. It's your cage.

Rats in the Park

After the first phase of Rat Park, Professor Alexander then took this test further. He reran the early experiments, where the rats were left alone, and became compulsive users of the drug. He let them use for 57 days—if anything can hook you, it's that.

Then he took them out of isolation, and placed them in Rat Park. He wanted to know, if you fall into that state of addiction, is your brain hijacked, so you can't recover? Do the drugs take you over? What happened is—again—striking. The rats seemed to have a few twitches of withdrawal, but they soon stopped their heavy use, and went back to having a normal life. The good cage saved them.

When I first learned about this, I was puzzled. How can this be? This new theory is such a radical assault on what we have been told that it felt like it could not be true. But the more scientists I interviewed, and the more I looked at their studies, the more I discovered things that don't seem to make sense—unless you take account of this new approach.

Here's one example of an experiment that is happening all around you, and may well happen to you one day. If you get run over today and you break your hip, you will probably be given diamorphine, the medical name for heroin. In the hospital around you, there will be plenty of people also given heroin for long periods, for pain relief.

The heroin you will get from the doctor will have a much higher purity and potency than the heroin being used by street-addicts, who have to buy from criminals who adulterate it. So if the old theory of addiction is right—it's the drugs that cause it; they make your body need them—then it's obvious what

should happen. Loads of people should leave the hospital and try to score smack on the streets to meet their habit.

But here's the strange thing: It virtually never happens. As the Canadian doctor Gabor Mate was the first to explain to me, medical users just stop, despite months of use. The same drug, used for the same length of time, turns street-users into desperate addicts and leaves medical patients unaffected.

If you still believe, as I used to, that chemical hooks are what cause addiction, then this makes no sense.

But if you believe Bruce Alexander's theory, the picture falls into place. The street-addict is like the rats in the first cage, isolated, alone, with only one source of solace to turn to. The medical patient is like the rats in the second cage. She is going home to a life where she is surrounded by the people she loves. The drug is the same, but the environment is different.

The Opposite of Addiction Is Connection

This gives us an insight that goes much deeper than the need to understand addicts.

Professor Peter Cohen argues that human beings have a deep need to bond and form connections. It's how we get our satisfaction. If we can't connect with each other, we will connect with anything we can find—the whirr of a roulette wheel or the prick of a syringe. He says we should stop talking about 'addiction' altogether, and instead call it 'bonding.' A heroin addict has bonded with heroin because she couldn't bond as fully with anything else.

So the opposite of addiction is not sobriety. It is human connection.

When I learned all this, I found it slowly persuading me, but I still couldn't shake off a nagging doubt. Are these scientists saying chemical hooks make no difference? It was explained to me—you can become addicted to gambling, and nobody thinks you inject a pack of cards into your veins. You can have all the addiction, and none of the chemical hooks. I went to a Gamblers' Anonymous meeting in Las Vegas (with the permission of everyone present, who knew I was there to observe) and they were as plainly addicted as the cocaine and heroin addicts I have known in my life. Yet there are no chemical hooks on a craps table.

But still, surely, I asked, there is some role for the chemicals? It turns out there is an experiment which gives us the answer to this in quite precise terms, which I learned about in Richard DeGrandpre's book *The Cult of Pharmacology.*

Everyone agrees cigarette smoking is one of the most addictive processes around. The chemical hooks in tobacco come from a drug inside it called nicotine. So when nicotine patches were developed in the early 1990s, there was a huge surge of optimism—cigarette smokers could get all of their chemical hooks, without the other filthy (and deadly) effects of cigarette smoking. They would be freed.

But the Office of the Surgeon General has found that just 17.7 percent of cigarette smokers are able to stop using nicotine patches. That's not nothing. If the chemicals drive 17.7 percent of addiction, as this shows, that's still millions of lives ruined globally. But what it reveals again is that the story we have been taught about chemical hooks is, in fact, real, only a minor part of a much bigger picture.

This has huge implications for the 100-year-old war on drugs.

This massive war—which kills people from the malls of Mexico to the streets of Liverpool—is based on the claim that we need to physically eradicate a whole array of chemicals because they hijack people's brains and cause addiction. But if drugs aren't the driver of addiction—if, in fact, it is disconnection that drives addiction—then this makes no sense.

Ironically, the war on drugs actually increases all those larger drivers of addiction. For example, I went to a prison in Arizona—Tent City—where inmates are detained in tiny stone isolation cages ('The Hole') for weeks and weeks on end to punish them for drug use. It is as close to a human recreation of the cages that guaranteed deadly addiction in rats as I can imagine. And when those prisoners get out, they will be unemployable because of their criminal record, guaranteeing they will be cut off ever more.

How Portugal Halved Drug Addiction Levels

There is an alternative. You can build a system that is designed to help drug addicts to reconnect with the world—and so leave behind their addictions.

This isn't theoretical. It is happening. I have seen it. Nearly 15 years ago, Portugal had one of the worst drug problems in Europe, with one percent of the population addicted to heroin. They had tried a drug war, and the problem just kept getting worse.

So they decided to do something radically different. They resolved to decriminalize all drugs, and transfer all the money they used to spend on arresting and jailing drug addicts, and spend it instead on reconnecting them—to their own feelings, and to the wider society.

The most crucial step is to get them secure housing, and subsidized jobs so they have a purpose in life, and something to get out of bed for. I watched as they are helped, in warm and welcoming clinics, to learn how to reconnect with their feelings, after years of trauma and stunning them into silence with drugs.

One group of addicts were given a loan to set up a removals firm. Suddenly, they were a group, all bonded to each other, and to the society, and responsible for each other's care.

The results of all this are now in. An independent study by the *British Journal of Criminology* found that since total decriminalization, addiction has fallen, and injecting drug use is down by 50 percent. I'll repeat that: injecting drug use is down by 50 percent.

Decriminalization has been such a manifest success that very few people in Portugal want to go back to the old system. The main campaigner against the decriminalization back in 2000 was Joao Figueira, the country's top drug cop. He offered all the dire warnings that we would expect: more crime, more addicts. But when we sat together in Lisbon, he told me that everything he predicted had not come to pass—and he now hopes the whole world will follow Portugal's example.

Happiness in "the Age of Loneliness"

This isn't only relevant to addicts. It is relevant to all of us, because it forces us to think differently about ourselves. Human beings are bonding animals. We need to connect and love. The wisest sentence of the twentieth century was E.M. Forster's: "only connect." But we have created an environment and a culture that cut us off from connection, or offer only the parody of it offered by the Internet. The rise of addiction is a symptom of a deeper sickness in the way we live—constantly directing our gaze towards the next shiny object we should buy, rather than the human beings all around us.

The writer George Monbiot has called this "the age of loneliness." We have created human societies where it is easier for people to become cut off from all human connections than ever before. Bruce Alexander, the creator of Rat Park, told me that for too long, we have talked exclusively about individual recovery from addiction. We need now to talk about social recovery—how we all recover, together, from the sickness of isolation that is sinking on us like a thick fog.

But this new evidence isn't just a challenge to us politically. It doesn't just force us to change our minds. It forces us to change our hearts.

Loving an addict is really hard. When I looked at the addicts I love, it was always tempting to follow the tough love advice doled out by reality shows like Intervention—tell the addict to shape up, or cut them off. Their message is that an addict who won't stop should be shunned. It's the logic of the drug war, imported into our private lives.

But in fact, I learned, that will only deepen their addiction—and you may lose them altogether. I came home determined to tie the addicts in my life closer to me than ever—to let them know I love them unconditionally, whether they stop, or whether they can't.

Critical Thinking

1. Has the war on drugs worked—nationwide or worldwide?

2. Do you agree that the opposite of addiction is not sobriety, but human connection, or do you believe that drugs have a chemical "hook" which causes addiction?

3. Should all drugs be decriminalized, or should they be legalized and controlled, as tobacco and alcohol are?

Internet References

Bruce K. Alexander
http://www.brucekalexander.com/articles-speeches/rat-park

Spiegelonline international
http://www.spiegel.de/international/europe/evaluating-drug-decriminalization-in-portugal-12-years-later-a-891060.html

Stuart McMillen
http://www.stuartmcmillen.com/blog/cartoon-blog/globalization-addiction-bruce-alexander/

JOHANN HARI is a British journalist whose work has appeared in the *New York Times, Le Monde, The Guardian, The New Republic,* and other publications.

This article is adapted from *Chasing the Scream: The First and Last Days of the War on Drugs* by Johann Hari.

"The Worst of the Worst" Aren't the Only Ones Who Get Executed

SIMON MCCORMACK

Learning Outcomes

After reading this article, you will be able to:

- Summarize the findings of Smith's study of people who have been executed.

- State some of the criticisms of the study.

- Discuss the Eighth Amendment requirements for the death penalty.

A new study suggests that the people put to death in America are hardly the worst of the worst offenders. The study, published in *Hastings Law Journal*, looked at 100 executions between 2012 and 2013. Some of the most striking results are displayed in the graphic.

Robert Smith, the study's lead researcher and an assistant professor of law at the University of North Carolina, told *The Huffington Post* his research provides evidence that many of the people who are actually put to death are not cold, calculating, remorseless killers.

"A lot of folks even familiar with criminal justice and the death penalty system thought that, by the time you executed somebody, you're really gonna get these people that the court describes as the worst of the worst," Smith said. "It was surprising to us just how many of the people that we found had evidence in their record suggesting that there are real problems with functional deficits that you wouldn't expect to see in people being executed."

One of the people in Smith's study is Daniel Cook. Cook's mom drank and used drugs while she was pregnant with him. His mother and grandparents molested him and his dad abused him by, among other things, burning his genitals with a cigarette.

As Harvard Law Professor Charles J. Ogletree, Jr. documents in the *Washington Post*, Cook was later placed in foster care, where a "foster parent chained him nude to a bed and raped him while other adults watched from the next room through a one-way mirror."

The prosecutor who presented the death penalty case against Cook said he never would have put execution on the table if he had known about the man's brutal past. Nonetheless, Cook was put to death on Aug. 8, 2012.

In various landmark cases, the Supreme Court has found that executing people with an intellectual disability or severe mental illness can be a violation of the Eighth Amendment, which bars cruel and unusual punishment.

The court has also found that severe childhood trauma can be a mitigating factor in a defendant's case, according to a press release accompanying the report.

But Kent Scheidegger, legal director of the Criminal Justice Legal Foundation, said there are serious flaws with the study's methodology. He noted that the authors count someone as intellectually disabled if they score below a 70 on at least one IQ test. However, he said, looking at the lowest score in a series of tests can be misleading.

"How fast can you run a mile? If you run on several different days and have several different times, the speed at which you can do it is your fastest time," Scheidegger said in an email to HuffPost. "Various factors can make you perform less than your best, including simply not trying hard, but nothing can make you perform better than your best. It's the same with IQ scores. The high score is a good indication of performance. The low score means practically nothing."

Scheidegger also said mitigating factors like intellectual disability or a traumatic childhood don't matter nearly as much as the brutality of the crimes that death row inmates have committed.

"Since 1978, defendants have had carte blanche to introduce everything including the kitchen sink in mitigation," Scheidegger said. "The actions of their attorneys in finding and presenting that evidence is scrutinized repeatedly in the years after the trial. What we see in case after case is that even after years of reinvestigation and relitigation, the horrifying facts of the crime remain far more than sufficient to outweigh the minimally relevant evidence in mitigation."

But Smith said the courts have found that, independent of the heinousness of the crime, the prosecution must also show that the defendant is "morally culpable."

"The Eighth Amendment requires that the death penalty be limited in its application to only those offenders who commit the most aggravated homicides *and* who possess the most aggravated moral culpability," Smith said.

"But our research showed that of the last 100 people we executed in America, most of them had severe functional deficits. In many cases, they suffered from several mental illness and years of horrific abuse. And the problem is that there is no standard measurement for these type of functional deficits. For instance, there is no IQ score equivalent for gauging the functional deficits that mark any particular person with a severe mental illness."

Smith also said those who ended up executed did not have adequate representation at the trial level. Juries were often not informed of defendants' intellectual or mental health problems or their family history of extreme abuse.

Smith noted that the reason traumatic childhoods are brought up is not necessarily to make juries feel bad for the person on trial, but because "decades of research" has shown that these types of trauma can trigger the kinds of "functional deficits" that were present in many of the cases examined in the report.

"We're executing people who get the worst lawyers, have the least resources and are the most vulnerable," Smith said.

Sometimes these mitigating factors come out during the appeals process, but by then it may be too late, since judges often give deference to the jury's verdict.

"It's often a tale told too late," Smith said. "How many of these people would have not even come close to dying if they had had good lawyers at trial or pretrial?"

With executions either being outlawed or rarely used in many parts of the country, Smith said the punishment's days may be numbered.

"We're not talking about reform," Smith said. "We're talking about it being on its way out."

Critical Thinking

1. In a death penalty case, should it matter to a jury that a defendant had a traumatic childhood?

2. When asking for the death penalty, isn't it enough for a prosecutor to prove that the defendant committed a heinous crime?

3. Why is it so important in capital cases that the defendant have good legal representation?

Internet References

Slate

http://www.slate.com/articles/news_and_politics/jurisprudence/2014/05 the_death_penalty_is_disappearing_in_america_except_in_the_south.html

The Washington Post

http://www.washingtonpost.com/opinions/charles-ogletree-the-death-penalty-is-incompatible-with-human-dignity/2014/07/18/c0849dea-0e6b-11e4-b8e5-d0de80767fc2_story.html